PREFACE

The decision to translate and revise Professor Franzen's *Kleine Kirchengeschichte* for the English-language reading public was not based entirely upon its successful publication in German. In spite of a number of similar works that have appeared during recent decades, none can compare with it in content and simplicity. Its special value stems from the fact that it restates modern historical research in terms that can be readily understood by students and general readers. Free from denominational bias, the work will serve as an absorbing study guide for the contemporary reader as well as an excellent source of material for study groups.

Simplification has been achieved by accepting established scholarship without lengthy substantiating data. Where interpretations are open to question, the position representing the most modern consensus is taken.

In revising the original work we have attempted to provide the reader with a brief treatment of new-world Catholicism without prejudice to the author's focus on the European background. Lord Acton, who first introduced the English-speaking world to the fruits of German historical scholarship, once remarked: "If history cannot confer faith or virtue, it can clear away the misconceptions and misunderstandings that turn men against each other." It is hoped that in the ecumenical spirit of our times these pages will achieve this end.

John P. Dolan,
University of South Carolina

v

CONTENTS

FOURTH EPOCH: 1300–1500
THE CHURCH IN THE TIME OF THE DISSOLUTION
OF WESTERN UNITY

THIRD ERA
THE CHURCH IN THE MODERN AGE

FIRST EPOCH: 1500–1700
REFORMATION AND CATHOLIC REFORM

SECOND EPOCH: 1789–1918
FROM THE FRENCH REVOLUTION TO THE FIRST WORLD WAR

THIRD EPOCH: 1918 TO THE PRESENT
FROM THE FIRST WORLD WAR TO THE PRESENT

FIRST ERA
CHRISTIAN ANTIQUITY

First Epoch: 1–311
From the Founding to the Constantinian Change

1
THE HISTORICAL JESUS AND HIS FOUNDING OF THE CHURCH

As a historical religion of revelation, Christianity derives from the historical person of Jesus Christ Incarnate and his work of salvation. The proof of his historical existence and the authenticity of the founding of his church is therefore prerequisite and basic to any presentation of church history.

1. Denials of the historical existence of Jesus have frequently been attempted since the eighteenth and nineteenth centuries in the name of enlightened and liberal science and historical criticism: for example, by H. S. Reimarus (d. 1768), F. Chr. Baur (d. 1860), D. F. Strauss (d. 1874), Bruno Bauer (d. 1882), and additionally around the turn of the century in particular by Robertson, Smith, Drews, and others. In their writings Christianity was portrayed as an invention of the apostles, and the figure of Jesus was presented as an imaginary mythical personification of religious longings and ideas, as a pious fraud of the disciples, or as adoptions and variations of the God-heroes of near-eastern Hellenistic mystery cults. Suddenly the blossoming science of comparative religion discovered similarities and parallels in the life of Jesus and those of the Sun-god Mithra (H. B. Smith, 1911), the hero of the Babylonian Gilgamesh Epic (Jensen, 1906), and the mythical figure of a dying and resurrected

God-savior (R. Reitzenstein, and others). It was believed necessary to interpret the picture of the life and teachings of Jesus as drawn in the gospels as a personified reflection of the social longings of the oppressed masses (Kalthoff, 1902).

All of these theories subsequently were settled scientifically and could be passed over in silence if they had not survived in Marxist-Communist propaganda. Seizing upon the new and radical ideas of their contemporary Bruno Bauer, Karl Marx and Friedrich Engels incorporated them into the theory of communism, and as such they are traditionally perpetuated without criticism.

Of more weight were the investigations and attacks on the historical authenticity and reliability of the gospels conducted by liberal theologians of the nineteenth and twentieth centuries in the name of textual criticism. Since then, modern biblical exegesis, conducted with the greatest conscientiousness and scrupulous exactitude, has newly confirmed the old foundations. R. Bultmann's attempts to de-mythologize the New Testament have led to a recognition of the complex thinking and expression of the early Christians which found its reflection in Holy Scripture. We have learned to differentiate the so-called "mythical" form of expression in many scriptural texts, a style which was conditioned by their time, from the essential content. From its wrapping has been isolated (demythologized) the historical nucleus with its central theme of the New Testament's message of God's work of salvation in Jesus Christ. By dealing critically and in detail with the literary form of expression in the texts, examiners have been able to extricate those sections and passages which may validly be regarded as primary sources for the life of the historical Jesus. If by this process traditional naive conceptions, which viewed the gospels as modern biographies of Jesus written with perfection of chronology and content, have been shaken, it has yet become possible to extricate from the New Testament texts a matrix of historically provable facts which can withstand criticism.

Although we now acknowledge that none of the four gospels is or intended to be a historical biography of Jesus, but rather presented that view of him which the apostolic description had formed in the hearts of his believing and loving followers, we can nonetheless state that many details in the gospels about him remain historically provable. Beneath this "Christ of Faith" as he is described in the New Testament, the "historical" Christ is ascertainable, and his historical existence cannot be denied. Most importantly, we can fit the beginning and the end of the mortal life of Jesus into their contemporary context with historical certainty. He was born under Herod the Great in 4/5 B.C. and he died on the cross under Pontius Pilate on the fourteenth or fifteenth Nisan in one of the years 30–33 A.D. Even if the four canonical gospels had obvious theological and kerygmatical intentions, they did not neglect to include references to contemporary events which thereby, even though they are not listed chronologically, establish historically the events of salvation. Only by studying the writings of these eyewitnesses can one obtain an uncommonly impressive and vivid picture of the personality, the teaching, and the death of Jesus.

Non-Christian sources also attest to the historical existence of Jesus. To be sure, contemporary reports of non-Christians are missing; but the statements of Tacitus around 117 (Annales XV, 44), of Pliny the Younger around 112/113 (letter to Emperor Trajan), and of Suetonius around 120 (*Vita Claudii*, ch. 25) are reliable and historically conclusive, and we may admit them as trustworthy evidence. We also possess statements by the Jewish writer Josephus Flavius from around 93/94 which permit us to accept his knowledge of the historical personality of Jesus (*Antiquitates* XVIII, 5, 2 and XX, 9, 1), while another passage (*Ant.* XVIII, 3, 3) is very dubious in its authenticity.

2. Since the beginning of modern times, the question of the historicity of the founding of the church by Jesus Christ has been very much disputed also. The dispute has concentrated on the problem of whether Christ preached only a general Christianity or gave to his religion a firm organization in the form of an institutional church, which he wished to be entrusted exclusively with the preaching of his gospel and the continuation of his work

3

of salvation. The spiritualistic concept of the church *(ecclesia spiritualis)* in the late Middle Ages led during the Reformation to a rejection of and intense struggle against the papal church which the Reformers accused of falsifying the original intent of Christ. Even in modern times, the Protestant teacher of church law Rudolf Sohn *(Kirchenrecht,* I, 1892), with his Lutheran understanding of the church concept, defended the thesis that Christ did not intend the founding of a church but preached a purely spiritual Christianity. For this reason, Sohn asserts, early Christianity was without any external order and organizational bond, and was guided and held together solely by the spirit of love exclusive of any churchly institution. It was the post-apostolic time that had misunderstood Christ's intention and had falsified his work. From this misinterpretation had grown the early Catholic Church in which the free belief of the initial period later had stiffened into dogma and in which the charismatic and spirit-filled life of the early Christians had been trapped by deadening laws and disciplinary rules.

Even in the argument and the ecumenical talks of the present, the question of the church founding occupies a central place. Sohn's ideas linger on in the writings of others, such as Emil Brunner *(Das Missverständnis der Kirche,* 1951), and Hans von Campenhausen *(Kirchliches Amt und Geistliche Vollmacht in den ersten drei Jahrhunderten,* 1953). Therefore, it is necessary to examine in detail the question of what the Scriptures say about the founding of the church and how the early church understood and realized the will of Christ.

The gospels report on every page that the essence of Jesus's sermon of salvation was the cheerful message of the kingdom of heaven. This kingdom is realized in two steps:

a) in a secular stage which started with the preaching of Jesus (Luke 11, 24; Matthew 11, 12) and

b) in a stage of completion at the end of time.

Did Jesus imagine the first stage, with which we are dealing here exclusively, as only an invisible realization or also as a visible one? Did he desire a visible outward kingdom of heaven in this world, divided and organized into offices? The answer is difficult, as Christ did not, as far as has been handed down to us, give a clear order for such a founding. Yet the biblical reports and the parables used by Jesus to characterize his concept of the church allow recognition of his very concrete church image and an awareness that the apostles understood this view.

When Jesus compares his church with a house or with a flock (Mt 16, 18; 21, 42; 1 Cor 3, 11; Acts 4, 11; and Mt 26, 31; John 10, 16; 1 Cor 9, 7) he explains quite clearly also that the house requires a strong rock foundation and that a firm shepherd is necessary for the guidance of the flock. From his disciples Jesus ordained the "Twelve" especially chosen ones, with Peter appointed as the shepherd with the major responsibility for his flock (Mk 3, 14f; Mt 16, 17ff; Lk 22, 31ff; John 21, 15ff). Thus Christ himself established the first "offices". An office is more than a transitory service; the official appointment invests it with a permanent character, and the union of the service function with a permanent commission continues beyond the death of the individual holder. The office gives the holder the power to speak and act in the name and authority of him who appointed him, and the office must include, therefore, the successorship. In this way the apostles regarded their office as a "God-given grace to fulfill the service of Jesus Christ and to perform the holy work of the gospel of God" (Rom 15, 16) and appointed assistants and successors to their office. The early church also held this view, and from this office the church was built. Since Christ himself holds the office and is active in it, one can say that the church evolved from and with this trait of office.

c) Although it is correct that the church which was founded by Christ can only be understood through faith and by the faithful, and that as a supernatural and transcendent magnitude it is necessarily spiritual and therefore invisible, it is just as emphatically true that it has occurred at this time and has been established for the people of this visible world. Jesus wanted his church to be a historical and visible community, and his entire activity was directed toward that end. He not only taught but also lived in

5

community with his disciples. His religious teaching is not directed toward the establishment of a school, but toward encompassing all creation within a real and vibrant community with himself as its very heart and center (John 14, 20 ff). From him the community was to receive its vital principle.

Paul sees this living community of the faithful with Christ symbolized by the body (1 Cor 12, 12 ff) of which Christ is the head and the faithful the limbs (Eph 2, 15 ff; 4, 12 ff; Col 3, 15). In becoming man and through his salvation and surrender to the cross, Jesus continues to live in the church. As the church participates in his incarnate being and his work of salvation, so it also lives his life. Paul reminds us continually that Christ's life, death, and resurrection are not only objective historical facts, but that we must participate in his life, in his suffering and death, and partake of his resurrection, if Christ's death is to have meaning.

The fundamental question which we have to ask is: "What think ye of Christ, whose son is he?" (Mt 22, 42). The answer can only be an answer of faith: God's son! The incarnation is the central concept of Christianity, but here the competence of purely historical research ends and one must rely on a theology which presupposes and demands a decision of faith. God became man in Jesus Christ in order to draw closer again to mankind and to form a bond with it. Through Christ's everlasting participation in the church, God continues to be a part of humanity in all eras and nations in order to lead it to salvation.

The deepest mystery of the church lies in its identity with Christ. The work of Jesus Christ Incarnate, begun during his historical life on earth, is continued in the life of the church until his future return in the eschatological completion. In this way the incarnation of the Logos in the world renews itself forever, and it is the living church to which J. A. Möhler refers as the "continual incarnation of Christ". In this sense the church itself is a deep mystery of faith and salvation (Letter to the Ephesians) and incorporates into its relations the tension between divine holiness and human failure. Divinity, holiness, and indestructibility it receives from its heavenly founder; human failure, sinfulness, and inconstancy it owes to humanity. Through this polarity, peculiar to its nature, the essence and activity of the church in history contains an uncommon excitement. Not only outside of the church but within its center and within the core of each of its faithful there takes place the dramatic struggle between the divine and the human, between the sacred and the profane, and between good and evil. It is the church of saints and the church of sinners. As the life of the individual believer, so church history is a struggle with spiritual peaks and declines, depending on how the church speaks its "ecce ancilla Domini" to God and Mary in whom the first historical incarnation of the Logos took place.

The salvation and sanctification of mankind is the obligatory program with which Christ charged the church. Its specific situation in history can be measured by the manner and competency with which it carries out this divine order in life. Means and methods of implementation often have altered and been adapted to the actuality of the human factor, but the mission and goal have remained unchanged. The call for reform and return to the early church which has sounded repeatedly during two thousand years of history cannot mean the repetition and rejuvenation of an anachronistic way of life, but only the recollection of the mission postulated in the beginning: The continuation of the work of salvation through Christ's word and sacrament, and the evangelical conversion of the world for Christ.

2
THE EARLY CHURCH AND THE APOSTOLIC ERA

More than any other epoch of history, the time of the founding and establishment of the church in the initial "apostolic" era was of decisive consequence for its historical development.

1. After the ascension of Christ the disciples were confronted with a totally new situation. To be sure, the departing master had left them an unequivocal mission (Mt 28, 18; Mk 16, 15), the content of which was the continuation of the preaching of salva-

tion and the proclamation of the gospel message of the eschatological kingdom of Christ. It seems that concrete directions were not provided, however, regarding their future life together and concerning the details of the organizational structure of their community. With respect to Christ's wishes in this regard, the opinions of exegetes vary considerably. But if Protestant theologians want to paint a contrast between what Christ really wanted and what actually developed, it must be pointed out that the apostles and the first disciples who, after all, were eye- and ear-witnesses of his revelation, certainly must have been in a better position to interpret the will of Jesus than contemporary scholars two thousand years later.

Yet the Scriptures alone are not adequate to interpret the events (*sola-scriptura*-principle), and it is imperative that the early Christian apostolic tradition be included as a vital factor in the calculation. Christ did not reveal his will in abstract norms and instructions, but rather passed it on to his apostles as a living command. If the apostles after the ascension, when they were suddenly deprived of their master and were faced with the uncommonly difficult task of continuing the work of Jesus, established a firm order for the community and a hierarchical structure for the church, they most certainly acted as the authentic interpreters of his intentions. Hierarchy (= sacred origin, divine domination) meant that the order was of divine origin, because it was given to the church by Christ himself.

It is impossible that the apostles could have been mistaken in their actions, because according to the principles of faith of the church the "Twelve" themselves were still bearers of divine revelation which they had received directly from Christ. Just as they acted under the inspiration of the Holy Spirit when they passed on their revealed teaching and the Holy Scriptures, they also performed this inspired function with regard to their manifold practical instructions in the cultic, disciplinary, and institutional areas. Since Christ himself did not leave any written word, the oral and written instructions of these twelve apostles, transmitted either personally or through their direct disciples, contain the essence of Christianity. These divine revelations incorporate all that is important for man concerning the steward-ship of salvation. Nothing new has been added since and nothing will be added in the future. The general divine revelation of salvation is embodied and completed in the apostolic tradition. Therefore the criterion for the authenticity of a religious doctrine is and will remain that its existence can be traced to the *traditio apostolica*. The apostolic tradition was reflected in the doctrine, the worship, and the life of the early church to as great a degree as it was in the inspired canonical writings of the New Testament which came into being during this apostolic era.

Because it is clearly discernible that the body of revelation was not simply conserved in a sterile fashion by the first genera-tion of Christians, it is often not easy to decide which of these early Christian-apostolic thoughts have to be regarded as direct divine revelation and which have been added through the theological reflection of the early communities. The revelations were thought through by the early Christians and continued with independent understanding. In this fashion there arose early a theological penetration of the truths of revelation, primarily with respect to the incarnate person of Jesus and his work of salvation, which we normally designate as the "communal theology" of the early church. This early period is admired today as one of the theologically most creative epochs of church history. As the "communal theology" is reflected in both Holy Scripture and tradition, exegetes and historians are working together to understand it better and to differentiate it from the direct divine thoughts of revelation. The final decision, however, on what was and is the essential content of faith is incumbent on the magisterial office of the church.

The closeness of the apostolic era to the revelation explains why Christianity has always lived in and from the conviction that it is tied to the *traditio apostolica* for existence or non-existence. But this sanction can not consist of a rigid and impossible repeti-tion of early Christian forms of life and thought, but must contain the principle of a living oral and written transmission and a law of organic development. An uncreative traditionalism would not do justice to the principle of life and spirit inherent in the church. If at all times in church history the call for reform has been heard and in the future will be heard, then the correct fulfillment of the demand cannot consist of the naive return to early Christian forms of life. Spiritualists, sectarians, and heretics have always held that such a return was possible and have denied the law of historical progression and the organic development of all living things. Reform means the continuous realization and recollection of the original mission of Christ given at the beginning. The early church accomplished this with a special manner and purity which established certain standards and examples; but that does not prevent the essential continuing development. In this deeper sense the Catholic Church knows itself to be still absolutely one and identical with the church of the apostles despite its universal dissemination and tremendous internal development.

The chronological limitation of the apostolic period of revelation creates some difficulties. It is usually regarded as having lasted from the ascension of Jesus "to the death of the last of the (twelve) apostles". But the delineation must not be regarded as rigidly fixed. We may also extend the boundaries of the period to include the first and second (!) Christian generations as long as the direct witnesses of the risen Lord still lived and carried on his revelation. The inspired canonical Letter to the Hebrews of the New Testament, for instance, according to the judgment of Catholic exegetes, was written by an unknown Alexandrian Christian of the second generation.

Our sources for the knowledge of churchly life in this time are primarily the New Testament writings, particularly the Acts of the Apostles and the Letters of Paul. Additionally, other witnesses are at our disposal, such as the writings of the Apostolic Fathers who in part themselves belong to this early period (Didache, Letter of Clement) or who have handed down to us reports on the condition of the early church.

2. What picture of the church does the early apostolic Christian period provide?

10

The Acts of the Apostles and the Epistles of Paul clearly demonstrate that from the beginning of the early church the spiritual "office" was regarded as an essential structural element of community order. A constitution based on a purely charismatic and free spiritual force without offices, without rule of law, and without a firm body of faith never existed and is incompatible with the Pauline church concept. This is true for the local community as well as for the whole church. Just as the first apostles received their official appointment to spread the gospel from Christ himself (Mk 3, 13ff; Mt 10, 1ff; Lk 6, 12ff), so they in turn also laid hands on their special associates and successors in official appointment. The organization of the early communities was not uniform, but always contained the structured principle of the unity of head and body. The officials are appointed and called to represent the spiritual Master and to continue in his name the work of salvation by word and sacrament. They exercise the governing functions alone by virtue of their office, be it in the service of the whole church as apostles, prophets, and evangelists, or in the service of the local community as bishops, elders, deacons, teachers, and shepherds (1 Cor 12, 28; Phil 1, 1; 1 Tim 3, 2ff). A rigorous gradation governs everywhere, based on the principle of succession in office as derived from Christ and the apostles *(apostolica successio)*.

The function of office was not opposed to that of charisma which was a gift of God for the accomplishment of special tasks. Often we encounter those in office who were charismatics at the same time (2 Cor 8, 23; Titus; Phil 2, 25; Rom 16, 1; Gal 1, 19; 1 Cor 15, 7); and conversely, charismatics were entrusted with the guidance of a community. Paul himself was a pneumatic and charismatic, yet as an office-holder he was sober and impartial enough to know that his newly founded communities were in need of observant, realistic, and strict authoritative guidance. The charismatics had to subordinate themselves to their office in the normal direction of the church. More and more, the ordinary direction of the community was concentrated in the bishops and deacons. The bishops had grown out of the

11

college of presbyters in which they had the leadership as heads and overseers *(episcopos)*. In some local communities we encounter in the beginning several presbyter-episcopes at the same time; but at the latest in the second century the monarchical episcopate prevails everywhere. In this tendency toward a monarchical system, which is discernible early in the local communities, it is justified to see the first stirrings of the principle of primacy which later becomes pronounced in the whole church (H. Schlier).

The intense awareness of faith of the early church corresponded to the group of pure charismatics who are frequently mentioned. Their function consisted in building the community and being available to it for special services, but not in directing it. Occasionally we hear of serious dissension between charismatics and officials in the early communities (1 Cor 1, 10ff; 14, 1ff), but these were overcome through love. Later on, the importance of charismatic gifts receded into the background without, however, ever completely disappearing from the church.

3

THE TRIUMPHAL PROGRESS OF THE YOUNG CHURCH FROM JERUSALEM TO ROME

The Acts of the Apostles describe the triumphant progress of the gospels "from Jerusalem unto the uttermost part of the earth" (Acts 1, 8). They provide us with deep insights into the overpowering and enthusiastic missionary activity as well as into the love-filled internal life of the early church. We can distinguish three periods:

1. The Jewish-Christian period with Jerusalem as its center (ch. 1–9, 31).
2. The period of transition from Jewish to Gentile Christianity with Antioch as its center (ch. 9, 32–15, 35).
3. The period of St. Paul's missionary journeys to the Gentiles (ch. 13–28).

1. *The Early Community at Jerusalem*

The Mother church at Jerusalem enjoyed special respect from the beginning. Here the first apostles under the leadership of Peter directed the community and acted as living witnesses of the Lord. Many were still alive who as eye-witnesses of the activity, death, and resurrection of Jesus proclaimed with enthusiasm the gospel of salvation.

It was in Jerusalem that the first steps toward a separate Christian terminology and procedure of service were taken. At first the young community still regarded itself as the fulfillment of Judaism, participated in Jewish worship, lived with the traditional Jewish forms of piety, and adopted the basic principles of Jewish organization (structure of the community, direction by elders and presbyters, and office-holders with permanent authority). At the same time, however, there formed a separate community with the apostles which conducted its own worship in grateful memory *(Eucharistia)* and cultic representation of Christ's sacrificial death. Thus they celebrated holy communion by "breaking bread from house to house" and "eating their meat with gladness and singleness of heart" (Acts 2, 46). Community life and constitution, piety and order of prayer of the church were decisively influenced by the Jerusalem community. It was also during the so-called Council of Apostles in Jerusalem (ca. 50) that the first difficult decision was made that the Gentiles would basically be free from Jewish law (Acts 15, 6 ff, 19). This decision became of the greatest importance for the future of the young church.

Even though the internal structure of the community at first was determined by the college of the twelve apostles, it is clearly discernible that Peter had a leading role. Next to him, Paul describes James and John as "pillars" of the community (Gal 2, 9). Only after the departure of Peter from Jerusalem (around 43/44, Acts 12, 17) did James take his place. By tradition, James is regarded as the first "bishop" of Jerusalem. During the Council of the Apostles we encounter the "presbyters" for the first time. Prior to this, the seven deacons are mentioned (Acts 6, 1 f), with Stephen as their leader. Thus the hierarchical order of the office-holders is complete: the apostle-bishop, the presbyters, and the deacons as authoritative leaders of the Jerusalem community.

Although the Jerusalem community participated in the Jewish cult and strictly observed Jewish law, and therefore at first appeared to be a Jewish sect, almost immediately a parting of the ways was necessary, because the typically Christian traits of the community brought the followers of Jesus into insurmountable opposition to the synagogue. Christian baptism; prayer, which was directed to Christ as the Kyrios (= God); the celebration of the Eucharist; and the exclusive Christian community of love which went as far as the surrender of private property to the community of the faithful (Acts 2, 44 ff) called forth the suspicion, the rejection, and finally the hostility of the Jews. Especially the belief in Christ led to open conflict and two brief periods of persecution. The first outbreak in 32/33 led to the stoning of Stephen, to the expulsion of the Hellenistic Jewish Christians from Jerusalem, and to their further persecution by Saul. Saul, who was converted on the way to Damascus in 33/36, then, as Paul, became the "chosen vessel" for the dissemination of the Christian message (Acts 9, 15 f). The second wave of persecution, kindled by King Herod Agrippa I (37–44), led in the year 42/43 to the martyrs death of the apostle James the Elder and to the arrest of Peter who miraculously escaped from prison (Acts 12, 1 ff).

The persecution in the main was directed against the Hellenists, i.e. against the Jews of the Diaspora who had been converted to Christianity, and thus had the positive effect of carrying Christianity into the world. The Hebraic Christian Jews remained in Jerusalem and through especially loyal conduct toward the Jewish cult and temple service attempted to retain the favor of the Jews. Yet in the long run it was not possible to hide the contrast. It had to lead to new explosions. Around 62/63 the apostle James the Younger was stoned. According to Josephus Flavius (*Antiquitates* XX, 9, 1, v. 4–6), the high priest Ananias, during a procurator vacancy, at Easter 62 accused the successfully acting "brother of Jesus" and a few other Christians of violating the laws and had them sentenced. According to an old source (Hegesippus, in Eusebius *Hist. Eccl.* II, 23, 12, 10–18), he was first thrown off the top of the Temple and then bludgeoned to death.

When the Christians early in the Jewish War (66–70), heeding the warning and prophecy of Jesus about the destruction of Jerusalem, left the city (Mt 24, 15 ff), they were branded by the Jews as deserters and traitors. The growing hatred in ca. 100 caused the synagogue to place the Christians under official anathema. The new and final revolt against the Romans by the Jews under Bar Kochba (132–135) brought the Christians in Palestine a renewed bloody persecution by the Jews. And so the line of separation between Jews and Christians was finally drawn, and that unfortunate enmity began which was to have such evil consequences for both sides. During the persecutions of Christians in the Roman Empire, the Jews again and again played an ominous role in inciting and stirring up the people against the Christians. After the Constantinian Change and primarily during the Middle Ages, the Jews were the victims. Of course, modern racist anti-semitism has no connection with this religious conflict.

With the destruction of Jerusalem in the year 70, the special pre-eminence of the Jerusalem community was at an end.

2. The Community of Antioch

As the first Gentile Christian community and as a Christian missionary center, Antioch in the beginning occupied an eminent position. The so-called Antiochian case of dissension (Acts 15 and Gal 2, 11 ff) provided the impulse for the clarification of relations between Hebrew and Gentile Christians. Other than this, not too much is known about the internal structure of the community and it is not possible to say to what extent it was responsible for the establishment of the numerous communities which Paul founded during his three long missionary journeys from Antioch. Obviously the Antioch community consisted chiefly of non-Jews and therefore no longer appeared as a Jewish sect. For the first time it was designated as a religious community in its own right and its members were regarded as "Christians" (Acts 11, 26).

It was chiefly Paul who detached Christianity from its Jewish-Palestinian native soil and carried it into the world from Antioch, a center of the Greek-Roman culture of Hellenism. After his conversion (ca. 33) he withdrew into the Arabian desert for three years (36–39) in order to prepare himself for his apostolic calling and then followed the invitation of Barnabas to Antioch. Together with Barnabas, "being sent forth by the Holy Spirit" (Acts 13, 4), he undertook his first missionary journey (45–48) which took him to Cyprus and Asia Minor (Perga, Antioch in Pisidia, Iconium, Lystra, and Derbe, cf. Acts 13–14). On his second missionary journey (49/50–52), Paul advanced beyond Asia Minor to Europe, where he founded the communities of Philippi, Thessalonica, Athens, and Corinth (Acts 15, 36 – 18, 22). The third missionary journey (53–58) went through Galatia and Phrygia to Ephesus, from there to Greece, and back again to Troas, Miletus, Caesarea, and Jerusalem, where it ended with his first arrest (58) (Acts 18, 23 – 21, 27). During these years he wrote his magnificent letters to the Corinthians, Romans, Galatians, and others. He was also already looking toward Rome and the West (Spain).

3. The Origins of the Roman Community

The Roman community was already flowering when Paul wrote his Epistle to the Romans in the winter of 57/58 (Rom 1, 8). Several years before (ca. 50), according to the reports of the biographer Suetonius (*Vita Claudii*, ch. 15, 4), there had occurred tumults over Christ among the Roman Jews (*"Judaeos impulsore Chresto assidue tumultuantes Roma expulit"*). Paul had met two of these expellees, the couple Aquila and Priscilla, on his second missionary journey in Corinth (Acts 18, 2), and must have heard more about the Roman Christians from them. Even then he must have planned to travel to Rome himself. Romans had already been present at the first Pentecost in Jerusalem (Acts 2, 10), and therefore it is not impossible that very early there may have been in existence a Christian community in Rome. Who founded it?

The oldest tradition of the Roman community has always traced its origins to Peter. After Peter's flight from Jerusalem from where he had gone "into another place" (Acts 12, 17) in the year 42/43, had he gone directly or at least soon thereafter to Rome? This is entirely feasible even if, for example, he was back in Jerusalem again in the year 50 for the Council of the Apostles. This is not inconsistent with the fact that he was not present in Rome when Paul wrote his Epistle to the Romans (57/58) or when Paul was in Roman captivity. For certainly, driven like all apostles by missionary fervor, Peter will have continued on after founding the community. The report of his twenty-five-year stay in Rome which was first mentioned in the fourth century (Eusebius and *Catalogus Liberianus*) does not deserve much credence and, most of all, need not be understood as an uninterrupted stay. On the other hand, it is clearly established that Peter was in Rome. The First Epistle of Peter, which was written by him in the year 63/64 in Rome (1 Pet 5, 13), as well as his martyr's death in Rome during Nero's persecution of Christians, probably in July 64, testify to it. Especially the latter is no longer in doubt after the recent excavations under St. Peter's in Rome. Even if exact identification of Peter's grave has not yet been made and can scarcely be made without some question remaining as to which grave it is among several graves lying one above the other, it is nonetheless unequivocally established that he was buried in that spot. Consequently the fact of his Roman martyrdom, which unanimous tradition traces to the earliest time, has to be regarded as historically assured.

This tradition points to Peter as the founder of the Roman Church in an unbroken line of witnesses from the first letter of Clement (ca. 96), to the martyr-bishop Ignatius of Antioch (Letter to the Romans), to Irenaeus of Lyon, who was the first to record

17

a complete Roman line of succession (*Adv. haereses,* III, 1, 1; 3, 2), to Dionysius of Corinth (Eusebius, *Church History,* II, 25, 8), to the Roman presbyter Caius (Eusebius, *Ch. H.,* II, 25, 7), to Tertullian (*De praescriptione haereticorum,* 32; *Adv. Marcionem* IV, 5), and many others. Together with Paul, who also died a martyr's death in Rome during Nero's persecution, Peter is mentioned as the founding apostle at the head of all lists of Roman bishops. To this direct apostolic origin, the Roman bishops knew very well, they owed their special position and meaning within the whole church; a fact, which the other churches always acknowledged as well. This origin insured the security and absolute reliability of the apostolic tradition in the Roman Church and safeguarded it through the chain of successors of St. Peter on the Roman bishop's chair. Through it the purity of Christian dogma was guaranteed.

Peter was followed by Linus, Anacletus, Clement, Evaristus, Alexander, Sixtus, Telesphorus, Hyginus, Pius, Anicetus, Soter, Eleutherius, etc. Hegesippus found this sequence already established in Rome in ca. 160 when he came to obtain information about the pure and true teachings of Christ and the apostles to combat the Gnostic heresy. Irenaeus also discovered this Roman order of succession in ca. 180 when he came to Rome to look for the most positive guarantee of Christian truth. Both of them had less a historico-chronological interest in this Roman bishop list than a dogmatic one. They were searching for the genuine and unadulterated truth of faith. At a time which left few writings, reliable oral transmission was of the utmost importance. If one could refer to reliable authority and could trace a chain of transmission back to the Lord himself, then the purity of dogma was guaranteed. We encounter such striving also in the non-Christian world; in Judaism (cf. the Old Testament genealogies, Gen 5, 11, 10 ff; 1 Chron 1, 9), in the Greek schools of philosophy, and in the Islamic schools of theology. The addition of years of birth and death mattered little. The very line of names possessed a dynamic character which bestowed surety of faith and firmness of dogma.

We must not be surprised that the oldest Roman bishop's lists have no dates. Historical interest awakened only much later and it is significant that it was a historian who first attempted dating. Eusebius of Caesarea (d. 339), the "Father of Church History", in his ten-volume *Church History,* written at the beginning of the fourth century, correlates the term of office of each of the twenty-eight popes with the dates of emperors. Here also is the first assertion that Peter had been bishop of Rome for twenty-five years after his flight from Jerusalem (42) until his death in Rome, which Eusebius put near 67. The same procedure was followed by the so-called *Catalogus Liberianus* of the years 336 and 354 and then perfected according to a purely schematic point of view by listing even days and months for the start of each accession. These indications do not, of course, have historical validity. One can attempt, however, by using the results of historico-critical scholarship, to obtain certain bases for the terms of office of the individual popes. The oldest list would then look as follows: Peter (d. 64?), Linus (64–79?), Anacletus (79–90/92?), Clement I (90/92–101?), Evaristus (101–107?), Alexander I (107–116?), Sixtus I (116–125?), Telesphorus (125–138?), Hyginus (138–142?), Pius I (142–154/155?), Anicetus (154/155–166?), Soter (166–174?), Eleutherius (174–189?), Victor I (189–198/199?), Zephyrinus (199–217?); from here on dates can be given with relative reliability.

4
FURTHER SPREAD OF CHRISTIANITY TO THE THIRD CENTURY

Many factors contributed to the noticeably rapid spread of Christianity, which represented a mystery of grace. The Acts of the Apostles show to what strong degree the Diaspora Jews in the beginning acted as transmitters of Christian preaching. At first Paul addressed himself everywhere to the Jewish communities throughout the whole Roman Empire. His preaching found special reception in the "God-fearing Gentiles", i. e.

within those groups which had become spiritual adherents of Judaism without belonging to it officially. By way of this bridge, the gospels soon reached the unadulterated Gentiles.

In addition to Paul, the other apostles also were active missionaries, but unfortunately we do not know about their activity with much certainty. What the later legends tell us about it is worthless. On the other hand it can be said that without their intensive missionary work it is impossible to explain how as early as the second century Christianity had been disseminated in the countries ringing the Mediterranean and had penetrated from these to the more distant regions of the Roman Empire. Besides the original apostles there were also professional missionaries, apostles in the extended sense. But they also are not at all to be regarded as the sole carriers of Christianity. The Christians in their totality became active in the world which surrounded them and spread the gospel of Jesus Christ. So the gospel of salvation traveled with merchants, soldiers, and preachers along the roads of the Roman Empire. At the junctions of traffic, in the cities, the first communities sprang up. Under the protection of the Pax Romana and in the atmosphere of the uniformly directed Empire, Christianity was able to gain a footing throughout the whole civilized "ecumenical" world.

The center of dissemination lay in the East. We possess the reliable testimony of the pagan governor Pliny the Younger, a Roman consul and senator (of the year 100), who as imperial governor (111–113) in Bithynia and Pontus in Asia Minor had encountered such a large number of Christians that he had to inquire of Emperor Trajan what his conduct toward them should be. "The matter seemed to me to be well worth referring to you", he wrote, "especially considering the numbers endangered. All ranks and ages, and of both sexes, are and will be endangered. Not only the cities, but also the villages and the rural districts have been infected by this contagious superstition (of Christianity). It seems possible, however, to check and cure it; for it is already noticeable that the temples which had been almost deserted are being visited again, that the sacred festivals after a long intermission are again revived, and that there is again demand for sacrificial animals for which there had been few buyers lately. From this it can easily be imagined that many people could be reclaimed if one gave them an opportunity to repent" (Pliny, *Epistola* 96).

If the countries of the Black Sea offer this picture, it is not surprising that in the western provinces of Asia Minor and Syria there was already at the end of the first century no important town which did not have a Christian community. In the main, these communities had an apostolic foundation (Paul), and by the second century there were cities with a majority of Christian inhabitants, as well as large numbers of Christians throughout the countryside. Because of this it is understandable that in Phrygia in the latter half of the second century Montanism could develop into a kind of popular movement which seized the whole country. Even before the end of the persecutions, toward the close of the third century, there seem to have been cities which already had become completely Christian. In them, even the terrible persecution under Diocletian was no longer effective.

From Asia Minor and Syria Christianity spread to Mesopotamia. Edessa became a missionary center and when in 200 King Abgar of Edessa with his family converted to Christianity, the further missionary work in the country was allowed full reign. The oldest Christian chapel known to us has been found in Duro-Europos on the Upper Euphrates. Built around 232, it is decorated with splendid frescoes of biblical content.

Unfortunately we lack information about the beginnings of Christianity in Egypt. But everything indicates that the Christian mission was active here as early as in Asia Minor and Syria. Alexandria was its starting point and soon became its spiritual center, chiefly through its famous school of theology. As Bishop Demetrius of Alexandria (188–231) was able to organize the Egyptian church and inasmuch as about 100 bishop's sees were soon established, it appears conclusive that Christian missionary efforts had been largely successful.

In the West, Rome was the ecclesiastical center. Pope Fabian

21

in the middle of the third century undertook a reorganization of the Roman municipal community which enables us to calculate its membership at this time at several tens of thousands. To Emperor Decius (249–251) the size of the Roman community appeared so threatening that he is supposed to have said that he would receive the news of the revolt of a rival with greater calm and equanimity than the message that a new bishop of Rome was being elected (Cyprian, *Epistola* 55, 9). In spite of all oppressions during the time of the persecutions, the Roman community developed enormously. Eusebius reports that for the condemnation of the rival bishop Novatian in the year 251 about sixty Italian bishops gathered in Rome for the synod (Eusebius, *Ch. H.,* VI, 42, 2).

In North Africa in the second century Christianity was also strongly represented. However, the first reliable knowledge we receive is from the report of a martyrdom in Scillium (Numidia) around 180. From the writings of Tertullian (d. after 220 in Carthage) we learn that the number of Christians in North Africa in the year 212 must have been rather large (Tertullian, *Ad Scapulam,* 2, 5). Around 220, bishop Agrippinus of Carthage could gather around him a synod of more than seventy bishops; twenty years later there were ninety, and toward the end of the third century the cities of North Africa seem to have been predominantly Christian.

In Gaul it was probably Marseilles which had a Christian community by the first century. During the second century the communities of Lyon and Vienne, in the Rhône Valley, are of importance and in the year 177, forty-nine Christians suffered a martyr's death in Lyon. In the third century the number of communities grew throughout all of Gaul. According to Irenaeus of Lyon (d. ca. 202), there were also during this time already Christian communities in Roman Germany (Irenaeus, *Adv. haereses* 1, 10, 2). The most recent results of excavations in Trier, Cologne, Bonn, and Augsburg have ascertained Christian places of worship dating from the third century. Yet only by the fourth century did Christianity become strong in the Roman cities of Germany. Bishop Maternus of Cologne is known to have participated in the Roman synod of the year 313 and was also in Arles a year later where he signed the synodal documents. Three Britannic bishops were also in Arles in 314.

Outside of the Roman Empire, in ca. 226, there were some twenty bishoprics in the area of the Tigris. Armenia under its king Trdat II was largely Christian by 280 and could be regarded as a Christian country toward the end of the third century. Even if it can not be proved with certainty, there is the possibility that the apostle Thomas was the first to preach the gospel in India. It is more probable, however, that the Christian religion was carried to India only later from Persia and that the name "Thomas-Christians" originated not with the apostle Thomas but with Mâr Thomas in the eighth century.

This certainly impressive survey should not induce one to misjudge the number of Christians as excessively large. Statistical indications concerning actual numbers are impossible, and only approximate estimates are available which will always remain problematical. Ludwig von Hertling has undertaken such an approximate estimate (in *Zeitschrift für Katholische Theologie* 58 [1934] and 62 [1938]), separating occident and orient, and has come to the following result:

In the Western Empire around the year 100 there were presumably only a few thousand Christians; around the year 200, however, several tens of thousands; around the year 300 about two million; and around the year 400 perhaps four to six million. In the Eastern Empire not even vague guesses can be made for the first three centuries. By the year 300 there could have been five to six million, and around the year 400 perhaps ten to twelve million Christians. The East was Christian to a much larger degree than the western part of the Empire. If one looks at these figures in relation to the total population of the Roman Empire, which in the year 200 came to about seventy million but to only fifty million in the year 300, one recognizes that Christians constituted only a small minority. The open countryside continued to be primarily pagan for a long time.

5

THE FIRST SPIRITUAL UNFOLDING OF CHRISTIANITY

The early internal unfolding and the organic spiritual growth of the young religion corresponded to its rapid spread. The epoch of the founding of the church in the "Apostolic Era", which encompassed the first and second generations of Christians, was now followed by the so-called "Post-Apostolic Era". This era was characterized by having to pass on, after the actual period of revelation had ended, the body of belief that had come down from the apostles to the third and all following generations. Thus began the tradition in the narrower sense which constituted a bridge between the apostles and the later church and formed the first link in the chain of transmission. The development of Christianity could not, of course, be arrested at this point. The young religion had to fight for its position in the world and to defend and maintain itself both internally and externally. Thirdly there was a need for theological elaboration and permeation of revelation; an expansion which corresponded to the spiritual-mental growth of the Christian communities.

These tasks were undertaken first by the so-called Apostolic Fathers, then by the early Christian apologists, and finally by the Church Fathers.

1. As "Apostolic Fathers" we designate a group of writers of the immediate post-apostolic era who in their own persons embody the living connection with the apostles. More particularly, they are "the writers of the early Christian era who according to contemporary knowledge can positively be identified as students or hearers of the apostles who together with the apostles, but even without personal acquaintance with them, can be regarded in their whole teaching to a high degree as carriers of apostolic information, but who cannot be included with the New Testament authors" (J. A. Fischer, *Die Apostolischen Väter*, 1956, IX).

According to this definition we certainly should have to include Clement of Rome, Ignatius of Antioch, and Polycarp of

Smyrna in this group. The issue is not so clear in the case of Quadratus (Kodatrus), whom Fischer includes but Altaner does not, and in the case of Papias of Hierapolis, whom Altaner considers a student of the apostles but whom Fischer does not include. Uncertainty also reigns in the case of the so-called presbyters of Asia Minor, whom Irenaeus of Lyon and Eusebius occasionally mention without naming them as having received their doctrines from the apostles (Irenaeus, *Adv. haereses* IV, 27, 1 and IV, 32, 1). In this case it can be presumed that on their part they only repeated sayings of students of apostles and thus constituted the second link in the chain of tradition.

Besides the first group of actual Apostolic Fathers, there is a number of early Christian writings which according to the above definition do not really belong here, but which because of their age and closeness to the apostolic era are usually treated in this context; they are the epistle to Diognetus, the epistle of Barnabas, the Didache, and the "Shepherd" of Hermas.

All of these writings are of inestimable value for knowledge of early Christian life and thought. They show how the transition was effected from the apostolic founding of communities to the early Christian constitutional form, and how the institutional character, which originally was strongly covered by the charismatic spirit, became more pronounced with time. They also give information about the formation of canons of the New Testament. Part of these writings in the beginning was counted among the contents of the New Testament and was used during the service and regarded as guiding principle (canon) of the revealed faith. Among these, for example, was the First Letter of Clement, the "Shepherd" of Hermas, and the letter of Barnabas in Syria and Egypt. The use of these writings shows that the process of separation was still going on. Only when the concept of inspiration, which had been sketched by the Apostolic Fathers themselves, was more clearly worked out, were the post-apostolic writings separated from the inspired New Testament writings of Holy Scripture. Here we can also see how numerous other theological concepts were formed or continued to develop.

25

We have to regard the first letter of Clement as the "first most precisely datable work of Christian literature outside of the New Testament". It was written in Rome around the year 96 and is a petition and admonition from the Roman community to the community of Corinth with the demand to stop quarrelling and to reestablish peace and harmony. According to the unanimous testimony of the oldest tradition, the letter was composed by Clement, bishop of the Roman community and third successor of St. Peter in Rome. It provides the oldest literary testimony of the martyr's death of the apostles Peter and Paul "here", i.e. in Rome, and also contains other valuable historical news about the first two persecutions of Christians in Rome under Nero and Domitian. With regard to the Corinthian dispute, the author treats the issue in such a way that one cannot overlook a certain self-assurance based on higher authority; an authority which cannot be explained solely with the Roman character in general, but which is plainly tied to Peter and his position of pre-eminence. Even if a brotherly admonishing tone is preserved throughout, there "seems to be evident not only a normal *correctio fraterna*", but more (Fischer, 12). "To be certain, nowhere is the primatial position of Rome explicitly asserted, but there is also no passage which contradicts it. On the contrary", Fischer continues by relying literally on B. Altaner (*Patrologie,* [6]1960, 81) and Adolf von Harnack (*Einführung in die alte Kirchengeschichte,* 1929, 99), "one may see here announced the spirit, the force, and the claim of Rome to a special position among all communities. The high esteem which this letter was accorded as early as the second century points in the same direction". The letter is still far away from the decretal style of the medieval papacy, but already it speaks authoritatively. Just as Clement of Rome, according to the believable testimony of Irenaeus, was a faithful student of Peter and Paul, so the same seems to have been true of Ignatius of Antioch. As bishop of Antioch in Syria, whose Christian community for a time was also led by Peter, he was Peter's second successor as reported by Origen and Eusebius. In Ignatius's early years, he must have been personally acquainted with Peter and

26

Paul. That he was a direct pupil of St. John is only a very late assertion (Jerome in the fourth century), but it could be true as it is known that John spent his old age in Ephesus.

We possess seven genuine letters by Ignatius which were written only a few years after Clement's letter. During the reign of Emperor Trajan (98–117), probably around 110, he was arrested as a Christian and taken to Rome where he was killed by wild beasts. During the journey to his martyr's death, guarded and tortured by soldiers, Ignatius wrote letters of thanks from Smyrna and Troas to the communities of Ephesus, Magnesia, and Tralles which had consoled him during his passage, as well as to the churches of Philadelphia, of Smyrna, to their bishop Polycarp, and to the Christian community of Rome "which takes preference also in love". All of these letters are filled with magnificent thoughts. From the point of constitutional history it is clear from Ignatius's letters that in his area the monarchical episcopate had prevailed. Only a single bishop now stands at the head of the community and Ignatius exhorts "all of you follow the bishop as Jesus Christ the Father, and the presbyterium as the apostles; the deacons, however, respect like God's command! No one shall act regarding the church without the bishop. A celebration of the Eucharist is only authentic when it takes place under a bishop or one of his representatives. Where the bishop appears, there shall be the community, just as where Jesus Christ is, there is the *Catholic Church*" (Letter to the Smyrnans, 8, 1). Already he develops a theology of the bishop's office in which he finds embodied the unity of the church. Christ, bishop, and church are one.

In Ignatius's letter to the Romans he also with certainty assigns a special position to the Roman church. He praises not only its profession of love, but also — probably in connection with Clement's letter which he must have known — its firmness of faith and doctrine so that "the special repute and actual pre-eminence of the Roman community is already clearly to be perceived" (Altaner, 86). From Troas, Ignatius reminds his brother-bishop Polycarp, who had attended him in Smyrna, of his duty as a shepherd and exhorts him to stand as firm during the persecution of Christians as an anvil under the blows of a hammer.

We also possess a letter to the Philippians from Polycarp, the bishop of Smyrna, who in his youth had still heard the apostle John and had been appointed bishop by him. The letter actually consists of two pieces, of which the first was written at the time of Ignatius's journey to Rome around 110, the second a few years later, approximately in 111/112 (Fischer). Polycarp suffered a martyr's death in Smyrna at the age of 86, either in 155/156 or in 167/168. His moving death on the pyre in the arena is reported in an essentially genuine, reliable letter which was written by a direct eyewitness and sent to the church of Philomelium in Phrygia by request of the community of Smyrna.

Of Quadratus we have only a few lines of an otherwise lost apology which he had sent around 125 to Emperor Hadrian (117–138) in defense of Christianity. Whether the letter is identical with that written to Diognetus, as has been asserted recently (P. Andriessen), remains questionable. Also only a few fragments of the "Explanation of words of the Lord", written by bishop Papias of Hierapolis around 130, have been preserved.

From the second, figurative group of writings of the "Apostolic Fathers", the letter of Barnabas belongs to the first half of the second century and the letter to Diognetus, a wonderful "testimony of spiritualized Christian belief of revelation and self-assurance" was sent by an unknown author to an eminent Gentile by the name of Diognetus in the second half of the second century. The Didache or Twelve-apostle-doctrine, which encompasses the oldest church order known to us and provided information about the liturgical life of early Christianity, originated in the first half of the second century, but its matrix (Did. 1–6) goes back to the first century. The "Shepherd", written by Hermas, a brother of the Roman bishop Pius I (142–154/155 ?), came into existence in Rome around the middle of the second century as an impressive apocalypse of penance, and forms an important part of the history of sacramental penance.

2. The early Christian apologists of the second century took upon themselves the task of the literary defense of Christianity. By this time the church had attained historical magnitude and could no longer be ignored by the world around it. The increasing number of men of position and education who entered the Christian communities sought stimulating discourse with the educated pagans, partly to justify their conversion, partly to refute the existing prejudice and slander exercised toward Christians.

In the attempt to explain themselves to the world around them, the apologists used the concepts of their time extensively. They wanted to proclaim the Christian message in a time which was characterized by the spirituality of Platonism and the later Stoa, and by the concepts of the Hellenistic Near Eastern mystery cults. They had grown up with these ideas before their conversion to Christianity as, for example, in the case of Justin who had found the way to Christian truth only after a long search. No wonder, then, that the apologists interpreted the gospel in the language which was spoken by their world and which was their mother tongue. It is unjustified to reproach them with "Hellenizing" God's word and thereby falsifying it. The aim of the apologists was the winning of the world for Christ, and they courageously sought the dialogue with the world around them with the intention of testifying for Christ and acting as his missionaries. It is to their everlasting fame that they did not permit themselves to be pushed into a ghetto.

The Hellenistic world indeed provided sufficiently valuable starting-points for a conversation. After all, the idea of the Logos in the prologue to the gospel of John, which itself seems to stem from late Jewish Gnosticism, had its counterpart in the philosophy of Zeno and the Stoa. The divine force which was here acting as the creative Logos and to which the whole universe owes its origin and animation had already been applied to Christ by the Apostolic Fathers (Ignatius, Epistle to the Magnesians 8, 2). The famous martyr and philosopher Justin who long taught Christian Gnosticism in Rome until he was executed around 165/167 for his testimony for Christ, in his two apologies developed the thought that all human beings in their reason already possess germs of the eternal Logos *(Logoi spermatikoi)*. All human beings are by nature, i.e. by the creator, directed toward divine truth. In the revelation of the Christ-Logos, this divine truth experienced its last and highest disclosure. Not only the men of God of the Old Covenant, but also the great Greek thinkers who were searching for truth, were close to Christ and partook germinally of him, the Divine Logos. In a sense these men were Christians before Christ. Christianity is the true philosophy and wisdom; it is the fulfillment of the yearning of man for perception of the last and deepest knowledge, the real Gnosis.

Other apologists continued the argument, just as Justin had; some of them argued with Judaism, some with the polytheism of paganism, and others with the promises of salvation by the mystery cults. All of them had in common the striving to show Christianity as the only fulfillment and the eternal destiny of man.

Besides Justin we include in this group of early Christian apologists the philosophers Aristides and Athenagoras of Athens and the Syrian Tatian who in addition to his "Speech to the Greeks" also wrote a harmony of the gospels *(Diatessaron)*. Tatian, who was Justin's pupil in Rome, also founded a heretical Gnostic-Encratitic sect around 172 after his return to the East. Additionally, there are the bishops Theophilus of Antioch, Apollinaris of Hierapolis, Melito of Sardis, Aristo of Pella (around 140), the rhetorician Miltiades, and the previously mentioned Quadratus and Hermas who also have to be listed here as apologists.

3. The distinguished name "Church Fathers" is given to those great theologians who did not stop with the defense, but who instead had as their aim the deeper theological permeation of the articles of faith on the basis of revelation. Most of them were bishops; thus arose the name "Father" which originally was reserved to the bishops in communities. Some of them, however, were only priests, such as Jerome, or laymen, such as Tertullian. Later doctrine lists as attributes for belonging to the group of

Church Fathers: 1) orthodoxy in doctrine; 2) saintliness in life; 3) ecclesiastical recognition; and 4) belonging to Christian Antiquity. With the help of the last characteristic, the Church Fathers are distinguished from the church teachers who lived and taught during the Middle and Modern Ages.

The topics of the Church Fathers were often provided by their environment and filled a genuine need of the time. The close contact with Hellenistic philosophy and Gnosticism, for example, had created for Christianity the danger of being regarded not as pure divine revelation, bound to Scripture and apostolic tradition, but as a syncretistic basis for Gnostic speculation. Very early, Gnosticism, thoroughly pagan at its core, tried to invade Christianity. For its muddled trains of thought on the creation and salvation of the world, it utilized an allegorical interpretation of Holy Scripture, and mixed Christian elements of revelation with pagan ideas, particularly dualistic concepts. In defense of Christianity it became necessary to fix exactly Christian beliefs and the sources of revelation, to designate finally and unequivocally in a "Canon of Holy Scripture" those writings which alone could provide a guideline (= canon), to define more closely their inspirational character, and to reserve their authentic interpretation exclusively to the bishop. The arbitrary interpretation of the Scriptures by heretics was countered by the understanding of the Scriptures in the spirit of the apostolic tradition as the standard of exclusive validity. The sole guarantee for maintaining the purity of the body of revelation transmitted by the apostles is its transmission by the bishop, assured through uninterrupted succession since the time of the apostles. Thus the Church Fathers stressed that the real Christian Gnosis could only be the one which understood the faith in the sense of the *"traditio apostolica"*. Only through the bishops, the legitimate successors of the apostles, can orthodoxy be found, and whoever separates himself from the bishop, goes astray.

Out of the discussion with Gnosticism and other heresies grew a scientific Christian theology. Its subjects were in the main the person and work of Christ (Christology), Christ's work of salvation (Soteriology), and his relationship to the Father and the Holy Spirit (Doctrine of the Trinity). For the next several centuries these subjects remained at the center of theological investigation.

The first important theologian of the second century was bishop Irenaeus of Lyon (d. ca. 202). In his principal work *Adversus haereses (Against the Heresies)* he defined, between the years 180 and 184, among other things, the meaning of the genuine apostolic tradition for the maintenance of purity of the true faith. He sees purity of faith most clearly guaranteed by the Roman bishop as the successor of Peter in the community of Rome and hurls this argument against the Gnostic heresies (*Adv. haereses* 3, 3). Irenaeus has given us the oldest list of Roman bishops.

At the same time, Tertullian (d. after 220 in Carthage), jurist and theological writer, worked in North Africa. He also opposed the Gnostic heretics with the genuine principle of tradition as a standard of faith. In his main work *De praescriptione haereticorum* (ca. 200) he refutes them curtly with two "claims" (= "prae-scriptiones" in juridical terminology): 1) Christ has handed down his doctrine only to the apostles for dissemination and to no one else; there was no special revelation of secret information to anyone else, as the Gnostics claim. 2) The apostles on their part have handed down their doctrines only to the bishop's churches founded by them. All Christians must agree in belief with these apostolic churches. A doctrine which is not in the apostolic tradition is heretical. Therefore, concludes Tertullian, the Gnostics are heretics. In his numerous writings he coined many theological terms which are still in use today. Unfortunately he himself went astray in his later years (ca. 207) by adhering to the rigoristic sect of Montanism.

In Rome at the beginning of the third century the presbyter Hippolytus (d. 235) wrote many theological tracts, such as *Refutatio omnium haeresium* ("Refutation of all heresies"), which he directed after 222 against the Trinitarian heresies of the Modalist Sabellius and the so-called Patripassians. He composed a very effective ritual, the "Apostolic Transmission" (ca. 220). Because of jealousy and wounded pride, Hippolytus also opposed the church when he was passed over at the papal election of 217 and Callixtus (217–222) was elected. He even permitted himself to be elected by his adherents as the first antipope and thereby brought about the first schism in Rome. Later he became reconciled again with the church and together with Pope Pontian died a martyr's death in 235 while in exile.

Also in Carthage lived and taught bishop Cyprian, only baptized in 246, but by 248/249 already a bishop and martyred in 258. Cyprian was a strong representative of ecclesiastical unity, and in his tract *De ecclesia unitate* (ca. 251) is the sentence: "He who does not have God as his father cannot have the church as his mother." The sentence from the fourth chapter of the tract, which often has been attacked without justification, is also authentic: "Primacy was given to Peter. How can anyone who separates himself from the see of Peter, in which the church is based, believe that he is still in the church?" (*De ecclesia unitate*, 4, 7). Of course, one must not read into these words an admission of Roman jurisdictional primacy. Cyprian himself quarreled with Pope Stephen I in 255. Regarding the question of the validity of the baptism of heretics and starting from an erroneous concept of the sacrament, he took the position that the efficacy of baptism depended on the condition of grace of the officiating priest. According to Cyprian, whoever did not himself possess the Holy Spirit could not pass it on in baptism; consequently, not Christ would be the dispenser *(ex opere operato)*, but man by virtue of his charisma.

33

6

THE BEGINNINGS OF THE CHRISTIAN SCHOOL
OF ALEXANDRIA

The number of converts in the large communities of the metro-
poles of the time, Rome, Antioch, Alexandria, etc., necessitated
the establishment of special catechumenates for the baptismal
candidates. The duration and the intensity of the preparatory
instruction demanded much from the candidates, but even more
from the instructors. Teaching institutions to supply the catechumenates also had to be created, the so-called catechetical
schools, in which were offered advanced theological education
and Christian instruction. It is assumed that such a school existed
already in Alexandria by the second century.

However, the type of school with which we are concerned
here was not of this nature. Rather it grew out of the teaching of
Christian Gnostics who, quite like the Stoic, Cynic, and other
philosophers, presented their Christian view of life privately.
When Justin was asked about his activity by the pagan judge, he
answered according to the official transcript: "I live on the second
floor of the house of a certain Martin near the bath of Timotheus.
There I have been staying since I have come to Rome a second
time. I know of no other meeting place. All of those who visited
me there I have instructed in the doctrine of truth. Yes, I am a
Christian."

A similar procedure was followed by the Sicilian Pantaenus
when on his own private initiative he opened a school of Christian
Gnosticism around 180 in Alexandria, the spiritual center of
Hellenism, and presented there the doctrine of the gospels
within the framework of philosophical lectures. Pantaenus
appealed to all who were desirous of knowledge, not only to
Christians, but also to those among the pagans who were seeking
truth. By way of his thorough and at the same time inspiring
expositions, he won many a pagan for Christianity and lifted many
Christians with him to the heights of theological speculation. In
this fashion, the Athenian Clement (b. 140/150, d. before 216) was

34

introduced to Christianity and soon was so gripped by it that in ca. 200 like Pantaenus he settled in Alexandria and enjoyed growing success as a Christian philosopher and Gnostic. His greatest pupil was the young Origen (b. ca. 185 in Alexandria, d. ca. 254). When Clement left the city during the persecution by Septimius Severus, Origen continued his teaching. He also began instruction as a free private teacher. Finally around 215 bishop Demetrius of Alexandria officially turned over to him the clerical instruction of catechumens of the large Alexandrian Christian community. Soon after, Origen transferred the actual catechist office to his friend Heraclas and again devoted himself to his former work with the greatest success. Now, by order of the bishop, he was an officially appointed teacher of the church. A break with Demetrius occurred in 230 when Origen had himself ordained a priest by other bishops without the permission and dispensation of his bishop. He had to leave Alexandria and went to Caesarea in Palestine where he continued to teach. Imprisoned and tortured during the persecution by Emperor Decius, he was released, but only to die soon as a result of the mistreatment.

What were the peculiarities of this Alexandrian school? The very fact, which recent scholarship has shown, that it was not an institution with a clerical purpose, neither a catechist school nor a clerico-theological university, but instead rested on private initiative, conferred a special note on it. If one thus sees the school in the midst of its time "there opens up an imposing vista: In the metropolis of the Hellenistic scientific world a teacher in philosopher's garb, driven by an unmanageable missionary eagerness, who was himself converted to Christianity in this way, runs a 'school' altogether in the style of his time for the young and old seekers of truth and lovers of wisdom of his pagan environment", as A. Knauber describes this enterprise. Clement is "to be regarded as the first Christian scholar". He was versed not only in the Holy Scriptures but also in the whole profane knowledge of his time, including Greek philosophy and classical literature. Clement understood the questions and problems of the young people who came from such educational centers of the time as Rome, Athens, and Antioch. They were just as dissatisfied with their instruction as he had been and now sought and found the last and highest wisdom in the Christian revelation. Perhaps the students had encountered Christianity before in the form of Gnostic syncretism. Clement had to enter their world, disentangle their conceptions, and lead them slowly from error to the pure and true knowledge of Christianity. He lived and taught like a philosopher and used the forms and the language of the Gnostics of his time. Origen followed him in this.

It was "an outright revolutionary action" that these men seized not only the external garb and forms of expression of the contemporary pagan philosophers, but also their problems. If, for example, they discussed cosmology, so beloved by Gnosticism, they did not do it with the intention of proving these ideas wrong *a priori* and discarding them quickly, but instead pointed out how the fundamental religious questions about the creation of the world, the creator, the existence of evil in this life, and the salvation through the God-Logos Jesus Christ found their last and deepest answer in Christian revelation. They wanted to be "messengers of Christianity in philosopher's garb". Especially Clement "was nothing more and nothing less than the missionary of the Hellenistic intellectual world who for the first time with the full force of his neo-Christian conviction of victory . . . undertook . . . a conquering advance of large design . . . into the contemporary pagan academic circles" (Knauber). His interest here was not purely or even primarily theological, but pastoral. He wanted to win his auditors for Christ and lead them to salvation.

But, we ask, did he not go too far in this accommodation to the Hellenistic environment? Did not with the language and the concepts the contents of Greek philosophy and mystery cults also enter the young Christianity and did the syncretism of late antiquity not lead, after all, to a falsification of the original pure gospel? These questions must be taken seriously, for it is certain that at no time, out of love for accommodation, can alterations be permitted in the revealed articles of faith.

Upon closer inspection it is quite clear that such alterations were not made, and also that no pagan thoughts and customs were permitted to adulterate Christian content. These men were too much aware of their essential opposition to the pagan-Gnostic environment to have fallen prey to this danger. Even though they took the accommodation seriously and involved themselves earnestly in the spiritual world of their listeners, they were cognizant of the living mission of salvation of him who through the church becomes human again in every age. Just as Christ in his incarnation affirmed and adopted all of man's being — with the exception of sin —, i.e. how among the Jews he became a Jew, so he adopts in the course of the history of the church the humanity of all peoples and civilizations, being incarnated in them ever anew. As in the case of Paul, who was "all things to all men" (1 Cor 9, 22), Clement repeatedly declared: "For the Hellenes one must become a Hellene in order to win them all. One must offer to those who demand it the kind of wisdom with which they are familiar so that as easily as possible they can make their way through their own world of ideas to the belief in the truth" (Clement, *Stromateis* I, 15, 3 ff; V, 18, 6 ff).

Subsequently, Greek thinking united closely with Christian thought. In the great saints and theologians of Greek patrology this bond found its glorious sanction and completion. Without it, the immense theological accomplishment of the first councils would not have been possible. After Clement, the great Origen continued to lay the foundations for this union.

7

INTERNAL CRISES: SCHISMS AND HERESIES

The mutual existence of the spiritual nature and ideas of the Christian truths of revelation together with the principle of the incarnate church through which it participates in history and exercises within all humanity its internal and external development, make the frequent appearance of erroneous opinions and heretical falsifications understandable. Precisely because the church was aware that it had to carry the precious treasure of pure divine truth in a fragile earthen vessel and preserve it unadulterated, it was required by this responsibility to devote special care to the refutation of false doctrines. Particularly in times when there was the tendency toward syncretistic amalgamation, which leads to a dangerous relativism in questions of faith, the church was strongly opposed to the rise of separate opinions and heresies. Such was the case with the young Christianity and its situation, which was severely threatened from the outside, became often almost tragic. Eusebius, the father of church history, noted that during the second century the internal threat to Christianity through heresies and schisms was far greater than the external one posed by persecutions. The remarkably rich anti-heretical literature of the early church, of the apologists, and of the Church Fathers proves with what great concern and attention this development was regarded.

1. After the death of St. James (62/63), Judaistic schisms developed, especially in Jerusalem and Palestine, among those Jewish-Christian circles which could not separate themselves decidedly enough from the old Jewish cult. These schismatic groups finally joined the heresies of the Ebionites, Nazarenes, and Elkesaites, groups which continued to believe in the messiahship of Jesus but denied his divinity. Cerinthus (end of the first century), a contemporary of the apostle John, connected Gnostic speculations with a harsh Judaism. Irenaeus reports that John wrote his gospel to confute Cerinthus's errors.

2. The various Gnostic systems are products of syncretism and go back to pre-Christian times. The discovery of a large Gnostic library in Nag Hammadi in Egypt in 1946 enables us to grasp a bit more clearly their essence and their confusing thoughts. Greek religious philosophies and the promise of salvation of the Near-Eastern-Hellenistic mystery cults united in them to produce a peculiar mixture of worldly and other-worldly conceptions, insights into which were permitted only to the initiated.

The Gnostics promised their followers mysterious answers to

the final great questions of man about the origin and destiny of life, about the creation of the cosmos, and about the meaning of evil and malevolence in the world. The "true knowledge" (= gnosis) which they imparted did not rest on rational cognition and factual instruction, but was attained through mystical immersion and certain religious practices. The Gnostics claimed to be in possession of secret revelations and a veiled knowledge, open only to the elect.

It was the revealed nature of Christianity which early had interested the Gnostics. We hear of them already in the New Testament writings, where Paul especially turns against them (1 Tim 1, 4; 4, 7; 6, 4; 6, 20; Col 12, 8 ff; Apoc 2, 6, 15). It could not be prevented, however, that in the course of time they adopted the Christian doctrine of revelation and adjusted it for their purposes. In their fantastic allegorical interpretation of the Holy Scriptures, they combined Platonic and Pythagorean speculations with the concept of salvation of the pagan mysteries and with the mythological cosmogenies and astrologies of the old orient. The Christian doctrine of faith and salvation through the incarnation of God's son blended with the teaching of emanations and aeons. Further amalgamation also took place with dualistic conceptions, according to which there exist two final principles, good and evil, which are struggling with one another.

The following thoughts form a common basis for the various Gnostic systems: From the supreme concealed God, living in an inaccessible realm of light, the universe has been created by emanations in such a way that numerous spirits (Aeones, up to 365) have emerged from this God and receded farther and farther from their divine origin. The wider the distance grows, the more they lose of their essence and the less light they possess. On the last and lowest step they finally merge with matter which belongs to the empire of darkness and evil. In this lowest region our earth took form; it is the work of the least of all aeons, the demi-urge. This demi-urge or "world-shaper" is equated with Yahwe, the God of the Old Testament.

"Salvation" now consists of the liberation of the divine sparks from matter and their return to the realm of light (pleroma) of the supreme God. At this point the blending with Christianity occurs. Christ appears as such a spirit (aeon); his task it was to reveal the so-far unknown supreme God to men and to teach them how one can separate from matter, surmount darkness, and return to the pleroma of God. In Jesus of Nazareth God assumed human form in appearance only. Christ only appeared to work and suffer (Docetism); in reality he could not suffer and die on the cross; some Gnostics even taught that the Christ-Logos had descended on Jesus the man only at the baptism in the Jordan and thereby had made him into the Messiah. Before the passion God had left Jesus again and consequently Jesus of Nazareth had died on the cross as nothing more than a human being. No atoning significance could be attached to the death on the cross; only his teaching was important, and only those who understood and followed the esoteric doctrine of the Christ-Logos would really be "saved". But the essence of the doctrine was to overcome matter. Only the true "Gnostics" or "pneumatics" would be able to understand this. The mass of the people, the pagans, the "material men" (Hylics) would get lost in the eternal darkness together with matter. The average Christians, the "psychics", who were incapable of higher knowledge, were admitted to a lesser salvation and a limited bliss. They asserted that Christ had left a dual revelation, a lower one, which was being proclaimed in the Holy Scriptures of the church, and a higher, veiled one, which he had entrusted secretly to only a few select persons and which was now possessed by the Gnostics.

The chief representatives of the so-called "Christian" Gnostics were Satornil in Antioch (beginning second century), Basilides in Alexandria (ca. 120–145), and Valentinus in Rome (ca. 136 – ca. 160).

It is easy to see that this gnosis is entirely un-Christian in its totality, because it denies the essence of Christianity, the belief in the actual divinity of Christ. Gnosticism represents an attempt to pull Christianity into the dangerous wake of syncretism. Its attraction rested mainly in the lure which the mysterious and the pseudo-mystical exercises on numerous people; in the cosmic speculations and revelations, connected with cultic forms, which created a new understanding of the world and salvation; and in the seemingly strictly ascetical conduct of life, a conduct which in reality contained a non-Christian dualistic denial of the world and hostility to the body. Through propaganda, Gnosticism was able to create some damage in the young congregations, primarily among the newly baptized converts from paganism. The Gnostics made extensive use of religious novels, pious cultic hymns, and apocryphal "Holy Scriptures" which allegedly were derived from special revelations and secret traditions of hitherto concealed sayings of Christ. Gnosticism in the form of Manichaeism survived into the Middle Ages by continuing to exist in the sects of the Paulicians, Bogomils, and Cathari. It even experienced a new life in modern times (Spiritism, Theosophy, Anthroposophy, etc.), and actually has never been overcome completely. This fact permits the assumption that in some way it has answered a deep human longing.

3. Manichaeism goes back to the Persian Mani (215–273), who as God's last messenger after Buddha, Zarathustra, and Jesus wanted to bring the divine revelation to full fruition. His doctrine has very little in common with Christianity. Mani taught a strict dualism and regarded the development of the world as a permanent struggle between light and darkness, between the principles of good and evil, and between spirit and matter. In this process man is supposed to overcome evil within himself and to amplify the light by avoiding all evil matter, such as meat and wine and sexual lust. During the last decades of the third century Manichaeism advanced into the Roman Empire and then spread rapidly during the fourth century. It became a great danger to Christianity by absorbing many Christian elements. Even St. Augustine was in its power before his baptism.

4. In the second century, Marcionism, for a time, offered the most dangerous competition to the Christian church. Marcion, born around 85 as the son of the bishop of Sinope on the Black Sea, came to Rome ca. 139, to preach his own ideas to the Roman

41

congregation. When he was rejected and excommunicated he founded his own church which quickly spread because of his strict direction and organization. In his teaching, Marcion rejected the Old Testament and preached a strict dualism. The Yahweh of the Old Testament to him was the wrathful God of evil; the Christ of the New Testament he saw revealed as the supreme God of good. When the followers of Yahweh, the Jews, had persecuted the God of the New Testament, Christ, they had only apparently been able to kill him, since he had only seemed to assume a human body. The strict ethical rigorism of Marcionism, resting on dualistic hostility to the flesh, enlisted many fanatical followers.

5. Irenaeus (*Adv. haer.* 1, 28) and Clement of Alexandria (*Stromateis* I, 15, 71, and elsewhere) designated the representatives of an ascetical group, strictly hostile to the flesh, as "Encratites" (Abstainers). Around 170 it found a wide hearing and assumed threatening proportions. Tatian, whom we had met earlier as an apologist, belonged to the group. Dogmatically, the Encratites were correct, but they went so far in their ascetical demands, apparently under Marcion's influence, that they expected *every* Christian to practise complete abstinence not only from meat and wine but also in marriage. Justifiably, this interpretation was rejected as heretical. Encratistic tendencies often did survive, however, and played a role in the pre-history and early history of monasticism.

6. Montanism contained encratistic features which were combined with an early Christian enthusiasm. Montanus, a former Cybele priest, since 156/157 (according to others only since 172) accused the church in general of having already become too secular. He preached asceticism and a strict reform of morals, and condemned the flight from martyrdom even to the point of demanding that Christians must volunteer and even press for martyrdom. Montanus also recalled to life the eschatological tension of the primitive church and announced the immediately imminent beginning of the millenium of Christ (Chiliasm). Referring to special revelations, he passed himself off as the

prophet of the Holy Spirit in whom now, beyond Christ, divine revelation had reached its completion. He was supported by two ecstatic women, Priscilla and Maximilla, who also claimed to have had prophetic visions and to have received revelations. In Perpuza in Phrygia they gathered their followers, there to await the arrival of Christ for the Last Judgment. The strict morals of the sect won it many adherents. Later it spread to North Africa where, around 207, even as intellectually eminent a man as Tertullian became a member. Now Tertullian on his part furiously attacked the church for its allegedly lax morals and practice of penance.

In view of the variety and frequency of heresies, the question about the meaning of schisms poses a real problem. "For there must also be heresies among you", writes Paul to the Corinthians (1 Cor 11, 19), "that they which are approved may be manifest among you." J. Lortz speaks of a "felix culpa" and emphasizes that "error and guilt may very well have a deep significance in God's plan of salvation". K. Rahner is of the opinion that the church learns "to recognize more clearly its own truth by listening to opposition . . . and rejecting it". Nothing could be more wrong than simply to equate heresy with malice and not to see that "sometimes it is founded in a particularly zealous personal search after the right truth of salvation" (Lortz). Jerome writes: "No one can establish a heresy who does not possess a burning spirit and gifts of nature which have been created by God the artist", and Augustine admonishes: "Do not believe, Brethren, that heresies could arise through small minds. Only great men proclaimed heresies" (In Psalm 124).

In the same breath, Augustine calls them malicious and compares them to large cliffs, the more dangerous because of their size, and cautions against them. The Pauline remark also is not explained by his desire to attach positive significance to heresies in the sense that they promote the knowledge of truth. Rather, Paul sees in the heresy a terrible threat to salvation not only of the individual person but also and even more so for the church which heresy wants to divert from its true goal. There can be only a single valid divine truth of revelation, and because of its universal task of salvation and its eschatological destiny, the church must never separate itself from this truth. By repeatedly sowing weeds among the wheat, the "evil one" attempts to overgrow the fruit and choke it. The victorious exposition of truth comes only at the end of time together with the great judgment. But until that day the church must always fight the weeds in order to protect its children. Looking at heresy in this manner, Augustine also calls heresies and their originators the "eliminations of the church" ("quos partim digessit Ecclesia, tamquam stercora", *Sermo V: Opera Omnia,* Paris, 1837, V, 42).

The church had to fight not only against external syncretistic falsifications of belief, but also as vehemently against the narrow abridgements of faith demanded by encratistic-rigoristic sectarians such as Montanus and the older Tertullian. It has accomplished this since the end of the second century by the exact definition of the apostolic principle of tradition, by fixing the canon of Holy Scripture, and finally by joint councils of the bishops. The bishops of Phrygia gathered for a synod for the first time against the Montanistic movement. Soon larger gatherings grew out of these local synods and around the middle of the third century provincial synods developed, at which the bishops of a whole province gathered around their metropolitan. Examples are found in the bishops of Africa at Carthage, in those of Egypt at Alexandria, those of Asia at Antioch and Caesarea, and those of Italy at Rome. When, for the first time after the Constantinian turning point, the bishops of the whole Roman Empire, the "ecumene", were permitted to gather in order to consult on universal ecclesiastical problems, the first "ecumenical council" of Nicaea (325) met under Constantine's direction to decide on the Arian heresy and the schism of Meletius (Egypt) and Donatus (North Africa).

8
THE PERSECUTIONS OF CHRISTIANS IN THE ROMAN EMPIRE

1. The Basis of the Persecutions

The Roman Empire was a state based on law. If it took forcible action against Christianity, we must assume that it had reasons for doing so. Unfortunately we possess only a very few official pronouncements which can provide us with information on the legal basis for the official persecutions of Christians. Did the state offices act on the basis of special legislation against the Christians? Or did they simply make use of their right to police supervision because they regarded Christianity as a "forbidden religion" *(religio illicita)*? This old controversial question is still undecided. If Tertullian occasionally spoke of an *"institutum Neronianum"* (*Ad nationes* 1, 7, 14), then we must not understand this as a lawful foundation in the sense that Nero had passed a law against the Christians, but simply as the fact that Nero began the persecutions. For the same Tertullian also accuses the Roman state of proceeding against the Christians inconsequentially and without the foundation of law.

This reproach of inconsequence was concerned chiefly with the ordinance which Trajan in a rescript had directed to Pliny: the Christians should be punished *as Christians ("propter nomen ipsum")* if they were accused; but the state should not actively pursue them. If they are criminals, asks Tertullian, why are they not pursued? If they are not criminals and need not be hunted, why are they then sentenced and punished? Hadrian also stuck to this imprecise position (Rescript to Minucius Fundanus, ca. 125). Only Decius (249–251) passed laws which based the actions against the Christians on a juridical basis.

The Christian sources on the persecutions allow us a deeper insight into the whole story. Three kinds of such reports are available to us:

a) Original files of martyrs which rest partly on official court transcripts and partly on eyewitness accounts such as the martyrdoms of Polycarp, Ptolemaeus, Lucius, the martyrs of Scillium, Apollonius, and Perpetua and Felicitas. Their value is very high, because even if their form has often been revised for didactic purposes, their content has remained true. They are concerned primarily with the interrogations and they report the sentencing by the judge with meticulous accuracy.

b) *"Passiones"* or "Martyria"; these are descriptions by usually creditable contemporaries, which partly go back to eyewitnesses, but in general report from second hand.

c) Legends and stories of a later period, which essentially are worthless and often do not show their historical kernel if they have one at all.

Other literary testimony of *Christian* origin is very numerous. All Christian writers mention and report the persecutions, for the most part from personal experience. The silence of the pagans, then, becomes even more astonishing. The first pagan literary reports we owe to Tacitus (*Annales* 15, 14ff) and Suetonius (*Vita Neronis* 16, 2), and they are meager enough. Some of the writings attacking Christianity are important; the pagan Celsus, for example, around 178 wrote an anti-Christian polemic, the answer to which, written by Origen, shows well the reasons and motives of the opponents.

The refusal to participate in the official pagan worship, which was necessarily connected with their exclusive monotheism, made the Christians appear as "atheists" (= "without Gods", not God-less), and thus as enemies of the state. The absolutism of the Christian religion, in which Christ is revered as the only master and God (= Kyrios), also denied the Christians the recognition of the emperor worship, whose forms had become steadily more bizarre since Domitian. By placing the "Kyrios" Christ in opposition to the "Kyrios" Emperor, the Christians became more and more enemies of the state as the religious form of emperor worship was made the test of loyalty to the state. Even if generally tolerant of alien religions, the Roman state rested on a religious foundation and demanded from everyone that he revere the emperor in suitable fashion and acknowledge the gods of the state. Toward the Jews the state remained tolerant even in spite of their monotheism, because the Jews only involved a small number of adherents, limited to a particular national group. The direction of Christianity, however, was supra-national and universal. Even if until the middle of the third century Christianity was a minuscule minority in the Roman Empire, this universal appeal tended to upset the foundations of the universal empire. Therefore, conflict was inevitable. It was brought about by the very emperors of the second and third centuries who were able rulers and who attempted to rejuvenate the state and strengthen the empire internally on a religious basis.

The Christians on their part acknowledged the state as a regulatory power, obeyed the laws of the state with faithful exactitude, and prayed *for* the emperor, but not to him. There was thus hardly any reason for action against them in normal times. As a matter of fact, persecutions occurred only sporadically and varied in extent and duration in the individual provinces. Especially in the second century they were more like volcanic eruptions of stopped-up hate than systematic state operations, prepared long in advance. Only the Emperor Decius began to act according to a clear plan.

From the beginning, the mob actively took a large part in the persecutions. What is the explanation for this hate against the Christians which was noticeable everywhere until the middle of the third century?

The first and most important reason was the instinctive dislike which primitive and uneducated people always have for those who are and live differently from the mass and who stand higher religiously and morally. The withdrawn life of the Christians created suspicion and awakened the desire for slander. People whispered about criminal activities during their secret meetings, about thyestic meals (as once Thyestes in Greek legend who was given to eat the flesh of his own slaughtered children) at which the participants ate human flesh (i.e. partook of the body and blood of Christ), and about incestuous fornication, for which the usual address among Christians of "Brother" and "Sister"

47

may have been responsible. Natural catastrophies, public disorders, accidents, and defeats in war were attributed to the
Christian refusal to sacrifice to the gods of the state. In general,
they were accused of hating the whole human race *(odium humani
generis)*. This accusation seems to have been so wide-spread that
as early as the time of Nero he was able without difficulties to
divert the suspicion that he had burned Rome to the Christians
as the "scum of humanity".

2. The Course of the Persecutions

Three stages can clearly be distinguished:

First Period: until about 100 Christianity was ignored or
tolerated by the state. It was regarded as a Jewish sect and shared
the official toleration of the Jewish religion *("religio licita")*. The
first great persecution by Nero (54–68) was nothing more than
the monstrous act of a brutal tyrant who incited it in order to
shift the guilt for the burning of Rome in July 64 from himself
to the Christians. He had a great number of Roman Christians
put to death by torture and made a public spectacle out of it in
his gardens. Among the victims were Peter and Paul. This
persecution was limited to the city and was devoid of any lawful
foundation. It was fateful that through Nero's action the stigma
of the *"odium humani generis"* was attached to the Christians and
for almost two hundred years provided not the lawful but certainly the factual or, better said, the permissive basis for actions
against them. The various measures of Domitian (81–96) were
also the murderous acts of a tyrant. In the year 95 the consul
Flavius Clemens, a cousin of the emperor, was executed and his
wife Flavia Domitilla was sent into exile together with her sons.
According to oldest tradition the apostle John was exiled to
Patmos (during the reign of Domitian), where he wrote the
Apocalypse (Irenaeus, *Adv. haer.* 2, 22, 5; 3, 1, 1).

Second Period: From 100 to 250. Christianity was now
recognized as a religion in its own right, but was persecuted as
a *religio illicita,* hostile to state and man. The foundation for this

view was the correspondence between Pliny and Trajan (98–117) which, though at first private, soon was circulated by Pliny, regarded as semi-official, and finally became common law. As the new governor of Bithynia in 112, Pliny had asked the emperor for rules of conduct; for, he writes, "having never been present at any trials of the Christians, I am unacquainted with the method and limits to be observed either in examining or punishing them. Also I am not certain whether any difference is to be made on account of age; whether to treat younger people the same as older persons, whether to grant pardon in case of repentance; or whether, if a man has once been a Christian, it avail him nothing to recant; whether the *mere name,* even if no crime be attached, or only the crimes associated with it are punishable; in all these points I am greatly doubtful."

"In the meanwhile", he continues, "the method I have observed toward those who have been denounced to me as Christians is the following: I asked them whether they were Christians; if they confessed it, I repeated the question for a second and a third time, adding the threat of capital punishment. If they still persevered, I had them executed. For I had no doubt that whatever the nature of their creed might be, their contumacy and inflexible obstinacy deserved punishment in any case. A few Roman citizens who were also obsessed with the same delusion I have directed to be taken to Rome.

These accusations spread (as is usually the case) and several cases came to light. An anonymous informer sent in a list with the names of many persons. Those who denied they were or ever had been Christians I thought it proper to discharge if they repeated after me an invocation to the Gods and offered adoration, with wine and incense, to your image, which I had ordered to be brought for that purpose, together with those of the Gods, and finally cursed Christ, acts, to whose performance real Christians cannot be forced under any circumstances. Others who were named by that informer immediately confessed themselves Christians and then denied it; true, they had been Christians, but were so no longer; some had been Christians three years ago or more, some even twenty-five years ago. They all worshipped your image and those of the Gods and cursed Christ. They affirmed, however, that the whole of their guilt or their error was that they were in the habit of meeting on a certain fixed day before sunrise when they sang in alternate verses a hymn to Christ, as to a God, and did not bind themselves by a solemn oath to commit a crime, but rather not to commit a theft, robbery, or adultery, not to break their word, and not to deny a trust when called upon to return it. Then it was their custom to separate and to meet again later to partake of food — but food of an ordinary and innocent kind. But after my edict in which according to your order I had forbidden associations, they had abandoned even this practice.

I judged it so much the more necessary to extract the real truth, with the assistance of torture, from two female slaves, who were called deaconesses. But I discovered nothing more than a depraved and excessive superstition. I therefore adjourned the proceedings and turn to you for advice . . ." (then follows the passage quoted on p. 20).

The emperor answered: "You, my dear Secundus, have pursued the right method. It is not possible to lay down any general rule for the treatment of all cases: No search shall be made for these people; when they are denounced, however, and found guilty, they must be punished. But whoever denies being a Christian and gives proof that he is not by praying to our Gods shall be pardoned on the ground of his repentance, even though he may have incurred suspicion because of his past. Accusations without signature must not be admitted as evidence in any trial: For that would be a bad precedent and not worthy of the spirit of our age."

According to this ordinance, simply to be a Christian was punishable; no further crimes need have been committed by the accused. Only anonymous denunciations should no longer be accepted. The implementation of the rescript, which was not a law of the state, was left in the hands of the provincial governors. Indeed, subsequently there occurred numerous territorially limited persecutions whose instigators often were fanaticized mobs. Emperor Hadrian (117–138) in a similar rescript in the year 124/125 to C. Minucius Fundanus, governor of Asia, actually forbade him to follow such desires of the mob and anonymous denunciations of Christians, and the Christians welcomed it as a relief. But also under Antoninus Pius (138–161), Marcus Aurelius (161–180), and Commodus (180–192) numerous Christians were executed either singly or in groups. Under Marcus Aurelius, the philosopher-emperor, an increase in hostility to Christians is actually noticeable.

Famous martyrs of the second century are: Ignatius of Antioch (ca. 107/110); Justin, the philosopher, and six companions (ca. 165/167); Polycarp of Smyrna (dates fluctuate from 155 to 177; probably around 167); the martyrs of Lyon (177); and the martyrs of Scillium in Numidia (ca. 180).

Septimius Severus (193–211) in the beginning tolerated the Christians, but suddenly in the year 202 made the conversion to Christianity punishable and thereby started a furious persecution which raged especially in North Africa, Egypt, and the Near East (Martyrs: Perpetua and Felicitas in 202 in Carthage; Leonidas, the father of Origen, also in 202 in Alexandria).

Under Caracalla (211–217), Elagabalus (218–222), and Alexander Severus (222–235) the Christians in general were left alone; the mother of Alexander Severus, Julia Mammaea, was even kindly disposed toward them and corresponded with Origen and Hippolytus of Rome. Maximin Thrace (235–238) decreed an edict hostile to the church and chiefly directed against the clergy, but Gordian (238–244) and particularly Philippus Arabs (244–249) were again friendly to the Christians. The latter may have been inwardly a Christian who just could not publicly show this at the time, for Christianity was not yet ripe. Then occurred again a relapse into fanatical hostility toward Christians. Military defeats and threats on the borders; a rise in the cost of living and famine in the interior of the empire; and the strongly blazing Roman nationalism in connection with the millenary celebration of Rome in the year 248, which occasioned a simultaneous revival of the traditional religion; all caused in the population a renewed hatred of Christians.

Third Period: From 250 to 311. Emperor Decius (249–251) aspired to an internal rejuvenation of the Roman state. He saw the religious foundations of the empire threatened by the Christians who refused to worship the state religion, and he passed for the first time general laws whose goal was the extirpation of Christianity and the return of all citizens of the empire to the Roman state religion. The first wave of arrests occurred in December 250. On January 20, 250, Pope Fabian died a martyr in Rome. In the middle of the year 250 an edict decreed that all inhabitants of the empire had to sacrifice to the Gods in order to ward off an epidemic. Special commissions were appointed which were supposed to supervise the sacrifice and issue a certificate to those who had complied. By this method the Christians would be uncovered when they refused to sacrifice, and those who had caused the wrath of the Gods, and thus the epidemic, would be put to death.

The number of those who weakened under the persecution was alarmingly high. The long preceeding period of calm was in part the cause; people were no longer used to the dangers. There were those who really sacrificed *("sacrificati")* and those who merely put up incense before the images of the Gods and the emperor. One cause of the "failure" of so many Christians was probably the ease with which they could squeeze by the sacrifices. The upright Christians considered as apostates and deniers of Christ even those who through bribery of the sacrificial commission had obtained certificates without actually having sacrificed *("libellatici")* and those who somehow had their names smuggled into the list of sacrificers *("acta facientes")*.

A grave dispute soon broke out among the congregations over the question of the churchly reconciliation with these fallen ones *("lapsi")*. In Rome, the presbyter Novatian advocated unrelenting severity in the punishment of the apostates, and there arose a conflict with Pope Cornelius (251–253) who practiced mercy. Novatian, highly respected as a theologian, went as far as schism in the Roman church by appointing himself as a rival bishop and founding a rival church. He appealed to the strict ideal of sanctity and championed rigoristic attitudes in the whole practice of penance. The "catholic" church of Pope Cornelius was accused of laxity and betrayal of the faith. Novatian's followers soon called themselves the "pure ones". Although they were excommunicated at a Roman synod in 251 by sixty assembled bishops, they maintained themselves into the fourth century. As the "Church of the Saints" their later rigorism excluded all mortal sinners.

In Carthage and Alexandria similar tension arose. The bishops Cyprian and Dionysius made every attempt to find a reasonable tolerant solution to the question (Cyprian wrote his tract *De lapsis* in 251), but they could not prevent the founding of a rival church in Africa under the leadership of a certain Novatus. This church soon contacted Novatian in Rome. Ever since this time, fanatical rigorism has been the characteristic of all heresies and sects. These narrowing tendencies, which always appeared under the label of special piety and sanctity, have been combatted rigorously by the church in order to retain its "catholicity" which, according to Christ's commission, consists of bringing God's salvation to all men *(kat'holon)* and not merely to a small sect *(haeresis)* of the elect and saints.

After the early death of Decius, who was killed in 251 in battle against the Goths, his successors Gallus (251–253) and Valerian (253–260) continued the persecutions only mildly. Pope Cornelius was exiled to Centumcellae (Civitavecchia) where he soon died, and his successor Lucius (253–254) was also exiled. Then, under the sustained pressure of straitened internal and external conditions in the empire (war at the borders, epidemics, rise of cost of living), hatred and persecution of Christians was renewed in the year 257. Emperor Valerian was methodical. A first edict in 257 concerned only the clergy, and all bishops, presbyters, and deacons were obliged to sacrifice to the Gods. Whoever of them continued to hold services or secret assemblies in cemeteries or catacombs was punished by death. In North Africa and Egypt

53

the leading bishops Cyprian of Carthage and Dionysius of Alexandria were imprisoned, and many Christians were sentenced to hard labor in the mines. A second edict of 258 ordered the immediate execution of all clerics who refused to sacrifice. Christian senators and members of the nobility were demoted, and if they continued to refuse to sacrifice they were subject to confiscation of estates and finally to execution. Christian court employees and imperial servants, the so-called *Caesariani,* were tortured and sent to hard labor or executed. All Christian churches and cemeteries were confiscated and destroyed. Now blood ran in torrents. In Carthage, Cyprian died a martyr. We possess official authentic files concerning his trial, in which we find his sentence: "Because for a long time you have led the life of a traitor and have started a sinister conspiracy with several others; because you are a declared enemy of the Gods and the laws of the Roman State, and not even the pious and illustrious Emperors Valerian and Gallienus and the supreme Caesar Valerian could induce you to serve again the Gods of the state; and because you are the actual originator of detestable crimes and have seduced others to iniquities; an example shall be made of you as a warning to all those whom you have caused to become your accomplices. At the price of your blood, decency and morals shall be preserved. Thus we order Thascius Cyprian to die by the sword" (*Acta proconsularia Cypriani,* IV, 1–2).

In Rome at that time, Pope Sixtus II with his deacons and priests, among them Laurentius, died as martyrs. Everywhere men and women, clerics and laymen, were executed in great numbers. The purification under Decius had had the effect that the number of apostates and weak ones was now much smaller. The Christian church offered a picture of solid inner strength as never before. Perhaps this is one of the reasons why after Valerian's catastrophe in the Persian War and his death in Persian captivity his son and successor Gallienus (260–268) was persuaded to rescind the persecution edicts.

For the Christians there now came a forty year respite. It was the lull before the last and most severe storm.

Emperor Diocletian (284–305), the able and deserving restorer of the Roman Empire, had for a long time tolerated Christianity even in his closest surroundings. His wife Prisca and his daughter Valeria were considered Christians. Then, in the year 303, he suddenly started the bloodiest of all persecutions. A decisive battle between Christianity and the Roman Empire developed which ended with the victory of Christianity through Constantine the Great.

The persecution began with an imperial edict of February 23, 303, which ordered the destruction of all churches, the surrender and burning of all copies of the Scriptures, and banned all Christian meetings. All Christian officials were dismissed and the Christian employees at the imperial court, the Caesariani, were demoted without consideration of rank and position. Soon after, the latter ones, under the accusation of arson in the imperial palace, were cruelly tortured and executed. The priests and deacons of the imperial residence Nicodemia were also executed together with their bishop Anthimus. Two subsequent edicts extended the persecution to all clerics of the empire and ordered their immediate arrest, torture, and execution. A fourth edict in the spring of 304 contained a strict general order for sacrifice in the whole empire, and carried the terrors of persecution to the whole Christian population. This last edict, probably instigated by Caesar Galerius, had as its undeniable goal the complete extermination of Christianity.

The implementation of the edicts, which were decreed for the whole empire, was different in each of its four regions. In the West, under Augustus Maximian and the Caesar Constantius Chlorus, they were not strictly followed; the persecution was generally completely stopped by 305, after the Augusti Diocletian and Maximian had retired from the government. But in the East, the persecution reached its peak in the years 305–311 under the new Augustus Galerius and his new Caesar Maximinus Daia. Here not only was the number of martyrs very high, but the cruelty during the executions was particularly brutal and inhuman. Finally Galerius had to admit the futility of his campaign, and shaken by a serious illness, he stopped the persecution.

In April 313 Galerius decreed from his residence in Sardica the famous Edict of Toleration which finally granted Christianity the right to exist, and whose most important sentence ran: ". . . and may they from now on be Christians" *(ut denuo sint christiani)*. Actually, Maximinus Daia continued the persecution for a while, but the political events of the succeeding years ignored him and brought with the victories of Constantine the victory of Christianity in the Roman empire.

Second Epoch: 312–604
From Constantine the Great to Gregory the Great

9

THE CONSTANTINIAN TURNING POINT

Constantine's conversion to Christianity was a historical event of the greatest dimensions and introduced a new epoch, not only for the Roman state but also for the church.

1. Constantine, the son of Constantius Chlorus and Helena, was born at Naissus (Nish in Serbia) in approximately 285, and spent his youth at the court of Diocletian in Nicomedia. When the latter announced his abdication on May 1, 305, before the assembled army, Constantine stood next to him on the platform. Not only Constantine but also the soldiers who loved him expected that the old emperor would appoint him as Caesar and his father, Constantius, as First Augustus. But Diocletian passed over Constantine entirely and raised the younger Galerius to First Augustus, while Constantius became Second Augustus only. Diocletian appointed Maximinus Daia and Severus, two relatives and favorites of Galerius, as Caesars. Dissatisfied with this arrangement, Constantine fled from Nicomedia and made his way to his father in Gaul. When Constantius Chlorus died in the following year, his troops in Britain proclaimed Constantine as Augustus on July 25, 306. During the intrigues of the following years, Constantine was able to maintain himself in the West through political astuteness and military strength. In the spring of 312,

after the death of Galerius, Constantine advanced across the Alps to dislodge Maxentius from Italy and to capture Rome. It was a daring gamble; and when he came upon the militarily superior enemy at the Milvian Bridge in Rome, he turned for help to the God of the Christians in his need and uncertainty over the outcome of the battle. In a dream he saw a cross in the sky and the words "conquer in this sign", and this convinced him to advance. When on October 28, 312 he achieved his brilliant victory over the troops of Maxentius, Constantine looked upon his success as proof of the power of Christ and the superiority of the Christian religion.

The "conversion" of Constantine has frequently been regarded as a purely political maneuver without an inner change of mind. As proof, it has been said that during his whole term of office (306–337) he did not fight paganism at all but continued to grant it toleration, and that he himself was baptized a Christian only on his death bed. Contemporary research, however (J. Vogt, H. Dörries, H. Kraft), evaluates the change of the emperor much more positively. It attributes no absolute importance to the events of the year 312, but nevertheless sees them as a real, true, and inner change in Constantine's life. It is pointed out that as a believer in the monotheistic sun god Mithra, as his father had been, he had long been prepared for Christianity. In his victory he saw the confirmation of the correctness of his turn towards monotheism, whose purest form he regarded as Christianity.

From 312 on he consistently declared his faith in Christianity and supported it in every way, even if he did not touch the pagan state religion and the other cults. In the year 313, together with Licinius, he drafted the Milan program of toleration and sent it to the governors of the eastern provinces in the form of a rescript (not edict!). The rescript accorded Christianity full equality with the religions in the empire. In addition, he decided immediately after his victory over Maxentius to give to his army a standard with a cross (labarum) and to his soldiers the monogram of Christ on their shields as a sign of victory. He was also greatly interested in internal questions of the church. When in the year 311 the rigoristic sect of Donatism in North Africa — named after their leader Donatus — caused a schism, he tried to mediate. Constantine charged a synod at Rome (313) with the investigation of the case and convoked a council for the following year at Arles (314) at which for the first time all western provinces were represented by their bishops. Because the Donatists were unwilling to heed the decision of the council, Constantine even intervened with troops to restore unity in Africa.

From the year 312, Constantine favored Christianity openly. He permitted the Christian clerics to enjoy the same exemption from taxes as the pagan priests (312/313), decreed the abolishment of the death on the cross (315), gave the church permission to accept bequests (321) and in the same year, by imperial decree, made Sunday a public holiday. In 319 the haruspices, i.e. the pagan inspection of the entrails of slain victims to deduce the will of the gods and the future, together with a few other immoral cults, were forbidden and in 321 the battles of the gladiators were discontinued as a punishment for criminals. In addition, the magnificent church buildings illustrate the emperor's public acknowledgement of Christianity. In 313 he gave the pope the Lateran Palace and began the construction of the Basilica Constantiniana. Around 320 he founded the Church of St. Peter over the tomb of Peter on the Vatican Hill, in the midst of a pagan necropolis near the Via Cornelia. Soon there followed the foundation of the basilica over the Holy Tomb in Jerusalem and also the Church of the Nativity in Bethlehem (by his mother Helena), the double church in the imperial palace at Trier, and several others. In 330 Constantine founded Constantinople as his new Christian residence, because Rome with its distinct pagan character no longer pleased him. All this took place even though he continued to be Pontifex Maximus of the pagan state religion.

Soon after 312 Constantine also called Christian bishops to his court (Ossius of Cordova; Eusebius of Caesarea, the church historian; and others). He transferred powers of legal jurisdiction to the bishops of his empire and through laws strove to incorporate the church into the state. After defeating his co-emperor

Licinius (324 at Chrysopolis), he immediately suggested the adoption of Christianity in the new-won eastern part of the empire. This last war for universal domination against Licinius, who had persecuted Christianity, was fought by Constantine as a religious war. Universal Christianity was to provide the foundation for the universal empire. Because of this, Constantine was very much concerned with restoring the ecclesiastical unity which was then threatened by far-reaching schisms (Donatists in North Africa, Meletians and Arians in Egypt). Therefore in the year 325 he summoned the bishops of the whole empire ("ecumene") to a general council at Nicaea, the first "ecumenical council". The function of the council was to resolve the schisms. As "marginal" bishop *(episkopos toon ektos)*, Constantine felt that he bore a responsibility for the church equal to that of the other bishops. He even claimed an intellectual-spiritual role of leadership in the Christian Church similar to that which he possessed as Pontifex Maximus in the pagan religion. Therefore he did not hesitate to intervene in the appointment of bishops, and directed the work of the synods.

In his private life, Constantine also made no secret of his Christian conviction. He had his sons and daughters brought up as Christians and led a Christian family life. The Arian bishop Eusebius of Nicomedia baptized him shortly before he died at Whitsuntide in 337. After his baptism, Constantine refused to wear again the imperial purple and thus left this life dressed in his white baptismal dress. In the East he is revered as a saint, as "one equal to the apostles", and as the "thirteenth apostle".

2. It is almost impossible to comprehend today what this change in the supreme secular leadership meant *for the church*. Until then, the church had been outlawed, persecuted, and its members tortured; suddenly it was favored, privileged, and spoiled. Constantine made Christianity a part of public life and because of this the church faced a totally new world situation. To the church, this man who overcame paganism and made room for Christianity in the official arena, appeared to be the pioneer of a new Christian world. Under a Christian emperor

the Roman Empire received a different function. Even in the time of the early Christian apologists the thought occasionally had been mentioned that God had so arranged it that the Christian Church should be able to proclaim its message of salvation at the very moment when the Roman Empire provided the world with political, economic, and cultural unity. Thus the Roman Empire had the providential task of preparing the way for Christianity to fulfill its mission. It is true that by defeating the many warring states and uniting them in the Pax Romana and by embracing the numberless national gods and cults in the universal Roman state religion, Rome prepared the way for universal monotheism. With Constantine the goal seemed to have been reached. In the empire of Constantine the prerequisites had been met which would lead to the conversion of the world, and nothing seemed to stand in the way of the "gathering of the world" for Christ which had been the dream of so many for so long.

It was not only the isolated personal opinion of the church historian Eusebius, but probably that of the majority of his contemporary bishops and Christians when, in his *Vita Constantini,* he represented the emperor as the ideal Christian ruler and saw beginning with him a new time of salvation for the church. Eusebius has left us a wonderful description of the atmosphere at the conclusion of the council of Nicaea when Constantine, who was just celebrating his twentieth anniversary in office, gave a banquet for the assembled bishops on July 25, 325. "No bishop was absent from the table of the emperor", Eusebius writes, and continues enthusiastically: "What happened beggars every description. Bodyguards and soldiers stood guard, with sharp swords drawn, around the outer court of the palace, but among them the men of God could walk fearlessly and enter the deepest parts of the palace. At dinner some of them lay on the same couch as the emperor, while others rested on cushions on both sides of him. Easily *one could imagine this to be the kingdom of Christ* or regard it as a dream rather than reality" (*Vita Constantini* III, 15).

With how much greater ease could the church now fulfill its task, favored by the imperial sun! Through the new alliance with the state, Christianity, only recently threatened in its very existence by the state during the last and most cruel persecution and still numerically only a small minority, was suddenly in the position to preach its belief publicly, to develop its religion, and to make known its maxims. Masses of people joined the church. Their registration and care required completely new forms of organization and ministry. The internal and external expansion of the catechumenate, the new attention paid to preaching and Christian instruction, the liturgical development, and the controversy with the still existing paganism gave valuable impulses to Christian theology. These people who now became Christians were not religiously disinterested and did not find their way to the church only out of political opportunism. To the contrary, the persecutions had made the question of religion a decision of life or death for pagans and Christians. The religious problem in the epoch of Constantine was "the most exciting question of the age" (J. Vogt) and remained so for a long time to come. The emperor's radical decision for Christianity caused passionate discussion in the centers of paganism, Rome and Athens, and was no less criticized there than it was greeted with excitement and enthusiasm by the Christian Church.

Who can think ill of the bishops of this religiously agitated time for welcoming the aid of the state? They could only be glad if ecclesiastical canons, which now were worked out more explicitly, found official recognition as well and were supported, if necessary, by the "secular arm". Soon council decrees were published as imperial laws and thus incorporated into the political life. Constantine's sons continued on his course. Constantius (337–361) as early as 341 fought superstition and pagan sacrifices and in the year 346, together with his brother Constans (337–350), ordered the complete closing of the pagan temples. There was a brief reaction under Emperor Julian the "Apostate" (361–363) who broke with Christianity and revived paganism, but his successor Jovian (363–364) returned the church to its privileged position in the empire. Emperor Gratian (375–383) in the western half of the empire and Emperor Theodosius the Great

(379–394) in the eastern half (394–395 in the whole empire) finally raised Christianity to the exclusively legitimate religion of the Roman Empire. In the year 380 an imperial edict demanded that all subjects accept the religion "which the saintly apostle Peter transmitted to the Romans and which Pope Damasus (in Rome) and bishop Alexander (in Alexandria) practise". Conversion to paganism was made punishable in 381 and the Roman Senate, so far a refuge of the old state religion, solemnly had to disavow the belief in the gods. In 392 an imperial ordinance declared participation in pagan sacrifices in the temple as high treason. After that, paganism rapidly disappeared from public life. Christianity had become the official religion and the church had become an imperial church. The tide had turned.

3. Was the church right in agreeing to such close union with the state? The question raises a grave age-old uncertainty which to this day has not been resolved.

Even the contemporaries found many different answers to the question. Some of them looked with gratitude and joy on the participation of the church in the empire (Eusebius); others feared the "secularization" of the church. In the reform literature of the Middle Ages the pre-Constantinian *"Ecclesia primitiva"* appears as the desirable prototype. Apostolic simplicity, the ideal of poverty, and distance from the world are the characteristics to which the church must return, according to the demands of the eleventh and twelfth centuries. Joachim of Flora (d. 1202) and the Franciscan Spiritualists of the thirteenth and fourteenth centuries saw nothing but a decline in the church since Constantine. Luther soon made the papacy alone responsible for this deterioration, and from this time on the so-called "Theory of Decadence" became a dominant theme in Protestant historiography. Even if the evaluation has changed in isolated instances, this basic concept has remained. The period of the Enlightenment saw the root of all evil in the hegemonial aspirations of the clergy, which had basked in the imperial favor since the end of the persecutions, fallen prey to the lust for power, and sacrificed the purity of the evangelical doctrine to its own egoistic interests.

63

By willingly permitting itself to be incorporated into the structure of state power, the clergy had betrayed its original destiny and committed a wrong to the gospel of Christ. In the nineteenth and twentieth centuries the only disagreement with this view was concerned with whether the decay had begun as early as the end of the Apostolic Age, with the "Hellenization" of Christianity by the early Christian apologists, or only with Constantine. In any case, the later Catholic Church had obviously erred by misinterpreting the intention of Christ and deviating from the valid primitive Christian ideal.

The chief accusations were always directed against Constantine. The gift which he had given Christianity in liberating it from persecution and incorporating it into the state was considered a dubious gift indeed. Certainly one cannot very well deny that much concerning the person of Constantine and his role is problematical. For even if he liked to call himself only a "co-bishop" and showed himself condescending, as at the banquet at Nicaea, nonetheless he always remained the emperor. Very soon he ruled the episcopate as he did his civil service and demanded unconditional obedience to official pronouncements, even when they interfered with purely internal churchly matters. Athanasius, the great bishop of Alexandria and fighter against Arianism, was put under the imperial ban in 335 when he refused to follow Constantine's order to accept the heretic Arius and his followers in the congregation. With time, Constantine's interference in internal church affairs became even more stringent.

Chief among the uncertainties with regard to Constantine is the theological depth and justification of his Christianity. Very probably he never completely understood the final meaning of the Christian mystery of salvation. At the beginning of the Arian troubles in 324 he wrote to the two exponents, Arius and bishop Alexander of Alexandria, in order to reconcile them: ". . . I have considered the outbreak and subject of your dispute and have come to the conclusion that it concerns a trifling matter only. In no way does your case justify such lamentation!"

Constantine never comprehended that the attack by Arius on

the divine nature of Christ was in reality a question of the very existence of everything Christian, and that the doctrine of salvation itself was questioned. He did not even sense that in "the intellectual situation of the age there was no problem that could have been more exciting for the Christians or more important for the educated among the pagans" than precisely this question of the eternal being of the divine Logos who became man and who came into the world to save it and to reestablish its connection with God. Through the introduction of his demi-urge Arius had denied the essence of Christianity. Not only had he undermined monotheism, but had adulterated the Christian religion by placing it on the same level as the pagan cults of gods and mysteries. Just "at a moment when ancient philosophy had spoken its last word in Neo-Platonism" and all yearning was directed to the salvation by the God-Logos Christ who had become man, but had remained God, Arianism signalled a relapse into paganism. Although he was not aware of this, it was Constantine who at the council of Nicaea in 325 played the decisive role and felt called upon to participate in the decision of such a vitally important question of faith.

Constantine forcefully supported the decision of the council to excommunicate Arius and his followers by exercising the imperial ban and sending them into exile. A few years later, however, with the same use of official force, he tried to have Arius readmitted into the church. This time he exiled Athanasius to Trier when he refused to obey the imperial order. Only a few decades later the continued official intervention in religious questions resulted in the first official burning of heretics. In January 385, the imperial usurper Maximus in Trier (383–388) had the prominent Spanish layman Priscillian, the founder of an ascetic movement in Spain and Gaul, executed together with six companions. Political intrigues also played a role. The leading representatives of the church, the bishops Martin of Tour, Ambrose of Milan, and Pope Siricius in Rome, condemned this gruesome act most strongly. Particularly St. Martin did everything he could to prevent it. Unfortunately other bishops, led by

Ithacius who suffered from a persecution mania, were actively involved. Thus began one of the saddest chapters in church history which finds its roots in the mixing of politics and religion.

With the beginning of this symbiosis of state and church, the position of the latter was to become most problematical. The epocal event of the first positive encounter between the church and the Roman state, which had come about so suddenly through Constantine's conversion, created the impression in many Christians that the church should now willingly put itself at the disposal of the state and positively help with its tasks. The general flush of victory which had seized many circles in the church all too soon transformed the hitherto existing distance from the world into a worldly-minded cultural optimism. The right God-willed moment was thought to have arrived to imbue all of public life with the spirit of Christianity according to Christ's missionary order. Constantine himself invited this attitude by transferring rights and powers to bishops and priests and by heaping honors upon the church. These ministers of the church, however, lacked any experience in dealing with the state. Indeed, they had successfully resisted the hostile state in the time of persecution; but the friendly state was new to them and they were unaware that under certain circumstances this could be more dangerous than the former condition.

The dangers were great, and masses now streamed into the officially favored church, confronting it with totally new tasks. The church of the elite to which hitherto only those had gained access who were convinced believers and prepared for martyrdom now became the church of the masses, which also included those who were politically ambitious, religiously disinterested, and still half-rooted in paganism. This threatened to produce not only shallowness and permeation by pagan superstitions, but also the secularization and misuse of religion for political purposes. Did the church succumb to these dangers?

The answer can be given only with great care and differentiation. Above all, the enormously complex situation of the time must be kept in mind. Little can be achieved with easy generalizations.

Only the superficial observer and biased critic, who lacks any historical understanding, can assert that the church betrayed its original mission in this epoch and exercised "power without a mission". Only those who have an insufficient understanding of the problem can maintain that Christ had not assigned to the church any secular political function in society, since the New Testament had excluded "any utilization of secular power for the achievement of the Christian mission" (Hernegger).

If the incarnation is taken seriously and the church is recognized as the continuation of the life of Jesus and the fulfillment of his work of salvation among the people of all ages, nations, and civilizations, then the Christian ideal can not be found in inflexible adherence to original functions, but must permit room for a real historical development. The church has its genuine historicity; it does not exist separate from the time or parallel to it, but rather it becomes enmeshed in time and temporal in it. This does not happen in such a way that the church becomes amalgamated or identified with any particular time. It must not stop with any time, neither with that of early Christianity, nor with that of the persecutions, neither with that of the Constantinian turning point nor with that of the Greek-Hellenistic civilization. The church is not committed to any individual civilization; this does not imply indifference, but rather openness and nearness to each. The task of the church is to carry Christ into every age and civilization and there to let him take form.

The church must steer a middle course between the denial and the affirmation of the world. It realizes itself only in the continuing fulfillment of the mission with which Christ charged it. The measure of the evangelical Christian content of an age is the success of the church in this mission. Within the wide band of variation between world-distance and world-nearness, there is room in the bosom of the church for saints and sinners, for victories and defeats. Although it is a scientific and theological error to deny or to overlook the negative aspects of a period, it is equally unhistorical and unscientific to deny its positive side. Only biased blindness can therefore "lead to the scientifically impossible global condemnation of the post-Constantinian history of the church, particularly that of the medieval 'papal' church" (Lortz).

The missionary drive of the time, the passion with which religious questions and theological problems were discussed, and especially the large number of saints and the development of monasticism invested the post-Constantinian age with the character of a great epoch in church history, an epoch full of dynamic and genuine Christian spirit in spite of its many weaknesses and dangers.

10
THE DOGMATIC CONTROVERSIES
AND THE GENERAL COUNCILS IN THE EAST

At the very moment when Constantine decided to make the universal Christian Church the foundation of his universal empire, he discovered that this church was not nearly as united as he had believed. Bitter internal struggles left it hopelessly torn. Donatism in North Africa, the schism of Meletius in Egypt, and finally the heresy of Arianism caused splits in the unity of Christianity. Many other unsolved questions and theological problems were present also and demanded an answer. As soon as he became sole ruler (324), Constantine planned to restore church unity and solve the difficulties by means of an imperial council.

Three large topics were theologically of interest and were to occupy the next three centuries: the doctrine of the Trinity, Christology, and the doctrine of justification; that of justification concerned chiefly the West.

1. In the doctrine of the Trinity it was necessary to define more precisely the internal relation between the Father and the Son, and to illuminate it from the standpoint of revelation. The Holy Scriptures speak only in general terms about the Trinitarian mystery. The dogmatic problem which consisted on the one hand

of maintaining a rigorous monotheism and the unity (= *monarchia*) of God, and on the other hand of also adoring Christ as God in addition to the Father, did not occupy the first Christians. Only for the apologists and the early Christian Fathers did the Christological question become a matter of reflection. The doctrine of the Logos did not solve the problem, but only left it more pronounced. In order to oppose the false speculations of the Gnostics who with their doctrine of aeons and the demiurge transformed the Logos into a creature, it was necessary to reconcile the divine nature of Christ with the unity of God. In an effort to do this there developed toward the end of the second century the two "monarchian" schools of thought: Adoptianism and Modalism.

The Adoptianists looked on Christ as a mere man who at some time, probably on the occasion of his baptism in the Jordan, was filled with divine power, transformed into a God, and thus "adopted" by God. The real and original God was, therefore, only the Father, and Christ was an adopted God.

The Modalists saw in Christ only one form or mode of the one and only God who manifests himself at one time as Father, at another time as Son, and at a third time as Holy Spirit. They maintained that in reality the Father had suffered for us (*"pater passus est"*, and because of this Tertullian derisively named them "Patripassians").

Both forms of monarchianism were rejected by the church, with the first decisions being made in Rome. Around 190, Pope Victor (189–198/199) excommunicated the Adoptianist Theodotus who had attempted to teach his doctrine in Rome, but the pope seems to have been uncertain with respect to the Modalist Praxeas who taught there at the same time. Only when Sabellius represented Modalism in Rome in ca. 215, did Pope Calixtus (217–222) reject and condemn this doctrine. A few decades later the Modalist heresy was finally refuted by the Roman theologian Novatian in his work *De Trinitate* (before 250). (After 251, Novatian himself became the founder of a rigoristic sect and, according to ancient tradition, became a martyr under Valerian (253–260)).

69

In the meantime the Logos-Christology prevailed and was especially carefully studied by Origen in the Alexandrian school. But even Logos-Christology had great difficulties with regard to the inner Trinitarian order. Although it followed the Holy Scriptures and maintained the divine nature of the Logos Christ, it nonetheless subordinated Christ to the Father, just as it subordinated the Holy Spirit to the Son. Thus the Holy Spirit and the Son had the same divine nature, but this nature was of a derived and inferior form. The result was a pluralistic monotheism which in reality was none.

In this way Origen, "probably the greatest scholar of Christian antiquity" (Altaner) and one of the founders of the Alexandrian school, unequivocally explained the relationship of the three persons in the Trinity as subordinational. Origen emphasized that the Son was of the same essence *(homooúsios)* as the Father and also eternal, but maintained that only the Father was a "Self-God" *(autótheos)* and the essence of goodness *(haplós agathós)*, while the Logos was only a "secondary God" *(deúteros Theós)* and the reflection of this goodness *(eikōn agathótetos)*, and the Holy Spirit was in turn even less than the Son. By assuming a real body, the eternal Logos had become "God-man" *(Theánthropos,* the expression was coined by Origen) and, therefore, one could truly call Mary the "God-bearer" *(Theotókos;* this term also stems from him or at least from the Alexandrian school).

In the future course of events, Origen's views provided a point of departure for two entirely different theological schools of thought. One emphasized the consubstantiality of the Son and the Father and the unity of the human and divine nature in Christ; it was cultivated chiefly in Alexandria. The other stressed the differences, emphasized that the Logos was only a secondary god, and separated the divine from the created in Christ; this opinion was developed in the school at Antioch.

The Antiochian school of theology owed its existence to the activities of the presbyter Lucian in the middle of the third century; Lucian died a martyr in 312. In a sober and rational manner, he interpreted the Scriptures from the standpoint of their literal and historical content and rejected the allegorical and mystical exegesis of the Alexandrians. With respect to Christology, Lucian taught a strict subordination. Arius and the other leaders of Arianism came from the circle of his students, the so-called "Syllucianists". This group stood in professed contrast to the Alexandrian theology.

Around the year 318, Arius (ca. 260–336), who had been pastor at the Baucalis Church at Alexandria since 313, came into conflict with his bishop Alexander of Alexandria, because he defended an extreme subordinational Christology in his sermons, in his letters and songs, and in his tract *Thalia* (= Feast). As a strict asceticist and overpowering speaker, with a good portion of vanity and a touch of fanaticism, Arius enjoyed the favor of the people. Soon his rationalistic opinion, presented as a conscious polemic against the Alexandrian school, created attention. After accusing the Alexandrian theologians of Sabellian Modalism, he dissociated the Logos from God. Arius asserted that the Logos was not the true God and that it had an entirely different nature, neither eternal nor omnipotent, but created in time, imperfect, and able to suffer. Because the Logos was the first created being and far superior to human beings, one could regard it as a half-God (Demiurge), but it was not in itself divine.

With this denial of the Godhead of Christ, Arius placed himself outside of Christianity, and a synod at Alexandria condemned his teaching as heresy (318/319 or 323) and excommunicated him. Now Arius went to his Antiochian friends and special help was given him by bishop Eusebius of Nicomedia. The church historian Eusebius of Caesarea also belonged to this Antiochian group. After Arius's friends had effected his return to Alexandria, furious disputes, street riots, and nocturnal meetings soon took place. Constantine finally intervened and summoned all the bishops to a general (ecumenical) synod at Nicaea.

The first imperial synod met in Nicaea from May 20 to July 25, 325, and transportation for all of the attending bishops was provided by the emperor. The reports of the number of participants vary: 220 names have survived in one list; others speak of

318, in keeping with Abraham's 318 servants (Gen 14, 14); and Eusebius speaks of about 250. Mostly the bishops came from the eastern part of the empire, with only five bishops present from the West. Pope Sylvester had not made the trip because of his age and sent two presbyters in his place. Some bishops still showed scars on their bodies from the last persecution. "Like a messenger of God, sparkling with the splendor of gold and purple" (Eusebius) the emperor mingled with them, kindly chatting with all of them, but particularly with the martyr bishops. He presented his address in Latin.

Arius defended his doctrine and seventeen bishops were on his side, among them bishop Eusebius of Nicomedia. The young deacon Athanasius was present also in the company of his bishop. After long and heated debates, the orthodox party won. In the Creed of Nicaea the right doctrine was defined: Christ was "the only begotten Son from the substance of the Father, God from God, light from light, true God from true God, begotten not made, of one substance *(homoúsios)* with the Father". The emperor informed all of Christendom that Arius and his adherents, as the worst enemies of the true faith, had been excluded from the church and exiled. He ordered their writings to be burned.

Other questions were also dealt with by the council and fixed in twenty short ordinances (canons). The celibacy of bishops, priests, and deacons was also discussed. Celibacy was practised already in some areas, but the martyr bishop Paphnutius strongly advised against it, saying that too heavy a yoke ought not to be laid upon the clergy. The synod therefore did not order celibacy and permitted a valid marriage, but condemned concubinage.

The result of this "great and holy synod" would have been satisfactory, if it had remained unaltered. But Constantine soon changed his opinion and in 328 recalled the exiled bishop Eusebius to Nicomedia. Even Arius was permitted to return and by imperial decree was restored to office and communion after he had formally signed the Nicene Creed. When Athanasius, who since 328 had been bishop of Alexandria, refused to readmit Arius to his clergy, he incurred the displeasure of the emperor, who exiled this courageous fighter for the Nicene Creed to Trier. A new period of suffering began for the church, which can best be inferred from the fate of Athanasius. Four additional times he had to shoulder the burden of banishment under the Arianistically inclined sons and successors of Constantine. In the year 340 Athanasius fled from Constantius to Pope Julius I in Rome, and in 356 he hid from the emperor among the monks and hermits in the desert. Hardly had he returned to his bishop's residence after the death of Constantius (361), when he was driven out again in 362. The speedy death of Julian (363) renewed his courage, but he had spent only two years with his congregation when he was sent into exile for the fifth time in 365 by Emperor Valens who also sympathized with Arianism. Only because Alexandria was threatened with a rebellion by the people was he permitted to return after only four months. Until his death in 373 he remained in Alexandria as a stalwart champion of the orthodox Nicene faith.

During these decades the struggle for the Nicene *"homoúsios"* was steadily continuing. A moderate group, the Semi-Arians, broke away from the strict Arians. They attempted to give a new interpretation of the "one substance" to "similar" *(homöios)* and agreed to the formula that the Son was "in everything similar" to the Father, the term *"homoúsios"* to be avoided at any price. Imperial synods at Rimini and Seleucia, called by the emperor in the year 359, brought no agreement. Yet in the meantime the internal decay of Arianism could not be stopped. Calm appeared again when Emperor Gratian (375–383), who sympathized with Catholicism, took over the leadership of the empire. Theodosius (379–395), whom Gratian had elevated to Emperor in the East, in 381 summoned the second general council of Constantinople to complete the clarification of the Arian disputes.

By this time the theologians had more clearly defined the terms "person" and "nature" in God. In addition to St. Athanasius, this achievement is owed primarily to the three "Cappadocian Fathers": Basil (ca. 330–379), Gregory of Nazianzus (329/330–ca. 390), and Gregory of Nyssa (ca. 334–394). They saw the distinction between the three divine persons as existing solely in their inner divine relations. According to them there is only one nature, but three carriers: one Godhead in three persons. This definition also emphasized the Godhead of the Holy Spirit which was disputed by the Arians. The relation of the Holy Spirit is that it proceeds from the other two divine persons. The creed adopted at Nicaea in 325 received the addition: "... and in the Holy Spirit, the Lord and the life-giver, *who proceeds from the Father,* who with the Father and the Son is together worshipped and together glorified, who spoke through the prophets ...". In this form the creed later became part of the liturgy. In antiquity it was used at first solely in connection with baptism, and only in the sixth century was it introduced into the Mass for the first time by Patriarch Timotheus (d. 517) of Byzantium, then in Spain through the third synod of Toledo (589), and finally in Rome in 1014 upon the demand of Emperor Henry II. Controversies arose again, because the East understood the emanation of the Holy Spirit as proceeding *from* the Father *through* the Son, and the western church asserted that it proceeds *from* the Father *and* the Son. When the *"filioque"* was added in the West it was not considered an expansion but merely an interpretation. The East, however, regarded it as an unauthorized addition and accused the West of heresy. Thus the *filioque,* beginning with the uncertainty of the first council of Constantinople (381), was one cause of the schism of 1054, and has remained an issue to this day.

After 381 the doctrine of the Trinity had come to a certain conclusion and it was now possible to turn to Christological questions.

2. Christology attempted to explain the exact relation between the divine and human natures in the person of Christ. The Holy Scriptures did not define this and mention at the same time the divine and human aspects of Christ. In the interpretation of the relevant passages the two famous schools of theology at Alexandria and Antioch diverged; the Alexandrians emphasized more strongly the divine nature and the Antiochians more the human one.

Origen had coined the term "God-man" Jesus Christ. Through an allegorical interpretation of Scripture together with theological speculation influenced by Platonic thought, Origen developed a deep, fervent Logos mysticism. This view found its completion with the idea that in Christ the encounter between God and mankind had taken place with utmost perfection and that Christians must strive to imitate it. The monks later liked to link their position with the views of Origen. The same mystical concept was developed also by Athanasius, Basil, Gregory of Nazianzus, and Gregory of Nyssa, the last three of whom were monks who belonged to the Alexandrian school. Gregory of Nyssa pointed out clearly that unity could be found in the divine person alone, and not in a completely impossible blending of the divine and human natures. He taught that in Christ the *one* divine person of the Logos had united in itself the divine and human natures. Both natures existed by themselves and distinct from one another, yet they were not separated but arranged in such a way that their attributes were mutually exchangeable *(Communicatio Idiomatum)*. One could say with justification, therefore, that the Son of God had been born and that this applied to his human nature but certainly not to his divine nature which is eternal.

Patriarch Cyril of Alexandria, bishop of the city since 412, attempted to present the connection between both natures as being highly intimate and real. He spoke of physical union and of the *"one* nature of the incarnated Logos". After the union of both natures in Christ one could speak de facto only of *one* nature, the whole or hypostatic one. He rejected the idea of union in the sense of the heretic Apollinaris of Laodicea (d. after 385) and instead used an image; the glowing coal. In a live coal, the fire and the coal form a unit; and in a like way the divine and human natures of Christ formed a union. From this point Eutyches was later able to begin the formation of the monophysite heresy.

At the same time the Antiochian theology had also developed. Diodorus of Tarsus (d. before 394), who had long taught at Antioch, used the critico-exegetical method of this school to expressly emphasize the complete humanity of Christ and so independently placed the human nature next to the divine that only a rather superficial connection between the two remained. According to Diodorus, the divine Logos had lodged in the man Jesus as in a temple.

The Patriarch Nestorius of Constantinople (since 428), himself an Antiochian, concluded therefrom that Mary in truth could not be called the "God-bearer" *(Theotókos)*, but merely had been the "Christ-bearer" *(Christotókos)*, since she had given birth to only a human being, Jesus. Nestorius strongly polemicized against the Alexandrian school.

The controversy became more and more concentrated on the title *"Theotókos"*, but behind it was the whole Christological question. In addition to the contradictory opinions of the schools, there existed the immediate rivalry between the patriarchs of Alexandria and Constantinople. In letters to the Egyptian bishops and monks at Easter in 429 Cyril strongly attacked Nestorius, after having assured himself of the support of Pope Celestine I (422–432), and composed twelve anathemas which he sent to Nestorius in the name of the pope with the strict demand to recant. But Nestorius wrote twelve counter-anathemas, won the Byzantine Emperor Theodosius II (408–450) to his side, and persuaded Theodosius to summon a council with the West Roman Emperor Valentinian II (425–455).

The third ecumenical council of Ephesus in 431 took a stormy course. At the opening session on June 22, Nestorius and his followers were absent. Cyril read a doctrinal statement which he had drafted on the hypostatic union of the two natures in Christ. The statement was approved by the 198 bishops present, and they signed the condemnation of Nestorius. The *Theotókos* designation was thus accepted, and the people waiting outside agreed jubilantly. A few days later, however, 43 bishops from Antioch arrived with their Patriarch John. They took the side of Nestorius immediately and constituted a counter-council. Now began a distasteful game of intrigue with mutual malicious attacks. The emperor was compelled to intervene and the two leaders, Nestorius and Cyril, were arrested. Finally Cyril was permitted to return to Alexandria, and Nestorius was banished to Upper Egypt, where he died around 451. It is unclear to this day to what extent Nestorius's teachings were actually heretical or whether he became a victim of misunderstanding and erroneous representations.

The followers of Nestorius fled to Persia and there founded the Nestorian Church which soon enjoyed an active life. A vital monasticism, an eminent theology (schools of Seleucia and Nisibis), and an imposing missionary activity testify to its strength. Its missionaries penetrated to Malabar, India (Thomas Christians), and Turkestan. Under the Nestorian Catholikos Timotheus I, Christianity between 780 and 823 even made its way beyond Chinese Turkestan to Tibet and central China. At the beginning of the fourteenth century the Nestorian Church in central Asia alone could count ten metropolitan sees and had a numerous native clergy. Unfortunately, during the bloody persecution of Tamerlane (1380) this mission was destroyed. In the sixteenth century many Nestorian churches adhered to Rome (the Chaldaeans and the Malabar Christians). Today the Nestorian Church in Iraq, Iran, and Syria still counts ca. 80,000 members, 5,000 in India, and 25,000 in America.

In his autobiography which he titled *Book of Heracleides* (edited 1910), Nestorius gives the reasons which caused him to enter the theological controversy with Cyril. He had seen in Cyril's doctrine of the *"one* nature of the incarnated Logos" the danger of a Docetic and Manichaeistic evaporation of Christ's human nature and regarded the Apollinaristic blending of the two natures as a great threat to the orthodox evangelical faith. Repeatedly he emphasizes the integrity of each of the two natures in Christ. He states that when he opposed the *Theotókos* title of Mary he did not do it to deny the Godhead of Christ, as Arius had done, but in order to emphasize that Christ had been born by Mary as a genuine human being with body and soul. Mary had not given birth to a Godhead, but to a man connected with the Godhead. In order to save the integrity of the manhood of Jesus, Nestorius separated the human nature too much from the Godhead. Thus he arrived at a dualism of natures without recognizing their indissoluble union in the one person of Jesus (also called hypostatic union).

That Nestorius's fears were not unfounded was soon shown when Eutyches, abbot of a monastery near Constantinople and a strong opponent of Nestorianism, continued Cyril's doctrine of the *one* nature in Christ (*mía physis* = monophysitism) and so intimately combined the two natures that the human nature appeared completely absorbed by the divine one. Just "as a drop of honey, which falls into the sea, dissolves in it", so the integrity of the human nature in Christ was cancelled. Factually this nature no longer existed; for the humanity of Christ was of a substance different from ours. Thus was lost the central prerequisite for the mystery of Christ and his activity as saviour and redeemer, of which the Holy Scriptures speak constantly, and the whole Christian doctrine of redemption was in danger.

Patriarch Flavian of Constantinople called Eutyches before a synod and condemned him as a heretic when he refused to recant. However, Eutyches was supported by Dioscurus, Patriarch of Alexandria and successor of Cyril, who followed Cyril's ideas. On Dioscurus's request, Emperor Theodosius II once again summoned an "imperial council". It assembled under Dioscurus's leadership in Ephesus (449) and rehabilitated Eutyches, even though it was not recognized by the rest of the Church. Pope Leo I (440–461) termed it the "Robber Synod". In his famous *"Epistola dogmatica ad Flavianum"* he placed himself behind the patriarch of Constantinople and authoritatively summarized the orthodox doctrine of the union of the two natures in the one person of Christ (hypostatic union). This has been called the first infallible ex-cathedra decision of a pope. At the same time he asked the emperor for a new council. The successor of Theodosius, Emperor Marcian (450–457), granted the request and called the fourth ecumenical council of Chalcedon in 451.

About 350 bishops assembled at this largest of synods in antiquity. It was chaired by the delegates of Leo the Great, and

Dioscurus was indicted at the very first session (October 8, 451) and deposed at the third (October 13). According to Leo's epistle *(Ep. ad Flavianum)* the synod rejected the monophysitic doctrine of the one nature in Christ and defined at its sixth session as dogma: In Christ *two natures* without confusion and division are united in *one person* or hypostasis. Thus Leo I, on the basis of western theological clarification since Tertullian, had declared the hypostatic union. Without confusion the divine and human natures of Christ retain their identity (counter to Cyril and Eutyches); they are not separated from one another and are indissolubly united in the person of the divine Logos (counter to Nestorius). On this union rests the whole redemption by Christ. These statements on the person of Christ (Christology) are the foundation for the doctrine of salvation (soteriology) and of central importance for the Christian faith.

This conceptual and linguistic clarification provided a solid basis for the future development of western theology, but not for the East. Already during the fifth session of the council severe tensions had arisen between eastern and western theologies and precipitated a serious crisis. The tensions were aggravated by the ecclesiastical rivalry between Rome and the eastern patriarchates, especially by the rivalry of long standing between the Byzantine patriarch and the pope.

Even after Chalcedon, eastern thinking, always having been directed strongly toward unity, tended toward monophysite thought. This unity was not limited only to theological fields, but also extended toward the political sphere (viz. the typically Byzantine imperial theology) and even to the private Christian life of the believer. The area of the divine had so much preference that it practically absorbed human concerns. Religion and politics, church and state fused with one another; and the personal life also merged with the theologico-religious atmosphere. While the West took as its own the fused dualism, based on the Christological formula of Chalcedon, according to which the human and the divine, politics and religion, retained their distinctiveness and peculiarities in Christ as in life, "unmixed" and yet also "unseparated", the East moved toward the so-called "political mono-physitism".

In spite of its condemnation, monophysitism maintained its position in Palestine, Egypt, and Syria. In the year 475 the imperial usurper Basilicus who was sympathetic to the mono-physites granted them official toleration by the so-called Encyclion (= edict). Emperor Zeno published a compromise formula in 476 which was later called the Henoticon (482). When Patriarch Acacius of Constantinople assented to the Henoticon, Pope Felix III (483–492) excommunicated him and dissolved the ecclesiastical bond with the East. The so-called Acacian schism between East and West lasted for thirty-five years (484–519). Around 490 the three patriarchates of Alexandria, Jerusalem, and Antioch were occupied by monophysites, and under Emperor Justinian I (527–565) the monophysite heresy was permitted to spread. In Nubia, Ethiopia, and Armenia they established their own hierarchy under the bishops Jacobus Baradai and Theodore of Arabia (Jacobites; Copts).

In order to appease the monophysites and to restore the threatened unity of the empire, Emperor Justinian in 543/544 condemned the three heads of the Antiochian school from which Nestorianism had sprung: Theodore of Mopsuestia (d. 428), Theodoret of Cyrus (d. ca. 458), and Ibas of Edessa (d. 457). The so-called Three-Chapter controversy, which concerned itself with the acceptance or rejection of the imperial policy, was long drawn-out. Although Pope Vigilius managed to preserve the Chalcedon formula, he was persuaded to agree to the condem-nation. Because of the stormy protests which his yielding caused in the West, Pope Vigilius finally was forced to withdraw his consent. When in 551 the emperor again attacked the Three Chapters, Vigilius more decisively refused to consent and was severely manhandled by imperial soldiers in a church. Because of this mistreatment, the pope refused to participate in the Fifth General Council which Justinian called at Constantinople in 553.

The council served to accomplish the emperor's planned

condemnation of the Three Chapters. The pope was neither present nor represented by delegates, and he rejected the action of the emperor as unjustified interference with the supreme ecclesiastical doctrinal authority. Following this, Justinian had Vigilius excommunicated by the council. In February 554, Justinian was finally able to wring the ratification of the decisions of the council from the old and weak pope by threats of exile and deportation. Dogmatic decisions were not involved.

The results were terrifying: The unity of the church suffered severe damage, the differences between East and West were deepened, "the prestige of the papacy sank enormously, and all through the fault of an ultraconfident and theologically incompetent emperor and of a wavering pope who lacked the strength to perform his duty" (Baus). The council finally found universal recognition even in the West, however, and it is regarded as ecumenical.

Still, the Christological question was not yet solved. To reconcile the monophysites with the imperial church again, Patriarch Sergius of Constantinople (610–638) made a renewed attempt to clarify the relationship of the two natures in Christ. In place of the union of natures posed by the monophysites, he predicated a union of wills. According to Sergius, the human and divine wills were so intimately connected and attuned that in reality only one natural human-divine energy and only one will (= monothelism) had been active in Christ. By assigning the principle of union not to the person but to the natures his system remained monophysitic, but this was not immediately noticeable. Sergius succeeded in presenting his thesis so convincingly to Pope Honorius I (625–638), whose knowledge of Greek theology was limited, that Honorius in a personal and rather general answer regarded it as acceptable. Honorius obviously had in mind less a physical union of natures than a moral accord of the divine and human will in Christ. Still, in his personal opinions, even a pope can err; the letter of Honorius was definitely not a magisterial statement *ex cathedra*. In later centuries this statement was often used as an argument against the "infallibility" of the papacy, and we encounter it during the time of the Reformation and the First Vatican Council. However, the argument is not a justified one.

In 638 monothelism was generally proclaimed by an imperial edict. When Pope Martin I (649–655) at a synod at the Lateran opposed and rejected it as heresy, he was maltreated and banished to the Crimea where he soon died as a result of this treatment. The course of events was only reversed with Emperor Constantine III (668–685) who summoned the Sixth General Council, the third at Constantinople. The council met from November 7, 680 until September 16, 681 in the cupola hall (= *trullus*) of the imperial palace and therefore received the name "Trullanum". Under the chairmanship of papal legates it condemned monothelism together with its originators and supporters, among them Pope Honorius, "because in everything he bade Sergius's will and confirmed the godless dogmas". Pope Leo II (682–683) approved the decisions of the council and the condemnation of Honorius "who did not illuminate this Apostolic Church (Rome) through the apostolic magisterial tradition, but permitted through ignominious treason that the pure faith was stained". Shortly afterwards Leo defended his predecessor insofar as he did not accuse him of direct participation in the heresy but simply reproached him because "he had not smothered the fire of the heretical doctrine in the beginning, as became his apostolic authority, but had promoted it through his negligence". This judgment comes closest to the truth of the matter.

In addition, the council confirmed the result of the council of Chalcedon: Corresponding to the two natures which are united without confusion and separation in the God-man Christ, there are also two wills and two energies, divine and human, which without confusion and separation act together for the redemption of mankind.

Two additional councils took place in the East during the first one thousand years which received general recognition as ecumenical councils. The seventh general council, the second council of Nicaea in 787, was concerned with the worship of images and confirmed that images deserved reverence but not adoration which was due to God alone; and the Eighth General Council, the fourth council at Constantinople in 869–870, ended the Photian schism and rehabilitated Patriarch Ignatius of Constantinople.

Visible evidence of the fact that the center of speculative theology throughout the first millenium was located in the East is that all eight councils took place there.

11
The Theology of the West.
Augustine and the Struggle for the Doctrine of Grace and Justification

While the East fought over Trinitarian and Christological problems, the West was agitated by soteriological questions. The concern here was less metaphysical speculation, which so strongly appealed to the Greeks, than practical and quite personal problems of salvation which immediately affected Christian life: Human free will and sin, predestination and original sin, and necessity and efficacy of grace in the process of justification of the individual.

One encounters the trend to the moral-ascetic attitude early in North Africa. Montanism had experienced there its greatest acceptance and even its intensification by Tertullian, who preferred to deal in his writings with religious-ethical topics. Tertullian's rigorism could still be felt around the middle of the third century in the dispute over the re-admittance of the backsliders to the church in Carthage. Cyprian, too, had taken a hard line in the dispute over the baptism of heretics. At the beginning of the fourth century Donatism in North Africa fought for similar rigoristic tendencies. Despite the intervention of Constantine and the condemnation by the council of Nicaea, it continued to split North Africa for more than another century.

In Rome also we have seen the same forces at work. Novatian and his followers, the "Pure Ones" (katharoi), accused the church of laxity and worldliness. In Spain, Priscillian created an ascetic movement toward the end of the fourth century which soon expanded and caused offense. The Spanish movement existed even after the cruel execution of its founder (385) and for a long time to come agitated the Spanish Church. Finally around 400 there appeared the British monk Pelagius, a morally zealous and educated man, with his ethic which relied too much on the strength of man's will. He lived in Rome until ca. 410/411, then moved to North Africa, and from there to the Near East. The doctrines of Pelagius testify to a high ethical standard. He had conceived them in opposition to Manichaeism, which denied the ethical good, and they were purely pragmatical and without any dogmatic depth. Grace scarcely played a role in his doctrines, as man is not in need of it to perform the good, but requires it solely to perform the good more easily. According to Pelagius, ethics were basically a matter of good will. Augustine entered the lists against him.

No important theologian had come out of the West in the hundred years since Cyprian, but the second half of the fourth century saw in Ambrose of Milan, Jerome, and most of all in Augustine a triumvirate whose brilliance was more than equal to the Greek theologians of the time. The triumvirate was followed by Leo the Great and Gregory the Great.

1. Ambrose (339–397), born at Trier as the son of the praetorian prefect of Gaul, was governor of Aemilia-Liguria and not yet baptized when in 374 he was unexpectedly chosen bishop of Milan by the populace. Upon becoming bishop he devoted himself to the church and became one of the first great doctors of the Western Church. In his sermons, speeches, and writings he fought Arianism and helped the Nicene Creed to victory. A westerner and Roman by background and tradition, his mind was always directed toward the practical. His interpretation of Scripture and his whole theology emphasized ethical and social aspects, and he was concerned with the questions of penance, sin and grace. Ambrose promoted the ascetic movement and became one of the pioneers of western monasticism. As friend and advisor of the Emperors Gratian (375–383), Valentinian II (375–392),

and Theodosius I (379–395) he exerted a decisive influence on church policy and thus became the leading figure of the western church. He is also a typical westerner in that Ambrose opposed political monophysitism in both directions: he denied the political power the right to intervene in the clerico-religious sphere, but he acknowledged the autonomy and the ordering function of the power of the state in the civil sphere. Thus Ambrose moved away from the Byzantine system in which the emperor as God's deputy laid claim to the rule over both areas of life (theocracy) and he represented western thinking, which even in the political region is dualistic. Later Pope Gelasius (492–496) in his letter to Emperor Anastasius clearly formulated the relationship between church and state in his doctrine of the two powers which emphatically differentiated between the sacred authority of the priesthood and the authority of kings. Ambrose already practised it.

In several conflicts with the imperial court Ambrose dared to reject any attempt at a theocracy and compelled penance even from Theodosius the Great who in 390 had been guilty of murder during a cruel massacre in Saloniki. And yet Ambrose always remained a priest and pastor who was not bent on politics, but instead looked upon his ministry as his highest principle. "Even the emperor is part of the church, not above it", when it is a matter of faith and salvation. Ministry, divine service, and charity filled Ambrose's life so convincingly that through his inner strength he was able to dominate all who came into contact with him. Augustine was one of his converts, and he also lives on in the church as a great composer of hymns.

2. Augustine was born on November 13, 354, at Tagaste in Numidia as the son of a pagan father, Patricius, and a devout Christian mother, Monica. He was raised a Christian, but was not baptized and later he attributed the errors of his youth to this lack of grace. During his years as a student he deviated completely from his Christian faith. In the *Confessions* (written around 400) Augustine described his sins in somber colors. In 372 he had an illegitimate son whom he named Adeodatus (d. 389), and only around 385 did Augustine separate from the mother of his child.

Augustine became a follower of Manichaeism in about 374 and for nine years remained in this sect which impressed him with its dualistic conception of good and evil, with its criticism of Christianity, and with its rejection of faith through authority. During this time he even broke with his Christian mother. After finishing his studies of rhetoric in Carthage he settled at Tagaste for a short time as a teacher of grammar, and then was a teacher of rhetoric in Carthage until 383. He lived in Rome for one year and then assumed a professorship in rhetoric at Milan in the fall of 384. Here Augustine met Ambrose, listened to his sermons, and through him found the way back to the church. At Easter 387 he was baptized by Ambrose together with his son Adeodatus. In 388 Augustine returned to Africa and together with friends lived a withdrawn monastic life in Tagaste. During a visit to Hippo early in 391 he was persuaded by bishop Valerius to accept ordination as a priest. His teaching of the baptismal candidates and preachers was so superior that in 395 Valerius appointed him his coadjutor and associate bishop. In 396 he succeeded Valerius as bishop of Hippo, an episcopate in which he labored for almost 35 years. Augustine died on August 28, 430, while the Vandals were besieging his episcopal city.

Both Augustine's personality and his meaning for history are equally imposing. He is "the man of Christian antiquity best known to us". In his *Confessions* he praises the guidance of God's grace which in spite of Augustine's many detours had led him to the right goal. Because he had experienced in himself human weakness and wretchedness, Augustine felt that he could and must counter with all his might the willful pride of Pelagianism. The controversy with Pelagius which began in 412, was conducted by Augustine with a passion which clearly reveals his own background and experiences. In 418 he achieved the condemnation of Pelagianism, and beyond even the grave of Pelagius (d. ca. 422) he fought this heresy, often with a polemicism which overshot the mark and spoke in harsh terms of the universal efficacy of grace and absolute predestination. In this respect Augustine became on the one hand the "Doctor of Grace", but on the other provided future heretics with a basis for heresy. The ideas of Luther, Calvin, and the Jansenists can be traced back to his writings. By ignoring the fact that Augustine's formulations were intended to be antitheses to a heresy, which attributed to man the ability to achieve righteousness by his own efforts, these men reached conclusions which Augustine had not drawn.

Augustine was first of all a minister. With untiring effort he administered his episcopal office through sermons, charity, and divine service. For the sake of the souls of those entrusted to his care, he fought the heresies of Pelagianism, Manichaeism, and Donatism. He did not avoid controversies with the world around him, even though he always lived his life with monkish simplicity and became one of the fathers of western monasticism (the Augustinian Rule goes back to him). More than this, Augustine was a speculative spirit and combined acuteness of thought with creative force. In his knowledge he embraced all ancient philosophy and culture and passed them on to posterity through his immense writings. The ideas and concepts of Augustine became in the Middle Ages one of the great shapers of western civilization and in many respects are still effective today. He remained dominant in medieval theology until he found his equal in Thomas Aquinas. Certainly he is the greatest of the ancient doctors of the West.

In yet another respect Augustine assumed importance for later developments. The minister Augustine, whose whole being revolved around God and the souls in his care and whose work breathed nothing but love, in many ways determined the future attitude of the church toward heretics. In his early years he had himself experienced how difficult it is to search for truth and to find it, and when he entered the episcopate he was willing to exercise utmost leniency toward all who had lost their way. Then Augustine experienced the terrible damage of the schism and witnessed the split in the North African Church caused by Donatism. The rival Donatist Church, with its own hierarchy and well-functioning organization, regarded itself as the church of the "Pure Ones", of the pious and the saints; it spread suspicion,

87

hostility, and contempt toward the members of the Catholic Church, particularly toward its bishops, and carried the spirit of a low, spiteful polemicism into each congregation. Augustine also encountered in Hippo a rival Donatist bishop and he saw daily that a church schism is the worst of all evils. Yet he was powerless to alter the situation.

Augustine tried to be amicable. He sought personal and written dialogue with his Donatist colleague, and he negotiated and entered into literary discussions with the Donatists. The other side remained uncooperative and the fronts hardened over a period of time. Religious fanatics among the Donatists, called Circumcellions, who regarded themselves as saints, fighters for the faith, and soldiers of Christ, roamed begging or even as armed hordes through the country. They did not stop at force and terror and demanded social laws in the civil sphere (abolition of slavery, welfare for the poor, etc.,) and rigoristic Donatist reforms in the ecclesiastical area. Everywhere they struggled for the dissemination of Donatism; destruction of Catholic churches and maltreatment of ministers and laymen happened repeatedly. For almost a century the state was powerless against the fanatics, and only with the Vandal invasion did the movement finally come to an end (430).

Augustine ultimately had to acknowledge that the language of reason and love found no echo in the face of this fanaticism, which was stoked by the Donatist bishops. He arranged and conducted a conference at Carthage in 411, and the participating 286 Catholic bishops were confronted by an iron front of 279 Donatists. Even the greatest concession fell on deaf ears. For the sake of the highest good of unity and peace in the Christian Church, Augustine and the other bishops went so far as to offer their resignation from office if only the Donatists would return to the community of believers. Their magnaminity only met scornful rejection and new threats of violence. The Catholic bishops knew only too well what it would mean if religious fanatics were exhorted to new terrorism and became martyrs fighting against Catholics.

In this situation Augustine became aware of "the justification of the bitter *'Compelle intrare'"* (Lortz). In the last analysis, would truth be better served if love were subordinated to law and the use of force, or if force were subordinated to love? Thus Augustine out of bitter experience became the first who justified through Scripture the use of force in questions of faith. In the parable of the great supper when the invited guests refused to come to the meal, Christ had had the master say to the servant: "... go out into the highways and hedges, and *compel them to come in (compelle intrare),* that my house may be filled" (Lk 14, 23). Completely misinterpreting this passage, Augustine saw in it the justification for forcing reluctant heretics to enter the church (*Corpus scriptorum ecclesiasticorum latinorum* 53, 226 f). He could not know what terrible consequences his false interpretation would produce. Soon the concept was formulated into law: "Heretics have to be forced to their own salvation even against their will" (*Decr. Gratiani,* c. 38 C. 23 q. 4) and finally became, based on Augustine's authority, the foundation for the medieval Inquisition. Luther, in his unfortunate stand against the peasants in 1525 and a few years later against the Anabaptists in 1529, also relied on this maxim, and Calvin used it to justify his bloody judgments in Geneva. Yet one looks in vain in the New Testament for a justification of the use of force in the religious sphere. The Scriptures speak of faith only as a voluntary surrender to God's call. It is an unfathomable mystery that Augustine, who himself experienced his conversion as a call of grace after a long straying from virtue, should be the very man responsible for this disastrous development. However, Augustine did not approve of the death penalty for heretics. It was the product of an extension of secular power — of the *bracchium saeculare,* as it was called in the Middle Ages — to the religious sphere. The death penalty was then not only enforced because heresy was viewed as a violation of faith, but also because it destroyed the common weal which was based on a unity of faith.

3. Jerome was born ca. 347 in Stridon (Dalmatia). He came to Rome in about 354 and received an excellent education. On a trip to Gaul he became acquainted with a colony of monks and

decided to lead a monastic life. For a time he lived at Aquileia with a group of ascetic friends; then he undertook a journey to Jerusalem, became ill at Antioch, and there devoted himself to exegetical studies and learned Greek and Hebrew. From 375–378 he lived as a hermit in the desert of Chalcis. Jerome had himself ordained as a priest in Antioch in 379 and then went to Constantinople (380/381) to study with Gregory of Nazianzus. There he also became acquainted with Gregory of Nyssa. Pope Damasus invited him to Rome, and from 382–385 he lived at the papal court and by papal request worked on a revision of the Latin Bible. The Vulgata was the fruit of his labors. Jerome was the private secretary of the pope and apparently designated by him as his successor. Yet after the death of Damasus (December 11, 384) he was ignored in the papal election. Owing to his ascetic views — he was the center of an ascetic coterie in Rome — and his pitiless castigation of the defects of the Roman clergy, he had become thoroughly disliked. Jerome left Rome in 385 and by way of Antioch visited the various monastic settlements in Palestine and Egypt. In 386 he settled permanently in Bethlehem, where he died on September 30, 419 or 420.

Jerome had been accompanied on his departure from Rome by the pious and wealthy Paula, who supplied the funds for the construction in Bethlehem of three cloisters for women and one monastery for men, which was put under Jerome's direction. During thirty-four years of unceasing work, Jerome created in Bethlehem a literature of vast dimensions and impressive content. He was "without a doubt the most learned of all Latin Church Fathers and the greatest polyhistorian of his age" (Altaner). In spite of certain defects and weaknesses in his excitable passionate nature and his nervous irritability, he was a noble, upright warrior of God, completely imbued with the monastic ideal of piety.

4. Pope Gregory I the Great (590–604) is ranked since the eighth century as the fourth of the four great doctors of the western church. He was born around 540 and stands in time on the border between antiquity and the Middle Ages. Descended

from the senatorial aristocracy, Gregory assumed the office of prefect of Rome as early as 572/573. After the death of his father Gordian he renounced a brilliant secular career (ca. 575) and remodeled the parental palace into a monastery which he dedicated to St. Andrew. Later he endowed another six monasteries from his estates in Sicily and lived there himself in monastic seclusion. However, Gregory was soon torn from his quiet life. In 579 Pope Pelagius II dispatched him to Constantinople as his resident ambassador *(apocrisarius)*, where he remained until 585. In the midst of the courtly life at the Byzantine imperial court he lived like a monk, totally devoted to prayer and theological studies. After his return Gregory entered the monastery again, but remained the advisor of the pope. After the pope's death in the year 590, Gregory was chosen as his successor despite his honest and vigorous resistance.

History has awarded Gregory the epithet "the Great". His fourteen years in office were indeed of universal historical impact. The extant 854 letters provide an insight into his far-reaching internal and external activities and illustrate his noble personality.

Gregory's first task as pope was the skilful organization of the land holdings *(Patrimonium Petri)* of the church to produce an increase in crop yield so that aid might be provided the Italian people who were suffering hunger and epidemics as a result of the barbarian invasions and migrations. Out of feelings of pastoral, priestly, and social responsibility, the pope did everything to ease the life of the despairing people. He had grain distributed, protected the peasants on the latifundia of Italy and Sicily from exploitation, and even assumed, since Byzantium failed to do so, the political and military protection of Rome and the country. When the Lombards besieged Rome in 592 and 593 he succeeded through friendly negotiations in persuading them to withdraw.

Gregory's western orientation was epochal and significant for the future. He broke the one-sided dependence of Italy and the Roman Church on Byzantium and pursued an independent policy. He clearly recognized the importance of the Germanic peoples for the future. First he established good relations with the

Frankish dynasty, and then he looked across to England and began the Christian conversion of the Anglo-Saxons. He sent the prior of his St. Andrew monastery, Augustine, together with about forty monks on a mission to England. In the Arian kingdom of the Visigoths a change had occurred with the ascendance to the throne of King Reccared in 586. Gregory was eager to profit from this turning-away from Arianism and to unite the Visigothic Church with the Roman Church. He also paved the way for the successful conversion of the Lombards to the Catholic faith with the help of the Catholic Queen Theodelinda. By finally doing away with the schism which had existed between the Milanese and Roman Churches since the Three Chapter controversy, Gregory laid the foundations for a new ecclesiastical development in Upper Italy. Through the efforts of Pope Gregory the papacy attained a position of leadership previously unknown in the West.

Gregory's influence on the inner life of the church was of even greater magnitude. He reformed the clergy and for this purpose wrote at the beginning of his reign the *Liber regulae pastoralis,* a great instruction for the priestly life and work of ministers. Throughout the entire Middle Ages this treatise was the basis for the training of priests. His work *Moralia in Job* (595), a theological and pragmatical commentary on the book of Job, became the basic handbook of moral theology and aesthetics during the Middle Ages. In his four books, *Dialogi,* Gregory included the picture of the great western father of monasticism, Benedict of Nursia, and thereby helped to establish him as the actual "Father of Western Monasticism". In the Roman liturgy Gregory reformed the celebration of the Mass and brought the Canon to its present form (Gregorian Sacramentary). He probably also reformed the liturgical music, but it is uncertain to what extent he may be regarded as the creator of the so-called Gregorian chant. The assertion that he wrote and composed new hymns and even wrote a treatise on music is certainly an untenable later attribution which perhaps goes back to the idea that he may have founded the Roman Schola Cantorum.

Augustine and Gregory the Great together became the spiritual father and teacher to the Middle Ages. Although he did not attain the greatness of Augustine, Gregory's effectiveness in an age of transition and as the pioneer of a new future was enormously great.

12
ASCETICISM AND MONASTICISM IN THE OLD CHURCH

1. The problem of interpretation: Not only was the existence of monasticism shaken to its depths by the Reformation of the sixteenth century, but also its prestige was seriously diminished. Luther, who like many of the Reformers had himself been a monk, declared passionate war on monasticism after his break with the church. For a long time afterward no one dared to treat the history of monasticism seriously. Finally the blossoming historiography of the nineteenth century again turned to the subject, but the negative evaluation of the Reformers still remained unwritten law. Monasticism was understood as nothing but pure denial of the world and flight from reality (Weingarten, 1876), and it was believed to have had its origins in the "recluses" of the pagan Sarapis temple at Memphis. The young comparative history of religion supplied news of monk-like institutions in other religions, and thus it was taken for granted that Christian monasticism also had been copied from paganism and was therefore a foreign body within Christianity. Some believed that they had discovered the direct model in Buddhist monasticism. Jewish models also were claimed, such as the Essenes, the fraternity at Qumrân, or Philo's Therapeutae! Even the motivation for monasticism seemed to be quite clear: An internal protest movement had been started by the more spiritually and intellectually inclined Christians against a church which had become secularized during the Constantinian change. The numerous men and women who had not approved of the dilution of evangelical Christianity and its universal character had protested and consciously turned their backs on the official hierarchical church of priests which had

surrendered to the temptation of an imperial church. They had renounced divine service and liturgy, even the Eucharist, and hurried into the desert "finally to be alone with God".

All of these conceptions sound rather plausible; unfortunately they are only figments of the imagination and reflect the mentality of those who dreamed them up. They have no basis in historical reality and the sources speak an entirely different language.

For the last forty years there has been a renewed attempt to understand the deeper meaning of monasticism. Its origins and its Christian substance have been outlined more clearly. By this process it has been shown that during ancient times there were many small trickles from which the river of the movement flowed. It does not matter that ascetic ideals of a similar kind were noticed outside of Christianity; the desire for solitude, for quiet and intensification, and for ethical perfection is a universal human craving to which the best people have always responded. The Christian desire for perfection has its natural place within this universal longing. Analogies to monasticism in the non-Christian world therefore no longer disturb us. It is much more important to see what has become of this human need within Christianity under the influence of revelation and grace.

2. Christian monasticism can only be understood by referring to the essence of Christianity and the church. It is part of the self-realization of the church. Monasticism owes its origin to the gospels and wants to represent the total commitment to God by the imitation of Christ. It faithfully puts into action the three "evangelical counsels". "If any man will come after me, let him deny himself, and take up his cross, and follow me. For whosoever will save his life shall lose it; and whosoever will lose his life for my sake shall find it. For what is a man profited, if he shall gain the whole world, and lose his own soul?" (Mt 16, 24 ff).

The aim of this imitation of Christ is to exist only for God and to live from his holy charisma (= grace). In order to reach this goal and not to be deterred by anything on their way, the true disciples of Jesus divest themselves of their possessions (poverty), their bodies and their marital happiness (celibacy; the single life for the sake of the heavenly kingdom), and finally of their own ego (obedience, submission to others). The degree of renunciation depends upon the individual, for no absolute standard was defined by the gospel. Only to him who "is able to receive it" (Mt 19, 12) is complete commitment suggested, and then only as advice and not as a duty. Salvation is there for all. Where would mankind be if redemption could be achieved only by a limited few?

The church is big enough to have room for both the ascetics who strive for perfection and the weak and small who shall be redeemed because Christ died for them also. If the church affirms and promotes the striving for perfection, this does not mitigate its duty to be prepared for the masses at all times and with complete love. Any kind of one-sidedness means a denial of its obligatory mission of redemption and is heresy in the narrow sense of the word. Nothing is more damaging to the church than that which makes it small and narrow.

Repeatedly during the first centuries the church had to guard against the danger of such narrowing. The temptation to give in to it was great, because there is, after all, something striking about seeing human beings stride along the path of perfection with enthusiasm and radical commitment. Quite certainly only enthusiastic, deeply religious, "charismatic" personalities were inspired by such idealism. In the primitive church we encounter such ascetics again and again. They were in the service of the communities, were regarded as examples, and were shining stars during the times of persecution. Paul addresses such a group in his epistle to the Corinthians (1 Cor 7). For him *encráteia,* abstinence for the sake of the heavenly kingdom, is a special gift of grace which acquires significance in view of the imminent end of the world. But Paul also emphasizes: "Let every man abide in the same calling wherein he was called" (1 Cor 7, 20).

Heresy began when the "evangelical advice" became obligatory law for all. In the general Christian enthusiasm of the second century "encratites" appeared again and again who asserted that *all* Christians *must* abstain from marriage; that to live a Christian life plainly meant to live as an encratite; and that whoever was unwilling or unable to do so did not belong in the church. They conjured the ideal of a "Church of the Saints", of the "Pure" (*katharoi,* heretics), and of the "Perfect Ones", from which all the weak and sinful should be excluded. All heretics such as Tatian, Marcion, Montanus, Tertullian, and Donatus made such demands and wrote perfection, holiness, and strict religiosity on their banners. In the whole course of history up to the present these words were used by heretics in their struggle against the Catholic Church which they accused of laxity, apostasy, and falsification of the gospel.

It is important to point out, then, that the church has always had a legitimate space in its heart for a justified striving for perfection, without ever falling prey to a one-sided heretical generalization. Ascetiscism and monasticism represent an essential ingredient in the life of the church. They are not just any form of Christian realization, but through their calling they represent in Christianity the holiness, the charisma, and the longing waiting for the second coming of Christ. The church stands in need of them, it receives life from them and strength to continue its work for and in the world. With all its openness to the world and all created beings, the church must never for a moment lose itself in them. According to the formula of Chalcedon, the church must arrange its life in this world and fulfill its task of continuing the incarnation of Christ "without separation and without confusion".

It is the task of monasticism to represent a model of the distance from the world which is a necessary part of everything Christian. This signifies neither hostility to the world nor flight from it, but is simply an essential direction of Christian self-realization in the church. At all times monasticism fulfills the task of protecting the church against the danger of losing itself in the world. At certain times this temptation was and is greater than at others. Perhaps it was never as great as in the fourth century.

The Constantinian change had liberated enormous forces within Christianity. Partially these forces were transformed into a powerful missionary drive for the conquest and penetration of the world by the Christian spirit. Activists believed that they would be able to reach this goal by superficial political methods, but the Christian faith is not a political instrument and does not suffer dilution. From within Christianity, as God's answer to the need of the age, monasticism developed. It made its appearance with unprecedented elementary power in the Constantinian epoch and during the fourth and fifth centuries swelled into a movement which affected all levels of the Christian population. This age in general contained a strongly ascetic element which stemmed from the period of the last persecutions. The best among the Christians felt the obligation to seek sanctification according to the words of the gospel. Something of the early Christian charisma and enthusiasm and of the eschatologically directed piety of Christian antiquity was revived in these ascetics and monks. The spirit of martyrdom was transformed into the final full commitment to God and the ascetic imitation of Christ. People went into the desert to testify for Christ and to give themselves completely to God.

Anyone who reads the lives of St. Anthony and of St. Pachomius, the two "founders" of monasticism, or looks into the monastic literature and apophthegms of later times, will be continually astonished to find in these hard, ascetic figures such uncommonly kind persons whose deep inner natures and openness make them lenient and generous with their fellow-men. Such men do not deserve a negative interpretation. They stand in the middle of the church and the world and fulfill a positive task in both. From the religious dynamism of monasticism the forces which were necessary to fulfill the religious mission of the time received their impulse and deepening. All great saints and Church Fathers of the age were either monks themselves or were closely tied to monasticism.

3. The transition from the early community-bound charismatic to the solitary Anchorite who withdrew to remote regions and deserts is first noticeable among the Egyptian ascetics around the middle of the third century.

The first hermit known to history was Anthony whose life Athanasius the Great described from personal knowledge (*Vita S. Antonii*, 357). Born around 251 in Kome (Middle Egypt), Anthony, after the death of his parents, sold or gave away his rich heritage according to Mt 19, 21, and placed his little sister in a house for Christian maidens. In around 271, at approximately the age of twenty, he withdrew to solitude. At first Anthony lived close to his native town, but then moved deeper into the desert and finally, when he could not escape the stream of visitors, withdrew to a mountain range beyond the Nile which was accessible only with great difficulty. Athanasius has reported to us Anthony's struggle for saintliness and his combat with the demons (Grünewald illustrated the agony of the hermit on his Isenheim altar in 1512/14). Athanasius also described the powerful attraction which Anthony had for people of all ages. Young men who wanted to follow in his footsteps, the sick and people in distress, bishops and priests who sought guidance for the soul, and even Emperor Constantine and his sons, turned to him. Anthony did not hesitate to intervene in life, not as a politician but as a charismatic and speaker for a higher will and as God's prophet. Anthony died in 356 at the age of 105. By this time, a large hermit settlement had grown up around him; he is known as the Father of Hermits.

Pachomius (287–347) went one step further. He also began as a hermit (ca. 308); but then around 320 he founded the first "cloister" by connecting cells which were near one another and uniting their inhabitants in a communal life (= *koinos bios, coenobium,* cenobitism). The first monastery was created at Tabennisi on the Nile and consisted of a house with many cells, surrounded by a wall. Pachomius established another nine monasteries and two nunneries and finally had a total of ca. 9000 monks in his monastic association. He established a rule for prayer and work for the community and through skilful organization took care of the communal needs. The name "monk" (*monachus* = living by one-self) actually no longer fitted this mode of life but was nonetheless accepted because every

98

inmate was expected to live a solitary life in his cell with silence and meditation. Pachomius became the Father of Cenobitism.

From Egypt both types of monasticism quickly spread over the whole East. Basil the Great (d. 379) drew up a rule for cenobitic monasticism which quickly became accepted in eastern monasticism. The hermit life also persisted in the East and developed some strange and extreme forms (stylites standing on top of columns; incluses = voluntarily immured; etc.).

The West first became acquainted with monasticism through Athanasius who, when he was banished to Trier (335), was accompanied by two monks. The circulation of Athanasius's *Vita S. Antonii* also spread the idea in the West. Bishop Ambrose of Milan, Jerome, Augustine, and Martin of Tours were eager supporters of monasticism. Augustine wrote the first western monastic rule for his community of clerics at Tagaste in 388/89 and at Hippo in 391/393. After being supplanted temporarily by the Benedictine rule, it regained acceptance in the High Middle Ages and survives in the modern Augustinian rule. Subsequently the monk Johannes Cassianus, who had visited Egypt, founded the monastery of St. Victor near Marseille around 415 and wrote two valuable books of meditation which could be regarded as rules. But only Benedict of Nursia provided the correct form for western monasticism.

Benedict (480–547?) fled from his studies in Rome to solitude. In Affile (Enfide) near Rome he first belonged to an ascetic community and then spent three years as a hermit in a cave in the Anio valley near Subiaco. After undergoing some trying experiences as the abbot of a hermit community, he gathered the monks in monasteries in order to have them under better control. In 529 Benedict moved to Monte Cassino and there wrote his monastic rule. This rule, which testifies to his sagacity and moderation as much as to his seriousness and depth, soon gained great influence.

13
ROME AND THE PATRIARCHATES OF THE EAST:
THE QUESTION OF PRIMACY

1. From the beginning, the Roman community assumed an eminent position in the church as a whole. In the West it was always the recognized leader, if for no other reason than that it was the oldest, largest, and the only western apostolic community. Since the rank of a community was commonly measured according to its (apostolic) founder, and since the apostle Peter had always been named by tradition as the founder of the Roman community, its pre-eminence was as undisputed as the special position of St. Peter in the body of apostles. Thus it came about that Rome "from the beginning had a position of leadership in almost all areas of ecclesiastical life" (H. E. Feine).

Despite persecutions of all kinds, the Roman congregation quickly grew in numbers and significance in the second century. By the middle of the third century its numbers can be estimated at at least 30 000 souls; it counted 151 clerics and 1500 widows and poor people. The position of this community in the capital of the empire provided it with far-reaching connections. Early it could count eminent and wealthy men and women among its members and was even able to exert its influence at the imperial court in order to protect persecuted and oppressed Christians. Its charity and welfare for the needy have always been praised. Other communities felt both the need and the desire to maintain communion with the Roman Christians. Rome was the focal point for all Christian love.

Particularly the bishop of Rome assumed a special position which rested on the fact that according to the list of bishops he could trace his apostolic succession directly to Peter. This meant that the doctrine of revelation as transmitted by Christ and the apostles was preserved by the bishop of Rome in its most reliable and purest form, because direct continuity with the apostles and the early church was the best guarantee for an unadulterated faith. Since early times the Roman bishop had enjoyed magisterial authority. As early as the second and third centuries it was the custom of heretics to go to Rome in order to justify themselves; this was done by Marcion in 139, Montanus, and the heads of Gnosticism. The defenders of orthodox belief such as Athanasius in 339/340 also sought and found protection in Rome. This does not alter the fact that the center of theological work lay always in the East, where the great councils assembled. The intellectual achievement of the theologians is not identical with the magisterial office of the church, and it is this office alone which has to decide whether a theological opinion is within the apostolic tradition and therefore belongs to the revealed tenets of faith.

In juridical and disciplinary questions also the Roman bishop enjoyed early a certain authority. An initial indication of this is found in the first letter of Clement (ca. 96) which is concerned with the settlement of a dispute in the Corinthian Church. The intervention of Pope Victor (189–199) in the Easter dispute and the controversy of Pope Stephen I (254–257) with Cyprian of Carthage over the question of the baptism of heretics mark further steps in this progression. No one will want to see in these examples alone a claim to the primacy of jurisdiction, but since, like everything historical, the position of the bishop of Rome underwent a long, slow development, the initial steps must not be overlooked.

2. The question concerning the primacy of the Roman bishop is more complicated than often portrayed. In order to understand the problem, one must differentiate exactly between his position 1) as bishop of Rome and metropolitan of the Roman church province, 2) as patriarch of the Latin Church of the West, and 3) as the keeper of Peter's office, which he holds as Peter's heir and successor in Rome. Therefore each case must be examined to see whether he exercised his authority as bishop, patriarch, or successor of Peter. The greatest difficulty is to separate primacy from patriarchate.

The development of the ecclesiastical constitution proceeded roughly as follows: The individual episcopal church as an apostolic foundation provided the nucleus. Very early several

101

of these formed an organized association. In most cases the political metropolis also became the ecclesiastical metropolis for the episcopal towns of the province, and usually the provincial capital became the starting point of missionary activity, so that the provincial towns became daughters to the mother church of the metropolis. The metropolitans exercised certain supervisory functions, for example during episcopal elections and in matters of discipline. They confirmed and ordained the chosen, called and directed provincial synods, and acted as agencies of appeal for episcopal courts. Rome exercised these rights for Italy, Carthage for North Africa, Alexandria for Egypt, Antioch for Syria, etc. The reorganization of the empire by Emperor Diocletian was not without repercussions on the ecclesiastical organization. Diocletian divided the empire into 100 provinces, and these in turn into 12 dioceses. Finally he dissolved the monarchy into a tetrarchy by appointing Maximian as Second Augustus and adding two Caesars, Galerius and Constantius Chlorus. Despite the quartering, unity was preserved by Diocletian's claim of the highest authority for himself. Even if each of the regents ruled autonomously in his own area, he was also acknowledged in the empire as a whole, co-signed all imperial laws, and participated in the minting of coins.

It was at this time that the ecumenical patriarchates developed in the church. The council of Nicaea (325) sanctioned the "old custom" that Alexandria, Antioch, and other "eparchies", should exercise the same authority as Rome over the bishops in their districts, Jerusalem being allowed a primacy of honor. The creation of effective patriarchates had thus been confirmed by conciliar law. The language of the council shows that the patriarchal claims of Rome were the oldest and were transferred to the others.

A new situation was created in 330 when Constantine moved his residence from the Old Rome to the New Rome, the Greek Byzantium, which now was called Constantinople. Thus the political center of gravity was moved to the East, and as Constantinople's power increased, the political importance of the Old

Rome declined. Very soon the bishop of Constantinople expanded his influence. This took place at first in connection with controversies among the patriarchates of the East, and at the second general council of Constantinople (381) the bishop of Constantinople was expressly given precedence of honor over Alexandria and Antioch and directly after Rome. But Rome's preeminent position among the patriarchates was still acknowledged. In addition, Constantinople did not yet claim a patriarchal district of a jurisdictional nature.

Another controversy also began to develop regarding the dogmatic struggles of the fourth century, and tensions arose repeatedly between East and West. In the midst of the Arian controversies, during which Rome steadfastly adhered to the Nicene Creed, Athanasius sought protection with Pope Julius in Rome in 339 when his episcopal see was taken by an Arian. It was from Rome that he fought for his rights. In 341 Pope Julius directed a letter to the eastern bishops in which he took the side of Athanasius, but he met strong resistance. The synod of Sardica (342–343), which was supposed to restore Athanasius to his rightful position, for the first time made public the split between East and West. The eastern bishops denied Athanasius their recognition and left the council in protest. The western bishop solemnly granted the supreme decision of appeal (for the West) to the Roman see, restored Athanasius, and excommunicated the (Arian) heads of the East. The eastern bishops rejected the claims of the West and in turn excommunicated the western synodalists. Thus eastern and western churches inimically confronted one another and even if the schism was removed in 381, the tension remained as a malignant heritage. During the subsequent centuries the gap widened and finally led to a complete break in the year 1054.

The departure of Constantine meant a reduction of political influence for the West, but it also assured the Roman bishop of an independent development in the ecclesiastical area. As there was only one patriarchate in the West, its development became identical with the insistence on primacy. The Popes Damasus (366),

Siricius (384–399), and Innocent I (402–417) knew how to use this to their advantage. In contrast to the political claims of Constantinople, the popes increasingly emphasized the primacy of Peter on a religious basis. The passage Mt 16, 18 became increasingly significant (". . . Thou art Peter, and upon this rock I will build my Church . . ."). Pope Leo I the Great (440–461) left no doubt that the Roman bishop was entitled to primacy over the eastern church as well, and asserted this claim emphatically. It was his legates who presided at the fourth general council of Chalcedon.

But at this very meeting the papal legates were unable to prevent canon 28 from granting the patriarch of Constantinople the same rights that the Roman bishop possessed. As long as it was only a question of patriarchal rights, Rome had no objection; but when it became a question of the rights of primacy which in Rome were connected with the episcopal see, the situation became critical, and Leo the Great protested vigorously against canon 28.

3. Subsequently the primatial position was strengthened in both Constantinople and Rome. Constantinople relied exclusively on its political position and was increasingly drawn into the orbit of the Byzantine imperial power. The more religion and politics became intertwined in the East, the less independent became the position of the patriarch.

In the West the conditions were quite different. The weakness of the West-Roman Empire in itself led to a mounting independence of the ecclesiastical position. Emperor Honorius (395–423) was powerless when in 410 Rome was conquered and sacked by Alaric and his Visigoths. When the plundering and murdering Huns approached in 451, the weak Emperor Valentinian III (425–455) was no less helpless. It was Pope Leo the Great who courageously faced King Attila of the Huns and succeeded in having Rome spared (452). His prestige in the eyes of the people grew enormously. In 455 the Vandals stood before Rome and again the people looked toward Leo the Great. Even if he was unable to avert the sacking this time, at least he persuaded

Geiseric to spare the populace and to refrain from burning the city. The position of the papacy was so strengthened by Leo that it was able to survive the fall of the West-Roman Empire (476) without difficulty.

Pope Gelasius I (492–496) on the basis of this papal strength developed his doctrine of the two powers: the spiritual power is independent from the secular power, and each is competent for its own area. The greater authority rests with the spiritual power, however, as even kings must account to God. Conversely, the governors of the church must obey the imperial laws required to maintain public order. Gelasius wrote this doctrine to the East-Roman Emperor Anastasius and thus formulated the dualism on which the subsequent western development was to rest.

SECOND ERA
THE CHURCH OF THE MIDDLE AGES

14

The Division and Basic Structure of the Western Middle Ages

1. Periodization and Terminology. Since history flows in a continuous uninterrupted stream, all attempts at periodization are dubious; at best they serve to define a partial aspect, but never the whole.

The term "Middle Ages" for the period 500–1500 is unfortunate and largely devoid of content. It is borrowed from linguistic philosophy and rests on a misunderstanding of the true values of the period. The humanists of the fifteenth century were eager to link their knowledge of Latin with classical Latinity. They regarded everything which was spoken and written after antiquity as a degeneration of language and were convinced that only they had produced a new age of pure forms of expression. The whole intervening epoch they characterized simply as the "barbarian Middle Ages".

The Reformers of the sixteenth century had similar attitudes. The early church was for them the everlastingly legitimate form to which all ecclesiastical reforms had to return. To them the Constantinian Age was already a degeneration and the subsequent centuries constituted a decline of the religio-ecclesiastical life of even greater dimensions. The Reformers believed that with them a new flowering of the Christian religion was to begin. The Reform Churches wished to revert directly to the forms of Christian antiquity, and the time in between, the epoch of the anti-Christian papal church, was to be overcome. The division into

Antiquity, Middle Ages, and Modern Times was first used in this sense in the historical writings of Christoph Cellarius (1634 to 1707), Professor at the University of Halle. The Enlightenment later painted an even darker picture.

Only the Romanticism of the nineteenth century rediscovered the magnificent achievements of the Middle Ages, especially in art and literature. The flowering science of history in conjunction with the enthusiasm engendered by the enormous publication of sources for the national past, especially the *Monumenta Germaniae Historica,* opened the gates for a renewed concern with this period. Bright and shadowy sides became revealed through research. On the whole we regard this epoch today with admiration, and only ignorance and prejudice can still speak of the "dark Middle Ages".

Now as then the temporal delineation of the age remains a problem. If one accepts the fall of the West-Roman Empire (476) and the migration of tribes as a watershed between antiquity and the Middle Ages, it can be argued that both events contributed little to the shaping of the new age. Especially the Germanic kingdoms of the migratory period were of relatively small importance for medieval history. They belonged completely to antiquity and disappeared with it. Even the invasion of the Mediterranean area by the Moslems cannot be viewed as decisive for the new shaping of Europe, as has been attempted by Henri Pirenne. This invasion delivered the deathblow to the ancient Mediterranean civilization, but it did not start the new medieval civilization. Rather, the one and only bond between antiquity and the Middle Ages was the Catholic Church. Only at the moment when the bond between Catholic Christianity and the Germanic tribes was concluded, was one of the most essential prerequisites established for the creation of that western community of peoples and civilization which characterizes the Middle Ages. Not the Arianization of the German tribes, but only the Catholic baptism of Clovis (496) was epochal. The turning of the Franks to Catholic Christianity made their cultural and religious amalgamation with the native Romance population possible, an event which had always been prevented by the Arian religion of the earlier Germanic tribes.

It is also difficult to determine the end of the Middle Ages. Neither the Renaissance nor the fall of Constantinople in the year 1453 was such a profound break as to introduce a new epoch. Rather, one could view the Reformation in the sixteenth century as such a decisive breach, because it finally destroyed ecclesiastical unity, but even it did not remove the common Christian basis of the West. The peoples of Europe remained in close contact through the bonds of culture, science, art, technology, and social forms, despite the separation of churches. Even in the internal life of the church, medieval forms (feudal order, benefices, piety, etc.) were retained beyond the Reformation and in part were eliminated only during the French Revolution, the Enlightenment, and the period of secularization.

2. The triad Antiquity, Christianity, and Germanic Tribes forms the basis for the historical development of the West during the Middle Ages. It was important that during this time the center of church history shifted from the Mediterranean to the North. The effect of the entrance of the young Germanic peoples into the church was particularly strong. It is certainly wrong to imagine the Germans as "savages" or "half-savages". Certainly they often appeared to the Romans as "barbarians", who during their wars and conquests destroyed the culture and civilization of the empire. Yet one cannot deny that in peaceful times the Germanic tribes respected and admired the cultural and civilizational achievements of the *Imperium Romanum* and that on the whole they faced this culture with an open and educable mind.

These people were, however, of a different and more primitive civilization than that of the Roman population. One can only correctly grasp the extent and the significance of the change between Christian antiquity and the Middle Ages, if one bears in mind the enormous contrast between the spirituality and the highly developed urban civilizations of the Greek-Roman region and the agrarian environment of the Germanic tribes. This tremendous contrast could not fail to produce repercussions in the life of the church and the whole cultural development of the Middle Ages. The more intimately German culture and Christianity became intermingled, the stronger this mutual influence had to become.

In the first epoch (500–700) there occurred only a highly superficial missionary encounter. Even after Clovis had been baptized in 496 and his people had followed him on this way, pagan customs, morals, and conceptions survived for another two hundred years and determined the life of the Franks. Gregory of Tours (538–594), the historian of the Franks at this time, tells us many stories about them. For a long time the mass baptisms did not effect an inner change, and the lack of pre- and post baptismal care permitted the opinion to grow among the baptized that the acceptance of Christianity did not require a break with their old philosophies of life.

Only in the second epoch (700–1050), after the Anglo-Saxon monks had prepared the ground with a second missionary wave, did a deeper penetration come about. Boniface and Charlemagne created the necessary conditions for the development of western Christianity by helping to establish the union between the universal Roman church and the kingdom of the Franks. At first the physically stronger and more primitive German nature still dominated. Pre-Christian and pagan conceptions also were still effective and included the belief in spirits, magic, incantations, trials by ordeal, duels, water tests, and blood feuds. These ideas could be supplanted only slowly by a more spiritualized conception and survived for a long time in the subconscious of the people.

Some basic structures of Germanic life survived and had the effect of "Germanizing the organizational forms of Christianity" (W. Neuss) in the following manner:

a) The Germans were an agrarian people. The church, which had grown within the ancient urban framework, under the Germanic influence soon adopted an agrarian structure (benefices, system of parishes in the country).

b) The Germanic conception of the rights of the landowner

had its effect in the system of local churches, according to which the church which was built on his plot belonged to the owner of the land, together with all its secular (tithes, income from gifts) and ecclesiastical rights (administration of the sacrament, pastoral care, etc.); the bishop had no jurisdiction over it. This system of local churches soon spread to the whole West, including the Romance countries. The whole Christian order was affected by the change, with particular influence felt in the ministry and the ecclesiastical administration.

c) The strict separation of the Germanic social estates into princes, nobility, freemen, half-freemen, and slaves was carried over into the Christian Middle Ages and also found expression in the church. The sharp separation of classes into lower and higher clergy favored an aristocratic rule in the church.

d) The attitude of the Germans toward battle and war led in medieval Christianity to the development of Christian knighthood and the idea of the holy war and the consecrated soldier for God. From this beginning, the knightly orders and the crusades evolved.

e) The Germanic idea of kingship was invested even in pre-Christian times with a strong sacral and mystical aura. This survived in Christian kingship and was heightened by ecclesiastical consecration. The anointment of Pippin (751/754), the crowning of Charlemagne (800), and the crowning of Otto the Great as King and Emperor (962) served the sacral justification for the concept of ruling. In the Ottonian Empire it was soon transformed directly into that of a priest-king possessing high honors.

f) This sacral formulation for kingship led in all Germanic countries to the early development of a regional church with the king at its head. Later the emperors also regarded their position as an ecclesiastico-religious one and strengthened it as such. They not only awarded and gave away church property, but also appointed and deposed bishops and freely disposed of the so-called "imperial church property".

g) The interference with the ecclesiastical right of appointment, which even saintly and pious emperors like the Ottonians or Henry II and Henry III did not regard as wrong, simply had to create ecclesiastical reaction. The struggle against "lay investiture" and simony became the rallying point of the reformers in the eleventh century. The great theme of the investiture struggle was the liberation of the church from the embrace of the state and the magnates, and this struggle began the

Third epoch (1050–1300), in which the ecclesiastical reaction occurred. Now the church stepped increasingly into the foreground, and the battles between papacy and empire kept the age in suspense. The conflicts between Henry IV and Gregory VII, Barbarossa and Alexander III, and Frederick II and Innocent IV represented the high points of the controversy. Under Innocent III the papacy became a world-controlling institution: the Christian western community of peoples was united under the church; the crusades sent European knighthood into battle for the Holy Land; and the religious orders flowered. Intellectual life as well developed to an admirable height; universities were founded, and Scholasticism, canonics, mysticism, and piety developed an intense life. But heresies grew also, especially in the twelfth century. As a whole, the High Middle Ages was a great and exciting time which found elevated expression in the wonderful works of Romanesque and Gothic art.

The peak was reached, however, around 1300. Once more the claims of the church for domination were compiled by Pope Boniface VIII in his bull *Unam Sanctam,* but the papacy was no longer in the position to enforce the claim against the French kingdom of Philipp the Fair. The politics of Boniface were condemned to failure, and thus began the

Fourth epoch (1300–1500), the time of the disintegration of the western community. Various forces were at work to expedite the process:

a) the rising national states, particularly France, escaped from the unified leadership of emperor and pope.

b) The unified culture of the early and high Middle Ages became differentiated and an increasing individualism expressed itself in art, science, and politics, as well as in theology and the attitude toward piety *(devotio moderna)*.

c) The laity exerted itself and removed itself from the leadership of the clergy. The territorial lords claimed episcopal rights for themselves and established their sovereignty over the national churches.

d) The tension between papal primacy and the college of bishops, between curial centralism and the general church, found expression in the so-called "conciliarism", which in its most extreme form wished to replace the hierarchical structure of the church by a democratic one (Marsilius of Padua, William Ockham).

e) The Ockhamistic philosophy and theology (Nominalism, *via moderna*) with its skepticism shook the closed medieval picture of the world based on Thomistic realism *(via antiqua)*.

f) The whole intellectual attitude of the Renaissance and of Humanism, especially in Italy, served to explode the medieval unity of mind.

The Reformation was the final step in this development. With the schism of the sixteenth century the western world lost the spiritual tie which had held its peoples together, and unity disappeared.

3. In conclusion, the following features can be singled out as characteristics of the Middle Ages:

a) The western community was based on a unified religio-philosophical attitude which was shared by all and whose basis rested on the universal recognition of the religious and meta-physical commitment to God. There was only one binding truth to which all men deferred: the supreme undeniable ethic, the ultimate highest moral authority on earth, the church. The existence of sinners and heretics did not contradict the dominating concept of community. Their existence could be proved as "necessary" by the Bible (1 Cor 11, 19). Society was on guard and saw to it that they did not destroy the unity of the West. Inquisition and persecution of heretics had the aim of protecting the inevitable and necessary Christian unity against all attempts at schism.

b) The internal life of the community was determined by the symbiosis between church and state. This relation between the two was viewed as dualistical, graphically represented by an ellipsis whose two foci were the papacy and the empire. In contrast to the eastern Byzantine centralism (caesaropapism), dualism in the West formed from the beginning the foundation and the determining factor for the development of all western thought. Tensions and battles between papacy and empire arose as soon as the balance was disturbed. The fall of the Staufic Empire necessarily involved the decline of the papacy, because since both universal powers had held the West together, the disintegration of one must result in the decline of the other. Universal empire and universal papacy implied one another.

c) The organization of public life by estates was regarded as the God-willed order on earth. The lower classes could accept this condition, because the Christian principle stated the inherent dignity of all men and their equality before God. Fiefdom and feudalism were founded on such an order by estates and had their analogy in the system of ecclesiastical benefices. The feudalization of the medieval church determined the external face of the church until the great secularization and resulted in a monopoly of the episcopal sees by the nobility. The richest prebends of the church were almost solely controlled by the higher estates.

d) The church as the strongest civilizing force had a monopoly on education which remained undisputed until the thirteenth century. Everyone who was intellectually active was a cleric. Clerics were in charge of the chancellories of royal and princely courts, and the universities established around 1200 were also ecclesiastical institutions with papal privileges, whose professors were clerics endowed with prebends. The laity achieved an independent education only gradually. Toward the end of the Middle Ages one can speak of an educated laity with influence in its own right as lawyers, doctors, or humanists.

Following this outline, we will deal now with the individual epochs of history.

First Epoch: 500–700

15
THE CHURCH AS CHAMPION OF THE DEVELOPING WEST

At first it was not easy nor at all a matter of course for the church to gain access to the Germans. Since the Constantinian Change the church was accustomed to being the imperial church which supported the Roman state. This responsibility which the church shared with the state was associated intimately with the political fortunes of the empire, and there was the risk that it might identify itself with the state or that others, such as the Germans, might do so. That, however, could result in rejection.

The Germanic tribes appeared as enemies and destroyers of the empire, and Rome had to suffer much under them. The tragedy began around 375 when the Huns, who were invading eastern Europe from Asia, pressed upon the (eastern) border populations and forced them to migrate to the south and the west. The first to cross the imperial frontiers were the Visigoths. The East-Roman Emperor Valens accepted them as confederates and let them settle on imperial territory (376); but soon difficulties arose; war broke out, and in the battle of Adrianople (378) Valens was totally defeated and killed by the Visigothic king Fridigern. His successor Emperor Theodosius the Great (379–395) was able to master the situation once more, but soon after his death the Visigoths under their king Alaric renewed their raids of conquest and plunder. First moving into Greece (396), the

Visigoths, skilfully diverted from Byzantium into Italy (after 401), soon stood before Rome. The conquest of the "eternal" city by Alaric (410) shook the whole Roman Empire. It moved Augustine to write his monumental *De Civitate Dei* (413–426), in which he attempted to provide a Christian explanation of the catastrophe.

Now the fall of the West-Roman Empire could no longer be stopped. After 425 the Vandals devastated Spain. In 429 they crossed over to North Africa and conquered the "granary" of Italy. During the siege of Hippo the great bishop Augustine died in the enclosed city (430). The Huns began to move again; burning and looting, they moved up the Danube into Gaul. On the Catalaunian plains they were defeated in 451 by a combined force of Romans (Aetius) and Visigoths. In 452 they turned to Italy and fear of death spread through the peninsula. This time no army stood ready for the defense of the country, but Pope Leo the Great faced them at Mantua and was successful in persuading the feared king Attila to leave Italy. No wonder that the population ascribed the rescue to the direct intervention of God through his high priest Leo. In 453 Attila died, but only two years later the Vandals, coming from Africa, besieged Rome (455). Again all eyes were directed to Peter's successor and Leo negotiated with the Vandal king Geiseric. This time he was able only to have the lives of the Roman citizens spared and to prevent the complete burning of the city, but Rome had to endure looting and sacking. In 472 the German master of the soldiers, Ricimer, patrician of the West-Roman Empire, prepared to attack the city and stormed it with his Germanic mercenaries; in 546 and 549 it suffered the same fate at the hands of the Ostrogoths under Totila; and it did not fare any better when the Byzantine commander Narses reconquered it three years later (552).

Meantime, German troops had deposed the last West-Roman Emperor Romulus Augustus in 476 and had replaced him with the Sciri prince Odoacer. From now on the whole west of the empire was under German domination. After he had personally murdered Odoacer, Theodoric the Great established the Ostrogothic kingdom in Italy from 493 to 526. Only the East-Roman

Emperor Justinian (527–565) was able to win Italy back after a bitter war of annihilation against the Goths (535–553). Italy was invaded again in 568 by the still pagan Lombards from Scandinavia who established their power from 568 to 774. Pressed upon and threatened by the Lombards, surrounded by hostile Arian German kingdoms (the Visigoths in Southern France with the capital at Toulouse, 418–507, and in Spain; the Vandals in Africa, 429–534; and the Burgundians on the Rhone), and cut off from all help by Byzantium, the condition of Rome and the church in Italy was deplorable. To whom should it turn? Only in the East did the church see any guaranteed permanence for the Roman Empire.

The political difficulties in the West were aggravated by the religio-ecclesiastical antagonism between the Romans and the Germans. The half-Goth Ulfilas (ca. 312–382) had become acquainted with Christianity in its Arian form when he resided at Constantinople under Emperor Constantius. Patriarch Eusebius of Nicomedia who at Nicaea in 325 had been the most zealous defender of Arius and who together with him had been banished by Constantine, meanwhile had become bishop of Constantinople. Eusebius consecrated Ulfilas as the Arian "bishop of the Christians among the Goths" (ca. 341). Thus Ulfilas preached Arian Christianity to the Goths even long after Constantinople had returned to orthodox Catholic Christianity. In time, Arianism spread from the Goths to all the other Germanic tribes. Among the Visigoths, Ostrogoths, Vandals, Gepids, Rugians, Heruli, Burgundians, and Lombards, Arian regional churches grew up, as they did among the Bavarians, Swabians, and Thuringians. Arianism was regarded as the German national religion and was defended by the Germans in harsh opposition to the orthodox Catholic denomination. Everywhere this religious contrast placed the German kingdoms in hostile opposition to the native Catholic populations. No less a person than the Ostrogothic king Theodoric the Great (489–526) conceived the plan to unite all Arian German tribes into an alliance against the Catholic Greeks and Romans and to found an Arian Germanic Empire on

117

Roman soil. By all human reckoning, if this enterprise had been successful, it would have sounded the death knell of the Catholic Church in the West.

The movement failed only because of the young rising Frankish king Clovis who could not be won for Theodoric's plan. Around 496 at Reims (historical scholarship is not yet unanimous on place and date; possibly it took place in 498/499 at Tours), Clovis was baptized by the Catholic bishop Remigius, and by this conscious turn to the Catholic faith foiled Theodoric's intentions. This step was a "statesmanlike act of supreme significance" and one of the "most momentous events in world history". It made possible the amalgamation of the Germanic tribes with the Christian-antique civilization and established the prerequisite for the birth of the Christian West.

Only the Catholic Church could convey to the Germans the cultural tradition of antiquity together with Christianity. Arianism was unable to do so, because it neither had a really religious potency nor was it rooted in the cultural world of antiquity. Long ago it had lost contact with this culture and had become an alien element in the orthodox Catholic Mediterranean area. Largely owing to Arianism, the German peoples had remained isolated from Roman culture during the foundings of their states. But Rome had continued to exercise its attraction as the carrier of the idea of empire and civilization, and the Roman Church perpetuated this heritage.

For a long time the pope had carried out in Italy a function which went far beyond the strictly ecclesiastical framework. During the total collapse of the West-Roman Empire, Leo the Great and his successors had seized the leadership. The people had learned to look to the popes as their only protectors and providers during the disorders of war and famines, and they in turn had not hesitated to conduct highly political negotiations at their own risk (Leo the Great during the sieges by Huns and Vandals). The papacy even provided grain and food from the ecclesiastical estates for the starving people and thereby assumed an ancient and traditional function of the emperors. In the consciousness of the native population, Catholicism and national Roman sentiments blended during this period, and the Roman Church was transformed, as A. von Harnack once expressed it, "into the religiously transposed West-Roman Empire, while its bishop was the secret West-Roman Emperor".

Now this Roman Church was faced with its greatest and most significant task in world history: to undertake not only the conversion of the Franks but also the civilizing of the German peoples as a whole and the construction of a new world out of the remnants of the old. Although one must presuppose a certain natural continuity of cultural, economical, and political institutions, most recent research shows that this stream alone would have been inadequate to shape the future. Not only had the political power of the ancient Roman Empire disappeared, but the ancient stream of civilization also had congealed. "Without transformation by Christianity and the Germans, antiquity would have had no future" (Steinbach). The birth of the Christian West was a merit of the Roman Catholic Church which brought both the Christian religion and ancient civilization to the peoples of the North to whom the future belonged.

16
THE FIRST ENCOUNTER OF THE GERMANS
WITH THE CHURCH

The external course of the encounter, the conversion, is relatively easy to describe, but it is much more difficult to grasp correctly the development of the inner Christian life and the momentousness of this process.

The first mission centers were the old Roman episcopal towns. They had largely survived the Germanic conquest and remained focal points of ecclesiastical life even under the new rulers. Strong personalities among the bishops were able to command the respect of the conquerors and to give the native population protection and security. Thus, for instance, almost all of the approximately 125 Gallic episcopal sees survived the Germanic flood during the fourth and fifth centuries. Among these prominent bishops were Martin of Tours (d. 397), Liborius of Le Mans (d. 397), Severinus of Cologne (d. ca. 400), and later Avitus of Vienne (d. 518), Remigius of Reims (d. ca. 533), and Caesarius of Arles (d. 542). Because of them the Roman population was able to survive for a long time, even though the country-side had long been settled by Germans. The old Roman cities of around 400 stood like oases of Roman civilization and Christianity in the midst of an area occupied by pagan Germanic settlers. The *Lex Ripuaria* (633/634) of the Franks in the seventh century still is considerate of the *cives Romani* in the cities and permits them to live according to their traditional Roman law, which remained in force in the Frankish empire as the civil law of the Roman population.

The church also lived according to Roman law *(Ecclesia vivit lege Romana),* and until the sixth century almost all episcopal sees in Gaul and Germany were occupied by bishops of Roman descent. At the synod of Paris in 614 we encounter German names in larger numbers for the first time. By the end of the seventh century most names were of German origin, and the fusion of Roman and German was complete.

Avitus of Vienne worked zealously for the conversion of the Burgundians, and Remigius of Reims devoted himself to the conversion of the Franks (baptism of Clovis in 496 or 498/499) and the establishment of additional episcopal sees (Arras, Laon, Thérouanne, Tournai, Cambrai). The conversion of the Frankish people not only laid the foundation for the fusion of the native and Roman populations, but also was decisive for the winning of the other Germans to the Catholic faith. The subjugation of the Alemanni (496) and their incorporation into the Frankish kingdom (506); the conquest of the Thuringians (531) by the sons of Clovis (d. 511); and the incorporation of the kingdom of the Burgundians (523–534) as well as the Provence, which was taken from the Ostrogoths (537), opened the gates to Catholic Christianity among the other Germanic peoples.

The Catholic religion provided the Frankish empire, which soon became the most uniform and most powerful of all German kingdoms, with internal stability and external prestige. Now, in contrast to the Arian German states, Clovis had the native Catholic population on his side, including the highly respected Catholic episcopate, and could even enjoy the sympathies of the East-Roman emperor. When Emperor Anastasius (491–518) pitted Clovis against the Ostrogothic king Theodoric the Great and awarded him the rank of a Roman Honorary Consul, Clovis became in the eyes of the Roman-Gallic population the legitimate governor of the *Imperium Romanum*. Clovis, therefore, felt himself obliged to exercise the supreme *Auctoritas Romana* for the protection of the Roman Catholic native population in Gaul and Germany and to the limits of the Frankish sphere of influence.

With naive pride the Franks expressed their joy over the new situation and their Christian duty. They praised their Catholic faith as the source of their power and regarded themselves as special proteges of Christ who, since they had turned to him, had granted them victory and domination. The *Lex Salica,* drafted in the last years of Clovis (ca. 510), recorded the old Salic-Frankish code of law and began with the words:

"Long live Christ, who loves the Franks! May he guard their kingdom, fill their rulers with the light of his grace, protect their army, provide the supports of faith, and grant peace, joy and happiness, he, the Lord of Lords, Jesus Christ."

Here is the beginning of the idea which Charlemagne later defended so zealously: The Franks are the new imperial people, called upon to represent and to bear the *Regnum Christi* in western society after the fall of Old Rome.

Unfortunately, the ideal picture corresponded only very little to the rough reality. Bishop Gregory of Tours (538–594) in the ten books of his *Historia Francorum* (completed in 591) left us a rather sad picture of the religio-ethical conditions in the Frankish empire of his time. How could it possibly have been different! These people had become Christians less because of convincing Christian preaching than because of the example of the king and the pageantry of the Christian divine service. Baptism had been preceded by scarcely any instruction in the faith and no early Christian catechumenate. The mass conversions of whole peoples had only superficial effect, because baptism was not followed by any subsequent training. As a result, Christianity with its high ethical demands and its spiritualized concept of God could establish itself only slowly and with difficulty. The Merovingian royal house and the aristocracy provided a bad example. The sixth and seventh centuries of Frankish history are characterized by murder and fraternal quarrel in the royal family, war and rapacity among the leaders, moral degeneration, and a nadir of education.

The Frankish Church was almost fatally hampered in its effectiveness by royalty and aristocracy which interfered ruthlessly in ecclesiastical affairs. The king made himself lord of the church, appointed bishops, convoked synods, and determined all affairs. While in the East at this time subtle theological problems were discussed by theologians and councils, theological thought in the Frankish kingdom stopped completely and religious life reverted to rudimentary forms, permeated by many pagan residues. The most fatal aspect was that the Frankish Church increasingly degenerated into an internally torpid, externally isolated national institution which completely lost its connection with the universal church. Its relations to Rome, center of the western church, died completely, even if no formal separation existed.

17

The Irish-Scottish Church and its Continental Mission

1. Ireland, until the tenth century also called *Scotia maior* (in contrast to *Scotia minor,* the present Scotland), was never conquered by the Romans. The first Christianity seems to have reached the island from Britain sometime prior to 400, but it is possible that it was monks of Martin of Tours who planted the first seeds.

According to the reports of Prosper of Aquitaine, Pope Celestine I in 431 sent the deacon Palladius as "first bishop to the Irish who believed in Christ". The historically proven figure of the Briton Patrick (ca. 385–461) provided us with a closer understanding of Irish Christianity, and he may be regarded as the actual missionary of Ireland.

Around 401 Patrick had been carried off as a slave by looting Irishmen and had become acquainted with both the country and the language before he returned to England in 407. Later, Patrick probably became a monk in the famous monastery of Lerin (southern Gaul), then became a cleric in Auxerre, and in 432 took up the mission in Ireland where he acted as bishop in place of the recently deceased Palladius. When Patrick died in 461, Ireland was not only Christianized, but also ecclesiastically organized. Armagk in the north was metropolitan see and ecclesiastical center after 444.

A monastic character became typical of all churchly life on this cityless island. The external organization of the church was tied to the numerous monasteries which soon dotted the island. The large monastic communities represented the real ecclesiastico-religious center for each of the numerous tribes. The great holy founders of monasteries (Finnian, Columban the Elder of Hy, Comgall of Bangor, Brendan, Kevin, Columban the Younger) enjoyed high respect, and the abbots, not the bishops, were the responsible leaders of the Irish Church. These abbots were also in possession of ecclesiastical jurisdiction and they generally had one of their subordinate monks consecrated as a suffragan bishop to perform the purely episcopal functions of ordination and consecration.

In the sixth century in Ireland monasticism was extremely popular. Christian enthusiasm seized the whole people and created a monastic spring without equal. The monasteries grew and flowered and became advanced schools of intellectual life and piety. They produced countless saints and scholars, and the island was soon called the *Insula Sanctorum* and *Insula Doctorum*. This Golden Age of the Irish Church lasted until about 740.

The strong influence of monasticism naturally affected the religious life. The tribal monasteries attended to the spiritual needs of the tribe (Clan); its monks ministered to the people, conducted school, and celebrated Mass. The monks, therefore, had to be priests, and the monk-priest became in Ireland the very ideal of a ministering priest. The image of the priest was influenced by monkish habits and monastic forms and with the Irish-Scottish continental mission these characteristics were often transmitted to the European peoples. Celibacy and hourly prayer, the foundations of monastic communal life, which at first were peculiar only to the Irish monk-priests, in the future course of history in increasing measure became the obligatory norm for all priests in the West.

The ascetic exercises of monasticism, above all, strongly influenced the priests and the laity at this time, at first in Ireland, then also on the continent, and the harsh penitential discipline and mortification of the flesh were imitated. The monk-priests who served as ministers and spiritual guides transferred the private, secret, and voluntary penitence and private confession, which had become the custom in monasteries outside of Ireland as well, to the laity. Enthusiastic laymen themselves may even have taken the initiative and asked for it, because the traditional Christian penitence, which included only public penance for major lay offenders, was no longer enough for them. The individual guidance of the soul which the monk received in the monastery and which extended to the secret inner sins, permitted a more sophisticated and ascetic striving for perfection, and the monks recommended it to laymen when asked for advice in spiritual matters.

The confession of grave sins, even when they had remained secret, had previously been a common practice within the framework of old Christian penitence. The bishop imposed penance on the confessor who was normally given such an opportunity only once in his life, and received him to full communion only at the end of penitence. With this reconciliation, final remission of the sin was granted. The new private confession, which included also the admission of the secret inner sins, incorporated immediate absolution. This confession was performed verbally to the priest and could be repeated at any time, and the laity increasingly demanded this instrument of spiritual guidance. During the sixth and seventh centuries this practice became common throughout the West and ultimately exerted an enormous influence on the ideal of piety in the whole western church. Soon regular confession before communion was introduced, and in order to provide the fathers confessor with a guide for determining penance, there now were circulated, first in Ireland, books called Penitentials, which consisted of a catalogue of sins with the corresponding penances. After the seventh century such penitential rules were in the whole western world a part of the official library of any priest, and the possession and knowledge of them was required for the correct handling of the ecclesiastical penitential discipline.

The beneficial results of the introduction of private confession to the laity soon showed themselves in the flowering of a high development of religio-ethical conduct. A comparison of the Irish Church with that of the continent, particularly in the Merovingian Frankish kingdom, clearly delineates the tremendous difference.

2. Irish monasticism, in spite of its strong anchoritic character, was not at all opposed to the world, but rather was full of an enthusiastic spirit of action which expressed itself in a strong missionary spirit. The desire for solitude and separation drove them far away. Homeless for the sake of Christ and yet everywhere at home, they traversed Gaul, Italy, and Germany all the way to Pannonia. Holy pilgrimage, the *Perigrinari pro Christo,* was their ascetic ideal. These rugged bearded monks with their tonsured heads and long flowing hair and tall travelling staffs offered a strange picture. Over their shoulders on a strap they carried a water bottle and a leather bag in which they carried their books, and around their necks they wore a capsule with relics and a vessel for the storing of the holy consecrated bread. The ascetic drive toward self-sanctification never left them, and

125

even on their journeys they prayed and studied. With a restless missionary zeal they utilized every opportunity to win souls for Christ.

In all the countries of Europe these zealous Irish travelling missionaries worked by means of their example and their words. Generally they did not stay long in one place, and their mission, therefore, could not reach any depth. In its sporadic starts it did not achieve nearly the importance and effect of the subsequent systematic missionary activity of the Anglo-Saxon missionaries. The Irish mission was not, however, without results, and the monasteries founded by the monks became centers of Christian life in a semi-pagan environment whose conversion was yet to come.

Columban the Younger (530–615) was the most important of the Iro-Scottish travelling missionaries and founders of monasteries on the continent, and his effectiveness was the most lasting. In the year 590 he started on a holy pilgrimage *(perigrinatio religiosa pro Christo)* to the continent together with twelve companions, similar to Christ with his twelve apostles. In Brittany, Gaul, and Burgundy he worked with fiery missionary zeal and attempted to promote a religio-ecclesiastical rejuvenation, chiefly among the nobility and the clergy. Columban finally settled in the Vosges Mountains and founded the monasteries of Anegrey, Luxeuil, and Fontaine, for which he devised a rigorous rule. His severe ascetic personality not only deeply impressed the native population everywhere but also attracted flocks of young men whom he inspired with the ideal of monasticism. The monastery at Fontaine alone was later the source of another fifty monasteries, all of which lived according to Columban's rule.

Around 610, Columban boldly and energetically criticized the amoral life at the court of the Merovingian king Theuderich II and his feared grandmother Brunhilde, and was forced to flee from Luxeuil. From Burgundy he went to the still largely pagan Alemanni. For a time he worked near Lake Constance and settled in Bregenz. In 613 Columban moved on to upper Italy where he founded the abbey of Bobbio, and he died there in 615.

Columban's influence on the religious life of the Frankish kingdom was very great, particularly with respect to the confessional and penitential practices. His numerous pupils, who were not all Irish but also came from the native population, carried on his spirit. Only a fraction of them is known to us by name; most of them lived as unknown hermits somewhere in the wilderness. Their cells and monastic settlements became missionary centers for the population living in their vicinity, however, and they acted as catalysts.

The Irish monks were especially active in northwestern Germany, in Franconia, and in Thuringia, but also travelled in Alemannia, Swabia, and Bavaria. Among the better known missionary monks were St. Kilian of Würzburg (martyred in 689 with his companions Colonatus and Totnanus), Pirminius (d. 753) who in 724 founded the monastery at Reichenau, Corbinianus of Freising (d. 725; he probably was a Gallo-Roman), Fridolin of Säckingen (ca. 600), Trudpert of the Untermünster valley near Freiburg im Breisgau (d. 607 or 643), Rupertus of Worms, the apostle of the Bavarians (d. ca. 718 in Salzburg), Emmeranus of Regensburg (d. 715); also Findan of Rheinau (d. 878), Furseus (d. between 647 and 653) and his brothers Fullanus (d. ca. 655) and Ultan (d. 686), as well as Eligius (d. ca. 660), Amandus, Lambert, and Hubertus.

18
CHRISTIANITY IN BRITAIN
AND THE ANGLO-SAXON CONTINENTAL MISSION

As early as the time of the Romans, an ecclesiastical organization existed in Britain. The bishops of York, London, and Lincoln participated in the council of Arles in 314. When the Roman legions were recalled from Britain in 407, the pagan Picts from the north and the Angles, Saxons, and Jutes from across the sea invaded the country, drove the Christian population into the western areas (Wales) or to the continent (Brittany), and around

127

450 founded seven kingdoms (the Angles: Mercia, East Anglia, and Northumbria; the Saxons: Essex, Sussex, and Wessex; the Jutes: Kent). In these kingdoms every trace of Christianity completely disappeared.

1. At the end of the sixth century the mission to the Anglo-Saxons began at the same time from Rome and from the Iro-Scottish Church. In 596 Pope Gregory the Great (590–604) sent Augustine, the prior of the Roman monastery of St. Andrew, to England together with forty monks. King Ethelbert of Kent received them kindly, and at Christmas 597 Augustine baptized Ethelbert and 10 000 of his people. Augustine made Canterbury his residence. Pope Gregory continued to send more monks to England and took a great interest in the mission. Gregory was the first pope who consciously paid attention to the Germans and was able to empathize with these primitive people of nature. The letter which he sent to Augustine and Mellitus in England in 601 testifies to his sense of reality and his shrewd gift of adaptation. Gregory recommended that the missionaries use as much as possible the existing pre-Christian religious customs and fill them with Christian spirit and content. He advised also that the people be left their harmless joys: "For if one does not begrudge the people these external enjoyments, it is easier for them to find the inner joy as well. It is, after all, not possible to take away everything at the same time from still unopened hearts. Whoever wants to climb a high mountain does not do so in jumps, but step by step and slowly" (*Monumenta Germaniae Historica, Epistola* II, 1899, 331).

The success of the mission was surprising. The kingdom of Kent adopted Christianity first and in 624–633 Wessex and Northumbria followed. The pagan reaction in Northumbria after the death of king Edwin (d. 633) did not last long, and kings Oswald and Oswin renewed the mission. Oswald asked for reinforcements from the Irish monks of the monastery of Hy, and thereby tension arose temporarily between the Irish and the Roman missionaries, but the difference was adjusted at the synod of Streaneshalch in 664. The conversion of the whole Anglo-

Saxon people was soon completed. In 680–690 Sussex was also converted. Bishop Theodore of Tarsus (ca. 668–690), archbishop of Canterbury, introduced an incomparable flowering of the Anglo-Saxon Church and of Christian civilization in England. Theodore possessed a high education, which he had acquired in Athens, coupled with an excellent organizational talent and an unswerving loyalty to Rome.

The combination of Irish piety and Roman spirit soon proved to be extraordinarily fruitful. The uncompromising asceticism and penitential discipline of the Irish helped the establishment in the numerous new monasteries of a flourishing spiritual life and scientific endeavor. The Anglo-Saxon monastic schools, including those in the nunneries, developed an equally high intellectual, religious, and theological culture whose peak lasted well into the eleventh century. Thirty-three Anglo-Saxon kings and queens concluded their lives in monasteries, and twenty-three kings and sixty queens are venerated as saints. The Anglo-Saxon monk and theologian Beda Venerabilis (672–735) for the first time showed compellingly in his famous *Historia ecclesiastica gentis Anglorum* how the complete assimilation of a Germanic people by Christian thought and civilization had proceeded and to what wonderful successes it had led.

2. From the Irish, the Anglo-Saxon monks also inherited the irresistible desire for the *perigrinatio pro Christo*. The missionary zeal gained from the Irish became the basis for the continental mission which the Anglo-Saxon monks soon began with the greatest activity among the Saxons and Frisians, but their missionary work illustrates the contrast to the Irish way of thinking most clearly. While the Iro-Scottish missionaries had proceeded without plan or system and concentrated on winning individual converts, the Anglo-Saxons undertook their mission quite differently. Initially they had their work sanctioned by the pope and supported by the Frankish rulers and then, equipped with papal letters of recommendation and royal guarantees of protection, they first tried to convert the leaders of the people, the tribal dukes, because they knew very well that the people

would then be prepared to follow them. By emphasizing authority and ecclesiastical organization in their actions, these missionaries represented the Roman heritage. The "mission from above" only made sense if their success was maintained through subsequent care and organizational incorporation. The connection with the universal papacy gave the mission breadth and autonomy and guarded it against a relapse into regional narrowness.

The first notable Anglo-Saxon missionary was Bishop Wilfrid of York. In 678/679 while in Rome, where he had come to honor the "prince of the apostles and door-keeper of heaven", Peter, and also his successor, the pope, Wilfrid obtained the authorization to preach among the Frisians. Two of his pupils, Egbert and Wigbert, followed him in 689. One year later (690) Willibrord, together with twelve companions, came to Frisia after also having obtained authorization in Rome. The Frankish mayor of the palace, Pippin (688–714), assigned Willibrord the lower Scheldt as mission area. A second journey to Rome (695) gave Willibrord renewed papal sanction and consecration as bishop. He chose Utrecht as his episcopal see and in 697 founded the monastery at Echternach as spiritual support for the mission and he died there in 735. Under Willibrord's experienced guidance Wynfrith Boniface began his missionary work.

Second Epoch: 700–1050

19
WYNFRITH BONIFACE AND THE FOUNDATION
OF THE CHRISTIAN WEST

Boniface was the greatest of the Anglo-Saxon continental missionaries, one of the significant key figures of the West, and the pioneer of the Christian community of Europe. His importance lies less in the conversion of Germany — the title Apostle of Germany was given him only in the sixteenth century — than in his work of organization and reform and the determination with which he turned the views of the stagnating Frankish Church toward universal Christian thinking, freed it from its isolation, and associated it with Rome, the center of the universal church. In this way Boniface prepared the union between the Frankish empire and the papacy. This development found its crowning point in the coronation of Charlemagne in 800 and in the reconstruction of the western empire by Otto the Great in 962. Without Boniface the concept of a universal empire during the Middle Ages would have been unthinkable.

Wynfrith was born sometime between 672 and 675 in the kingdom of Wessex. He was reared as a monk in the monasteries of Exeter and Nursling, and received his higher education at Nhutscelle, where he also taught. He undertook his first missionary attempt in Frisia in 716 under the direction of Willibrord. The unpropitious political conditions, particularly the war which had broken out between the Frisian duke Radbod (d. 719) and the Frankish mayor of the palace Charles Martel (714–741), soon obliged him to return to England. In 718 he again went to the continent, and before resuming his missionary activity he journeyed to Rome in order to receive his commission from Pope Gregory II (715–731). Now he received the name Boniface, and from 719 to 722 preached as a missionary, at first under the direction of Willibrord in Frisia and then independently in Upper Hesse and Thuringia. Boniface founded the monastery at Amöneburg as his base of operations. The country was no longer completely heathen. Iro-Scottish and Frankish travelling missionaries were busy here, but their impermanency hindered the missionary work. Boniface recognized that he was in need of greater authority in order to be successful against these monks and the local magnates and he returned to Rome a second time in 722, in order to receive personally from the pope the consecration as bishop and letters of recommendation to Charles Martel. On this occasion Boniface swore the suburbicarian bishop's oath which was customarily taken by the seven bishops in the immediate vicinity of Rome (Albano, Ostia, Porto-Santa Rufina, Palestrina, Sabina-Poggio-Mirteto, Frascati (Tusculum), and Velletri). The oath pledged specially close ties and unity to Rome.

Between 723 and 732 Boniface resumed his missionary work in Hesse, this time supported by papal letters of recommendation and special guarantees of protection from Charles Martel. Near Geismar he felled the sacred oak of Thor. After 725 he devoted himself particularly to the organizing, strengthening, and deepening of Christianity, and to fortifying his positions. He remained in continuous correspondence with the pope and with his native country which at all times sent him aid as well as additional monks and nuns. In order to provide Boniface with even greater authority for organizational expansion, Gregory II (731–741) appointed him archbishop-at-large in 732 and granted him the privilege of consecrating bishops for the bishoprics that were to be established. During this time Boniface founded a series of additional monasteries (Fritzlar, and the nunneries at Tauberbischofsheim under the abbess Lioba and Kitzingen and Ochsenfurth under Thecla). He had not yet had any opportunity to establish bishoprics. Probably the Frankish episcopate and nobility obstructed him in this, because they saw their privileges threatened by Boniface, the stranger. Since the archiepiscopal dignity and authority still proved insufficient, Boniface journeyed to Rome a third time in 737/738 and was appointed by the pope as apostolic legate for Bavaria, Hesse, and Thuringia, with the special charge to institute in these areas a tighter ecclesiastical organization. In Rome he found additional assistants for his task: Lullus, Willibald, and Wunibald, who had just come from the abbey at Monte Cassino.

Between 738 and 747 Boniface devoted himself exclusively to the organization and reform in the Frankish kingdom. At first he re-ordered the ecclesiastical structure of Bavaria by setting new and definite borders for the bishoprics of Passau, Salzburg, Freising, and Regensburg, and later (745 ?) also for Eichstätt. Then he established the bishoprics of Würzburg, Buraburg, and Erfurt (after 741) in Thuringia. The new Frankish rulers Carloman in Austrasia and Pippin in Neustria assisted him in the reform of the church in the Frankish kingdom. This support enabled Boniface on April 21, 743 to preside over the *Concilium Germanicum I* which also reformed the Austrasian Church. We do not know its location, but Carloman proclaimed its decisions as royal law. In 743–744 further synods were held in Estinnes (Hennegau) for Austrasia and in Soissons for Neustria. An all-Frankish synod could be convoked by 745.

The reform work was undertaken by Boniface, legate for the whole Frankish kingdom since 741, in closest contact with the Frankish rulers who adopted not only the idea of reform, but also that of association with Rome. In 747 the bishops assembled at a synod under the direction of Boniface, sent to the pope a solemn promise of loyalty, and the alliance was concluded. Pippin, who since Carloman's entry into the monastery at Monte Cassino in 747 was sole ruler, soon negotiated directly with the pope. In

133

the persons of abbot Fulrad of St. Dénis and bishop Chrodegang of Metz, Pippin had at his side his own reliable Frankish advisors in questions of church reform. Boniface's work had borne fruit.

For Boniface himself the last years of his life seem to have been filled with personal disappointments. Pippin energetically proceeded with the reform, but he increasingly gave in to the Frankish opposition to Boniface as a foreign Anglo-Saxon missionary, and acted without consulting him. As a result, Boniface withdrew. Frankish nobles had prevented him in 745 from taking over the just vacant bishopric of Cologne, and thus in 748 he chose Mainz as his metropolitan see. There and in his favorite establishment, Fulda, which he had founded in 744 and turned over to abbot Sturmi, Boniface now lived for his ministerial and supervisory work. He no longer seems to have participated in the great political decisions. Presumably he was as little involved in the negotiations between Pippin and Pope Zacharias (741–752) over the dethronement of the Merovingian dynasty in the Frankish kingdom as in the anointing of king Pippin in 751 or 752 (T. Schieffer).

When Pope Stephen II (752–757) appeared as petitioner in the Frankish kingdom in 753/754 and solemnly repeated the anointment and coronation of Pippin, Boniface was just about to undertake his last missionary journey to Frisia. Together with fifty-two companions he was slain at Dokkum on June 5, 752 by pagan Frisians. The martyr's death of Boniface once more aroused the attention of the whole Frankish kingdom, and his corpse was solemnly escorted to Fulda. In the same year, the momentous bond was established between papacy and Frankish kingdom, a bond whose foundations Boniface had laid.

20

The League of the Papacy with the
Frankish Kingdom

In order to understand the meaning and significance of the alliance
we must examine briefly the concrete situation of both partners.

1. *The Papacy between East and West*

After the fall of the West-Roman Empire (476), Constantinople
as the New Rome *(kainé Róme)* had assumed the claim to sole
legitimate rule in the Roman Empire. Emperor Justinian I
(527–565), after defeating the Vandals and the Ostrogoths, was
able once more to restore the splendor and majesty of the Roman
Empire. But the following century brought new perils. Slavs and
Avars pressed upon the empire from the Balkans, and the old
hostility to the Persians took new life. It was the Persians who
brought Byzantium to the brink of destruction when in 605 the
Sassanids expanded to the Bosphorus, after 615 subjugated the
Mediterranean provinces to the borders of Egypt, and in 619
finally occupied Egypt proper. Emperor Heraclius I (610–641)
was able to defeat the Persians decisively in a "Holy War" in 627
at Niniveh. At that time he rescued the Holy Cross of Christ which
the Persians had taken away from Jerusalem (Feast of the Exul-
tation of the Cross). Only a few years later, however, new and
even graver afflictions had to be suffered.

The attack of Islam affected the Mediterranean world decisively;
the Arabs destroyed the old Hellenistic-Roman unity of civilization and thus created unsuspected political and cultural consequences. The Mediterranean, for thousands of years the
unifying element for the bordering peoples, as a result of the
Arabic conquests in the Near East and North Africa became a
dividing barrier between the Islamic world on the one side and
the Christian West on the other. To Byzantium fell the task of
serving as the outpost of the Christian faith and protector of

Europe in the East against the incursions of Islam. Increasingly, Byzantium found itself between the two fronts.

From insignificant beginnings, Mohammed (571–632) had created a religio-political movement among the Arabs of tremendous impetus. Born in Mecca and orphaned at the age of six, Mohammed grew up with an uncle. At the age of twenty-five he married the widow of a wealthy merchant and on his commercial journeys in Syria and Arabia came in contact with the different religious denominations, particularly Judaism and Christianity. When at the age of about forty he appeared as a religio-social reformer among his people, who in the majority still embraced a primitive polytheism, he had developed a religious body of thought which mixed in equal measure ideas gained from old Arabic, Jewish, Christian, and Gnostic concepts. The essential element of his theology was an exclusive monotheism. As the prophet of Allah, Mohammed preached submission to God's will (= Islam) and promised paradise after death as reward for the Moslems (= the faithful). The simple and clear doctrines, which he claimed to have received through divine dreams and which contained besides monotheism the idea of the predestination of all human acts and fates by God (Kismet, fatalism) and the retribution of all good and evil deeds on the day of judgment, strongly appealed to the eastern phantasy. The sensual images of a paradisical life after death for the Moslems, and its religious exercises (ablutions; five daily prayers; fasting during the month of Ramadan; and pilgrimages to Mecca) were well suited to these people. At first Mohammed had to flee from Mecca because of socio-religious tensions (622; the beginning of the new chronology, called Hegira) and, together with his followers, he went to Yathrib, the future Medina (= city of the prophet). From Medina he conquered and converted the Arabic tribes and in 630 returned to Mecca, which surrendered to him without resistance. Mohammed purified the Kaaba, the old Arabic shrine, of idols and made his new doctrine into the national Arabic religion. Soon he ruled over all of Arabia.

Mohammed's early death (632) threatened his work with collapse, but his first successor ("Caliph") Abu Bekr (632–634) managed to bring the disunited tribes together again and directed their desire for battle and booty toward the neighbouring countries. The collision with the adjoining great powers of Persia and Byzantium introduced a time of extensive Arabian expansion. Caliph Omar (634–644) became the founder of the Arabian Empire. In 635 he conquered Damascus and defeated the Persian Sassanids; in 637 Jerusalem fell into his hands; between 640 and 644 he occupied Persia; and his general Amru subjugated Egypt at the same time (639–641). Soon North Africa became part of the Arabian Empire, and the Mediterranean coast from Syria to Gibraltar was under Arabian control. Omar and his successor Othman, Mohammed's son-in-law, formulated the 114 suras (sections) of the Koran. These suras contained the "revelations" proclaimed by Mohammed. The dynasty of the Omayyad caliphs, who from 661 to 750 resided in Damascus, began with Othman.

The Byzantine Empire was not able to withstand the powerful Arabian drive for expansion, and extensive parts of its holdings were lost. Only Constantinople proper was defended successfully in heroic battles over the years (674–678) and thus saved the West from being overrun by the Arabs. In 717–718 the Moslems, attacking by water and by land, again suffered a crushing defeat before Constantinople.

In the face of this emergency it is understandable that Byzantium was no longer able to protect Rome and Italy against the Lombards. After 568 the Lombards founded a state in upper Italy ("Lombardy") with its capital of Pavia, and quickly expanded southward. In Spoleto and Benevent two Lombardic dukedoms were established in the immediate vicinity of Rome. When the Arabs conquered southern Italy, the part of Italy belonging to Byzantium shrank to the areas around Rome (*Ducatus Romanus*) and Ravenna (Exarchate of Ravenna, seat of the Byzantine governor). In 592–593 the Lombards besieged Rome and the city could not expect help from Byzantium. It was then that Pope Gregory the Great (590–604) faced the Lombards

137

— as Leo the Great had formerly confronted the Huns and Vandals — and was able to obtain from them an end to the siege and their withdrawal from the city. Soon Gregory was able to convert the Lombards to Catholic Christianity with the help of the Catholic queen Theodelind. Gregory the Great was the first pope to pay special attention to the Germans.

Even though the Lombards had adopted the Catholic faith, the political tensions nevertheless remained. When king Liutprand (712–744) finally resumed the old policy of expansion with the intention of subjugating all of Italy, East Rome was being shaken by the most severe internal and external crises. The popes called for help in vain — Byzantium could not send any troops. In 739/740, faced with war against the Lombards and deserted by the emperor, Pope Gregory III (731–741) turned for help for the first time to the Frankish mayor of the palace, Charles Martel. But Charles Martel was an ally of the Lombards and needed their support against the Arabs in southern France, and the bond which had been created by Boniface between Rome and the Frankish state was not yet effective. Thus help was denied to Pope Zacharias (741–752), and he could do nothing but conclude a twenty-year peace with Liutprand. After a brief respite under king Rachis (744–749), who became a monk in the monastery of Monte Cassino, king Aistulf (749–756) resumed the old plans for conquest. The renewed threat to Rome caused Pope Stephen II (752–757) to ask once again for help from the Franks. This time there was the greatest probability that he would find sympathy, because the situation had changed drastically. Pippin, Charles Martel's forceful son and successor, gave Stephen a willing hearing.

2. The Frankish State before new Tasks

For a long time the mayors of the palace had served as the actual governors of the Frankish state rather than the Merovingian shadow kings. When in 743, Childeric III, the last Merovingian, became king, his position was a completely hollow one. Charles

Martel (714–741), a forceful personality who had been successful in administering a devastating defeat to the Arabs in 732 at Tours and Poitiers, extended his power as mayor of the palace to the uncontested leadership of the whole Frankish state. In fact, Charles the "Hammer", who had saved Europe from Islam by finally stopping the victorious advance of Mohammed's fanatical followers who in 711 had invaded Spain via Gibraltar, had quickly destroyed the Visigothic kingdom, and had already conquered southern France, was the uncrowned king of the West.

Charles Martel's sons Carloman (741–747) and Pippin (741–768) also ruled autocratically. When Carloman renounced public life and became a monk at Monte Cassino (747), the time had come for the sole ruler Pippin to free his way to kingship by deposing the incompetent Merovingian dynasty. Yet in view of the strong religious roots of the German kingship, Pippin required a higher authority to justify the undertaking and to substitute spiritual anointment for his lack of blood line. Under the prevailing circumstances, such authority could only be supplied by the pope, whose esteem and recognition had greatly increased since the work of Boniface. Therefore Pippin addressed the crucial question to Pope Zacharias (741–752) as to whether he could dare take this great step. Having the pope's consent and thus supported by the supreme spiritual authority, Pippin convoked the Diet of Soissons (751–752) and had himself elected king of the Franks. The pope thereupon ordered Pippin to be anointed by one of the Frankish metropolitans. (Presumably it was not Boniface as often has been assumed).

The reorientation of the Frankish state toward Rome, begun by the reforms of Boniface and continued by Pippin, now was answered by the turning of the papacy to the Frankish kingdom. Byzantines and Lombards forced the pope to take this step. It indicated a truly "epochal change in European history" (T. Schieffer). The papacy, which despite numerous tensions had continued to look toward Byzantium, now dissolved its ties with the East and turned completely to the West and to its principal representative, the kingdom of the Franks.

When in the summer of 753 the Lombard king Aistulf once again threatened Rome and help could not be expected from Byzantium, Pope Stephen turned to the Frankish king. Stephen asked Pippin to invite him and provide a Frankish delegation to escort him to the Frankish court for negotiations. Pippin immediately acceded to the request, because this was not only an opportunity to repay a great debt to the pope, but also a test of his recently received Christian kingship. Pippin knew that this kingship involved the religio-ethical duty to use his political and military power for the protection of the church. If Stephen in his letter of thanks mentioned that Rome was not only the principal church of the West, but was also the foundation of the very prince of apostles, Peter, whom the Franks had chosen as their patron saint, he could be certain of appealing to the whole Frankish nobility and people in the most convincing manner. His journey to the Franks, which Stephen began in November 753, "symbolized the separation of the papacy from the (Byzantine) Empire and the transition from the Byzantine to the Frankish segment of its history" (Schieffer).

The friendship alliance between the papacy and the Franks was concluded on January 7, 754, at Ponthion. Pippin promised the pope help against Aistulf and also the "return" of the areas conquered by the Lombards, especially Ravenna. In connection with the return of these areas there was no longer any mention of the Byzantine Empire, to which they had so far belonged, but only of St. Peter. The Franks declared that it was not for the Byzantine emperor that they wanted to campaign, but only for St. Peter and his successors.

In April 754 the Frankish Diet at Quierzy resolved to protect the pope against the Lombards. In a famous title deed, which unfortunately did not survive, Pippin promised Stephen II all the territories of central Italy which were going to be liberated; Tuscany, Ravenna, Venetia, Istria, and the dukedoms of Spoleto and Benevent. By giving these territories to St. Peter, Pippin laid the groundwork for the development of the future Papal State.

Aistulf meanwhile had refused negotiations for a peaceful

solution of the conflict. In the summer of 754 he was defeated by the Franks and forced to relinquish the territories in question. When Aistulf rose again two years later and even moved against Rome, he was defeated once more by a Frankish army and this time subjugated completely. Now difficulties arose in connection with the implementation of the promise of title, and not all territories were handed over to the pope. Did the Franks hesitate to ignore the claims of the Byzantine emperor? The reasons for the caution are no longer entirely discernible.

In any case, the new church state still required a lawful foundation. The chief task was to repulse the old Byzantine legal claims, derived from Emperor Constantine the Great as the heir to the ancient Roman Empire. The Byzantines claimed not only Rome and Ravenna as Roman imperial territory, but basically all of Italy and the West. They regarded the alliance of the pope with the Franks as treason, and they refused to recognize the territorial agreements.

The creation of the so-called Donation of Constantine seems to fall into this period between 750 and 760. This early medieval forgery was in the form of a document according to which Constantine the Great, when he had transferred his residence from Rome to Byzantium around 330, had ceded to Pope Sylvester (314–335) and the Roman see the sovereign authority over the whole western half of the empire. It is based on an old Sylvester legend from the fifth century. According to this fantastic and completely invented narrative, Emperor Constantine attributed his miraculous cure from leprosy to Pope Sylvester and in gratitude transferred the control over Rome and the western countries to the Roman see. The basis for this early Sylvester story was possibly the intention to protect the papacy against the tutelage of East Rome and to guarantee its political and ecclesiastical independence in the West. Now there is recognizable the desire to award to the papacy in Italy the political leadership which after the fall of the West Roman Empire (476) and during the disputes with the East Roman Empire from the sixth to the eighth centuries the papacy had long since exercised de facto

141

and which it had been conceded by the native population. The forgery was to support this claim authentically and legally and to do so at the very moment when it became necessary to reject the East Roman claims to Ravenna, Rome, and Italy.

It has been speculated, therefore, that it was fabricated for this purpose in the chancellories of either Stephen II (752–757) or Paul I (757–767). Full clarity on time and place of its creation is unattainable. Because it was in good faith generally regarded as genuine, at least since the middle of the eleventh century, it served as the legal justification not only for the church state, but also for primacy and the universal dominion of the popes from Gregory VII to Innocent III and Boniface VIII. Only Nicholas of Cusa, Lorenzo Valla, and the humanists of the fifteenth century began to doubt its authenticity and recognized it as a forgery.

Pope Stephen seems to have exercised imperial rights based on the Donation of Constantine when on July 28, 754 in St. Denis he repeated the anointing of Pippin and his sons Charles and Carloman and awarded them the title *Patricius Romanorum,* a title which normally could be awarded only by the Byzantine emperor. For the Franks, of course, such honor meant the assumption of a new task: to be the protective power of the western church. It was the year in which St. Boniface died.

21

CHARLEMAGNE AND THE FOUNDING
OF THE WESTERN EMPIRE

Charlemagne (768–814), the most powerful ruler of the Middle Ages, finished uniting the Frankish kingdom to Rome, a work which had been begun by Boniface and Pippin, and created the western universal empire on this new basis.

1. In 754 at the age of twelve, Charles had participated in the meeting between his father Pippin and Pope Stephen II at Ponthion, co-signed the treaties, and been anointed. In 768 he had shared the rule with his brother Carloman, but after Carlo-

man's early death (d. 771) Charles became the sole ruler and was now able in successful campaigns to expand his empire over almost all of Europe and to strengthen it internally and externally.

In spite of Charles's marriage to Desideria, the daughter of the Lombard king Desiderius, which Charles had concluded at his mother Berthrada's insistence to foster peace, the old tensions between Franks and Lombards arose again. When Charles, for unknown reasons, finally returned Desideria to her father, war was inevitable. Desiderius attempted to form an alliance against Charles and tried to win Pope Adrian (772–795) to it. When the pope refused, Desiderius marched on Rome. Adrian called to Charles for help and he soon appeared in Italy with a strong army which defeated the Lombards (773–774). At Easter 774, while the siege of Pavia was still going on, Charles visited Rome and the king of the Franks and the pope swore an oath of eternal friendship at the grave of St. Peter. As *Patricius Romanorum*, Charles now assumed the military protection of Rome, and from now on the *Defensio ecclesiae Romanae* was the most distinguished task of the Frankish kingdom. The Frankish role of protector was soon expanded from Rome to the entire western empire.

Charles also renewed the promise of Pippin's donation to the pope at Easter 774. But after the victory over Desiderius, Charles himself had become king of the Lombards and now had to look after his own interests in Italy. He hesitated with the implementation of the donation, and negotiations continued until 781. Only in that year did Charles adjudge the dukedom of Rome and the exarchate of Ravenna, the Pentapolis, the Sabina, southern Tuscany, and a few other small territories to the papacy as its sphere of influence. Thus the Papal State was finally created, which existed until 1870. This state gave the church stability during its colorful history, but it often also became a burden. Neither Istria and Venetia, nor the dukedoms of Spoleto and Benevent were given to the Papal State. After Charles conquered them in 787, he retained them for himself to assure his domination of Italy.

The first decades of Charles's reign were spent in the construction and securing of the frontiers. Charles's ecclesiastico-religious position had been strengthened by his alliance with the papacy and the Roman Church, and he could now pursue his conquests with much more force as the authorized protector of religion and the church. This was particularly true because his campaigns were directed solely against the heathens and infidels who threatened the borders of his empire. All of Charles's campaigns, therefore, had an ecclesiastical and religious as well as a military and political character. This was so, whether he fought against the Mohammedans in Spain or against the pagan Saxons, Avars, Slavs, and Bohemians in the north or the east of the empire. Politics and religion became one: Subjection was coupled with the Christian mission, and conversion of these peoples meant for them also subjection to the sovereignty of the Frankish empire.

There is no doubt that Charles acted out of a sense of genuine responsibility. The spreading of the Christian faith and Christian morals was as much his concern as the extension of his political power. Understandably, it is no longer possible to determine which of the two weighed heavier. The question in itself is anachronistic in view of the all-embracing political religiosity of the age. In 778, Charles fought against the Arabs in Spain, and in 795 he founded the Spanish March for the protection of the regained territories in Northern Spain. He campaigned against the Slavs in 789 and in 791, 795, and 797 against the Avars, in 805–806 against the Bohemians, and in 808–811 against the Danes. The longest and bitterest of his campaigns was against the Saxons from 772 to 804.

The conquest of the Saxons was vital for the creation of a uniform Frankish state, but it was not favorable for the Christian mission that the conversion of the Saxons appeared so closely tied to politics. From initial police actions in reprisal for Saxon border raids, a bitter struggle developed which year after year required new Frankish expeditions to Saxony and lasted until 804. In 777 Charles held a Diet at Paderborn in the center of Saxony during which he ordered all Saxons to become Christians and divided the territory into missionary districts. After this,

144

numerous noble Saxons had themselves baptized and Christianity made speedy progress. But soon the reaction set in, and under the leadership of Widukind a great rebellion started (782–785) while Charles was in Spain. The rebels ambushed a Frankish army unit at Mount Süntel and destroyed it. Charles immediately returned and took bloody revenge. He defeated the rebels and had 4,500 of them executed by his troops at Verden/Aller. The bloodbath stirred renewed hatred. Widukind, who had escaped to Denmark, continued to agitate the rebellion until it finally collapsed in 785 and Widukind himself was baptized in Attigny.

Still further rebellions occurred in Saxony, and only the enforced transfer of thousands of Saxons to the Frankish heartland and of Frankish settlers to Saxony resulted in the pacification of the country early in the ninth century. New bishoprics were founded (Münster, Osnabrück, Paderborn, Minden, Bremen, Verden/Aller, Hildesheim, and Halberstadt) and monasteries sprang up. These bishoprics were subordinated to the Rhenish bishoprics of Cologne and Mainz, which thus became archbishoprics again. In addition to its suffragan bishoprics of Liège (formerly Tongern) and Utrecht, Cologne received as suffragans the Saxon bishoprics of Münster, Minden, Bremen, and Osnabrück. The archbishopric of Mainz, in addition to Speyer, Worms, Strassburg, Augsburg, Constance, Chur, Eichstätt, and Würzburg, received the Saxon dioceses of Paderborn, Verden, Halberstadt, and Hildesheim. In the process of episcopal organization Saxony was thus integrated with the land of the Franks in a very fruitful way. Christianity took root surprisingly rapidly in Saxony after the wars, and monasteries blossomed (Corvey in 822, Werden in 800, Essen). Around the middle of the ninth century an unknown poet composed the wonderful *Heliand* epic which described the passion as though it had happened in Saxony and as though Christ had been a Saxon duke to whom the Saxons had sworn loyalty. During the tenth century these same Saxons produced the imperial dynasty of the Ottonians. This dynasty with its deeply Christian convictions helped to establish the concept of a Christian German Empire, which characterized the

145

Middle Ages. One may boldly assert that without the integration of Saxony into the Frankish kingdom the Christian western universal empire scarcely would have come about.

2. Charles understood his royal leadership completely in the Christian spirit. His ideal was the realization of Augustine's *City of God* which he had had read to him at table. With great love and care he devoted himself to the religious and cultural elevation of his peoples. He first had to train and educate them before he could unify them and make them into an innerly strong Christian imperial people. He held firmly in his hands the threads not only of the political but also of the spiritual life of this gigantic empire which soon encompassed all of Europe.

The center of gravity of the empire shifted from the Seine to the Rhine. In 786, Charles began the construction of the palace at Aachen, and by the nineties it had become his favorite court. This court became the focal point for countless people who sought justice, help, or even intellectual training. Charles understood how to attract intellectually prominent men. The Aachen Court Academy soon developed into a superior intellectual center for the entire Frankish state. Among the large number of court and imperial officials who resided at Aachen were numerous clerics, and ecclesiastical synods were frequently conducted there after 789.

The Aachen palace chapel according to the Byzantine model (S. Vitale in Ravenna, Hagia Sophia in Constantinople) received an "imperial" dome in 795 and was probably consecrated on July 17, 800. This chapel was later to become the absolute symbol of the concept of the Christian western empire and emperor. In 936 Otto the Great received the symbols of his royal dignity on the throne of Charles in the Aachen cathedral, and until 1531 thirty other coronations of German rulers took place on this spot. The Aachen cathedral treasure, the depository of the Carolingian relics and, after the Ottonians, also of the imperial jewels, is currently still one of the richest in the West (Cross of Lothar, Evangelistaries, Palla d'Oro, golden Ambo, etc.).

Under the patronage of Charles science and art blossomed at the royal court and also in famous monasteries and numerous

146

cathedral schools. Science and art to a large degree still moved within the orbit of the inherited ancient body of knowledge, and Charles consciously utilized the tradition of Christian antiquity. Charles wished the young Frankish people to grow intellectually according to the precepts of the ancient model in order to arrive later at its own forms of creative thought and art.

We owe the preservation of most of the texts of the classics which we possess to the fervor with which Charles and his scholars collected from everywhere the writings of antiquity, studied them, and corrected errors in the manuscripts. A new, more beautiful script was used in copying the writings, the so-called Carolingian minuscule, a system of four lines which joined capital and small letters in well-arranged and clear word-forms. The script became the basis for medieval calligraphy, and even today is used in our so-called "Latin" script. In the famous schools at Aachen, Trier, and Tours, etc., a unique book art was developed with magnificent miniatures, which for the most part still imitated antique models; with precious book covers carved out of ivory; and particularly beautiful lettering (Viennese Evangelistary, Godescalc-Evangelistary, Ada-Manuscript in Trier, etc.).

Understandably, special attention was devoted to the Holy Scriptures and liturgical books. The Anglo-Saxon scholar Alcuin (d. 804) and the Visigoth Theodulf of Orléans (d. 821), whom Charles had invited to his court, worked on an improved edition of the Latin Vulgate. To revive the liturgy in the Frankish Church, Charles sent for a copy of the Gregorian sacramentary from Rome; between the Roman and the Frankish Churches a mutually beneficial liturgical exchange took place during Carolingian times. In general, Charles sought an inner spiritual and religious connection with Rome. What Boniface had begun, Charles continued with a clear recognition of the goal and how to accomplish it. Thus he asked Pope Adrian for the expanded collection of canons and decretals by Dionysius Exiguus, which was used by Rome, so that it might form the basis for the canons of the Frankish Church. For the necessary monastic reform in the kingdom Charles obtained from Monte Cassino a copy of the Benedictine rule. While campaigning in southern Italy, he had seen the (presumed) original of Benedict's rule when he visited the Benedictine mother house. Charles innate sense of order had immediately recognized the value of the original version of the rule with its balanced sober language and its prudent rule of life. The center for the reform which was adopted by the Aachen synods of 802, 816, 817, and 822, and whose implementation was entrusted to abbot Benedict of Aniane (d. 821), was the newly founded monastery of Kornelimünster near Aachen. The rule of Benedict became obligatory for all Frankish monasteries.

Charles continued vigorously the church reform begun by Boniface, in the course of which he increasingly assumed the direction not only of the external but also of the internal concerns of the church. He decreed imperial laws for the rejuvenation of the ecclesiastical life, held imperial synods, and constantly had his royal officials *(Missi dominici)* supervise not only governmental but also ecclesiastical affairs. Even if Charles may be regarded with justification as having completed the Bonifacian reform, it cannot be overlooked that he soon imprinted his own characteristics, shaped by his personal idea of a ruler, on the work of rejuvenation, characteristics which did not correspond completely to the concepts of Boniface.

3. Charles's view of kingship was quite theocratic, and this thinking was strongly influenced by Old Testament concepts. In the circle of his intimates he liked to be addressed as King David, and he performed his function like a divinely-sent and divinely-consecrated leader who is the protector of Christianity and of the new people of God. As early as the Frankfurt synod in 794 Charles had himself addressed as *Rex et Sacerdos,* and in 796 in a letter to Pope Leo III he summarized his royal task in the following way: "It is *our* task to protect by force of arms Christ's Holy Church externally everywhere against the attacks of the pagans and devastation by infidels, and to safeguard it internally by general acceptance of the Catholic faith. It is *your* task to support our campaigns like Moses with hands lifted up to God so that as

a result of your intercession the Christian people may everywhere win victory over its enemies."

In Charles's mind the distinction between the spiritual and the secular became less and less clear, particularly after he became acquainted with the Byzantine concept of emperorship. Just as the basileus of Constantinople viewed himself as the guardian of orthodoxy and therefore claimed the right to convoke synods and to interfere with the discipline and the doctrine of the church, so Charles also considered this his prerogative. He regarded himself as the supreme head of the Frankish Church, administered ecclesiastical property like secular royal property, and appointed men of his choice to bishoprics and monasteries. In elevating bishops and abbots and changing them into spiritual magnates, Charles committed them at the same time to the tasks of the state. They were soon no longer primarily shepherds and pastors, but became spiritual officials of the state. Soon they became accustomed to receiving secular directives and preferred to rely on the support of the state *(brachium saeculare)* in the execution of their spiritual duties. Again bishops and abbots could be found at the head of armed troops in the imperial army, and the secularization which had been fought so passionately by Boniface soon became common usage again.

Yet another danger lay in the overly strong emphasis of the cultural mission of the church, an emphasis which could easily lead to an obscuring of the primary religious duty. As long as Charles himself had the reigns in his hand, the situation was bearable, but later, under his weak successors, secularization was firmly established.

4. It was from Byzantium also that Charles received the impulse for his thinking on emperor and empire. As "Ruler of Europe" he had accomplished the political unification of the West by about 800. His immense empire could justifiably be compared to the empires of Byzantium and the Arabs. It was the third great power of the Mediterranean western world. Charles maintained diplomatic relations with Harun al Raschid, the caliph of Baghdad, and he contested the claims of East Rome.

Charles's position was determined on the one side by political and military considerations, and on the other by ideological questions. Through his Italian conquests in Ravenna and chiefly in Istria and southern Italy, he had come into military conflict with Byzantium. Owing to the weakness of the East Roman Empire Charles had little to fear, but the military encounter also brought him to a greater degree into spiritual conflict with the Byzantine Empire and its religiously founded claim to world domination. Byzantium derived its absolute and sole claim to leadership within the Christian family of peoples from Constantine the Great and the Christian *Imperium Romanum* which he had established. The title of emperor was clothed with a unique and religious brilliance. Because the Roman Empire was completely identified with Christianity, the conversion of a people meant at the same time their subjugation or at least ideological recognition of Byzantine preeminence. To such a subordinate position, however, Charles did not wish to be relegated. His political ambition and the power and the size of the Frankish kingdom, which could stand up to any other power on earth, could not be reconciled with the Byzantine claims.

Thus the question of Byzantine predominance and the problem of emperorship became Charles's chief concerns during these years. More was involved than mere words; the struggle for the title of emperor and for the Roman Empire has been described as the problem of world recognition during the Middle Ages (W. Ohnesorge). Just as today recognition as an atomic power carries great power status, so the possession of emperorship was of the highest political importance throughout the whole Middle Ages. It is on this basis that the imperial policy of the German kings finds its justification. The striving after the emperorship was also for Charles a highly political matter, even though at first it was not his intention to take the title of emperor away from Byzantium; Charles merely desired to be recognized as an equal.

In 781 in Constantinople the queen-mother Irene, who was the regent for her minor son Constantine VI (780–797), asked the hand of Charles's daughter Rotrud for her son. The Frankish king willingly agreed. He saw in the marriage the recognition of equality for the Frankish kingdom with Byzantium, while the queen-mother simply hoped for a return of Istria and southern Italy as well as protection against further conquests by the Franks. The marriage project came to nothing when Charles saw his expectations disappointed. He realized that Byzantium did not regard him as an equal, even though the inequality stemmed from a different area than the political one.

The area of conflict was a dogmatic question which had agitated the East for quite some time: the worship of images. We must deal with it because of its great ecclesiastical and political importance.

In order to protect the people of Israel against a relapse into the worship of idols and to accentuate sharply the spiritual essence of God, it had been ordered in the Old Testament: "Thou shalt not make graven images . . ." (Ex 20, 4; Lev 26, 1; Dt 4, 16). After God himself, however, had become man and taken visible form in Jesus Christ, the prohibition of images could no longer have the same meaning in the New Testament. Nevertheless, the early church exercised great caution for a long time. It preferred signs and symbols to the pictorial presentation of Christ, and the oldest crucifix portrayal known to us stems from the fourth century (S. Sabina in Rome). Even if it was not possible to do completely without the pictorial representations of biblical scenes and the saints, because many Christians could not read, opinions remained divided over the meaning and importance of the images of Christ. Christology became involved in the dispute, and here it was a question of whether it was at all possible and permissible to portray the human nature of Christ. The strict Docetists as well as the Monophysites rejected all portrayal of Christ, because they did not believe in the complete and true human nature of Christ. Even the more moderate thought it unnecessary to represent the human nature, as they did not attribute any redeeming importance to it. Any portrayal of the incarnate God should include his double nature, and since

151

the divine cannot be pictorially presented, any solely human presentation would play into the hands of a dangerous heresy, Nestorianism, even if it did not go so far as to join the Arians in completely denying the divinity of Christ. Therefore, it was argued, any picture of Christ was dangerous and suspect of heresy. Additionally, the common people tended to give all images, including those of the saints and particularly Mary, a superstitious veneration, and it would be better, therefore, to suppress images and the worship of images entirely.

Following the invasion of Syria and Egypt by the Arabs, and under the influence of their religious propaganda which was hostile to images, many bishops also began to attack the worship of images, a practice which was widely followed among the Christian people. The council "Trullanum II" of Constantinople in 692 still decided in favor of images of Christ, however. In spite of this, the hostile movement against images continued to spread and the battle was brought into the open in 730 when Emperor Leo III (717–741) finally decreed the prohibition of image worship in the whole empire. The people were divided, but the majority, under the leadership of the monks, was strongly in favor of retaining images. Political conflicts played a major role in some areas, especially in southern Italy, and when Pope Gregory III (731–741) at a Roman synod spoke out against the imperial decree, a noticeable intensification of the contrast between eastern and western churches occurred.

Under Emperor Constantine V (741–775) iconoclasm reached its peak. The synod of Hieria in 754 ordered the destruction of all religious pictures. Bloody riots, persecutions, and executions, especially of monks, who in some areas were almost entirely exterminated, shook the East Roman Empire. Finally Empress Irene gave in to the pressure in 787 and convened the seventh ecumenical council of Nicaea, the second one at Nicaea, and had image worship restored. The pope recognized the council and sent two legates. It was the last general council in which eastern and western churches were united. The council clarified the distinction between adoration and veneration: Adoration is given to God alone *(= Latreia)*; veneration (Proscynesis) can also be given to creatures, for, so the council declared, relying on St. John of Damascus (d. ca. 754) and Basil the Great (d. 379), "the honor given to the picture reflects the honor given to the model". The value of the holy picture, of the icon, rests not in itself, but in its reference to the portrayed saint or to Christ. "Whoever venerates a picture, honors the one who was painted."

In thus resolving the issue, Byzantium had overlooked Charlemagne. To Charles, the fact that the empress had called a general council and decided a question of faith without consulting him was an autocratic action that violated completely the rights of the Frankish kingdom to equality with Byzantium. His reaction was immediate and impetuous: he cancelled the marriage project. Charles then had a great state document composed, the so-called *Libri Carolini* (790), which declared itself against Nicaea II and against the worship of images. The author, Alcuin or more probably Theodulf of Orléans, fell victim to a fateful error. He did not know Greek, and the Latin translation for "Proscynesis" and *"Latreia"* gave only the one word *"adoratio"*; consequently, he did not grasp the distinction between veneration and adoration and polemicized unjustly against the alleged "adoration" of pictures in the East. The whole tract was an emotional reaction against Byzantium and it must be understood as the "protest of the Frankish empire against the East Roman claim to leadership in the dogmatic, ecclesiastical, and political sphere" (G. Haendler).

Charles's counteraction, the Frankfurt Synod of 794, must be understood in the same context. Even though it never found "ecumenical" recognition and remained simply a Frankish imperial synod, he wanted it to be regarded as a general council. Its agenda was concerned with the heresy of adoptionism of two Spanish bishops, Elipandus of Toledo and Felix of Urgelis; furthermore with the question of image worship, which it rejected, and with reform measures for clerics, monasticism, and the people. With this council Charles attempted to establish equality in these matters with the Byzantine empire.

5. Charles's striving for imperial recognition was not designed to abolish the Byzantine emperorship, but to obtain acknowledgement of his equality. Just as there had been a double empire in the fourth and fifth centuries, one in the East and one in the West, the western empire, which had disappeared in 476, now was to be recreated and the Franks were to be the new western imperial people. After 795 Charles consciously exercised imperial prerogatives. Having provided the Frankish empire with unity and power through his military successes, he now attempted to develop the new Frankish imperial people by enabling them to catch up in the field of education and to create a cultural unity.

He was thwarted twice in carrying out his plans, once by Byzantium and the second time by Rome. In Constantinople a struggle had broken out between the empress and her son. When Constantine VI resumed relations with Charles, Irene, who feared the loss of her rule, had him seized and in 797 even had him blinded in order to remove him permanently from the political scene. Irene then ruled alone, claiming for herself emperorship and power in the East Roman Empire. A legation was sent to Charles in an attempt to pacify him.

A woman on the Roman imperial throne was an innovation without precedent, and one which was as legally dubious as it was historically questionable. In the West, Rome drew the immediate conclusion that the Byzantine emperorship had been extinguished. Pope Leo III (795–816) struck the name of the Byzantine emperor from the liturgical prayers and replaced it with the name of Charles. The unspoken goal at this time appeared to be to regain the emperorship from the East and to invest Charlemagne with it. The situation seemed to demand the *translatio imperii,* and Rome seems to have felt this as early as 796 when Leo III invited Charles to Rome to have him receive the homage of the Romans.

When Pope Leo III was driven out of Rome during a rebellion in 799, he personally appeared before Charles in Paderborn. Charles promised his help, and the following year he went to Rome to investigate the case against the pope's opponents.

After Leo had acquitted himself of the accusations against him by an oath of purification before a synod, he was restored to full papal rights two days before Christmas 800. On Christmas Day, the pope, according to Charlemagne's wishes, was to anoint Charles's son as king.

On this occasion the pope surprised Charles by placing a crown on his head during the Christmas Mass and proclaiming him as emperor. The Roman populace enthusiastically concurred.

If we can believe Charles's biographer Einhard, Charles was not delighted by the surprise. Charles had conceived of a Frankish-western empire which was to take its place beside the East Roman one. The theory which was now represented by Pope Leo and the Roman people, namely that the imperial dignity of the *Imperium Romanum* by the *translatio* had been returned to Rome and therefore could be awarded *by them* to Charles, was obviously distasteful to him. It was a year and a half before he accepted the imperial title, and he carried it officially only after the summer of 801. It is not clear whether or not the resumption of the marriage negotiations with Irene, which occurred at this time, was responsible for his acceptance of the title. East Rome deigned to recognize Charles's imperial position only in 812, after the fall of Irene (802), by granting him a second emperorship in the West.

That step, however, revived the western empire once again. Even during the enormous political and cultural breakdown of the Carolingian empire under Charles's successors, the concept of empire survived and supplied western history with content and direction during the subsequent centuries.

Charlemagne died in 814 at Aachen and was buried in an antique sarcophagus in his palace chapel. History justifiably knows him as the "Great". In 1165 he was declared a saint upon the wish of Frederick Barbarossa by the antipope Paschal III, and although Rome did not accept this canonization, it has permitted Charlemagne's veneration to this day.

22

THE DECAY OF THE CAROLINGIAN EMPIRE AND THE "SAECULUM OBSCURUM" OF THE ROMAN CHURCH

1. The Empire

Louis the Pious (814–840), the son and successor of Charlemagne, did not lack the intellectual strength to continue the work of his father, but he did not possess the political farsightedness and the practical decisiveness to preserve the newly won imperial unity.

Recent discoveries and research reveal Louis's internal administration in a bright light. He had a profoundly Christian concept of the *Imperium Christianum,* based on a cultural foundation, and of the duty of the emperor. He implemented the great reform program of his father with the immediate consequence of a blossoming and flowering of the entire spiritual and intellectual life of the time. Some very recent scholarship has even designated the first years in office of Louis the Pious as the "absolute peak of the Carolingian empire" (T. Schieffer).

Louis gave ecclesiastical life his particular support. An encompassing reform of the laws concerning the canons regular, the secular clerics, and the monks was conducted. In 816 Louis decreed the *Institutio Canonicorum* which followed the rule of Chrodegang of Metz and newly ordered the life of the religious in the collegiate churches on the basis of the *vita communis.* The *Capitulare Monasticum* followed in 817 and decreed the observation of the Benedictine rule by all monasteries, appointed Benedict of Aniane (d. 821) as plenipotentiary for the monasteries of the whole empire, and made Kornelimünster a model monastery. The *Capitulare Ecclesiasticum* decreed in 819 deeply affected ecclesiastical life by protecting the clerics in the churches of landed proprietors. It was ordered that henceforth no one but a freeman could be ordained as a priest. Should a proprietor wish to have one of his serfs ordained as a priest in one of his churches, he first must give him his freedom and supply him with adequate means of support (in form of interest-free real estate in the size of one hide *(mansus)*. In addition, even in these private churches the clerics could be appointed or recalled in the future only with the permission of the bishop, and the church itself together with its clerics was subordinate to the visitation and the supervision of the bishop of the diocese. In this way the central position of bishops was strengthened after it had been weakened by the unauthorized activities of the landed proprietors.

The success of these laws became evident in all areas of spiritual and ecclesiastical life. The level of education was raised, cathedral and monastic schools flourished, and the first signs of a local theology in the Germanic area became visible. In Fulda, Rhabanus Maurus (d. 856) worked as abbot and teacher and in 847 became archbishop of Mainz. At the monastery at Reichenau, Walafrid Strabo (d. 849) wrote his famous *Glossa ordinaria* for the Holy Scripture which was highly esteemed throughout the Middle Ages, and at St. Gallen, Notger Balbulus (d. 912) composed his sequences. Religious poems in the vernacular such as the *Heliand,* the so-called Wessobrunner Prayer, and a harmony of the gospels by Otfried of Weissenburg (870) were created. The theological controversy over the Eucharistic doctrine which was carried on in the monastery of Corbie by the abbot Paschasius Radbertus (d. 859) and his monk Ratramnus (d. 868) testifies to a lively intellectual life just as does the discussion about the doctrine of predestination conducted by the monk Gottschalk. The son of a Saxon count, Gottschalk, while still a child, had been given to the monastery of Fulda as an oblate. The strict views of the age did not permit him later the desired withdrawal from monastic life. He found a meaning for his own tragic fate through the adoption of a rigorous doctrine of predestination based on Augustine's writings. Because of this doctrine, his former abbot Paschasius Radbertus, who in the meantime had become metropolitan of Mainz, had Gottschalk condemned as a heretic at a synod at Mainz (848). He was then turned over to the powerful Hinkmar, archbishop of Reims, who also denounced him as a heretic (synod of Quierzy in 849) and kept him in monastic custody until Gottschalk's death.

During the reign of Louis the Pious the missionary work in the north was continued under St. Ansgar, who in 826 accompanied the Danish king Harald to his residence and devoted himself completely to the conversion of Denmark and Sweden. In 831 St. Ansgar founded a bishopric in Hamburg which, however, had to be moved to Bremen after its destruction by the Normans in 845. Ansgar died in 865 while serving as bishop of Bremen.

After 864 the brothers Methodius (d. 885) and Cyril (formerly Constantine, d. 869 in Rome) worked in southeastern Europe among the Slavs. They translated the Holy Scriptures into the Slavic language and created an individual Slavic liturgy. Unfortunately the success of the brothers was ruined by the invasion of the Hungarians (906).

A healthy development of spiritual and intellectual life always presupposes an ordered external existence. The decay of political order in the ninth century, threrefore, soon had its effect on the newly flowered spiritual and ecclesiastical life.

Louis had three sons from his wife Irmingard (d. 818). As early as 817 he divided the kingdom among them: Lothar, the oldest, was awarded the emperorship, the sovereignty, and also the central part of the empire, from Italy to the Atlantic ("Lotharingia", of which present-day Lorraine represents a remainder); Pippin received the west of the Frankish kingdom with Aquitaine as center; and Louis, later called the "German", received the east, with Bavaria as its heartland. When Louis's second wife Judith bore the emperor a fourth son in 823 (called Charles the Bald), he gave in to Judith's entreaties and changed the division of the empire in such a way that the youngest son received Alemania as his heritage. The sons of the first marriage protested the new arrangement and started the sad fraternal strife which was to lead to the downfall of the empire.

In the treaty of Verdun (843) the empire was finally divided into three parts and the unity of the European family of peoples was once again abandoned. Charles the Fat (876–887) was able to unite the whole empire for a short time (885–887) through inheritance, but the internal dissolution of the empire and the hard times caused by the Norman invasions which reached their peak around 880/881 led to Charles's deposition. With Arnulf of Carinthia (887–889) the Carolingian dynasty died out completely. The emperorship fell into the hands of Italian magnates and was not won back until the time of Otto the Great in 962.

History does not tolerate a vacuum, and the decline of the central imperial authority exposed the once powerful empire of Charlemagne to its external enemies. In the south the Saracens robbed and plundered in Italy and along the Mediterranean coasts, and Pope Leo IV (847–855) was forced to build a wall to protect the Vatican against them. In the east the Hungarians pressed hard on imperial territory through continued invasions. In the north and the west the Normans, who penetrated deeply into the interior, created immeasurable damage and destruction. In 845 they burned Hamburg; in 846 they raided Paris; and between 881 and 883 they systematically devastated the Rhineland as Cologne, Neuss, Bonn, Aachen, Liège, even Cambrai, Arras, Amiens, and also Koblenz, Trier, and Reims were plundered and destroyed by them. In order to save Paris in 883, Charles the Fat bribed them with gold and silver and permitted them to ravage Burgundy. Charles was incapable of defending the empire against them, and only Arnulf of Carinthia succeeded in 891 in defeating them so decisively at Louvain that in the future they turned away from the empire and moved against England. The political collapse of the empire brought with it the total deterioration of western culture and the Church.

2. The Church

The Roman Church under Leo IV (847–855) and especially under Nicholas I (858–867) experienced a short revival, only to fall then to the nadir of the *saeculum obscurum*.

To his contemporaries Nicholas appeared as a second Elias who fearlessly and powerfully defended the rights of the church and of religion. He did not hesitate to oppose Emperor Lothar II (850–875) when the emperor divorced his rightful wife Theutberga (862 ff) in order to marry his mistress Waldrada. When the archbishops Gunthar of Cologne and Thietgaud of Trier obliged the emperor in this, Nicholas immediately removed them from office and excommunicated them. He also exercised his authority against the powerful archbishop Hinkmar of Reims (845–882), who on his own authority had deposed his suffragan bishop Rothadius of Soissons (863), and against archbishop John of Ravenna, who in 861 had improperly extended his jurisdiction. Because he was misled by Abbot Theognostus, who was a bitter enemy of Photius and gave a distorted account of the events in Constantinople, and because he was uninformed of the actual conditions involved, Nicholas intervened in the Byzantine struggles between the patriarchs Ignatius and Photius. Nicholas excommunicated Photius in 863 and restored Ignatius to his dignity as patriarch. Photius in turn now excommunicated the pope (Photian Schism) at an eastern synod at Constantinople (867). This incident is one of the many tragic misunderstandings which contributed to an increasing deterioration of relations between eastern and western churches and which prepared the way for the Great Schism of 1054. An anti-Photian synod at Constantinople in 869–870, which is counted as the eighth ecumenical council only in the West, confirmed the excommunication of Photius who had become meanwhile the victim of a change of rulers. Soon afterward Photius was rehabilitated and even recognized by Pope John VIII (872–882). He died at peace with Rome, probably in 891.

Nicholas I was the first great representative of the medieval papacy to whom the ecclesiastico-political conceptions of Gregory VII and Innocent III can be traced. His aim was the preservation of the independence of the church and its freedom against the inroads of the state in spiritual matters. To Nicholas it was still completely alien to meddle in the affairs of state, but as the spiritual head of the church and as guardian of religion and morals, he nevertheless felt entitled to watch over the morals of the rulers. It is understandable that such a view could easily induce him to issue directives. For this he was provided with

160

a pretext by the Pseudo-Isidorian decretals which probably had been produced between 847 and 852 in the province of Reims. These decretals, which constituted an extensive collection of mostly forged or distorted papal letters and decrees whose aim was to safeguard the independence of the suffragan bishops against the metropolitan Hinkmar of Reims, referred to the pope as the sole power entitled to judge bishops. The decretals also opposed transgressions of the secular power by emphasizing the supreme papal sovereignty which they supported with the forged Donation of Constantine; incidentally, this is the first mention of the Donation. Although it was not the direct intention of the decretals, the emphasis which they placed on papal power resulted in an immense elevation of the papal position. The popes were certainly not responsible for the forgeries, but they did believe in their validity. Nicholas I soon relied upon them, as did subsequent popes. Doubts concerning their authenticity arose only in the fifteenth century (Nicholas of Cusa, Torquemada, and others), and until then they had a tremendous effect on medieval secular and ecclesiastical thought. The claims of the papacy to power in political matters during the Middle Ages rest to a large extent on these documents.

If by these means Nicholas I stepped "for a short moment as the supreme authority into the gap left by the atrophying imperial power since 843" (Schieffer), after his death the papacy soon was pulled into the whirlpool of the general decline. Deprived of its support by the universal empire, the papacy quickly succumbed to the partisan interests of degenerate aristocratic families in the city of Rome, lost its universal importance, and became a plaything of local Roman interests.

Caesar Baronius (d. 1607) coined the designation *"saeculum obscurum"*, "dark age", for the period 880–1046, i.e. from the end of the Carolingian empire to the beginning of the Gregorian reform. Far fewer than all of the forty-eight popes of this time were bad; some of them were personally quite honorable men, such as Benedict IV (900–903) and a number of the popes of the period of the Ottonians after 962, but on the whole the picture presented by the Roman see was not at all commensurate with its universal significance. It declined to the level of an ordinary local bishopric and like so many other bishoprics of the time became the object of the political struggles of the unruly and tyrannical nobility. The nobility alone is responsible for the deplorable conditions, because in the absence of an emperor the papacy was delivered to it without protection.

Legend placed the existence of "Pope Joan" before the *saeculum obscurum*. We do not learn of her until the thirteenth century when she was mentioned in the tale by Martin of Troppau (d. 1278). According to it a girl from Mainz, dressed as a young man, studied in Athens, then visited Rome, and there was elected pope in 855 after the death of Pope Leo IV. The imposition was only noticed when after a pontificate of over two years she suddenly gave birth to a child during a procession to the Lateran and died on the spot. The untenability of this idle tale is proven historically by the fact that Benedict III followed Leo IV directly in the year 855 and that not even at any other time there was room for such a story in the sequence of popes known to us.

The ghastly desecration of the corpse of Pope Formosus (891–896) which occurred at the beginning of this epoch is, however, true. In 893, Formosus had appealed for aid to the German king Arnulf against the ruling Spoletan party. His successor, Pope Stephen VI (896–897), a puppet of the Spoletans, conducted a trial of the dead pope; Formosus's body was exhumed after having been buried for nine months, dressed in the papal gowns, sentenced, mutilated, and finally thrown into the Tiber. The Roman populace, angered by this desecration of the dead, seized Stephen, threw him in prison, and had him strangled.

The Tusculan party headed by Theophylactus came to power in Rome with the elevation of Sergius III (904–911). For several decades Theophylactus's tyrannical and unscrupulous wife Theodora together with her equally debased daughters Marozia and Theodora the Younger controlled Rome and the papacy. Disorderly party struggles, shocking moral brutalization, and naked lust for power were the order of the day. Popes were chosen and deposed, driven into exile, held prisoner, and assassinated, but it would go too far to speak of a "pornocracy". Marozia, who seized power after the death of her father, married Alberic, margrave of Spoleto, and after his death Wido of Spoleto and Tuscany. Finally in 929 she married a third time; her ambitious husband, Hugh of Provence, expected the imperial crown from her hand. Marozia became the ancestress of the counts of Tusculum, who contributed no fewer than six popes.

From 932 to 954 Marozia's son Alberic ruled Rome and the papacy, which now was no more than a Roman municipal institution. The nadir of the epoch was reached when Alberic's seventeen-year old son Octavian, as undisciplined a libertine as Nero, ascended the papal throne. He called himself John XII (955–964) and was the first pope to change his name. Much of what has come down to us concerning John XII is so unbelievable that there are doubts about the truth of the events; for instance, he is reported to have ordained a bishop and a deacon in a stable. The reports do show us at least that he was thought capable of anything, even of blaspheming the sacred things entrusted to his care.

Although God had permitted the papacy and the Roman Church to sink deep into ignomy and human guilt, he did show his omnipotence and care regarding the sacredness of the church, an institution which is able to use even evil for the accomplishment of the good. John XII unwittingly initiated an improvement by calling upon the German king Otto the Great for help. In 962 Otto came to Rome with a strong army and liberated the church from its worst enemy, the unworthy Pope John XII.

23
OTTO THE GREAT AND THE REJUVENATION
OF THE WESTERN EMPIRE

The East Frankish kingdom under Otto the Great (936–973) recuperated first from the general collapse. By establishing a strong royal power, Otto created the foundation for an internal renewal which affected the religious life in particular. By securing power in Italy and Rome he gave the imperial position in the West new form and content, and its universal importance once again became evident. For a time at least, he succeeded in rescuing the papacy from Roman party struggles and directing it toward its universal ecclesiastical duties.

1. *Otto's Imperial and Church Policy*

The effect of the reconstitution of order and security within the empire was decisive. Otto inherited favorable pre-conditions for reform from his father Henry I (919–936), the Saxon, but there were still many problems to be solved. In the interior of the kingdom local tribal self-interest had to be overcome, and the administration of the empire had to be put on a solid basis. The borders of the empire also had to be protected against the invasion of the Slavs, particularly against the Hungarians.

After fierce battles, Otto succeeded in subduing the rebellious tribal dukes of Lorraine and Franconia, of Swabia and of Bavaria. These he replaced with members of his own family. Bavaria he entrusted to his brother Henry, Swabia to his oldest son Liudolf, Lorraine to his son-in-law Konrad the Red, Saxony he entrusted to his loyal follower Hermann Billung, and Franconia he retained for himself. But a general family rebellion then taught him the bitter lesson that not even relatives were reliable. In 953 Liudolf rebelled against him and attempted to become the sole ruler of Swabia. Konrad the Red joined Liudolf and Henry was soon also allied with them. The rebels did not hesitate to make common cause with the Hungarians, who were again invading the empire, and Otto mastered the situation only with difficulty. After his victory over the Hungarians in 955 Otto was then able to make new plans.

Instructed in the sad results of nepotism, Otto made a completely new attempt to order the empire by creating in the imperial bishops reliable supports for a royal central power. Since the time of Charlemagne the episcopate had shown itself as an effective defender of imperial unity. The church was always in need of a strong central power to protect its possessions against the greedy nobility. Conversely, the king did not have to fear dynastic tendencies on the part of the celibate bishops, whose priesthood automatically precluded inheritance and the creation of local power. Additionally, most of the ecclesiastical possessions were derived from imperial gifts and so it was easy to regard bishoprics and abbeys as royal proprietary churches and as imperial territories and to treat them accordingly. Thus imperial and ecclesiastical interests met.

Otto began deliberately to add to the real property of the church and to strengthen the position of the bishops by awarding them princely privileges and rights formerly reserved to the crown. He transferred to them the rights of counts, jurisdiction, taxation, coinage, market privileges, and immunities. Thus Otto laid the foundation for the spiritual princely powers of the medieval feudal church, powers which decisively influenced the face of Germany until the great secularization in 1803.

By these measures Otto did not nationalize the church as Charles Martel had once done when he ruthlessly intervened in ecclesiastical affairs and subordinated the interests of the church to the interests of the state. On the contrary, Otto brought the state under ecclesiastical control, and his political conception was such that the Christian church and the state were one and their interests coincided to such a degree that they fused. The system served Otto well, because in the future the new imperial church, which at its height encompassed ninety-three archbishoprics, bishoprics, monasteries, and abbeys with their own territories, proved itself to be the most reliable support of the German kingship. Even during the investiture struggle and the conflict between *sacer-dotium* and *imperium* at the time of Barbarossa, the imperial church always stood on the side of the king. In spite of the selfish interests of the German lay princes, the German rulers were able to govern the country by means of this ecclesiastical system.

The church also won unforeseen new opportunities through this alliance. Because it was free to exercise its influence in all spheres of public life, it was able to create that religious and political unity of culture which shaped the following century. It was fortunate that in Germany at this time there was a large number of great bishops who were exceedingly able in combining political responsibilities with religious and ecclesiastical duties. At no other time were there so many saintly bishops as at the time of the Ottonians. Among these great ecclesiastics were archbishop Bruno of Cologne (d. 965), the brother of the emperor and his most loyal supporter during the family rebellion, who was also appointed duke of Lorraine; bishop Ulric of Augsburg (d. 973), the brave defender of Augsburg against the Hungarians in 955; the bishops Conrad and Gebhard of Constance (d. 975 resp. 995); bishop Wolfgang of Regensburg (d. 994); bishop Adalbert of Prague (d. 997); archbishop Willigis of Mainz (d. 1011); and the bishops Bernward and Godehard of Hildesheim (d. 1022 resp. 1038), Burchard of Worms (d. 1025), and Heribert of Cologne (d. 1021).

In the monasteries Christian art and culture experienced a new flowering (Ottonian Renaissance). Church building and book art reached their height, particularly in the impressive and expressive use of symbols at Reichenau. Around the year 1000 the new style of the Romanesque began and produced among its many impressive examples the magnificent construction of St. Michael's in Hildesheim.

Otto's church policy, however, carried within itself the seed of future complications. Even at this time there were people who pointed to the dangers of the experiment. Archbishop Frederick of Mainz, a representative of ecclesiastical reform, firmly opposed the innovation because it contained the danger of church secularization. Indeed, it is certainly true that the increased royal interest in the episcopate caused the king to influence the composition of the episcopate and claim for himself the right of awarding bishoprics and abbeys. The canonical election under Otto became a mere matter of form; the king decided on the candidate, gave him the bishop's staff as a sign of his investment with the episcopal dignity, and, after the time of Henry III, also the bishop's ring. In return the emperor received an oath of fealty. In the tenth century this procedure caused little offense, but with the reawakening of the ecclesiastical spirit, particularly that of the Cluniac reform movement, this royal interference was regarded as a limitation of ecclesiastical liberty. During the battle for the *Libertas Ecclesiae,* lay investiture was soon to provide a basic issue and to initiate an immense struggle between papacy and empire.

After Otto's decisive victory over the Hungarians on the Lechfeld near Augsburg (August 10, 955), his power in the empire increased enormously. He not only freed Germany forever from the dreadful plague of the Hungarians, but also freed his own way to something higher, the acquisition of real emperorship. After Lechfeld it was Otto's aim to reconstitute the western empire as it had been during the time of Charlemagne.

2. The Rejuvenation of the Imperial Power in the Year 962

At the time of his coronation in Aachen in 936, Otto was already deliberately evoking Carolingian tradition. In 951, Otto's assistance was sought by Adelheid, the daughter of Rudolf II of Burgundy and widow of Lothar, who had claimed the kingship of Italy. Otto illustrated his interest in reestablishing the empire by marrying Adelheid after he had freed her. From Pavia, Otto intended to march on Rome and thus to secure an imperial position, but the conditions in Rome at the time did not permit this.

Then, in 960, the degenerate Pope John XII himself called for Otto's help. Otto began the campaign in August 961 with the aid of a well-equipped and strong army. By January 31, 962, he was camped on Mount Mario before Rome. On February 2, Otto, together with his wife Adelheid, was summoned to St. Peter's by Pope John and there ceremoniously crowned emperor. He had attained his desired goal. Hardly had Otto left Rome, however, when John began to intrigue against him with Byzantium and even with the Saracens. In November 963 Otto hurriedly returned to Rome and had John, who had fled from Rome, deposed by a synod at St. Peter's (December 4, 963). Then Otto had a new pope chosen, Leo VIII (963–965), and required the Romans to swear that in the future no pope would be elected without imperial consent.

3. Otto the Great's Concept of Empire

The theocratic attitude of Otto toward empire and emperorship, taken over from Charlemagne, introduced a new epoch of German history. Otto the Great, the victor over Hungarians, Slavs, and Danes, lord of Rome and Italy, and protector of western Christianity, became a ruler who once again thought in universal categories. Imperial anointment and coronation were for him not means toward a goal, but a sacred ordination which bestowed on him quasi-sacramental participation in the priesthood of the church. Whenever Otto put the imperial crown on his head he fasted the day before. The church was the source of his religious and political concept of empire in which Christianity and the nationally unified West became one. Even so, he continued to acknowledge the double authority of papacy and empire. As long as he and his successors with their concept of empire were in power, they regarded themselves as responsible for the papacy, and the papacy as an institution in its own right remained in the background. In the following epoch, however, the papacy rediscovered its universal function, and of necessity tension arose between *regnum* and *sacerdotium*.

24

"Sacrum Imperium"
The Empire of the Ottonians
and the Salians until 1046

Otto II (973–983) was everywhere well received on his journey of homage through the empire. It is true that in the beginning he had to defend himself against the Danes, the Bohemians, and also the Bavarian duke Henry the Wrangler, who was allied with them, but when this was done and the wars with the Poles (979) and with king Lothar of France (978) were successfully concluded, he was able to begin his Italian campaign by 980. Unholy factional strife had broken out again in Rome after the death of Otto I. The family of the Crescentians now had the upper hand and managed to create such an unacceptable pope as Boniface VII (974). After Boniface was driven out, Benedict VII (974–983) was elected with the help of imperial protection. He was a deserving pope who was loyal to Otto and eager for reform.

Otto II married the Byzantine princess Theophanu in 972, and with her and his small son, the future Otto III, he arrived in Rome on Easter 981. Otto intended to resume the imperial policy of his father. From 982 on he called himself *Romanorum Imperator Augustus* and attempted to link Italy closely with Germany. In order to drive the Saracens out of southern Italy Otto started a great campaign, which after initial successes ended with the terrible defeat of the German army at Cotrone (982). Only with great difficulty was the emperor himself able to escape ruin. Otto's misfortune was the signal for rebellion of the enemies of the empire. The Danes and Slavs revolted, and the opposition gathered in upper Italy. Suddenly, in the midst of preparations for a new campaign, Otto died of malaria in Rome (December 7, 983) at the age of twenty-eight. He left behind as successor his three-year old son, whom only shortly before he had had elected king by the German and Italian magnates.

Otto III (983–1002) owed his rule to the church. Archbishop

Willigis of Mainz, who acted as his regent, defeated all attempts by Henry the Wrangler to gain the crown for himself. Now for the first time the system of the imperial church which Otto I had founded was tested and found sound. While scarcely of age, the young king journeyed to Italy in 996. He also dreamed of the *Renovatio Imperii Romani* and had great plans for ruling the world. He was requested by the Romans to fill the vacant papal chair, and he gave it to his young cousin Bruno of Carinthia who reigned as the first German pope under the name of Gregory V (996–999). He was anointed and crowned in St. Peter's on Ascension Day 996 and received the acclaim of the Romans. The new pope and Otto III together convened a synod and, filled with eagerness, began ecclesiastical reforms following the example of Cluny. Yet hardly had Otto begun the journey homeward when Crescentius once again usurped the power in Rome, drove out Gregory, and appointed an anti-pope. In February 998 Otto arrived in Rome once more, exacted severe punishments (Crescentius was beheaded), and now decided to remain in Italy. When Pope Gregory died in February 999, Otto appointed as pope the learned Frenchman Gerbert, archbishop of Ravenna, who took the name of Sylvester II (999–1003).

Otto now established his residence on the Aventine and intended to make Rome the center of his universal domination. At his court, Otto adopted both the ceremonial and theocratic ideas of Byzantium, and together with the pope, as *servus apostolorum,* he wanted to govern the Christian West. His government took on a serious and sacral brilliance from contact with such deeply religious movements as that of the hermits of St. Nilus of Rossano (southern Italy), St. Romwald of Ravenna and the Camaldoli (Camaldolese monks), and the reform activity centered in the monastery of Cluny. Unfortunately Otto neglected his sources of power, and a new rising of the Romans forced him to leave the city. Together with Pope Sylvester he waited at Paterno for the arrival of German help. Here he became ill with malaria and died on January 23, 1002, at the age of only twenty-two. He is buried in Aachen.

Henry II (1002–1024), the Saint, was a grandson of Otto the Great and a son of Henry the Wrangler, duke of Bavaria, the last member of the Saxon imperial dynasty. Henry had great difficulties in holding the realm together and fortifying his position, and it is a proof of his sober energy that within a short time he mastered all dangers and restored power and prestige to the empire. Many fierce battles filled his first years of office, but finally in 1014 Henry, together with his wife, St. Kunigunde, was able to have himself anointed and crowned as emperor by Pope Benedict VIII (1012–1024).

The symbiosis of church and state had now brought about the closest union of religion and politics in Germany. All life was religiously oriented, and a political and religious cultural unity of imposing greatness was created. The emperor himself had become a sacred person through his ordination and the holy imperial couple governed the sacral empire. Since the kingship of all Christian countries had become sacred in a new way through an ecclesiastico-liturgical act of supreme solemnity, which was arranged according to the ordination of bishops (anointment with Chrism), the kings together with the sacred emperor now formed a kind of political hierarchy which was comparable to the sacred order of the bishops with the pope at their head.

To protect the church internally and externally and to further the Christian mission, were regarded as aims which constituted the very essence of the duty of the state. It is surprising, then, that the internal policy of Henry II stressed to even a greater extent than that of his predecessors the expansion of the imperial church system. After all, Henry believed that he was only applying his sacred regal right when he appointed only men of his confidence to vacant German sees. These bishops were the strongest pillars of Henry's power and his most reliable aides in the administration of the empire. In the process of this administration, Henry dealt very autocratically with church property; wealthy churches were deprived of part of their possessions which he bestowed on poorer dioceses. In 1004 he restored the bishopric of Merseburg and in 1007 he founded that of Bamberg. The latter bishopric he thought of as a missionary see and chose it also as the center of his imperial power.

Henry's marriage with Kunigunde remained without children, not because it was a Joseph's marriage, as later legend related, but because nature denied him children for reasons of health. Thus on Henry's death (July 13, 1024, buried in Bamberg) the rule passed to a new dynasty, that of the Frankish or "Salic" emperors (1024–1125).

Konrad II (1024–1039) was a great-grandson of Otto the Great through a female collateral line. He was elected at the instigation of archbishop Aribo of Mainz and together with his wife Gisela was solemnly crowned emperor in Rome on Easter 1027. Konrad's personality was as religiously oriented as that of his predecessor, and he continued the ecclesiastical and political trends of Henry's reign with consistence and temperance. The monastery at Limburg a. d. Lahn and the cathedral at Speyer were founded by him. It is an incorrect interpretation to make him a "simonist" and "anti-clerical layman" because of his interference with the appointment of bishops and abbots and because of his imperial church policy. Konrad worked energetically for monastic reform.

Henry III (1039–1056) took over from his father a strong and consolidated empire and through his powerful personality brought it to the apex of medieval world importance. As *vicarius Christi* and Anointed of the Lord, Henry determined the religious and political unity of culture of the early Middle Ages. The imperial bishops were invested by him with ring and staff, and the monastic rejuvenation was supported by him with great diligence. Henry also enforced by imperial decree the idea of a general truce of God, the *Treuga Dei,* and emphatically supported the reform of the church. In 1051 he made the abbot Hugh of Cluny godfather to his son Henry IV. As a deeply religious person Henry was convinced of the necessity of church reform, and his energetic intervention in the chaotic Roman situation finally produced a reform of universal historical significance.

Meanwhile in Rome the scandalous behavior of the Crescentian and Tusculan families had continued with only occasional interruption. In the youthful Benedict IX (1032–1044) the Tusculans had succeeded in placing a highly questionable man on the chair of St. Peter. The picture of Benedict seems to be severely distorted by the later slanders of the opposing faction, and most recent research judges him less severely. His "elevation to the papal dignity at the age of twelve and his depravity are no longer to be believed" (Gebhard, *Handbuch der Deutschen Geschichte* [1960], 233), and the assertion that he "was a paragon of moral vileness is a later invention" (Schieffer). The Crescentian faction in 1045 elected an antipope, Sylvester III. Benedict, who was driven out of Rome, now sold his papal position for a great sum of money to the Roman archpriest John Gratianus who was induced to become a partner to this exchange only through his noble intention to free the church from Benedict. John called himself Gregory VI (1045–1046). Benedict soon returned to Rome, however, in spite of the arrangement, and now there were three popes who fought for the highest office.

At the request of reformers, Henry now undertook his first journey to Rome (1046–1047). After taking care of urgent imperial business in upper Italy, he conducted the synods of Sutri and Rome in December of 1046. The synods simply deposed all three popes and nominated Henry's candidate bishop Suidger of Bamberg, who was willingly elected by the Romans. Bishop Suidger took the name of Clement II (1046–1047). Henry also nominated the following popes from among the German bishops: Poppo of Brixen (Damasus II, 1048), Bruno of Toul (Leo IX, 1049–1054), and Gebhard of Eichstätt (Victor II, 1055–1057). The powerful position of the emperor is nowhere better illustrated than through this intervention in the papal elections. Henry was master of the church.

Third Epoch: 1050–1300
The Flowering of the Church in the High Middle Ages

The synod of Sutri signified the peak and at the same time the turning point of imperial power in the church. Western dualism in the second epoch had developed too one-sidedly in favor of the imperial position, and the field of tension between the two foci of the ellipses had been disturbed. If in the future there was not to develop a permanent and dangerous threat to the *Libertas Ecclesiae,* and a subordination of the religious and spiritual life to the power and tutelage of the state, then the existing relationship between pope and emperor had to be altered and the total position of the church toward the world had to be re-examined.

That is the meaning of the mighty struggle between the two great powers which soon occurred. The first evidences of an ecclesiastical reform movement had their origin in purely monastic considerations. This reform movement, by aiming at a fundamentally new attitude toward religious, political, and cultural questions and not at isolated innovations, expanded into all other spheres of religious and moral life and had its effect on the life outside of the monastery. It became necessary to re-orient the relationship between church and state and to assign to each its rightful place. In the investiture struggle the political accent which this attempt acquired within the church was chiefly the result of the goals of the Gregorian reform party. The ramifications of the reform movement were not limited to the controversy between church and state, however, but changed the forms of spiritual life everywhere.

25

CLUNY AND THE MONASTIC REFORM MOVEMENT

The most important monastic reform movement of the Middle Ages started in the monastery at Cluny. Duke William of Aquitaine founded this monastery in Burgundy in 908–910. William clearly recognized that one of the chief reasons for the ecclesiastical decline in the ninth century had been the failure to protect the independence of the monasteries from both worldly and spiritual magnates. The duke assured Cluny of liberty both internally and externally. Free election of abbots and exemption from the jurisdiction of the bishop of the diocese were guaranteed by the founding charter and by special papal privileges of protection. The spirit of the monastery was characterized by strict adherence to the Benedictine rule, severe asceticism, absolute obedience to the abbot, and special attention to liturgical worship. Under its great abbots Berno (909–927), Odo (927–942), Aymard (since 942/948; when he became blind in 954, he took Majolus as coadjutor), Majolus (954–994), Odilo (994–1048), Hugh (1049–1109), and Peter the Venerable (1122–1156), Cluny grew into the strongest religious force in the church.

Just as it had during the secularization of the late Carolingian epoch, it became the task of monasticism during the time of the Ottones to serve as a counterweight to a carefree attitude to the world. Christianity must maintain distance from the world or suffer the danger of secularization. Through its religious dynamism, monasticism has had the strength at all times to effect the reform of the church from the inside and to renew in it the necessary inward and spiritual freedom which it requires for the fulfillment of its essentially religious duties. In this context, western monasticism in contrast to the mystically oriented eastern monasticism always has been strongly concerned with its responsibility for all of Christianity. This dedication explains why the Cluniac movement did not remain a purely monastic phenomenon, but soon decisively affected the course of western history.

The Cluniac movement owed its brilliant rise and overwhelm-

175

ing influence during the tenth to the twelfth centuries to both its dynamism and its internal stability. Undisturbed by outside forces, the monastic life was able to develop depth and validity within the walls of the monastery. The silent, introspective monks, who lived exclusively for divine service, were known in the western community for their emphasis on prayer. Common prayers with other monasteries and the pronounced concern for all of Christianity, which is the main feature of all liturgy, guarded the Cluniacs against all egocentricity. The movement's strength was not founded in a pessimistic negation of life, but in the quiet assumption of the spiritual and intellectual task of praying for all of Christianity. Recent researches (G. Tellenbach, K. Hallinger) have shown that the Cluniacs, although filled with a fervent reform spirit, preserved a certain openness toward the world. The monks pursued scientific studies, were interested in political developments, and maintained contacts with emperors and kings. Abbot Majolus was highly esteemed by Otto I, Odilo was a friend of Henry II, and Hugh became godfather to Henry IV and later mediated between the emperor and the popes.

The second abbot of Cluny, Odo, began the expansion of the reform movement. More and more monasteries affiliated with Cluny or were re-ordered according to Cluniac statutes. Thus a great association of monasteries grew up which remained closely tied to the mother house and received its directives and stimulation from it. The Cluniacs reached their peak in the eleventh century and during the twelfth century about three thousand houses belonged to the association. The monastery at Cluny became the religious heart of the West, and in France, Burgundy, Italy, Spain, England, and in isolated parts of Germany the movement deeply influenced spiritual and intellectual life.

Soon, in addition to the Cluniacs, there were other monasteries working to make Christian life deeper and more introspective. The monastery of Gorze in Lorraine, founded in 933 by John of Vendière, was particularly effective in Germany, where 150 monasteries affiliated with it. Brogne, Hirsau, Siegburg, and Einsiedeln also became centers of reform movements whose independent importance has been recognized only by modern research. The German monasteries remained within the framework of the existing feudal order to a much greater degree than the Cluniac monasteries. The old and important imperial monasteries viewed the centrally directed, anti-feudal Cluniac reform with reserve and in some cases with opposition. These monasteries felt committed to the Ottonian imperial church and in the coming struggle between emperor and pope remained in large part on the side of the emperor.

The historical question of the influence of Cluniac reform on the so-called Gregorian reform has been reexamined recently by G. Tellenbach and his school, and investigations have shown that there can be no talk of a direct influence. The Cluniacs did not start the investiture argument, and they did not take an extreme position on the controversial points of reform (investiture, marriage of priests, etc.) or intended any political effect. The defense of the papal claim to leadership was as alien to Cluny as the development of the idea of the crusades or the spreading of the Christian mission. The Cluniacs were solely a monastic and ecclesiastical reform movement.

By deepening Christian life, however, the movement necessarily turned men's thoughts to the importance of religion in public life, the position of the church and the pope in the world, the existing grievances, and the great ecclesiastical tasks. Thus, historically, the Cluniacs prepared the way for future reform developments.

26
THE GREGORIAN REFORM AND THE INVESTITURE STRUGGLE

1. The position of the Gregorian reform in the church is differentiated from that of the Cluniacs by its political orientation. Both movements started with the concept of the *Libertas ecclesiae*. Cluny at first viewed this liberty as freedom from external pressure on and infringement of its internal life by princes and bishops,

but the concept soon expanded and was regarded more positively. *"Libertas"* in the medieval Germanic world was also understood as what the individual could positively do or omit. One spoke of *libertates* or the liberties as the sum total of rights and obligations which the individual could claim for himself on the basis of law or special privilege. If these rights were violated by anyone, the individual fought for their restoration.

Initially, the *libertas ecclesiae,* which became the goal of the Gregorian reform, was also the liberation of the church from infringement by the worldly magnates. The movement, which received its name and impetus from Gregory VII, attacked the way in which bishoprics and abbeys were bestowed by kings, princes, and noblemen (lay investiture) and often shamelessly exploited financially (simony). It demanded restoration of the free ecclesiastical right of election in order to safeguard religious and ecclesiastical independence, and at the same time demanded that the church be permitted the unhindered exercise of its positive rights. Since universally valid criteria in this field of law did not yet exist, it became the task of the movement to devise and implement them. Dissension between church and political powers was the consequence.

Meanwhile the Cluniac reform had reawakened an awareness of the spiritual life and of the dignity and independence of the church. The emphasis given to the political factor during the last centuries was realized to be a reversal of the correct order. The Gregorians argued that the church is superior to the state just as the mind is superior to the body. In this fashion church political reform developed out of monastic reform. Actually the new spirit had been brought to Rome by the German emperors themselves. The popes who were put into office by Henry III instituted the idea of papal reform. Particularly Leo IX (1049 to 1054) worked toward such reform and both returned to the papacy its universal meaning and emphatically defended its rights of primacy. In 1059 Nicholas II by papal decree removed the election of the pope, the most important act in the hierarchical church, from the influence of laymen and transferred it to the cardinal bishops. The ordinance was at first directed against the Roman noble factions, but it affected to an equal degree the German king and emperor. Imperial intervention at Sutri in 1046 had been greeted enthusiastically by Abbot Odilo of Cluny and Peter Damian, the most zealous fighter for reform, but now from the point of view of a cleansed church concept was thoroughly unacceptable. In his decree concerning papal elections, Nicholas II (1058–1061) in an ambiguous clause did concede to the German King Henry IV (1056–1106) the honorary right to confirm the papal election; but this privilege was so imprecisely defined that dissension could arise at a later date.

The decree was expanded several times, and after the year 1100 all cardinals participated in the election. The Third Lateran Council of 1179 decided that a two-thirds majority were required, and Pope Gregory X in 1274 introduced the conclave in which the electing cardinals were separated from outside contacts until the election had been completed. Regulations concerning the election were finally codified in the *Codex Iuris Canonici* of 1918, with a few additions by Pius XII in 1945.

2. In Henry IV (1056–1106) and Gregory VII (1073–1085) two men appeared on the historical stage who as the exponents of two opposed views decided the conflict.

The young king still embraced the view of a sacred, almost clerical kingship which had been fashioned by the Ottonian imperial theology and which not only had a place in the hierarchical church, but actually constituted its head. Henry firmly regarded himself as *Rex et Sacerdos*.

Gregory VII, as the young deacon Hildebrand, had accompanied the deposed Gregory VI into exile in Cologne in 1046 and after his death had become a monk at Cluny. Leo IX had recalled him to Rome in 1050, and after that date he became active in behalf of reform. After the death of Cardinal Humbert (1061), Gregory became the uncontested leader of the reform party at the papal court. The main points of his program were the fight against the marriage of priests, simony, and chiefly lay investiture. With respect to investiture, the king was for Gregory no more than a layman among other laymen in the church and as a Christian subordinate to the church and obliged to obey it. In the spirit of the time this meant a removal of the sacred element from kingship. Scarcely had Gregory become pope when he formulated his tenets in his *Dictatus Papae* (1075): The pope is the supreme head of Christianity. Not only can he limit the rights of bishops, but on the basis of his spiritual supremacy he also stands above kings and emperors whóm he can depose if for religious and ethical reasons it appears necessary. Even if these principles had been intended at first to apply only to the ecclesiastical and religious level, their political significance became clearly apparent.

A controversy over investiture soon provided the occasion and the opportunity to test the opposing principles of papacy and empire. Contrary to papal prohibition, the young king Henry IV had just used his royal rights of disposition in the Milan episcopal election (1072). At the Lenten Council of 1075 Gregory made the prohibition against lay investiture more severe and proclaimed, threatening the king with the ban, that he would remove from him *any* privilege in connection with appointments to bishoprics. That, however, would mean the overturning of the Ottonian imperial church system on which the order of the empire rested, and Henry paid no attention to the papal decree. At the synod (Diet) of Worms in January 1076 dramatic scenes took place. Henry incited the imperial bishops, who were concerned over Gregory's revolutionary demands, against the pope, and Gregory VII was proclaimed deposed.

Gregory answered immediately by excommunicating Henry and releasing his subjects from their oath of fealty. The ban, which placed the king outside the church community, made the change in the sacred character of kingship evident, and the world held its breath. Henry's following quickly melted away, and in October 1076 the princes gathered at Tribur and presented the king with an ultimatum: within one year he had to obtain the lifting of the ban or his throne would be forfeited and a new king chosen.

In the face of this ultimatum, Henry began his journey of

penance to Canossa in the winter of 1076–1077. Accompanied by wife and child and a small escort, he completed a perilous crossing of the Alps. The pope, meanwhile, had left Rome for Germany. Gregory had arrived at the stronghold of margravine Mathilda, when Henry appeared in Canossa on the northside of the Apennines. Dressed in the garb of a penitent, Henry waited three days to be admitted to the pope (January 26–28, 1077). Through the intercession of his godfather Hugh of Cluny and the margravine, Henry received absolution from Gregory under the condition that he would accept papal arbitration in his quarrel with the German princes.

For the moment, Henry was victorious and again in control of the situation, but, on the whole, Canossa meant a heavy blow for German kingship and one from which it never wholly recovered. The leadership of the West passed from emperor to pope. Gregory had proved to be the more powerful figure.

The German princes elected Rudolf of Swabia (d. 1080) as anti-king in March 1077 in spite of Henry's absolution. Henry had to fight for his crown, and civil war shook Germany. Soon Henry's relations with Gregory worsened again, and in March 1080 Henry was excommunicated and deposed a second time. Now Henry in turn appointed an anti-pope, Wibert of Ravenna, who called himself Clement III (1084–1100). Henry advanced against Rome and Gregory fled to the Normans in southern Italy. On March 25, 1085, Gregory died at Salerno, outwardly defeated but in reality the victor.

The basic problem of the relationship between church and state was not an easy one, and the struggle continued after Gregory's death. The question deeply touched the whole structure of the empire and society. Much was written concerning the question of what could replace the hitherto existing religious and political unity of church and state which had its peak in the sacred kingship. A separation of church and state was impossible. This was shown when Paschal II (1099–1108) agreed with Henry V (1106–1125) in the concordat of Sutri (February 1111) to reverse the feudalization of the church and with this its internal links to the empire. Under the terms of the concordat the German imperial church was to return to the king all fiefs and privileges which it had received from him and in return Henry was to stop the practice of investiture which then would be superfluous. The vehement opposition of both the German princes and bishops to this solution, which they regarded as completely out of touch with reality, illustrates how impossible it was to restore early Christian conditions. The wheel of history could not be turned back, and the suggestion was rejected.

There remained only the possibility of a compromise. In long discussions, distinctions were formulated between the spiritual office and the external secular administration (temporalities), without separating the two entirely. In the concordat of Worms in 1122 a solution of the investiture problem was attempted by providing a double investiture: the king retained the worldly investiture which included the conferral of fiefs and rights (regalia and temporalities) and which were symbolized by the sceptre, while the spiritual investiture was left to the church. The king was to respect the canonical right of election which was to be reserved to the clerics and nobility of the episcopal churches. After the thirteenth century the election was reserved exclusively to the cathedral chapters. Only after the canonical election and spiritual investiture with ring and staff would the king confer the worldly investiture. In Germany this was done even before the episcopal consecration, and in Italy and Burgundy following it.

3. A real solution to the central problem of church and state had not yet been accomplished. The feudal ties of the imperial church to the state continued to exist throughout the whole Middle Ages and until the time of the French Revolution and the great secularization (1803). Thus there continued to exist also the points of contact and friction which could kindle new controversy and struggle.

The Cluniac reform had only striven for the liberty and the independence of the church within the state, but the Gregorian reform placed church and state on equal footing. Gregory VII, as both monk and ruler as well as born *Imperator,* continued to develop this concept. From the idea of the general supremacy of the spiritual over the physical, Gregory derived the supremacy of the church over the state, and in his famous *Dictatus Papae* (1075) laid down in twenty-seven guiding principles the political program for the popes of the future. Relying on the Donation of Constantine, which he regarded as genuine, Gregory established the claim of the papacy to world domination. This question of power now increasingly governed all altercations between church and state. Even if the aims of Gregory VII were without the base element of egotism and were in fact deeply religious, and even if in the case of Innocent III (1198–1216) papal domination was still an outgrowth of purely religious goals, there nevertheless existed the danger of the abuse of power, and the church did not always escape it.

Again, when Emperor Frederick I Barbarossa (1152–1190) tried to put into effect the idea of the universal empire, the struggle between *imperium* and *sacerdotium* was renewed. Frederick found his antagonist in Alexander III (1159–1181). The bitter conflict lasted for twenty years, from the diet at Besançon in 1157 to the peace of Venice in 1177. This unhappy controversy brought four imperial anti-popes, wars, bloodshed, and inflicted much suffering on Christianity before finally peace was restored and the emperor was freed from the ban which Alexander had imposed on him in 1160.

For us today, much concerning these power struggles remains incomprehensible unless it is understood in relation to the outlook of the time. To it, Christ alone was the Lord of Christianity. From Luke 22, 38 it was concluded that he had appointed two powers for the governing of the world, symbolized by two swords (Two-Sword Theory). One of the swords, the secular one, rested in the hand of the emperor; the second sword, the spiritual one, in the hand of the pope. The canonicists and theologians of the Gregorian age, however, interpreted this theory quite one-sidedly in favor of the pope; they claimed that both swords were owned solely and exclusively by the church; the church wielded the spiritual one, the ban, and loaned the secular one to the emperor who held it for and in the name of the church.

From this one-sided ecclesiastical concept to the attempt to revamp the order of the Christian West into a supreme liege lordship of the pope over all states of Europe was only a small step. The taking of this step necessarily led to a conflict with the imperial power. Even though Frederick Barbarossa revived the old concept of empire and successfully defended himself against papal domination, the powerful Pope Innocent III (1198–1216) did succeed in erecting a kind of papal world domination over all of Europe on the basis of a papal system of liege states. Although the Staufic house lost the battle, not long after the collapse of the house of Staufen the universal papacy also declined. In retrospect we can say that Gregorianism was not of benefit to the church in its spiritual task.

4. The Gregorian reform of the internal life of the church produced an immense increase in the primatial position of the pope within the church. Following Leo IX the popes seized the reigns of church government with increasing firmness. Their influence and will prevailed with the help of reform synods held at Rome and elsewhere. The extension of the legate system permitted the implementation of the reforms and at the same time established the papal authority everywhere. Appellations to the Holy See increased, especially in the case of contested episcopal elections, and supplied the pope with the opportunity to intervene directly in the dioceses. In the event that the electors were unable to agree, the pope simply claimed for himself the right of appointment on the basis of devolution (transfer). The papal court also proceeded with penalties and depositions against bishops guilty of abuses. After the eleventh century the metropolitans had to go to Rome personally to obtain their staffs, and after the twelfth century they had to swear a special oath of obedience and appear in Rome periodically (every four years) for the *visitatio liminum apostolorum*. Additionally, the desacralization of the political element resulted in a sharper division between clerics and laymen. The clergy, which now was removed from

the direct jurisdiction of princes and kings, gathered into a kind of supranational corporation which was governed directly by the universal church. The papacy received important supports for its power in the thirteenth century from the world-wide mendicant orders, and the remaining clergy also transcended national borders. The universal church thus provided the Christian West with a new consciousness of community.

27

THE GREAT EASTERN SCHISM OF 1054

The views of the eastern and western churches had developed along diverging lines for a long time. Many contrasts were found in the areas of liturgy, discipline, politics, and dogma. The establishment of the western empire under Charlemagne and Otto the Great, the iconoclasm controversy, the territorial claims of the Byzantines in Italy (Ravenna and Southern Italy), and the Frankish expansion into Italy all heightened the tension. Finally the new feeling of self-awareness of the western church as a result of the reforms contributed to a further intensification of ill feeling.

A crisis was reached when the German Pope Leo IX (1049–1054) extended his political power into southern Italy just as the Normans were seizing it from the Byzantines. In this way new points of contact and friction were immediately created. The Byzantine Emperor Constantine IX and his governor for South Italy, Argyros, were inclined toward an alliance with the pope so that they might fight together with him against the Normans. Patriarch Michael Cerularius of Constantinople (1043–1058), however, feared an expansion of the pope's power into his sphere of jurisdiction and prevented an understanding by emphasizing the ecclesiastical conflicts. This he did by closing Latin churches and monasteries in Constantinople, and sharply condemning the Latin use of unleavened bread during the celebration of the Mass, clerical celibacy, and the inclusion of the *filioque* in the creed.

In an attempt to promote negotiations for an alliance and to repell the attacks of the patriarch, Pope Leo sent three legates, Cardinal Humbert of Silva Candida, papal chancellor Frederick of Lorraine, and Archbishop Peter of Amalfi to Constantinople. The first two, who were Lotharingian nobles, were particularly ardent defenders of reform.

From the beginning, the negotiations in Constantinople took an unfortunate turn. The legates faced the patriarch with great self-assurance. Relying on the Donation of Constantine — which was then regarded as genuine by Constantinople — and on the absolute primacy of the pope as derived from his succession from Peter, they demanded the recognition of the Roman primacy of jurisdiction. Western customs they designated as the only valid ones and as the only ones corresponding to tradition. The vain, ambitious, and calculating patriarch permitted the negotiations to be wrecked and finally refused to receive the legates. At this point Humbert delivered a passionate polemic against the patriarch and made out a bull of excommunication which on July 16, 1054 he placed on the altar of the Hagia Sophia. In the presence of the clergy and the populace who had assembled for the service, he protested loudly against the patriarch's conduct and exclaimed: "*Videat Deus et judicet*".

The bull of excommunication "shows clearly how much the western church had developed in a new and independent direction and how little the reformers understood the mentality of the Greek Church" (Dvornik). The whole occurrence is so much more disturbing because for the greatest part it was based on nothing but tragic misunderstanding, human failure, and a question of discipline. The controversy over the *filioque* certainly was not of central importance. It is contested to this day whether cardinal Humbert was empowered to take such a far-reaching step. When the excommunication of the eastern patriarch occurred, Pope Leo had already died on April 19, 1054, and his successor Hadrian IV (1054–1059) was not chosen until December 4, 1054. The fact that the papal chair was vacant explains why Cerularius in turn excommunicated neither the pope nor the

Roman church, but only the legates. The breach, however, was never mended, and in spite of often renewed attempts at unification, the schism has continued to this day.

28

THE NEW SPIRIT OF THE WEST

The rising religious tide which had begun in the monasteries and particularly with the Cluniacs soon affected the whole life of the Christian West. It is not easy to grasp the true Christian character of an age. It expresses itself in manifold forms of piety and charity, in the willingness of the faithful to make sacrifices for ecclesiastical and caritative purposes, in art and in literature, and through the participation of the people in the great duties of the community. But spirituality is not measured according to the visible achievements of an epoch, but rather by the quality of its inwardness and depth, by the degree in which Christ's life is imitated, and by the way in which it receives the message of the gospels.

1. The vitality of monastic life and the degree of striving for perfection are always the most reliable gauges for the intensity of the religious and ecclesiastical life of an epoch. The High Middle Ages produced such an abundance of new forms of monasticism and ascetic life among both clergy and laity that we can see not only the religious tendencies in general but also a clear desire for individual and personal shaping of the spiritual life. Religious men and women of all classes turned to monasticism in great numbers. Not all of these people found their fulfillment in the Benedictine rule of the early medieval orders. Many persons lived as hermits in the wilderness, either isolated or in colonies; others became wandering preachers and penitents. The ideal of life which guided these individuals was the *vita apostolica* of poverty and voluntary renunciation.

a) St. Romwald (951–1027), a religious firebrand and charismatic of old Christian format, worked in upper Italy. His biographer reports of him that Romwald would have liked to inspire the whole world with his sense of contrition and "to change it into nothing but a hermitage". After a wild youth, he had entered the monastery of S. Apollinare at Classe near his home town of Ravenna around the year 972 in order to atone for a capital crime which his father had committed. The atmosphere of the house and the Benedictine rule were not severe enough for him and he went to the harsh school of the hermit Marinus in the wood near Venice. From here Romwald moved to the Cluniac reform monastery of Cuxa in the Pyrenees and finally returned to his native land in order to find his own ideal in the fashion of the ancient desert fathers. He sought solitude for prayer in the deadly swamps near Ravenna and on the heights of the Apennines. From time to time, filled with zealous ardor for God and the care of souls and in order to preach penitence, Romwald would come among the people and spellbind them with his grave words and his burning devotion to God. Emperor Otto III, Adalbert of Prague, and Bruno of Querfurt were among those attracted and touched by him. Numerous young people followed him, and for them he founded Fonte Avellana, Camaldoli, and other monastic establishments. These communities contained a curious mixture of hermits and cenobites; only the beginners lived in a community under the Benedictine rule, while the advanced ones settled in hermitages around the main house. From these monasteries later came the most ardent zealots for reform of the church. Peter Damian (1007–1072), who after 1057 was a cardinal and leader of the Roman reform party, was a Camaldolese.

St. Nilus (d. 1005) also worked in lower Italy at this time with no less zeal. He founded the Basilian monastery of Grottaferrata near Rome. In Tuscany, St. John Gualbert (1073) created a center of spiritual rejuvenation at Vallombrosa near Florence.

North of the Alps we also encounter serious reformers. Itinerant preachers such as Robert of Abrissel (d. 1117), Vitalis of Tierceville (d. 1122), and many others roamed over Germany and France and lived the *vita apostolica* as an example for the people to whom they preached penitence and religious revival.

b) St. Bruno of Cologne (1030/1035–1101) became the founder of the order of Carthusians (1084). After a brilliant career in the bishopric of Reims, where the future Pope Urban II (1088–1099) was his pupil, he withdrew completely from public life and together with six companions founded the first *Cartusia* in the Grande Chartreuse, a wild mountainous area near Grenoble. When forced to accompany Pope Urban II to lower Italy, he also established monasteries there; among them were La Torre in Calabria and S. Stefano in Bosco, where St. Bruno died in 1101. The silent Carthusians, whose number never became very great, always preserved a spirit of genuine religiosity and inner strength through prayer and introspection. The order survived the late Middle Ages and the Reformation without loss; it was said of them: *"Cartusia numquam reformata, quia numquam deformata."*

c) But is not the continually renewed desire for reform the very essence of the itinerant church and its establishments?

The Cluniacs were to experience this. In the same century in which their penetrating spirit of reform had renewed the western church, there arose in their own ranks the call for a reform of Benedictine monasticism. The order of the Cistercians instigated this reform.

In 1098, abbot Robert of Molesme (d. 1111), under whom Bruno of Cologne had begun, together with twenty companions founded a strict Benedictine reform monastery in the wilderness of Cîteaux, and his successors, the abbots Alberic (1099–1109) and Stephen Harding (1109–1133), drafted the charter *(Charta caritatis)*. In the charter, apostolic poverty, solitude for prayer, and regular manual labor were especially emphasized. The Cistercians rejected the traditional feudal order in the monastic sphere because of the wealth which could so easily accompany it. The man who effected the acceptance of this new ideal was Bernard of Clairvaux, a young nobleman from Burgundy (1090/1091–1153).

Bernard was one of those great forceful personalities whom no one can resist. When he knocked on the gate of Cîteaux in April 1112, he brought thirty companions with him. Through

Bernard the monastery gained impetus and an unexpected strength to expand toward the new ideal. In 1115 Bernard moved to Clairvaux with twelve companions and established a new community. During his lifetime he founded another sixty-eight monasteries. At his death in 1153 the order had grown to 350 monasteries. By 1200, Cistercians maintained 530 monasteries, and around 1500 the number had increased to 700 monasteries and 900 nunneries. Female communities were formally accepted into this monastic league at the end of the twelfth century, although some isolated nunneries already were living according to its rule (Tart 1132). The emphasis on manual labor and agriculture gave the order a civilizing importance, particularly during the opening up and missionizing of eastern Europe.

Bernard's real task, however, lay in the spiritual area. The sanctification and intensification of Benedictine monasticism and the religious revival of the whole church were Bernard's goals. His advice and help were sought on all sides and he was continually in touch with popes, emperors, and princes. He wrote the rule for the order of the Templars, and during the papal schism of the year 1130 his word was determining. The crusade of the year 1147 was largely influenced by his sermon, but after its failure he also had to bear the blame. Bernard has been called both the oracle and the religious genius of his century, as well as a great reformer and theologian. Yet most of all Bernard must be remembered as a monk, saint, and mystic.

2. The secular clergy was not excluded from reform. Modern research has shown only recently how very strong the canonic reform movement of the eleventh and twelfth centuries really was, and how much it had as its goal a truly Christian renewal of the pastoral spirit among all secular clerics.

From the first, the members of the cathedral and collegiate chapters were captured by this spirit of reform. In an age when only a few independent parishes existed and when the majority of the clergy must perform their religious duties while still concentrated in the episcopal churches or at the central churches of the original parishes, it was imperative to design a good rule for these collegiate canonics. St. Augustine as bishop of Hippo had given the clerics who were living with him a firm rule (canon = rule). Later this mode of life was called the *ordo canonicus* after the canons, just as the *ordo monasticus* governed the monks. What was intended here was the continuance of the early Christian ideal of the *vita communis* in imitation of the apostles. The canons, unlike the monks, were not prevented from owning private property and they did not swear monastic vows. The communal life, however, did demand extensive subordination and obedience to the administration. Only in this way could the accomplishment of their duty, a particularly solemn performance of divine service in the cathedral or collegiate church, be guaranteed.

Because the communities of clerics enjoyed more freedom, they more easily fell prey to corruption, and ever new reform became necessary. Boniface and Charlemagne instigated such reform; in 768 Bishop Chrodegang of Metz wrote a new rule for canons; and a capitular of 805 required the whole clergy in France to live either *monastice,* i.e. as monks, or *canonice,* i.e. in the collegiate communities. In 816, Louis the Pious decreed his own rule from Aachen *(Institutio canonica),* but unfortunately the rule was not in effect very long in the general turmoil during the dissolution of the Carolingian empire. During the ninth and tenth centuries the property of the cathedral and collegiate churches was divided into individual prebends and the *vita communis* came to an end.

The Gregorian reform renewed some of the old demands. In 1059, a Roman synod led by Hildebrand, the future Pope Gregory VII, demanded from all cathedral and collegiate religious that they give up all private property and live according to a definite rule. The canons who agreed to this were called the canons regular, and the remaining ones were the secular canons. It was the aim of the reformers to persuade all collegiate canons to accept the Augustinian rule. We have learned only recently how effective the movement was: the existence of about 4500 such houses of regular canons has been determined for the Middle Ages. Among the centers of Gregorian reform were the canons of the Lateran, the Augustinian canons of the Great St. Bernard, the congregation of St. Victor in Paris, the canons of the Holy Sepulchre in Jerusalem, and the canons of the Cross. All of these groups had the aim of bringing the clergy closer to the apostolic ideals of this time. The Gregorian reform program called for the sanctification of the secular clergy and presupposed its inner renewal by the new emphasis on the sacramental priesthood and its position in the church. Apostolic poverty, celibacy, obedience to the spiritual leadership, hierarchical church consciousness, theological training, and an irreproachable personal life were to comprise the attributes of the new clergy.

Pope Urban II (1088–1099), himself a Cluniac monk, regarded the reform of the clergy as more important even than the reform of the orders. In 1140, archbishop Conrad I of Salzburg demanded from all of his clergy that they live according to reform regulations unless they belonged to the *ordo monasticus*. Gerhoh von Reichersberg (d. 1169), the zealous reformer, also wanted to make the Augustinian canon rule obligatory for all secular clerics, and for a time it looked as though the movement would encompass the whole clergy.

The largest and most influential of these canonical communities was that of the Premonstratensians, which was founded by Norbert of Xanten (1082–1134), a canon from the lower Rhine.

As a young nobleman with a great career before him in the service of Emperor Henry V, Norbert refused the bishopric of Cambrai when it was offered to him in 1113, and in 1115 suddenly decided to change his whole life. A stay at the Benedictine reform monastery of Siegburg and a visit with a hermit, who pointed out to Norbert the urgent need for a reform of the clergy, convinced him that he should devote himself to this task. As a penitent and itinerant preacher, Norbert wandered through France for a few years and then became aware that he could only fight the heresies spreading among the people in a successful manner by emphasizing the poverty of Christ. In 1120 Norbert founded the monastery of Prémontré near Laon which was to serve not as a community of monks but as one of canons who were to live according to the Augustinian rule. As its special duties he assigned it the sanctification of the clergy and ministerial work and preaching among the people. A thorough training was to prepare the ground for this endeavor. Already in 1156 the new order of the Premonstratensians counted over 100 communities. Norbert himself, personally concerned with the active life, in 1125 became archbishop of Magdeburg. He soon introduced his canons into his archbishopric and thereby provided them with a new field of activity. Together with the Cistercians, the Premonstratensians contributed much to the conversion and cultivation of the territories east of the Elbe.

3. The laity also was affected by the new spirit of reform. The tremendous religious buoyancy found its expression on the one hand in the crusades and in the poverty movement on the other. Both of these examples of lay spirituality will be examined in the following chapters.

29

THE CRUSADES

It is undeniable that the crusades had a religious core which grew out of the new Christian awareness in the West as a result of the Gregorian reform. But in addition to elements of lay piety, the crusades also contained a measure of knightly energy which at times expressed itself in a bloody and un-Christian frenzy which turned the crusades into the most cruel phenomenon of the Middle Ages. Both elements must be viewed soberly side by side, without an attempt to reconcile them at all times.

1. In the beginning, western knighthood viewed the reconquest of the Holy Land and a war against Islam in a deeply Christian and missionary fashion. The conquest of Jerusalem by the Turks (1071) and the moving complaints of the pilgrims about the manifold restrictions put upon them by the new lords of the Holy Land effected an appeal to the general Christian conscience. When in addition Constantinople was threatened and Emperor Alexius I

(1081–1118) sent an urgent call for help to the western church in Rome, Pope Urban II (1088–1099) directed an appeal to Latin Christendom in 1095 at the synods of Piacenza and Clermont. The appeal captured the imagination of the masses and awakened gigantic popular energies. The desire to go to the aid of the eastern Christians and to recapture from the Mohammedans the land in which Christ had walked and brought us salvation was able to unite the peoples of the Christian West despite all national barriers. With the stirring cry "God wills it", Pope Urban II placed himself at the head of the movement and carried the masses with him. Because Emperor Henry IV and the French king Philipp I were at that moment excommunicated and thus outside of the Christian community, the leadership of this all-western movement devolved upon the papacy, that same papacy which only fifty years previously at the synod of Sutri (1046) had been pulled from decline by Henry III and redirected into universal channels. The result of the papal appeal was completely unforeseen; it started a religious movement among the masses which in spite of many reverses remained alive for centuries and only lost its inspiration and strength with the dissolution of western unity at the end of the High Middle Ages.

First Crusade: 1096–1099. The actual crusade was preceded by the departure of disorganized and unenlightened bands of peasants. Moving through the Rhineland, these excited mobs started bloody pogroms of Jews, and as they continued leaderless through the Balkans they committed such excesses against the native populations that the Byzantine emperor refused to let them enter Constantinople. Most of the peasants perished during the trip, but a part of them reached Asia Minor under the leadership of the hermit Peter of Amiens who had preached the crusade. They were finally completely decimated and destroyed during the first attack of the Seljuk Turks.

The main army of the knights, recruited almost exclusively from Romance countries, reached Constantinople by various routes; it was led by the princes Raymond of Toulouse, Godfrey of Bouillon with his brothers Baldwin and Eustachius, and the

Norman Bohemond of Tarentum. After many hardships and bitter bloody battles they were able to capture Jerusalem in 1099. There followed a terrible bloodbath which severely reduced the lustre of their heroic actions. Contemporary reports indicate some of the causes for the massacre in which neither women and children nor old men were spared; the extreme hardships of the journey through scorching deserts and continuous ambushes had caused the knights exorbitantly high losses, and the pent-up bitterness and overstimulation had found its release in a totally un-Christian bloodlust against the "infidels" during the storming of the city. From the point of view of the gospels these actions certainly can not be excused, and such excesses, born of human inadequacy, later placed a heavy burden upon the conscience of the crusades. But who can judge what went on in the minds of these rough and semi-educated warriors whose religious fervor was mixed with the bitterness engendered by a fight for life and death?

As a result of the first crusade, the Christian kingdom of Jerusalem was founded. It was modeled after the French example as a liege state with the smaller crusading states of Antioch, Edessa, and Tripolis as principalities. Godfrey of Bouillon was chosen as the first "Protector of the Holy Sepulchre", and in 1099 he defeated the Egyptian sultan at Askalon. His brother Baldwin I (1100–1118) followed him and took the title of Christian King of Jerusalem. Under Fulco of Anjou (1131–1143) the kingdom achieved its greatest extension.

Second Crusade: 1147–1149. Bernard of Clairvaux was particularly active in bringing about this crusade and won for it the participation of the kings of France and Germany (Konrad III). The campaign ended in a terrible disaster for the Franco-German army which was decimated by the Turks during several battles. Jerusalem was lost again in 1187.

Third Crusade: 1189–1192. In order to regain the Holy City, a strong, well-organized and well-equipped crusading force was led by Emperor Frederick Barbarossa. At Ikonium Barbarossa won a brilliant victory over the Turks, but when the old emperor drowned in the Saleph in 1190, the leaderless army was unable to achieve any other successes. The further actions of the English king Richard Lionheart and the French king Philipp II did not result in the reconquest of Jerusalem, but in 1192 they were able to conclude a truce with Sultan Saladin which guaranteed the peaceful visit of Jerusalem by Christian pilgrims.

Fourth Crusade: 1202–1204. Pope Innocent III called the crusade, and for the last time all of western Christianity was united for such an undertaking. Quite contrary to the wish of the pope, Venetian merchants, because of selfish commercial interests, diverted the crusading army to Constantinople, where the crusaders seriously interfered with the internal political troubles of Byzantium. When after the first conquest of Constantinople (July 17, 1203) the agreed-upon reunification of the Greek and Latin Churches was not implemented, a second conquest followed (April 13, 1204) during which the city was ruthlessly plundered and destroyed. A so-called Latin Kingdom was then established which lasted until 1261. No religious unity was achieved, and the rough and irresponsible treatment only deepened and made unbridgeable the division between eastern and western churches.

The failure and senselessness of this crusade raised doubts in the West about the desirability of continuing crusades of armed men. The thought arose that God would rather use defenseless children than bloodthirsty warriors, and thus occurred the children's crusade in 1212. This crusade, incomprehensible to us today, included thousands of boys and girls from France and Germany and was led by the French shepherd boy Stephen and ten-year old Nicholas of Cologne. As was to be expected, the enthusiastic enterprise ended in terrible tragedy, and in Italy the group already began to disperse. The girls were cruelly abused by swindlers, and the remaining youths who gathered for the passage in Marseille and Brindisi were sold as slaves in Alexandria by unscrupulous shipowners. This was "a gruesome picture which appears like a malicious caricature of the crusading spirit, but which can be understood from the attitudes of the age in connection with the dislocation of the crusading enthusiasm into other social classes and age groups" (Waas). St. Francis of Assisi later adopted the healthy core of the crusading spirit and attempted peaceful conversion in place of crushing conquest. He visited the sultan himself near Damietta to bring him the message of the gospels. Unfortunately his sermon had no results and the hostile armies continued to tear one another to pieces. Although during the occupation of Damietta in 1219 the Christians committed wholesale murder in the city, when later the Christians were captured they were shown magnanimity and spared by the sultan. In spite of the many failures, the peaceful mission of the Franciscans in the Holy Land had its inception at this time.

Fifth Crusade: 1228–1229. This crusade was a private project of Emperor Frederick II who at this time was excommunicated. Through negotiations with the Egyptian sultan he obtained the return of Jerusalem to the Christians, but in 1244 the Holy City was lost for good.

Sixth Crusade: 1248–1254. King Louis IX, the saint, of France wanted to conquer first Egypt and then the Holy Land, but in April 1250 the French army was totally defeated near Cairo and the king was captured together with his troops. In 1270 Louis undertook a second crusade which also failed; the great age was past, and in 1291 Acre and the last vestiges of the crusading states were lost by the Christians.

2. The orders of knighthood. The deep religious dynamic which engendered the crusading movement also formed the basis of one of the most unique phenomena of the Middle Ages, the monastic knight. The three great orders of knights owe their existence directly to the crusading experience in the Holy Land. In addition to the three usual monastic vows of poverty, chastity, and obedience they included in their statutes the care of exhausted and sick pilgrims and the protection of the holy places against the infidels.

a) The Order of St. John was founded in 1099 as brotherhood of the Hospital of St. John in Jerusalem and was reorganized into an order in 1120 (habit: black coat with a white cross). In 1291 the seat of the order was transferred first to Cyprus, and then in

197

1309 to Rhodes. Finally in 1530 it was located in Malta, from which it received the name of "Maltese Order".

b) The Order of the Templars was founded ca. 1118 by eight French knights in the Temple of Solomon (habit: white coat, red cross). In 1291 it also was transferred to Cyprus and later, in 1311–1312 it fell victim to the intrigues of the French King Philipp the Fair and was dissolved by the Council of Vienne.

c) The Order of the Teutonic Knights was founded as a collegiate brotherhood in 1189/1190 by citizens from Bremen and Lübeck and reorganized into a knightly order in 1198. Under its Grand Master Hermann of Salza (1210–1239) it transferred its field of activity and its center to Prussia (Marienburg, since 1309). Here the order devoted itself to building a state and spreading Christianity in the Baltic (habit: white coat, black cross). In 1525 Grand Master Albrecht of Brandenburg seized the state and refashioned it into a secular Protestant dukedom.

3. The significance of the crusading movement as a whole is still contested. Although the military successes were small compared to the tremendous sacrifices in blood and strength, the ideological gain must not be overlooked. The expeditions greatly strengthened the consciousness of community in the West, expanded the European horizon, and promoted scientific learning through encounter with the Byzantine and Islamic cultures. A brisk exchange of goods and commerce was set up between the two civilizations, and the brilliant growth of western philosophy and theology in scholasticism would be unthinkable without this eastern influence.

The crusades most profoundly and lastingly marked western piety. The crusaders, who for the sake of Christ had taken the cross and survived endless dangers and hardships in the *perigrinatio religiosa,* by taking upon themselves the poor life of the cross-bearing savior also achieved respect at home for the idea of the imitation of Christ. A quite personal piety took the place of the early medieval religious communal experience; the holy Scriptures were read with new eyes; and the movement of Christian poverty awakened.

30

The First Mission in the Western Hemisphere

There are few phases in the history of Western Europe that have proven more fascinating, and at the same time remain more shrouded in mystery, than the European emigration to, and settlement of, the west coast of Greenland. The colonizing voyages of Erik the Red, begun in 985 and lasting for a period of less than twenty years, brought about the establishment of a Christian settlement in the western hemisphere five centuries before the voyages of Columbus. This fact is not only one of the least known of that remarkable and final stage of Nordic expansion which reshaped Europe during the Middle Ages, but is a chapter of history that would, were its secrets revealed, shed much light on the early missionary endeavors of the church in America.

The almost incredible fact is that, for a period of five hundred years, there flourished in the now still and silent fjords of Greenland, a community that far antedated the generally accepted notion of European westward expansion in modern times. Certainly, this phenomenon recommends itself to the sober consideration of anyone interested in the pre-Columbian history of North America.

The ruins of these settlements, of which many are still to be excavated, stand in the Julianehaab and Godthaab regions of Greenland as dumb witnesses of the days when a recently christianized Scandinavia sent its missionaries, priests and bishops across the vast stretches of the North Atlantic to bring the message of Christ into what was then the edge of the world. The beginning of a trans-Atlantic trade route, long before Columbus discovered the Bahamas, testifies to the fact that as the colony developed and prospered, it exercised a proportionately important influence on European trade. For example, it monopolized the ivory trade for almost three centuries. Croziers and other articles made from walrus tusks were found all over Western Europe. The demand of the medieval aristocrats for Greenland flacons and polar bears are but a few of the indications of the European contact with this outpost in the western hemisphere. Its products were exhibited at the Cologne fairs. Walrus rope for ships' rigging and anchor was used throughout Europe; trans-Atlantic lumber, unquestionably from North America, equipped the maritime fleets of Norway, France and England.

Even more fascinating than these commercial ties with Europe was the role that the church played in this remote and long forgotten colony of Norse Catholics. The Icelandic annals inform us that a bishop's see was established at Gardar and became one of the most flourishing of the scattered fjord settlements as well as the meeting place of the All-moot, or Althing, which was the governing authority in the small republic. Interest in the docese, collection of tithes, appointment of bishops and concern for its spiritual welfare kept it in focus for over five centuries in the curial records of far-off Rome. The disappearance of this once flourishing settlement, the oblivion into which it fell for over three centuries, remains one of those mysteries which neither the historian nor archeologist has solved.

The Reformation, severing, as it did, all diplomatic exchange between the Vatican and the church provinces of Northern Europe, did much to destroy the last links with this remarkable colony in the West. Yet it was common opinion in the sixteenth and seventeenth centuries that a European community and a Christian church still existed in Greenland. Its ghost continued to haunt the Protestant ecclesiastics who studied the church annals of the North. It is not surprising that the Lutheran churchmen of this period, familiar with the old episcopal provinces of Nidaros, would be interested in making contact with it and reforming it. The last communique of the Vatican with Greenland was a letter of concern dictated by Pope Alexander VI on 10 August 1494, which will be referred to later.

References in the sagas and annals centered about the see and the cathedral of Gardar; which of the many ruined churches was the cathedral has been difficult to determine. Investigation of the Norse remains with the aim of finding the cathedral of St. Nicholas began as early as the time of Hans Egede (1723), Protestant missionary to the Eskimos, who spent the greater part of his life in the quest for the lost Catholic colony.

It is true that the famous explorers of the 16th century, Sir Martin Frobisher and Sir John Davis, were both interested in Greenland. Yet it was in the 1720's before Hans Povelsen Egede, desiring to convert the descendants of the Norse from the evils of Romanism, began to probe into the location of the colony. He traversed during the years 1723–1724, some four hundred miles of coast from a southern point near Nanurtalik to beyond the present site of Sukkertoppen, but failed to determine the location of the see. Convinced that a colony of Norse still lived somewhere along the eastern coast of Greenland, the Norwegian government sent an expedition beyond Cape Farewell in 1724. It was at a later date that historians identified the so-called "East Settlement" of the sagas with the ruins found on the southern part of the west coast (near the present location of Julianehaab), and the more northerly "West Settlement" (near present day Godthaab).

More and more, as the Danish missionaries and historians became engrossed in the ruined remains of European habitation that they unearthed, the conviction grew that somewhere in the area of Igaliko there must have been a cathedral church — the center of this strange colony of Norse farm settlements. The famous historian of the north, Rafn, came close to discovering the true identity of Gadar in 1845, but it was not until recent times that the location and identification of the first cathedral in the western hemisphere was ascertained. This was accomplished in 1926 by Paul Norlund, in his work for the Royal Danish Commission for Geological and Geographical Investigation. The discovery of the remains of a buried bishop gave conclusive evidence to the suspicion that ancient Gadar was the present settlement of Igaliko.

The sources of our knowledge of the Norse colony in Greenland are somewhat limited, and are found, for the most part, in the various Icelandic sagas, which are not always historically reliable. Another source has been the well-known *King's Mirror,* written in Norway about 1130. We do have, however, in the various uncatalogued manuscripts in the Vatican, a picture of at least some of the personnel who established this first diocese in the western hemisphere, and something of the trials and difficulties that were theirs.

The archdiocese of Bremen, to which Greenland belonged during the eleventh century, was charged with sending the first bishop to this land. Archbishop Adelpert of Bremen, author of the *Gesta Hammaburgensis,* our source of the earliest church history of the far north, undertook to send a bishop to Greenland and even promised to go himself. The Icelandic annals tell us that a bishop was sent to Greenland about the year 1113. However, he did not take up residence there. It was not until 1125 that one Bishop Arnald, a cleric of German birth, was sent to Greenland by Archbishop Asser of Lund, and took up his residence there.

According to a description we have of Greenland about the year 1350, the episcopal estate had become quite extensive. The entire fjord where it was situated, as well as a number of the out-lying islands, were part of the church property. Extensive building operations must have followed the establishment of the diocese. Both the cathedral, which was dedicated to St. Nicholas, patron of sea-farers, and the bishop's residence must have been edifices of imposing magnitude, even by the standards of the more populated cities in Scandinavia and Iceland. The bishops of this remote diocese were not regarded as inferior prelates throughout the ecclesiastical provinces of Scandinavia. On the contrary, their arrival at Iceland and their journey to and from Europe were occasions of great pomp and ceremony.

After the establishment of the archbishopric of Nidaros (now Trondheim in Norway), bishops were appointed by the chapter of that archdiocese. The sagas tell us of a number of bishops who succeeded Bishop Arnald. The first successor to the see was Jan Knutr, who reigned from 1152 until his death in 1187. Jan Smyrill Armason, according to the Sturlunga Saga, was the next bishop. All in all, some twelve bishops resided there at one time or another during the years 1124 to 1377.

About the middle of the fourteenth century, the Eskimos began their relentless attack on the settlement. Ivar Baardson, a Norwegian priest who managed the property of the cathedral as a steward, and who led the expedition aimed at driving the marauding Eskimos out of the West settlement, wrote about the beginnings of the ravages that were to destroy the settlements.

Alf, who died in 1378, was the last residential bishop to sit in Greenland. Although appointments to this diocese continued until the eve of the Reformation, the Icelander, Bjorn Einarssen Joralatari, who visited Greenland before the death of Bishop Alf, stated that an old priest was attending to the diocese and performing all episcopal marriages. In 1409, the priest, Siru Eindride Andresson, was appointed as the bishop as *officialis* at Gadar and the last document that we have from this ill-fated diocese was a marriage certificate entered into in 1408 at Hvalsey church.

The identification of the extensive ruins along the west Greenland coast with the Gadar of the sagas and the papal tax reports, as well as the exact location of the ruins of the vanished episcopal church, was largely the work of the late Paul Norlund.

During the summer of 1926, Norlund proved beyond further doubt the location of the cathedral, lost for so many centuries, by unearthing the remains of a skeleton of a bishop in the north chapel of the church remains on Einarsfjord, near present day Julianehaab. The presence of a crozier and a gold ring on the man's finger gave definite proof that the remains were those of a Catholic bishop. Judging from an approximate dating of the ornamentation on the crozier (a twelfth-century motif: foliage work with a highly developed leaf termination) it can be assumed that the bishop was none other than Jan Smyrill (i.e. sparrow hawk) Armason, who constructed the church and died in his diocese in 1204. It is fitting that he should be buried in the cathedral he had erected as a monument to the Catholic faith at the edge of the world. It is one of the paradoxes of history that his bones were reinterred, according to the Lutheran rite, after they had been scientifically studied.

The skeletal remains of the bishop found in the north chapel of the cathedral were unfortunately in a bad state of preservation.

The skull, destroyed by a later burial, had only the lower jaw and some loose teeth remaining. The bones are rather powerful and give the idea of a man of about 6'4" in height, and who was still in middle age. The remnants of clothing clinging to the skeleton were undoubtedly fragments of a chasuble and an alb. Remains of leather shoes were found at the feet. The skeletal remains have the peculiarity that all the bones of the right foot were missing, an indication that the foot may have dropped off due to gangrene after frostbite, and that this was probably the cause of the bishop's death.

The remains of the cathedral itself indicate an edifice that was fairly well orientated east to west. The ground plan is a cruciform. To the broad nave is attached a narrower chancel that is flanked by two shorter chapels which stand out a little in front of the side walls of the nave and form the arms of the cross. The nave itself measures exteriorly some 59'0" in length with the west gable at 33'4". The breadth of the nave at the cross arms is 42'9". The total length of the cathedral is 88'9" and its greatest width is 51'7".

The building material is red sandstone, of which large quantities are found in the hillside just behind the settlement. In view of the fact that the only remains of the structure are the underground foundations, it is somewhat difficult to reconstruct the entire edifice. Yet what remains of the foundations indicates a cruciform church erected in the last half of the 12th, or the early half of the 13th century, a date that certainly fits the period when Jan Smyrill Armason sat on the episcopal seat of Greenland. The two small wings have not at all the character of transepts, but are merely side-chapels standing back from the chancel gable. Similar chapel wings are found at the Lyse Conventual church, a Norwegian Cistercian building commenced in 1146, and at Trondenes church in northern Norway.

The gradual disappearance of the Norse Catholics in Greenland is one of the saddest chapters in the annals of church history. Most historians admit that by the middle of the fifteenth century the Greenland colony was slowly cut off from Europe, and that it became extinct due to malnutrition and the incessant attacks of the Eskimos. Yet there is indication that trade continued with Europe almost until late in the 15th century, as witnessed in the style of clothing in the graves exhumed at Herjalknes during the 1930's. Hence, there must have been some contact with Europe even after the Eskimo attacks.

Certainly there was a continued concern on the part of the Renaissance popes for the Christian outpost. Pope Alexander VI writes, during the early years of his pontificate (1492–1503), what is the last known reference to this far-away diocese:

> Since, as we have learned, the Church of Gardar is situated at the ends of the earth in Greenland, and the people dwelling there are accustomed to use dried fish and milk for lack of bread, wine, and oil; and since the shipping to that country is very infrequent because of the extensive freezing of the waters — no ship having put into shore, it is believed, for eight years, or, if voyages happened to be made, it could have been only in the month of August, when the ice had thawed — and since it is likewise said that for eight years, or thereabouts, absolutely no bishop or priest governed that church in personal residence, which fact together with the absence of catholic priests, brought it to pass that very many of the diocese unhappily repudiated their sacred baptismal vows; and since the inhabitants of that land have no relic of the Christian religion, save a certain corporale, annually set forth, upon which a hundred years ago the Body of Christ was consecrated by the last priest then living there.

The religious articles found in the ancient graves, the devout writings on the rune stones unearthed there, show a people of great religious fervor. All in all, the bishops of Gardar were entrusted with the care of sixteen churches; twelve were in the Eastern Settlement and four in the Western. There were, in addition to the parish churches, four monasteries mentioned in the records. Excavations have unearthed the ruins of an Augustine monastery at Ketilsfjord and a convent of the Benedictine order near present day Unartag.

31

THE POVERTY MOVEMENT, HERESIES, AND INQUISITION

1. As early as the tenth and eleventh centuries, monastic reformers had demanded the return to the apostolic poverty of the early church, and the *vita apostolica* had been closely connected with the ideal of leading a simple life according to the example of Christ and the apostles. Under the influence of the crusades this desire developed into a veritable mass movement throughout the whole West. Not only the soldiers returning from the Holy Land but also those who had stayed at home had before their eyes the vivid image of the poor savior and were inspired to the imitation of Christ. All people became interested in the gospels. Monks and clerics devoted themselves to reading the Scriptures, and members of the laity also formed small circles where the Scriptures were read and explained to them. The laymen wanted to learn about the life of Christ and the apostles directly from the Scriptures and were literally starving for the word of God. Great preachers like Bernard of Clairvaux and Norbert of Xanten gathered listeners from great distances.

If the poor life of Jesus was compared with the existing conditions, it was easy for an opposition to the institutional church to develop. The medieval feudal church was wealthy, not only in Germany, where the bishops were also princes, but also in France, England, and Italy. Everywhere bishoprics and abbeys were in the hands of the nobility and the magnates. The clergy who determined spiritual life was also most intimately connected with the feudal lords. Now, however, a self-confident citizenry was developing in the expanding cities which no longer let itself be guided solely by the spiritual leaders. The laymen of the church were awakened and wanted to make up their own minds regarding religious questions by referring to the Bible. As long as this search took place within the limits of the church and could be utilized for an inward reform, its results would be beneficial, but there was also the danger that it would seize upon heretical and anti-ecclesiastical ideas and produce ill effects. The question was, therefore, whether the church could channel the movement or whether it would turn against the church.

The zealous Dutch reformer Tanchelm spoke out against any possessions of clerics and violently assailed the secular life of the clergy. His stance culminated in his spiritualistic opposition to the hierarchy and the sacramental church and a rejection of the Eucharist. In 1115 he was killed by the people, but his heresies did not die with him, and in 1124 Norbert preached against them near Antwerp. The radical Italian penitential preacher Arnold of Brescia also called for a church without property and violently criticized the papacy. By permitting himself to be used in the Roman municipal struggles he became enmeshed in high politics, and Emperor Frederick Barbarossa had him executed in 1155. His followers, the "Arnoldists", later often joined the Waldensians and the Cathari.

The Waldensians have their origin with the wealthy merchant Peter Waldes of Lyons. Around 1173/1176 Peter Waldes discovered the ideal of poverty during the reading of Mt 10, 5ff and gave away his fortune to devote himself to strict apostolic poverty and the preaching of penance. His followers called themselves *"pauperes Christi"* or the "poor men of Lyon". Certainly these men meant well, but their criticism was not free from exaggeration and also contained dangers for the faith. The bishop of Lyons expelled them, because as laymen they were not qualified to speak on questions of faith. Waldes turned to the pope and appeared at the Third Lateran Council in 1179. Alexander III applauded Waldes's ideal of poverty and permitted him to preach pure penance as long as he did not become involved in questions of faith. This regulation was both vague and flexible, and under the pretext that Waldes had not kept it, the bishop again denied him permission to preach. Once more Waldes appealed directly to

Rome, but this time Lucius III reacted sharply. In 1184 the pope forbade Waldes any activity as preacher and censured the whole movement which had meanwhile become more radical.

Now Waldes resisted; he justified his position by reference to his inner call and personal mission by Christ and asserted that only persons who had given away everything and lived in poverty were entitled to preach Christianity. The pope excommunicated Waldes, and persecution drove the movement underground. Waldensians became increasingly hostile to the church and adopted heretical doctrines of faith. Waldes died around 1217, and the remainders of his sect later joined the Italian Protestants.

Around 1170 the Beghines appeared for the first time in Belgium and the Netherlands. These pious women concerned themselves with prayer, the reading of Scripture, manual labor, the care of the sick, and the religious instruction of girls. They lived together without monastic vows and were totally devoted to active charity work for the sake of Christ. In the Milan area the cloth weavers united into similar religious communities, the Humiliati. In imitation of the early Christian community (Acts 2, 44) they formed production co-operatives and rejected private property. When the Humiliati also evinced gradually increasing radical tendencies, Innocent III succeeded in 1201 in bringing the movement under ecclesiastical control and spiritual leadership. Some of the Humiliati elected to live together in monastic communities under the Augustinian rule, others chose to remain in the world, but participated in the religious exercises of these monasteries. They were affiliated with them in communities of prayer and were the forerunners of the "Third Orders". In 1216 the diocese of Milan counted 150 such Humiliati monasteries and the order existed until 1571.

2. While all of these groups had a common Christian basis, the movement of the Cathari was based on a genuine un-Christian Manichaeic dualism. Armenian Paulicians, who in the ninth century had been resettled in the Balkans by Byzantium, had brought with them early Gnostic concepts. These ideas were

208

summarized in Macedonia by the village priest Bogomil in the first half of the tenth century: The world was created and ruled by the devil, i.e. by the evil God of the Old Testament, and in the process of creation, the pure souls of men had been enclosed in evil matter. Then the good God of the New Testament had sent one of his angels, Jesus Christ, to teach men how to liberate themselves from evil matter and to enter their real home, heaven, as the "pure ones" (*katharoi* = Cathari = *Ketzer* = heretics). To accomplish this end, asceticism and complete separation from the world were necessary; any contact with evil matter made a person unclean, as the whole of creation was sinful. The "Perfect Ones" were expected to avoid marriage, sexual inter-course, and the eating of meat, as well as any kind of manual labor, material possessions, and wealth.

Travelling merchants and returning crusaders brought these ideas to the West in the twelfth century and here they spread quickly to Germany (Cologne 1143), England, France, and Italy, where they were connected with the Christian thoughts of various individuals. The followers of the movement organized themselves according to the example of the Catholic Church, and provided themselves with a hierarchy and a division into bishoprics. In 1167 a large council of the Cathari took place near Toulouse, which contrasted the wealthy Catholic Church, laden with sinful possessions, with their own poor church which re-jected all possessions. This comparison only too well answered the desires of many radical reformers who dreamed of a "gospel-poor" church, and the Cathari succeeded in presenting to the simple people their un-Christian dualistic rejection of the world as the ideal picture of Christian asceticism. The movement presented its members as ideal Christians who led exemplary ascetic lives, while it designated the Catholic Church as the synagogue of Satan, stigmatized the priests as hypocritical sinners, and declared the sacraments to be the work of the devil.

With the same unwillingness to compromise, the Cathari also opposed the state and called the emperor the governor of Satan and his princes Satan's helpers. Their strong following in the south of France, particularly in the area of Albi (thus "Albigenses"), soon brought them together with the French barons who were then preparing for the fight against the French king. The resulting tension was released in the bloody, semi-religious, and semi-political Albigensian war (1209–1229).

3. The fight against the Cathari and the Inquisition must be viewed in the light of the dual position of the Cathari as enemies of both the church and the state. Because the Cathari attacked the political and social as well as the religious foundations of the Christian community, state and church acted together. Peter II of Aragon denounced the Cathari as enemies of the state as early as 1197 and ordered their burning. In 1179 king Louis VII of France and king Henry II of England put pressure on the Third Lateran Council to pass severe ordinances against the heretics who were to be punished by the confiscation of their property and imprisonment. If necessary, force should be used against them to crush the movement. Lucius III, therefore, in 1183 concluded an agreement with Emperor Frederick Barbarossa, according to which the heretics immediately after their excommunication should be put under the imperial ban and the agents of the state were to search them out and turn them over to secular courts. It is idle to speculate to what extent religious or political motives were decisive; a world which saw itself as a religious-political unit could only act as a unit when it saw its uniform Christian foundations attacked.

After attempts at conversion among the Albigenses had failed and the papal legate had been murdered in 1208, Innocent III called a crusade against them. The un-Christian killing went on for twenty years and much blood was shed on both sides. In the process, whole cities were depopulated, broad regions of the area were devastated, and the culture of the Provence was destroyed. Outwardly the heresy could be regarded as exterminated. But the Inquisition had to work for many decades in order to really master the situation. The profit accrued to the French monarchy, which was the victor in the war, for it was able to settle its political dynastic problems under the mantle of religion.

The procedures of ecclesiastical trial law for the Inquisition were perfected under Innocent III. According to it, the government in certain cases had to proceed officially against a sinner or criminal, i.e. it must not wait until someone had preferred charges against him, but ex officio had to search for him and put him on trial. The application of this procedure to heretics in 1231 led to the appointment of special papal inquisitors to pursue those suspected of heresy. In 1224, Gregory IX and Emperor Frederick II together passed a law against the heretics of Lombardy which required the secular power to arrest a heretic who had been convicted by the bishop and to execute him if he remained obstinate. The arrest by the secular arm thus automatically was followed by punishment, and if during the surrender of the convict by the ecclesiastical to the secular power the wish was expressed to see the life of the condemned man spared, this was nothing but a "ghastly formalism and pure fiction". If the secular court refused to execute the heretic, the court itself was suspected of heresy. In 1252 Innocent IV empowered the inquisitors to employ torture if necessary to obtain a confession.

The pope thereby introduced one of the most dismal chapters of church history. The inhumane practices of the brutal torturers no longer had any limits. Much innocent blood was shed and cruel excesses and desperate sorrow descended on humanity. When this "frightful institution" later was also put into the service of unqualified superstition, namely the absurd belief in witchcraft, the nadir was reached. In the name of Jesus, the merciful Lord of the Sermon on the Mount and of the gospel of salvation, blind fanatics brought immeasurable suffering on humanity. We can only note these events with profound shame and dismay; we can not understand them.

Nevertheless, if we examine the causes, much has to be considered. Medieval man regarded the religious heretic also as a political revolutionary, who through his attack on the foundation of western Christian society threatened the existence of both church and state. Theologians, especially Thomas Aquinas, rejected outright force in matters of faith, but medieval man regarded truth, particularly the truth of faith, as only Christian, and the question of what was to be done with those who denied it had an entirely different aspect from today. There exists only one objective truth; is it better served through severity or indulgent love? The medieval believer was convinced that severity served best. The Reformers Luther, Melanchthon, and particularly Calvin thought and acted in this same way. Trials of heretics and persecutions of witches occurred as frequently and as late in Wittenberg and Geneva as in Cologne and Paris. Only the eighteenth century Enlightenment put an end to this type of persecution.

Even at the time, monastics such as Francis of Assisi and Dominic demonstrated that other ways existed for spreading the gospel and overcoming threats to the faith.

32
THE GREAT MENDICANT ORDERS

Great saints are always God's answer to the particular needs and difficulties of an age. Francis of Assisi and Dominic by their inner calling and grace showed the way out of the dilemma in which church and society were caught: A wealthy and powerful church and an increasingly wealthy Christian society were in danger of becoming victims of their possessions and losing touch with the poorer elements of the population. Power and force could not save the unity; this tension could only be overcome inwardly through the spirit of the gospels. By perfectly living the ideal of poverty in imitation of Christ and at the same time refraining from blindly scolding others for their wealth or going so far as to call property "evil" in itself, these saints taught mankind the way to possess and to renounce at the same time. They were, as Paul said: "Sorrowful, yet always rejoicing; poor, yet making many rich; having nothing, and yet possessing all things" (2 Cor 6, 10).

1. Francis was born in Assisi in 1181/1182. After a carefree youth, full of ambitious plans, he was seized in the spring of 1205

by the ideal of poverty while on the way to a military campaign in Apulia, where he wanted to earn a knighthood for himself. Now Francis completely renounced the world and performed works of penitence and charity. When in 1206 his father expelled him from his house, Francis wandered happily through the country, singing and begging for his bread. In the spring of 1208/1209 while in the chapel of Portiuncula near Assisi the words of Mt 10, 5ff gave him the pattern for his future life: to preach the glad tidings of the merciful love of the savior to all men and all creation, and to lead them to a change and turn toward God. With a few disciples he went to Rome in 1209/1210 to obtain from Innocent III approval for his way of life and the authorization to preach. The pope granted both (legend of his dream), and Francis seems to have received his ordination as deacon at this time. He began his work, and his ideas spread with unprecedented speed. Preaching penance and God's love, Francis travelled through Italy, southern France, and Spain (1214–1215). He wanted to convert the Cathari and the Moors, not through power and armed force, but as an insignificant friar — he wanted himself and his companions to be known as *fratres minores*—, through love, humility, and joy. Illness prevented him from crossing over to Morocco, and in 1215 he returned to Assisi.

The order quickly became popular, and everywhere Francis's appearance caused a profound impression on the people at all levels of society. The young people thronged towards Francis, and he enjoyed the confidence of the simple people as well as that of the pope and the bishops. Francis exerted a peculiar attraction; when in 1219 he accompanied the crusading army to Egypt, he could in safety make his way through the battling warriors near Damietta to the sultan to tell him of the love of the savior. Thus Francis showed a new way for the mission of the cross; instead of conquering with weapons, it was to achieve conquest through love.

In 1221, Francis gave a rule to his order which sprang entirely from his spirit and the gospels. In order to make it meet the needs of the tremendous organizational tasks of a brotherhood which was already active throughout most of Europe, the rule was redacted in cooperation with cardinal Ugolino, the future Pope Gregory IX, and was then confirmed in 1223. Francis himself withdrew completely from the administration of the order so as to be able to live entirely according to his ideal. After 1224 he suffered from grave afflictions of eye and stomach. On Mount Alverno, in September 1224, while gazing up at the cross in mystical union with Christ, he received on his body the stigmata of the Lord. Thus Francis, the most Christ-like Christian, became one with the crucified Christ in the passion. In the midst of his suffering, Francis composed the beautiful song to the sun which overflows with love and gratitude to God, whom all of creation praises. Lying on the bare floor, poor and naked, Francis died on October 3, 1226, while singing the Te Deum with his brethren.

The ties which Francis had established with the people were maintained by the members of his order, and they remained the most popular missionaries of the Middle Ages. Closely connected with the Franciscans was the order of St. Clara, who, in 1212, had put herself under the spiritual guidance of Francis and had settled in S. Damiano near Assisi. In 1221 the so-called Third Order (Tertiaries) was added to the movement; its members remained in the world and at the same time participated in the ideals and the strength of the Franciscans. Francis had invested the church once more with love for poverty and made it believable in the eyes of those who had taken offence at its wealth. His disciples have preserved the ideals of poverty to this day, while the members have neither scorned the world nor been ignorant of it.

2. Dominic, born ca. 1170 in Castile, had a personality which was quite different from that of Francis, but he was quite closely related to him in intentions. Dominic was a canon regular who, on a trip to Rome in 1204, became acquainted with the destructive effects of the movement of the Cathari in southern France. He decided then to devote himself to their conversion by becoming an itinerant preacher and living in apostolic poverty. He accepted the strict Franciscan rule of poverty, but he felt the necessity for

adding something: A well-founded sermon required a good theological training, and Dominic wanted to emphasize this idea. When, in Rome in 1215, he asked for approval of his new priestly order, Innocent III demanded that he accept Augustine's rule, and in 1216 Honorius III confirmed the new order. As early as 1217 the first convent also existed at Prouille in the foothills of the Pyrenees. The convent had grown out of an association of pious women who had come together to support Dominic's mission to the Albigenses. Later a Third Order for secular disciples, similar to that of the Franciscans, was added.

The ideal of unconditional poverty was also adopted by two other orders; the Hermits of St. Augustine, who received papal approval in 1256, and the Carmelites, who had relocated in Europe from the Holy Land in 1228 and who in 1247 had become a mendicant order. The Carmelites also established an order for women after 1452.

These four mendicant orders acquired great significance in ecclesiastical life, because they not only provided the best-loved preachers, but also the most important theologians of the High Middle Ages.

33
THEOLOGY AND THE UNIVERSITIES

Although the early Middle Ages had been satisfied to continue theological studies in the spirit of the ancient Christian patristics, the intensification of ecclesiastical life in the eleventh century led to a stronger differentiation of theological thinking in the twelfth and thirteenth centuries. The more the Christian West developed unity under papal leadership, the more active became the spiritual intercourse of the people. This exchange of ideas stimulated a many-sided concern with tradition. The expansion of the European horizon by the crusaders also provided new aspects, and the centers of learning shifted from the monasteries to the newly developing universities.

1. The Benedictine Ruprecht of Deutz (d. 1135) was still entirely within the old tradition, but Berengar of Tours (d. 1088) opened a new field. In the doctrine of the Eucharist, Berengar denied the real presence of the body of Christ. He held that the bread and wine were mere symbols which were not changed in the consecration, but only received supernatural strength. However, when his doctrine was rejected in Rome in 1079, Berengar submitted to the decision of the church. The Fourth Lateran Council in 1215 decided that the consecration in Holy Mass effected a real change of the essence, and termed this change "transubstantiation".

Anselm of Canterbury (d. 1109) is regarded as the "Father of Scholasticism". Utilizing traditional ideas he attempted to penetrate all matters of faith rationally and to arrive at new conclusions. Faith *could* be supported by the intellect, and in fact required it: *fides quaerens intellectum*. The existence of God, for example, could be shown not only by revelation through the Holy Scriptures, but also could be recognized by the use of the intellect. Anselm introduced the so-called ontological demonstration for the existence of God. Here we have the first glimpse of the problem of "faith and reason", "revelation and natural knowledge". In the doctrine of redemption and in Christology Anselm also went a new way (doctrine of satisfaction). The most important theologian of early scholasticism was the ingenious but uneven Peter Abelard (1079–1142). His dialectical and critical method of *Sic et non (Yes and No)* attempted to fathom all depths, and in the process Abelard occasionally blurred the lines between faith and knowledge. He was opposed by Bernard of Clairvaux at the synod of Sens (1141), and a number of his propositions were rejected.

Around 1140, the Camaldolese monk Gratian (d. 1158), a professor at Bologna, tried to compile and to codify the diverse church laws (= canones). His *Concordantia discordantium canonum,* later simply called *Decretum Gratiani,* became the matrix of the *Corpus Juris Canonici,* which until 1918 remained the authoritative lawcode of the church. In the course of the Middle Ages several legal collections were added to the *Decretum Gratiani:* the *Liber extra decretum* of Gregory IX (1234), the *Liber sextus decretalium* of Boniface VIII (1298), the *Constitutiones Clementinae* (1317), and the so-called *Extravagantes,* i.e. the papal decrees of later times. Gratian is called the "Father of Canonics".

Peter Lombard (d. 1160), a lecturer at the University of Paris and a future bishop, wrote the definitive textbook of compiled and edited doctrines, and his *Sentences (Sententiarum Libri IV)* were used throughout the whole Middle Ages.

Theological development reached its absolute prime in the so-called High Scholasticism of the thirteenth century. Through the works of Arab and Jewish thinkers (Avicenna, d. 1037, in the East; Averroes, d. 1198, in Spain; Maimonides, d. 1204, a Jew), the West learned more about the Greek philosopher Aristotle (d. 322 B.C.) than it had hitherto known. The methods of logic used by Aristotle were taken as a model for the theological investigation of the Christian world of faith after they had been cleansed of pagan content and "Christianized". Aristotle's terminology seemed well-suited for the task and a "modern" philosophical and theological method was created which soon found great appeal among the young mendicant orders. The Dominicans Albertus Magnus (d. 1280), Thomas Aquinas (d. 1274), Meister Eckhard (d. 1328), and the Franciscans Bonaventure (d. 1274) and Duns Scotus (d. 1308) were the most important representatives of High Scholasticism.

Albert, a Swabian who had entered the Dominican order in 1223 and a scholar of universal erudition (he was called *doctor universalis,* the Great), taught in Cologne and in Paris. Thomas Aquinas became Albert's student in Paris (1243–1247) and later accompanied him to Cologne (1248–1252), where Albert had been sent to found a new school of the order *(studium generale).* Albert was probably the first systematically to apply the Aristotelian philosophical and theological method to Christian theology, but he was far surpassed in this by his great pupil Thomas Aquinas. Thomas Aquinas was born in Roccasicca near Naples in 1226/1227 and in 1244 entered the order of the Dominicans against the vehement opposition of his parents. Thomas listened to Albert's lectures (1245–1252) and was greatly stimulated by them. Thomas also taught in Paris (1252–1259, since 1256 as university professor), in Rome (1259–1269), again in Paris (1269–1272), and in Naples (1272–1274). In addition to the classical *Summa Theologica,* the unsurpassed universal representation of the Christian religion based on philosophical and theological Christian Aristotelianism, Thomas Aquinas was also the author of numerous other works, such as the *Summa contra gentiles* (1264), *Quaestiones Quodlibetales, Quaestiones Disputatae,* commentaries on holy Scripture, Aristotle, and many other works. Although he was the most gifted theologian of the Middle Ages, he was also a great mystic and saint *(doctor angelicus).*

The Franciscan Bonaventure, born in 1217/1218 near Viterbo and a member of the order since 1243, studied and taught together with Thomas Aquinas in Paris (1253, resp. 1257–1274). His theology was strongly influenced by mysticism *(doctor seraphicus)* and Augustinian and Platonic thought, particularly his compendium of dogmatics *(Breviloquium,* 1257*)* and his much-read devotional and mystical *Itinerarium mentis ad Deum* (1259). While Thomas Aquinas worked principally with the intellect, Bonaventure was more influenced by the will; if knowledge of God was the goal of Thomas, love of God concerned Bonaventure. He gave this spirit to the theology of the order, and as general of the order (1257–1274) was always concerned with practical pastoral work in addition to his teaching in Paris. To relieve the tension between the conventuals and the spirituals in the Franciscan order, Bonaventure wrote the *Vita maior S. Francisci.* Another Franciscan, Duns Scotus, continued his theological line. Born around 1265 in Scotland, Duns Scotus strongly influenced theology during his short but prolific teaching career in Paris (1305–1307) and later until his death in Cologne (1307–1308) through his incisive critical method and through his Christocentric and Marian speculations (Mary's immaculate conception as prior redemption by Christ). He also emphasized the primacy of the will, of freedom, and of love. Duns Scotus has been called the "last great figure of High Scholasticism" (Grabmann).

2. The centers of theological studies and of science in general at this time were the newly founded universities. Around 1200, the professors of various schools in Paris formed themselves into a corporation, the *Universitas Magistrorum,* which soon obtained ecclesiastical and official recognition as an independent organization. Gregory IX also gave the corporation independence from the bishop in 1231 and granted it numerous privileges. A *Universitas* also developed in Bologna at this time; but here the students conducted the incorporation *(universitas scholarium).* Subsequently many such corporations were formed, and these were simply called universities. Among the famous scientific centers were Padua (1222) and Naples (1224) in Italy; Montpellier and others in addition to Paris in France; Oxford and Cambridge in England, and Valencia and Salamanca (1220) in Spain. Germany followed this trend only around the middle of the fourteenth century with universities in Prague (1348), Vienna (1365), Heidelberg (1386), and Cologne (1388). Paris, the "Mother of Sciences", had the greatest prestige and the largest number of students. In 1258 Robert de Sorbon had founded a college for poor students of theology, and even though numerous other foundations were added in the course of time, the name Sorbonne became attached to the entire University of Paris. Primarily philosophy and theology were of importance in Paris, while at Bologna the school of law dominated. All students, some of whom were still quite young, at first completed the philosophical faculty *(facultas artium),* only then could they chose a specialty from one of the three higher faculties, theology, law, or medicine.

In contrast to local schools *(studium particulare),* the universities were characterized by accepting students and tutors from everywhere, and their degrees were universally recognized in the Christian West *(studium universale).* In the universities could be glimpsed the universality of the uniform western spirit, and university studies were regarded as an independent third power in addition to *sacerdotium* and *imperium.* The Cologne canon Alexander of Roes in his clever parable of the *Pavo* in 1284 attributed the *sacerdotium* to the Italians, the *imperium* to the Germans, and the *studium* to the French, as particular functions of these peoples in the service of the western community. The acquisition of a doctoral degree from one of these universities meant equality with the nobility. Learning truly ennobled a person!

34
THE PAPACY FROM INNOCENT III TO BONIFACE VIII

The development which had begun with Gregory VII led the papacy under Innocent III to the zenith of its power. With the pontificate of Innocent III, "the papacy achieved a dizzying and untenable height" (Gregorovius). It was no longer the emperor, but unequivocally the pope who now was acknowledged the supreme arbiter of western Christianity.

Europe experienced an abrupt change of scene in 1197 when Emperor Henry VI suddenly died at the age of 32, in the midst of the construction of a powerful empire, and left behind him a two-year old son, Frederick II, as heir. A few months later in Rome the senile Celestine III (1191–1198) was followed by the energetic thirty-seven-year old Innocent III (1198–1216), the most powerful pope of the Middle Ages. In Germany struggles over the succession broke out and the empire began to break down. At this very moment the papacy was able to fortify its primatial position in the whole western church and to exert a central, commanding, and guiding authority.

1. All that the Gregorian reform had striven for and Gregory VII had demanded in his *Dictatus Papae* (1075), was realized under Innocent III. As supreme legislator, judge, and administrator he fully possessed the *plenitudo potestatis* and exercised this wealth of power with sovereign assurance over the whole church. But since this church was one with western Christianity, the political destinies of the people could not remain unaffected by its increase in authority. The Augustinian idea of the city of God, together

with the Donation of Constantine, which was regarded as genuine, allowed the church to appear as the true *Imperium Romanum* and to develop the idea of papal world domination. This concept was deeply rooted in the religious and political thought of the age and also stemmed from the Christian responsibility which a reformed papacy felt for western Christianity. The *populus christianus* of the West was the supernatural and therefore also supranational community of all Christians. The pope, as *caput christianitatis,* therefore automatically became the head and guide of the western world which, though consisting of many peoples, was united in the same faith.

The picture which modern research has drawn of Innocent III shows him as a deeply religious, inwardly pious, and ascetically severe man who, although a born ruler and *imperator,* was a priest and pastor of the first rank. As vicar of Christ, Innocent administered his office solely in the knowledge of his responsibility to God, and since that time *Vicarius Christi* has been one of the titles carried by the popes.

Lothar of Segni was born in 1160 into an ancient family of counts. He studied theology and canon law in Paris and Bologna and became a member of the college of cardinals during the papacy of his uncle Clement III (1187–1191). Small and frail of figure and in delicate health, Innocent combined a comprehensive knowledge with a towering intellect, acuteness, shrewdness, and moderation. Above all, he gave a lofty spiritual interpretation to the office of a universal papacy. Far from being an ecclesiastical fanatic or a "purely political pope" (Heussi), Innocent actually showed a great openness to all the problems of an age which was filled with cultural, political, social, and religious tensions and contrasts. Through internal consistency and strength he forced the many diverse tendencies to conform to a uniform principle of order which, in light of the time, could only be papal order.

If Innocent interfered with secular matters, he did so out of responsibility and the conviction that all things in the world must submit to God's order, and that even kings and princes

221

were subject to God's judgment. The world appeared to Innocent as a *hierarchia,* i.e. as a "holy arrangement"; the fine distinction between the purely political and the purely spiritual, between church and state, had not then been so refined that overlapping and infringement could be avoided. *Ratione peccati* the pope always felt justified and even obligated to intervene wherever order was disturbed through moral guilt or objective injustice. Thus, as *caput christianitatis* he also must be *arbiter mundi* in all pending issues.

For these reasons Innocent intervened in the German struggle for the throne after the double election of 1198. He did not claim for himself the approbation of the election itself, but merely the judgment of the moral qualities of the candidates. At first he rejected the Staufen Philipp of Swabia because he considered him to be a violent man and regarded the Staufic concept of uniting lower Italy and Sicily with the empire as reprehensible and dangerous as well as illegal. However, when Philipp after his victory over the anti-king Otto IV turned out to be a moderate man and gave guarantees with respect to his Sicilian policy, Innocent was immediately willing to conclude peace with him. On the other hand, when, after Philipp's assassination (1208), Otto IV won recognition in the empire and was also willing to make concessions, Innocent did not hesitate to crown him emperor (1209). Consequently Innocent was severely diappointed when Otto did not keep his word and in 1210 began to follow the Staufic Sicilian policy. Because of this "wrong", Innocent disputed Otto's right to the crown and set against him the now adult Frederick II. Previously, Innocent had obtained a sworn oath from Frederick that he would never attempt to unite Sicily with the German crown.

What caused Innocent to be so concerned with the lower Italian policy of the German emperors? The problem was not a purely territorial one, but rather one which affected the whole church and was, therefore, universal. The unification of Sicily with the German Empire would of necessity have made the pope nothing but a subordinate imperial bishop and would have taken from the pope his independence from the universal empire. The typically western dualism would have been lost, and Innocent believed that only if the independence and sovereignty of the Church State provided the requisite freedom, could the papacy fulfill its universal function.

However, Innocent also had his own concept of the proper structure of the European world. Because of the pre-eminence of the spiritual over the secular, the states should be combined in a higher order under papal leadership. The idea of a papal liege lordship over the Christian peoples of the West corresponded with medieval feudal thought. There was no question of establishing a hierocracy. The *Christianitas* whose head was the pope, was not to be a state; it was "not at all a real *societas,* but that relationship of the papacy to the Christian world which seemed to be appropriate to the age" (F. Kempf). Therefore, the sovereignty of the secular rulers within this order was not at all excluded, and the papal claim to leadership was only of an indirect character. Papal leadership, then, merely demanded the acknowledgement of the supreme norms of the Christian faith and of the moral authority of the papacy. In this way, dualism was preserved.

Systematically Innocent worked on the structure of papal liege lordship. The beginning had been made with the contested Sicily, and already in 1198 Empress Constance recognized the pope as liege lord. In the following years, the kings of England, Aragon, Portugal, Denmark, Poland, Bohemia, Hungary, Dalmatia, and other smaller territories accepted their countries from the pope as fiefs. The preservation of law and peace, the traditional duties of the emperor, therewith passed to the papacy and a papal system of vassalage developed which was constructed entirely on the strong moral authority of the pope.

Innocent decisively established papal primacy in the internal affairs of the church by intervening energetically in uncanonical episcopal elections and by reserving the so-called *causae maiores* for the curia in Rome. Reforms of papal administrative offices, of monasticism, and of the clergy also helped to enforce good

223

order. By the authority of the papal office, i.e. ex officio, the pope proceeded against unworthy prelates and bishops and had them cited before his inquisitional court. At first Innocent was mild and lenient with heretics, but when his peaceful attempts at conversion failed, and his legate, the Cistercian Peter of Castelnau, was murdered by the Cathari in southern France (January 1208), he organized the crusade of 1209. However, he was not responsible for the terrible and shameful sanguine course of this enterprise; the blame rests above all on the fanatical papal legate Arnaldus Amalrici and on Count Simon of Montfort.

It stands to the honor of Innocent in the annals of his pontificate that he correctly evaluated the appeal and the significance of the poverty movement in the church. He gave his special concern to the Lombardic Humiliati (1201) and he also founded the alliance of the Poor Catholics (1208). But most far-reaching was his kind reception of Francis of Assisi, who had come to Rome in 1209/1210 to request papal authorization for his small society, and the mendicant orders soon became the strongest supporters of the church. In spite of all his power, Innocent had something in common with these orders in that he always maintained an inner distance from wealth and pomp and never felt its addiction.

The high point of Innocent's pontificate was the Fourth Lateran Council which he assembled in November 1215 and which was attended by about 500 bishops and 800 abbots. Not only was this council an imposing review of the whole Christian West, but it also constituted an unparalleled peak of ecclesiastical life during the zenith of the Middle Ages. Its reform decrees contributed much to the internal rejuvenation and consolidation of the church and were long effective in provincial councils and diocesan synods. The definition of the doctrine of transubstantiation and the ordinances regarding obligatory annual confession and communion at Easter were of lasting permanence.

2. Unfortunately this high point also became a turning point. Innocent died soon after the council (July 16, 1216), and his successors were unable to maintain the position which he had achieved for the papacy, primarily because the papacy was bur-

dened with such a heavy political mortgage. World domination, after all, can never be the task of the church, even though it must always be concerned that the life of the states is conducted according to the religious and moral principles of Christianity. Religion suffers when it is amalgamated with politics, and the pontifical office loses prestige if it is employed for worldly as well as spiritual aims. With the successors of Innocent III, the high ideals of a universal church receded more and more into the background, and in the High Middle Ages, the Renaissance, and the Reformation territorial and political problems and the maintenance and enlargement of the Papal States often outweighed general ecclesiastical concerns.

However, in the last great decisive battle between *regnum* and *sacerdotium*, that between Emperor Frederick II and the popes, the issue was still the question which of the two great universal powers had precedence. When the young emperor revived the Staufic policy on Sicily and, instead of going on crusade as he had promised, became totally enmeshed in the plans for southern Italy, which constituted a threat to the Papal States, Gregory IX excommunicated him in 1228. While under the ban, Frederick undertook the crusade (1228–1229) and was successful in obtaining the cession of the Holy Land to the Christians by treaties with Sultan Al Kamil. In 1230 Gregory lifted the ban, but soon the real differences over the imperial policy of the unification of Sicily with the empire and the concomitant encirclement of the Papal States by the empire came to the fore again. Frederick was excommunicated again (1239), and from Naples he advanced against Rome (1241). It was Frederick's goal to capture the city and to make it his residence for a universal empire. That would have meant the irreversible end of the universal papacy, which would have sunk to the position of a common imperial episcopate. This, then, was a matter of life and death for the papacy.

Innocent IV (1243–1254) recognized the danger, and the fight which was carried on during the following years was extremely bitter on both sides. At the first council of Lyons, Frederick was once more excommunicated. A flood of polemic pamphlets supported the war. It became even more clearly evident that the fundamental question was one concerning the order of the western world. In order to escape the danger of Staufic encirclement, Innocent transferred lower Italy, Sicily, and Naples as papal fiefs to Charles of Anjou. After Frederick's death (1250) the empire was again in terrible crisis, and in Germany elections and counter-elections disturbed the peace. Conrad IV (1250–1254) fought in Italy for the maintenance of his Staufen heritage and when he died at the age of twenty-six, his half-brother Manfred attempted to retain the crown for Conrad's two-year old son, Conradin. After Manfred's death (1266), the youthful Conradin courageously set out in the fall of 1267 to regain his lower Italian empire. Near Tagliacozzo Conradin was defeated by Charles of Anjou and together with twelve companions was beheaded in Naples on October 29, 1268. The Staufic dynasty had come to a tragic end and the imperial power had been cruelly destroyed.

The papacy also had been most severely damaged; it had won a Pyrrhic victory and could no longer maintain its universal position. It was not able to withstand the special interests of the rising national states, and the dissolution of the western community proceeded rapidly. France now became the strongest power in Europe. The time was not far when the papacy would be relieved of its newly attained predominant position by the national French monarchy and would fall into humiliating dependence on France.

3. The attempt by Pope Boniface VIII (1294–1303) once more to assert the papal claim to leadership in a completely changed world appears like a strange anachronism. An authoritative personality with an exaggerated awareness of power, but without religious depth and a sense of the realities of life, Boniface dreamed of the erection of a universal theocratic western state under papal leadership. He ignored completely the inordinately great damage which the prestige of the papacy had suffered in its struggle for power with the empire. A portentous battle ensued when Boniface tried to enforce a spiritual and political position of preeminence for the papacy against Philipp the Fair of France

(1285–1314), who himself had plans for the establishment of French world domination. With the bull *Unam Sanctam* (1302), which relied on the doctrine of the two swords (according to which Christ in Lk 22, 38 had given to the church both powers, the spiritual and the secular) and declared obedience to the pope a necessity for salvation, Boniface expected to achieve his goal. Philipp answered the papal ban by appealing to a council against Boniface and had the pope arrested by a handful of soldiers in the papal palace at Anagni in September, 1303. Even though the citizens of Anagni liberated the pope after only two days, this violent action revealed the complete lack of power and political insignificance of the papacy. The pope was helpless to defend himself, and he did not long survive the collapse of his dreams of world domination. Only a few weeks later Boniface died in Rome. With the death of Boniface VIII the universal medieval position of preeminence of the papacy irrevocably came to an end.

Fourth Epoch: 1300–1500
The Church in the Time of the Dissolution of Western Unity

35
THE "BABYLONIAN CAPTIVITY" AND THE
GREAT WESTERN SCHISM

From the time of Boniface VIII the papacy came increasingly under the powerful French influence. Because of pressure from the French crown, more and more Frenchmen were included in the college of cardinals with the result that the next popes were also Frenchmen. Clement V (1305–1314) did not think it necessary to go to Rome and he was consecrated at Lyons and remained in France. After some hesitation, Clement took residence at Avignon, where his successors also stayed.

1. The abandonment of the city of Rome and the transfer of the papal curia to Avignon were symptomatic of the general shift in the spiritual and political center of gravity. The "Eternal City" was connected in the consciousness of the European peoples through century-old tradition not only with the idea of the succession to the apostolic see of St. Peter and its attendant primacy, but also with the concept of a western universalism founded by the *Imperium Romanum*. Avignon, on the other hand, was situated completely within the sphere of power of the French monarchy, and even if Avignon was purchased in 1348 by Clement VI and thereby became an independent papal territory, it was nevertheless surrounded on all sides by the French kingdom and thus

hermetically closed off from the world. Thus the freedom from encirclement and the political superiority of the emperor, which the popes of the eleventh and twelfth centuries had defended so successfully in their bitter struggles against the Staufic Sicilian policy, was now voluntarily surrendered to the French kings by French popes. In this way the papacy renounced its freedom of decision and in the eyes of the peoples lost its supra-partisan universal ecclesiastical authority. Often the French popes became irresolute tools in the hands of rising and power-hungry French rulers and the toy of international politics. The concept of a universal church was destroyed, and at the end of the "Babylonian Captivity" (1309–1378) waited the great schism. The exile in Avignon served to introduce an epoch of the most weighty crises for both the papacy and the church.

The first of the Avignon popes, Clement V, already had to give in to the vengeful demand of the king to open proceedings against the late Pope Boniface VIII. Even more ignominious was Clement's acquiescence to the request of Philipp the Fair that he destroy the Templars, who had settled in France after the end of the crusades. The king coveted the wealth and privileges of the Templars which had once been employed in the crusades but which now had no such use. After 1307 Philipp slandered them and intrigued against them; he accused them of heresy and sodomy; and in October 1307 had about two thousand Templars in France arrested and their estates confiscated. By the use of torture Philipp exacted confessions, and fictitious accusations served to indict the knights. The feeble Clement V took no steps to save the order, and after initial hesitation he accommodated the king and made the accusations of heresy his own. Against the will of the majority, Clement dissolved the order of the Knights Templar on March 22, 1312 at the council of Vienne. The pope also looked on without comment as Philipp and the princes appropriated for themselves the possessions of the order although formally they had been made over to the Knights of St. John. Clement further tolerated Philipp's continued rage against the knights of the order; the king had the Grand Master Jacques de Molay burned

229

as a heretic in Paris in 1314 despite his protestations of innocence, and numerous other Templars were burned at the stake as well.

The French influence under John XXII (1316–1334) was fatal for papal policy toward the German Empire. The pope made an enemy of king Louis the Bavarian (1314–1347) by removing him from office in 1323 under a shabby pretext. In the following war, the last great battle between *sacerdotium* and *imperium,* the issue was no longer one of ideas, but of naked political goals. The papacy had become the handmaiden of French interests and was bitterly resented in Germany.

Now the struggle assumed fundamental proportions which were to an unexpected degree fateful for the papacy itself; for the first time the imperial counterattack was directed not against an individual pope but against the papacy as an institution. In 1324 Louis moved against John XXII by appealing to a general council, and all of the opponents of the pope gathered at his court. Among them were two scholars from the University of Paris, Marsilius of Padua and John of Jandun, who had fled from France. In 1326 they presented Louis with a polemic under the title *Defensor pacis,* which questioned the hierarchical order of the church and demanded a democratic structure. The divine origin of papal primacy was denied and the supreme power in the church assigned to the people alone. *Defensor Pacis* asserted that the church was the community of all believers and that the clergy was not superior to the laity. Neither popes nor bishops nor priests had received an independent function from Christ; they officiated merely as agents of the *congregatio fidelium* which was represented by the general council. Thus the highest representative organ of the faithful was the council.

This radical and revolutionary concept of the church transformed the papacy into a mere executive organ of the council, subordinated it to the council, and obliged the pope to be obedient to the council which had the right to demand an account from him at any time and, if necessary, to remove him from office. This theory, which basically placed the general council above the pope, was called conciliarism, and it was to have evil consequences for the future.

The financial conduct which the curia developed in Avignon was no less agitating. This change came about in part because the papal court had to replace the failing revenues from the Papal States, but also because in an age of transition from an agrarian to a money economy, a transition which was taking place because of the flowering of mercantile cities, the papacy was forced to adapt itself to new circumstances. The extent and the methods to which the Avignon papacy resorted in finding new ways to raise taxes and tributes to relieve its constant financial emergencies caused anger and disturbances. The fees for dispensations, privileges, and pardons often reeked of simony. In addition there were fees for provisions, reservations, and expectancies; the payments which had to be made by the archbishops for receiving the pallium; the annates and spoils which had to be paid to the curia from the revenues of the first year and the property of deceased prelates; the crusade tax which was still demanded although there had been no crusades for a long time; the feudal fees and taxes which were raised from the countries which had become fiefs under Innocent III; and many others. The bitter feelings against the curia were increased because these demands were exacted ruthlessly under threats of censure and excommunication. Especially in Germany, where the attitude of the papacy to Louis the Bavarian was considered hostile to Germany, resentment continued to grow. In the course of decades this resentment found reflection in the fifteenth century *Gravamina nationis Germanicae* and had its final effect in the sixteenth century in the form of mass defections at the time of the Reformation.

On the whole the Avignon Exile did the prestige of the papacy immeasurable damage; it affected the confidence which the papacy had enjoyed at the time of Innocent III and contributed to the great crisis which followed it: The great western schism (1378–1415) and the epoch of conciliarism.

2. The schism occurred with the death of Gregory XI (1370 to 1378). Influenced by the grave prophetic announcements of

231

St. Catherine of Siena (d. 1380) and of St. Bridget of Sweden (d. 1373 in Rome) as well as by the chaotic conditions which prevailed in the Papal States, Gregory had returned to Rome in 1377. Although disappointed with what he found, Gregory died in 1378 before he could leave again. According to the law concerning papal elections, the conclave had to be held in Rome for the first time in seventy years. Inasmuch as eleven of the sixteen cardinals were Frenchmen, the Romans were justified in fearing that another Frenchman would be elected pope. To prevent this, the electors in the Vatican were put under severe pressure. On the day before the election, armed bands made their way into the conclave and demanded that a Roman be elected. On the day of the election, the scene was repeated. The cardinals realized that they would have to acquiesce if they wanted to survive the conclave, and as a result on April 8, 1378, they elected not a Roman but an Italian as pope. He was the archbishop of Bari, who called himself Urban VI. The cardinals then fled the city to safety.

They returned for Urban's coronation on April 18, and swore the oath of allegiance to him, but three months later the eleven Frenchmen and the sole Spaniard, Peter of Luna, the future Avignonese Pope Benedict XIII (1394–1417), left Urban's court again and declared that because of the use of force the eclection was annulled. On September 20, 1378, they elected a new pope in Fondi, a Frenchman who took the name of Clement VII (1378–1394) and who made Avignon his residence. The three Italian cardinals (the fourth had died in the meantime), also renounced Urban and supported Clement; the church now had two popes.

Although French nationalistic and egoistic intrigues were a major cause of the double election, the fact of the riotous character of Urban's election also cannot be denied. New research (Přerovsky) has emphasized that the threats of the Romans were so massive and the peril to life so great that there could have been no assertion of genuine electoral freedom. There also cannot be any talk of a free subsequent assent by the cardinals, because it also has been shown that the oaths given the pope during his elevation were also gained by force, this time originating with Urban (K. A. Fink). If, then, all electors of Urban VI described this election as invalid because it occurred "under grave fear and coercion", their assertion cannot be flatly denied. Just as under such circumstances the validity of Urban's election cannot be proven, conversely the invalidity of Clement's election cannot simply be maintained either. In addition, Urban VI after his inauguration showed himself so overbearing, cruel, and fanatical that not only the cardinals but also his curial officials and supporters were of the opinion that his sudden elevation had left him mentally deranged. He was, indeed, guilty of acts which according to contemporary scholars certainly support a suspicion of mental disturbance. According to canon law the election of a mentally deranged person is invalid.

The confusion over the double election was so great and so widespread that even its contemporaries were bewildered. For Urban VI was not disturbed to the extent that it was readily obvious, and outsiders were even less able to judge the extent to which pressure had been exerted on the cardinals during the election. Because the striving for power among the cardinals was so well known, it was easy to suspect that they simply wanted to rid themselves later of an inconvenient pope. To this day this question of papal legitimacy is unsolved and will forever remain so. Saints were the supporters on both sides. St. Catherine of Siena defended Urban's sole legitimacy just as emphatically as the incorruptible preacher of penance St. Vincent Ferrer stood up for the exclusive validity of Clement's election. Additionally, both popes were so deeply convinced of their own legitimacy and the illegality of the other that they regarded it as a principle of conscience to defend the papacy with all means and to combat their opponent. To voluntarily resign from the papal office in order to free the way of the church to unity, which subsequently was suggested to them frequently, they rejected with *Non possumus;* given their conviction of conscience, such a step had to appear to them as treason to the legitimacy and validity of the

233

apostolic succession whose pure state they were obligated by God to preserve.

This explains the duration and the intractability of the schism which lasted for forty years and appeared well-nigh insurmountable. Urban VI as well as Clement VII established courts and had successors after their deaths. The Roman line consisted of: Urban VI (1378–1389), Boniface IX (1389–1404), Innocent VII (1404–1406), and Gregory XII (1406–1415); the Avignon line of: Clement VII (1378–1394) and Benedict XIII (1394–1417). The consequences of the schism were devastating; all Christianity was split into opposing obediences, and, as each pope excommunicated the followers of the other, no one could remain unaffected. De facto all of Christianity was under the ban. The influence of the schism extended to all countries, dioceses, and parishes and caused discord and conflict, as both popes appointed their own candidates and all offices and emoluments were filled doubly. The result was the most difficult constitutional crisis which the church has ever experienced. In 1394, the University of Paris finally suggested three alternatives for overcoming the schism: the *via cessionis* (voluntary resignation), the *via compromissi* (submission of the popes to arbitration), and the *via concilii* (decision by a general council).

36
The Council of Constance and Conciliarism

1. Antecedents: After it had been attempted in vain for thirty years to restore unity by means of voluntary resignation or compromise, the realization was reached that only a general council could solve the disputed questions. Although canon law had long provided for such an emergency, the principle that no one might judge the pope *(prima Sedes a nemine iudicetur)* and that he was only responsible to God had increasingly received recognition since the early Middle Ages. This concept had developed chiefly to protect the pope against deposition by emperors (Sutri, 1046),

but also as protection against the despotism of the Roman noble families in the *saeculum obscurum*. The development which primacy underwent during the pontificates of Gregory VII (*Dictatus Papae,* 1075) and those from Innocent III to Boniface VIII, resulted in the position of the pope becoming less and less assailable. On the other hand, however, there was an awareness that the possibility existed that even a pope as a private person could fall into heresy or mental illness, and for this purpose a heresy clause was added to the law: If a pope fell into heresy, it was concluded, there would have to be a board which could note the fact and draw the proper consequences; it was impossible that a heretic could be a legitimate pope; if, therefore, heresy were confirmed in a pope, then he simply was no longer pope and would have to be removed from the papal throne. This determination had to be made by a general council, and it was incumbent on the cardinals and also on the emperor as the protector of the Roman Church to convoke and conduct such a council.

Even strictly papally inclined canonists such as the papalists at the court of Boniface VIII, Aegidius Romanus (d. 1316), who decisively participated in the formulation of the bull *Unam Sanctam,* Augustinus Triumphus (d. 1328), and Alvarus Pelagius (d. 1349) agreed with this maxim; it was common property. Of course, in reality one could not imagine a council without a pope. In contrast to the eight general councils of the first millenium, all of which had been convoked in the East by Byzantine emperors, a new type of western council had developed in the Middle Ages. Gregory VII in the sixteenth proposition of his *Dictatus Papae* had reserved exclusively to the pope the right to call an ecumenical council. The First Lateran Council had been assembled in 1123 by Calixtus II; as an "ecumenical" council it served the purpose of extending the validity of the concordat of Worms to the whole church. The Second Lateran Council was used by Innocent II in 1139 to end the schism of Anacletus. The Third Lateran Council was called by Alexander III in 1179. The Fourth Lateran Council was conducted in 1215 by the great Innocent III and was of far-reaching significance for the reform of the church.

235

The next general council was assembled by Innocent IV in Lyons in 1245 and deposed Emperor Frederick II. At the second council of Lyons in 1274 Gregory X conducted negotiations for a crusade and regarding a union with the eastern church. This council also passed the famous rules for conclaves, which provided that the cardinals were to congregate ten days after the death of a pope at the place of death in strict privacy (conclave) for the election of a successor and should be forced to a quick conclusion of the election through increasing reductions of daily food rations. The next general council took place in 1311 in Vienne under the influence of the French monarchy and already evinced the weaknesses of the Avignon papacy (trial of the Templars). Even there, however, the pope was the organizer, and a council without a pope seemed to be completely unthinkable.

Therefore it is understandable that there was pronounced hesitation in proceeding against the two popes by way of a council. Finally thirteen cardinals of both obediences, and against the will of their masters, agreed to call a general council at Pisa in March, 1409. Even though the risk was great, more than 100 bishops assembled and another 100 sent their delegates with powers of proxy; additionally there appeared plenipotentiaries of more than 200 abbots, cathedral chapters, and universities. Thus the assembly found courage to try the two popes, pronounce them enemies of church unity, i.e. heretics, and declare them deposed. The members then chose a new pope, who called himself Alexander V. Alexander died in the following year, and the notorious cardinal Cossa, who took the name of John XXIII, became his successor.

It cannot be contested that according to the legal understanding of the time the council of Pisa and its actions were legally valid, and Alexander and his successor were therefore as legitimate as the other two popes. Unfortunately, since the Roman Pope Gregory XII and his Avignon counterpart Pope Benedict XIII refused to be replaced, there were now three popes, each of whom in equal measure could be viewed as legitimate or illegitimate.

Inasmuch as Gregory and Benedict had been deposed according to the rules of canon law, Alexander had the best prospects of maintaining his position; indeed, while the obediences of the first two were reduced, Alexander and then John had the greatest following in Christendom.

2. Constance, the council of unity. The German king Sigismund (1410–1437) therefore favored the Pisan Pope John XXIII, when he conceived a plan to heal the triple split in Christendom by calling a new council. It was Sigismund who wrung from John the agreement for the convocation of a general council at Constance in November 1414. Sigismund was and remained the very life and soul of the council.

John XXIII appeared in Constance together with numerous Italian prelates and opened the council on November 5, 1414. He hoped to be confirmed by the council as the sole legitimate pope, but this was not to be. Under the influence of the leading cardinals d'Ailly (d. 1420), Fillastre, Zabarella, and the chancellor of the University of Paris, Gerson (d. 1429), the council reached the conviction that unity could only be achieved if all three popes were forced to resign. In order to break the Italian majority, the French, Germans, and English forced the procedure of voting according to "nations", not according to number; each of the four nations should have only one vote during the general voting, with the fifth vote cast by the college of cardinals. This method succeeded in overcoming the superior strength of John and the Italians.

When he saw his chances disappear and realized that because of his former transgressions he would be put on trial, John secretly fled Constance during the night of March 20/21, 1415. From Schaffhausen he then attacked the council with accusations and threats. He had hoped to cause the dissolution of the council by his departure, and he almost succeeded. Everyone was preparing to leave when king Sigismund intervened and proclaimed that the council would continue its work even without the pope. On March 23, John Gerson made his famous speech to the council in which he established the reason why the pope had no right to dissolve the council and why he was bound by its decisions. The first session without the pope took place on March 26. Cardinal Zabarella submitted the motion that the council acknowledge that it had been duly summoned and that it would not disperse until it had fulfilled its task of removing the schism, clarifying the questions of faith which had been raised by John Hus, and reforming the church in both "head and members".

Because John continued to do everything in his power to disturb the council and to cause its dissolution, the council on April 6, 1415, passed the famous decree *Haec Sancta* in which it solemnly declared that it regarded itself as duly summoned, acting in the Holy Spirit, representing the whole church militant, and receiving its authority directly from God; therefore, every Christian, even the pope, had to be obedient to the council "in what it decided with respect to the faith, the overcoming of the schism, and a general reform in head and members."

The question has been much discussed whether this decree asserted a fundamental subordination of the pope to the council in the sense of Marsilius of Padua, i.e. whether it was heretical, or not. One can indeed put this construction upon it, but it can also very well be understood within the context of traditional canon law (heresy clause). Because the decree was ambivalent, the very problem was debated at the council. Since the three popes had tried the patience of their contemporaries greatly, particularly John XXIII through his troublesome interference, it is understandable that some participants were open to radical ideas. Their number, however, was demonstrably small. The overwhelming majority wanted the decree to be understood conservatively and moreover saw in the measure no decision of faith but simply a requisite protection of the church against similar cases of schism in the future. A definition of the fundamental superiority of a council over the papacy, such as Marsilius of Padua had advocated, was not considered. The decree, therefore, is certainly not to be evaluated as a dogmatic definition of faith.

Weeks of terrible excitement and passionate discussion followed the flight of the pope. What further action was to be taken against John? John was attempting to escape across the Rhine into Burgundy, from there to continue his attacks on the council, when Sigismund suddenly had him arrested. He was tried, and on May 29, 1415, he was deposed. On July 4, 1415, the Roman Pope Gregory XII announced his voluntary resignation. This nonagenarian, who remained unshaken in his conviction that he was the only legitimate pope, had previously stipulated the right to convoke the council once more in his own name. His request was granted, even though, or precisely because, no one attributed any importance to the act. The most difficult problem was how to deal with the obstinate Pope Benedict XIII. Sigismund negotiated with him personally at Perpignan without any result. At least, however, Sigismund succeeded in detaching from him most of Benedict's followers, principally Spaniards, who now also attended the council and constituted the fifth nation. Proceedings against Benedict were initiated in the council and ended with his deposition on July 26, 1417.

3. In the weeks after the flight of John XXIII, in April, May, and June of 1415, the council dealt with the issue of Hus. The events took an unhappy course and left the council with a burden which has lasted to this day. One can judge the problem justly only if one sees it against the background of the tense times and the passionate excitement which affected everything.

John Hus, born in 1370 in Husinec (southern Bohemia), studied in Prague and was ordained as a priest there in 1400. During his studies, Hus became acquainted with the ideas of the Englishman John Wyclif (ca. 1320–1384), who since 1374 had directed sharp attacks against the financial methods of the Avignon papacy, the wealth of the church of prelates, and the hierarchy, while at the same time contrasting it with a church of the predestined which was to renounce property and live in apostolic poverty. In the true church of Christ, Wyclif declared, only those had a place who, as the elect, lived in a state of grace; most of all, no mortal sinner could have a leading position in Christian society, be it church or state. A pope, bishop, or prelate who was a mortal sinner no longer had any authority, just as the rulers in a Christian state lost their governing authority if they were in a state of grave sin. Hus also denied the church as a sacramental community of redemption in Christ.

While preaching at the Chapel of Bethlehem in Prague after 1402, Hus adopted Wyclif's tenets and found a strong response among his Czech listeners. (More recent studies [De Vooght, Spinka] have shown the influence of Wyclif to have been doubtful.) National sentiments combined with a criticism of the ruling clergy in Bohemia, which was primarily German. This anti-German sentiment, which extended to all of Bohemia, became fused so strongly with the ecclesiastical and religious tendencies, which were determined by Wyclif's ideas, that Wyclifism appeared as a native nationalistic Czech matter. When by orders of Pope Alexander V the archbishop of Prague, a German, took steps against the dissemination of Wyclif's heresies in his diocese, it was viewed almost as political interference. Hus hotly opposed the episcopal ordinance and tried to defend the orthodoxy of Wyclif. When he was forbidden to preach, he appealed to Pope John XXIII, but the archbishop had also turned to John. Hus was cited to appear in Rome, but he did not comply and was then excommunicated by the pope. The Bohemian king Wenzel, however, protected him. John XXIII, who needed money for a war against Ladislaus of Naples, had a crusade indulgence preached in Bohemia in May 1412, and the disgraceful trade in indulgences heightened the tension. Soon all of Bohemia became agitated.

In order to settle the matter, King Sigismund insisted that Hus be dealt with at the council of Constance and offered him safe conduct. Hus agreed and arrived in Constance on November 3, 1414. The pope lifted the ban from Hus and he could then move around freely. On November 28, the first hearing was held and following it Hus was imprisoned, counter to the imperial guarantee upon the demand of the cardinals. On December 6, Hus was taken to the prison of the Dominican monastery, and although Sigismund protested vehemently, Hus remained incarcerated there. In the first months of 1415 the proceedings

240

against him receded into the background because of the over-shadowing question of unity; then, suddenly, they took an unexpected turn. In the wake of the events after John's flight from Constance and on the new basis which the decree *Haec Sancta* had created, the council actively concerned itself with the question of Hus. After all, here was an opportunity to prove independence in matters of faith.

The trial which followed can be comprehended only with difficulty today. The leadership of the council had fallen completely into the hands of the cardinals d'Ailly, Fillastre, Zabarella, and Gerson, the chancellor of the University of Paris, men who were among the outstanding personalities of the council and whose intellectual and moral qualities were not open to doubt; in addition, they were not even Germans but Frenchmen, so that national sentiments can not have been involved. Furthermore, these members were not "papalists" but moderate "conciliarists", as well as confirmed opponents of John XXIII and the other popes of the schism. And yet, objective investigation must accuse them of partisan bias and they must bear the blame for the conduct of the trial (P. de Vooght). Hus hotly defended himself against the accusation of being a heretic. He was confronted with thirty heretical propositions from his writings, and although he did not deny having written them, he disputed their heretical meaning and attempted to interpret them according to orthodoxy. When he therefore also refused to recant them, Hus was asked to recant at least their wrong meaning. He retorted that he could not recant what he had never taught or ever had had in his mind. The endless discussions which resulted were unprofitable and severely tried the patience of the judges. If the passionate excitement of those days and the tension of the atmosphere is considered, one can not be less willing to grant extenuating circumstances to the judges than to understand the defendant. Attempts were not lacking to provide ways for reconciliation and to enable Hus to "recant", but he obstinately rejected every such suggestion.

After the cardinals d'Ailly and Zabarella, at the express wish

241

of King Sigismund, had visited Hus in prison on July 5 and had vainly tried to persuade him to recant, final sentence was pronounced on July 6, 1415 before the whole council in the cathedral of Constance. Because Hus had "dogmatized, defended and preached" the heresies of Wyclif in his writings, he was sentenced to death. That very same day he was consigned to death by fire at the place of execution. When Hus was already standing on the pyre, Sigismund once more offered him mercy in return for recantation. Hus refused and died forgiving his enemies, invoking Jesus Christ, and reciting the confession of faith.

Guilt, tragedy, and failure — his own as well as that of others — are interwoven with his fate. The council, however, easily moved on to other business. The question of Hus was for most of the participants only a peripheral one, and they took little notice of it. Yet history avenged Hus terribly, and the fierce Hussite Wars (1420–1431) brought fear and terror to Bohemia and Germany for a long time.

4. Before the council could consider the election of a new pope, it was necessary to decide the question of reform. All were agreed on the necessity of reform in head and members, but should reform be considered before or after the election of the new pontiff? In the decree *Haec Sancta* the council had expressly reserved to itself the right of reform. Was the decree limited to this exceptional case or was it intended fundamentally to subordinate the pope to the council? The reform question was regarded by the strict "conciliarists" as a test case. They wanted to tie the pope to the council forever, by subordinating him to the reform decrees passed by the council. At regular intervals in the future general councils were to be held which could pass reform decrees on their own authority to which the popes would be bound. Especially the Germans and the English took this view, because meanwhile in their countries the conciliaristic ideas had made the most progress. This was not true, however, with regard to the other nations, and as soon as the basic issue of the debate became pronounced, they resisted most vehemently. As a compromise, five decrees which previously had been debated

were passed on October 9, 1417. Among them was the decree *Frequens,* which provided for regular councils every ten years. Otherwise the council emphasized most clearly that reforms as part of the normal administration of the church were reserved to the pope and that therefore a pope would have to be elected before further reforms could be discussed at the council. When the English finally agreed to this fundamental precept, the Germans had to give in as well, and the papal election could then take place.

5. The man who was acceptable to all participants and could count therefore on general recognition, was to be selected according to a special procedure. In addition to the twenty-six cardinals, six representatives from each of the five nations were included in the conclave which met on November 8, 1417, a total of fifty-six electors altogether. The Constance warehouse had been specially prepared for the purpose of the election. That an agreement was reached "in the conclave on a wave of religious exaltation" (Fink) after only three days, despite the complex electoral procedure, and while a procession passed outside, appeared to contemporaries as a miracle of the Holy Spirit. On November 11, 1417, Cardinal Odo Colonna was elected. He called himself Martin V, after the patron saint of that day.

Indescribable joy reigned not only at the council but in all of the West; the forty-year old schism had been bridged and the unity of the body of Christ had been restored. The church once again had a sovereign who was duly elected and acknowledged by all. Perhaps we in the twentieth century can understand this joy better than people in former ages, since we also long for this unity. We know, after all, that a split in Christendom is the worst that could happen to it.

6. After the papal election, the leadership of the council soon passed to the new pope. Martin V immediately assumed the direction of all matters, including reform, and thereby effectively overcame the grave crisis of the papacy which easily could have become a constitutional one. On April 22, 1418, he concluded the council. The much debated question whether and to what extent he confirmed the decrees *Haec Sancta* and *Frequens* in the

243

conciliarist sense and thereby raised them to decrees of faith, must without a doubt be answered negatively. The initial doubt stemmed from the fact that the content and the meaning of these two decrees was ambivalent; they could be understood in a moderate, orthodox sense or in a radical, heretical and conciliaristic one. Among the participants at the council there was only a small minority that was actually conciliarist. Incontestably, the overwhelming majority understood the decrees as being conservative and moderate, as did Martin V. The minority did not admit defeat, however, and conciliarist ideas continued strongly after the council and soon were to assume dangerous proportions again.

Eugene IV (1431–1447) called the seventeenth general council for July 23, 1431 at Basle. Dissension arose between him and the council members, who in keeping with conciliarist theories began to regard themselves as superior to the pope. The council demanded an account from the pope and established itself as the last resort in the legal and administrative concerns of the church. Finally the council curtailed the papal authority and claimed the rights of the executive for itself. When Eugene, in an attempt to end the problem, transferred the council from Basle to Ferrara in 1437, a small group of radical conciliarists remained in Basle in protest (until 1449). The radicals proclaimed the supremacy of the council over the pope as doctrine of faith, deposed Eugene, and elected a new pope by the name of Felix V. Once again a schism had occurred, but this one was to be the last in church history. The position of Eugene IV had been so strengthened in the meantime that the council of Basle (schismatic since 1437) and its anti-pope could not last for long; in 1449 Felix V gave up his claim and resigned. His resignation was the end of radical conciliarism in the church.

But the effects of conciliarism were to be felt for a long time, and fear of its revival governed the popes from this time on. Appeals to councils had a shocking effect upon them, and at the outbreak of the Reformation in the sixteenth century this fear was responsible for the delay in convoking a general council to eliminate grievances and undertake the urgently demanded reforms. Had the council of Trent met in 1525 rather than in 1545, the history of the Reformation very likely would have taken an entirely different course. The great western schism and conciliarism served in strong measure to prepare the schism of the sixteenth century.

37

THE RENAISSANCE PAPACY:
ALEXANDER VI AND SAVONAROLA

The fifteenth century had to solve two great tasks: internal reform and the support of the Greek Church in its struggle for existence against Islam. It failed in both.

The seventeenth general council was transferred from Basle (1431–1437) to Ferrara (1438) and finally to Florence (1439–1442). Its main task was reunion with the eastern church. The Greek Emperor John VIII Paleologus (1425–1448) himself arrived in Ferrara in March 1438 with a delegation of seven hundred; among them the patriarch of Constantinople and the metropolitan Bessarion of Nicaea. The pope also attended. Behind the wish of the Greeks for reunion with the western church was the burning desire to receive help against the irresistibly advancing Turks. Only a mighty crusade could save Byzantium from falling, and after long and difficult discussions an agreement was finally reached; the Greeks and the pope signed the decree of union *Laetentur Coeli* (July 6, 1439). An agreement was reached even on the primacy of the Roman Church and the *filioque*, but after the return of the emperor to the East it was discovered that his concessions to the western church found little sympathy at home. When the expected military help was not forthcoming either, union could not be maintained.

The West was no longer a unit. The crusade was not conducted, because the national states were motivated by selfish interests, and Emperor Constantine XI (1448–1453) sent another call for help to Rome in vain. The ring of Turks closed more tightly

245

around Constantinople, and on May 29, 1453, after having defended itself courageously, the city fell into the hands of the Turks. Constantine himself died in the final battle. The terrible blood-bath perpetrated by the conquerors and the enslavement of many thousands of citizens stirred the West, but now it was too late. In 1459 the heritage of Constantinople was assumed by Moscow, which soon was termed the "Third Rome", and union between eastern and western churches was formally retracted in 1472.

1. The Renaissance popes which succeeded the serious and noble Eugene IV (1431–1447) repeatedly tried to unite Europe once again in defense against the Turks who now threatened all of the West from the Balkans. Their attempts were without success and received little credence because the same papacy had lost sight of its universal role and in its concern for the Papal States had sunk to the level of narrow territorial politics. Men such as Innocent VIII and Alexander VI thought of the *Patrimonium Petri* merely as their private domain which, if possible, they wanted to retain as the possession of their own family. Nepotism and the family politics of the popes played a sinister role until long after the Reformation. Paul III (1534–1549) and even the fanatical reform pope Paul IV (1555–1559) operated under an unlucky star and their anti-imperial Papal State policy continued to abet the Reformation.

Above all it was the particularism of the Renaissance popes which kept them from devoting themselves in time and intensely enough to their actual and universal duty of church reform. Their concern for the Papal States and their striving to make Rome into a center of humanism and art was less an expression of the general "cultural creative force of the church" than petty princely thirst for glory and, therefore, treason to the universal church. One may admire in Rome the great cultural achievements of the Renaissance papacy; yet measured against the divine mission of the church they represent no equivalent to its failure in other respects. This is not due in the first instance so much to the personal moral failure of a few — not all — popes of the period as to a fundamental attitude which they all shared toward the religious and universal ecclesiastical functions of their high office. The actual responsibility falls in equal measure on the college of cardinals which elected the popes and on the popes who appointed the cardinals.

The Renaissance papacy began with the elevation of Nicholas V (1447–1455). Nicholas was personally irreproachable, a noble and educated humanist, and the founder of the Vatican Library. He also tried ardently to establish a defensive front against the Turks. Calixtus III (1455–1458) also used all his strength for a crusade against the infidels. The limitless affection of the seventy-seven year old man for his family, the Spanish Borgia, motivated him to appoint two nephews to the college of cardinals, among them the morally depraved Roderigo Borgia, the future Alexander VI. Pope Pius II (1458–1464), Aeneas Sylvius Piccolomini, was one of the most famous humanists of his age. Until the age of forty he led a lax life according to the way of humanists as secretary at the court of Emperor Frederick III, but then he repented, became a priest, then bishop of Trent, and finally pope. When during his attempts at reform his own past was held up to him, he openly acknowledged his former errors in a bull of "retraction" (1463) and requested: *Aeneam rejicite, Pium recipite.* The threat of the Turks did not permit Pius to bring his reform plans to fruition. His pontificate as well as that of Paul II (1464–1471) were free of nepotism, but Sixtus IV (1471–1484), who, as a former general of the Franciscans, covered his order with privileges *(Mare magnum)*, introduced the system of nepotism into the ecclesiastical government where it became firmly ensconced until the seventeenth and eighteenth centuries. "Like a suppurating cancer" (Schwaiger) nepotism can be traced through papal history from the Middle Ages to the modern age. Despite a fundamental prohibition by Innocent XII in 1692 it continued, in other forms, until the most recent past (Pius XII). It reached its peak under the Renaissance popes who soon gave territories of the Papal States as fiefs to their sons and nephews and who even attempted to separate them from the Papal States as independent principalities (Alexander VI, Paul III). The beginning was made by Sixtus IV who not only included two nephews in the college of cardinals, the ostentatious and worldly Giuliano della Rovere, the future Pope Julius II, and the morally unprincipled Franciscan Peter Riario (d. 1474), but also invested another nephew, Girolamo Riario, with the principality of Imola. By means of this last act, the pope permitted his nephew, an ambitious, powerhungry and unscrupulous man, to involve him in dangerous and morally objectionable political quarrels (Pazzi conspiracy against the Medici in Florence in 1478, wars with Florence, Naples, and Venice). Art history, however, remembers him as the builder of the Sistine Chapel in the Vatican. Innocent VIII (1484–1492) was elected through bribery by a totally worldly college of cardinals. His pontificate is characterized by corruption in the curial administration, lack of interest in church reform, and concern for his two illegitimate children who were born before he became a priest. He celebrated the marriage of his son Franceschetto to a daughter of Lorenzo de Medici with great publicity in the Vatican. He appointed the thirteen-year old son of Lorenzo, Giovanni de Medici, to the college of cardinals, and Giovanni was the future Pope Leo X (1513–1521) who in 1517 disposed of Luther's theses as "a monkish quarrel" and who wanted to "enjoy the papacy" with which "God had provided him".

Alexander VI (1492–1503) represented the absolute nadir of the papacy. Elected by a worldly college of cardinals as a result of shameless simoniacal machinations, he abused his papal office with such impudence that even contemporaries speculated that he was not a Christian at all but a disguised Marrano. Even though some modern investigators judge his administrative activity more favorably today, there remains his immoral and unscrupulous life during which he subordinated everything to his licentious nepotism and political goals. He used his position to provide principalities for his illegitimate children, four of whom resulted from adulterous relations with Vannozza de Cataneis, a member of a noble Roman family. First, Pedro Luis Borgia (1458–1488), the oldest, became duke of Gandia as early as 1485; then, when he died, his brother Juan Borgia, born in 1474, became his successor in Gandia; and finally Juan was assassinated (by Cesare?) in Rome in 1497 (his grandson was St. Francis Borgia, 1510–1572, a general of the Jesuits). The notorious Cesare Borgia (1475–1507) became protonotary at age seven, bishop of Pamplona at age sixteen, archbishop of Valencia at age seventeen, and cardinal (1493) at age eighteen. Cesare was never ordained as either priest or bishop, and received ordination merely as a subdeacon from which he had himself exempted in 1498 when he resigned his cardinalate. Morally uninhibited and driven by political ambition, Cesare tried to amass his own empire in central Italy through force, cunning, and trickery in the fashion of the condottieri. The pope, who after 1498 was totally under Cesare's influence, became an accessory to these designs. Lucrezia Borgia (1480–1519), who "wrongly has become the embodiment of the moral degeneracy of the Renaissance" (H. Rahner), was the victim of the marriage policy of her father; after two unhappy marriages she married Alfons d'Este of Ferrara in 1501 and lived with him happily, charitably, and piously as a member of the Third Order of St. Francis until her death. Jofre Borgia (1481 to 1533), the youngest son of Alexander VI, became prince of Squillace through his marriage to an illegitimate daughter of king Alfons II of Naples.

2. Alexander's clash with Savonarola reveals his own failings and at the same time shows that the Holy Church can be holy even when the chair of St. Peter is occupied by an unholy pope. The complete failure of the popes awakened the self-reform of the members. It must always remain the particular duty of monasticism to lead the church to repentance, contemplation, and Christian aloofness from the world. In times of extreme secularization the monk is the visible expression of disagreement. He is charged with giving the warning, "whether convenient or inconvenient", even if he must sacrifice his life in the process.

As a Dominican, Girolamo Savonarola (1452–1498) placed his life into the service of penance and reform. Owing to his powerful preaching he succeeded after 1490 in reforming Florence. As prior of San Marco he founded a reform congregation within his own order. Untiringly he applied the ideal of reform to himself and to others, and his criticism stopped short neither of the court of the Medici nor of Alexander VI. After the overthrow of the Medici in 1494, he ruled the city and without delay effected a complete moral reversal. He believed that he knew through an inner voice that the approaching French king Charles VIII had been chosen to lead humanity to repentance. This peculiar combination of the religious with the political was fatal for him, because his prophesies disturbed Alexander's political plans and caused him to attempt to rid himself of the troublesome friar. Savonarola was forbidden to preach, cited to Rome (1495), and excommunicated in 1497. At first Savonarola hesitated; then it came to him that Alexander, who had achieved the papacy through simony, could not possibly be the true pope. Just as he was about to ask the emperor and the kings to call a general council to determine Alexander's illegality, the pope struck. Alexander threatened Florence with the inderdict unless the city silenced the Dominican immediately. Savonarola's opponents gained the upper hand, stormed San Marco (April 8, 1498), and put the prior, together with two brethren, on trial. The dungeon, torture, interrogations without pause, lying prosecutors, and falsified minutes led to judicial murder. As "heretic, schismatic, and scorner of the Holy See", Savonarola was condemned to death. His last notes, written in his cell, show him as a saint. With hands tied and body flayed, he anxiously questioned himself again and again whether he had acted correctly. There is a holy right of opposition in the church; Savonarola used it against a pope who, according to his conviction, was not a true pope. He never attacked the church or Christianity, on the contrary, he sacrificed his life for them. By always keeping the person and the office separate, the friar of Florence essentially differed from the friar of Wittenberg. He recognized that the church was suffering before his eyes from the wretched person of Alexander, and to save it he and two brethren died on May 23, 1498, on the pyre which his enemies and Alexander VI had prepared for him. Before, he devoutly confessed and communicated.

Savonarola was a saint, not a heretic, and the Dominicans have been pressing for his beatification since 1955.

3. Unfortunately, Alexander VI did not change his life. He was followed for a short interlude of twenty-three days by Pius III (1503), then by Julius II (1503–1513), the nephew of Sixtus IV. Again simony, politics, and force ruled during his pontificate. Even though Julius was free of nepotism and moral transgressions, he devoted his entire term of office to enlarging Rome and the Papal States, beautifying them, and winning glory for himself. He commissioned Michelangelo to design his tomb and instructed him to personify him as the powerful figure of Moses. Julius conducted war without interruption, and Luther in 1520 called him a blood-sucker. Bramante designed for Julius the reconstruction of St. Peter's (1506), Michelangelo painted for him the ceiling of the Sistine Chapel, and Raffael painted the frescoes in the apartments of state in the Vatican at his commission. The peak of Renaissance art had been reached, but the Reformation was imminent also.

THIRD ERA
THE CHURCH IN THE MODERN AGE

The question of periodization entails the utmost difficulty with regard to the transition from the Middle Ages to the Modern Age. There are many new elements to be found, but as criteria none are so characteristic and encompassing that they embody a new era adequately and succinctly. Transition, therefore, may be placed at different times, according to the aspect which one considers. If the breakthrough of "modern" individual religiosity is considered to be decisive, then one has to begin as early as the fourteenth century. If the social structure becomes the yardstick, one must regard the French Revolution as the turning point, for only then was the feudal order of the medieval church overcome.

If we use the earlier division, then we are of the opinion that the Reformation was indeed such a profound caesura in the history of the church that the modern age can be said to have begun at that time. Not only was the Reformation the "greatest catastrophe which befell the church during its whole history to this day" (Lortz), but it also influenced all of modern times so decisively that nothing else is of the same importance. The Reformation not only shattered the unity and the common foundation of faith, it also divided religious thought into denominational thought. Since that time, Christian thought has no longer been unified, but is separated into Catholic, Lutheran, Reformed, and sectarian thinking. It seems to be the task of our time to rediscover the common roots; at least we sense that the split must not endure and that once again Christians must think "ecumenically", or in a "catholic" (not in the denominational sense) manner.

The modern age is divided into the following segments:
1st Epoch: Reformation and Catholic Reform (1500–1700)
2nd Epoch: From the French Revolution to the First World War
(1789–1918)
3rd Epoch: The Recent Past (from 1918 to the present).

First Epoch: 1500–1700
Reformation and Catholic Reform

38
THE BACKGROUND OF THE REFORMATION

The coming of the Reformation is a many-layered problem which cannot be reduced to the equation: *because* there were so many grievances in the medieval church, the Reformation *had* to occur. Indeed, *reform had* to come, but not *Reformation!* Instead of a movement *against* the church, a reform movement *in* the church could and should have developed and effected an internal recovery. That this did not happen was not the product of logical necessity but the result of the incidental occurrence of many isolated facts which in their totality we can designate as causal prerequisites in the extended sense.

Modern Reformation scholarship has corrected the previous black-white portrayal of this period and adjusted the former frequently distorted picture of the absolute corruption of the late medieval church. The result has not been a softening of the outlines but a better understanding of the relationships. It is still considered true that the church was never more in need of reform than at that time; but the church had not become so degenerate and rotten that it was no longer worthy of reform and therefore simply had to become extinct. A proportionate picture would be:

1. Grievances had become widespread, and excesses in the religious life of the period were reflected in a frequently unhealthy

veneration of saints and relics, disorganized pilgrimages, and in multiple other peripheral forms of worship. Extreme credulity, a mania for miracles, superstition, fear of hell and devils, and a pathological obsession with witchcraft resulted in a severe distortion of piety. Reform was also needed in the ecclesiastical administration, which frequently was calcified in formalities and seemed to see its justification for existence in a wholly materialistic system of taxes and fees. The misuse of excommunication for non-spiritual purposes, simony connected with the awarding of benefices, and nepotism existed not only in Rome but also in the episcopal and archdeaconal administrations of the dioceses. Grave moral grievances and transgressions were committed by both clerics and laymen, and numerous complaints about the immoral life of priests, monks, and nuns have come down to us. The worst aspect of all was that whole estates and communities and whole institutions such as convents were infected.

This last consideration was precisely the most alarming. There has always been and there will always be individual human failing, but here the evil seemed to have been truly institutionalized. The papacy was defect and seemed unable to escape from its *circulus vitiosus:* bad cardinals elected inferior popes and inferior popes appointed bad cardinals! Additionally, the papacy was so involved with its secular concern for the Papal States that a pope who might have been willing to alter the course was often the victim of circumstances. The well-meaning Adrian VI (1522 to 1523) earnestly attempted reform and simply foundered in the surrounding sea of secularism.

The episcopate also was so enmeshed in its feudal ties that it was incapable of freeing itself. The cathedral chapters were staffed by the egoistic aristocracy; the chapter members then selected the bishop from their midst, who in turn also belonged to the nobility and was obligated to it. To breach the monopoly of the nobility in the church was impossible; it had become sacrosanct. This monopoly also entailed political ties; Geneva, for instance, became Protestant because its bishop belonged to the dynasty of the princes of Savoy. Political opposition, therefore, necessarily also involved the ecclesiastical as well. Everywhere such a correlation could be noticed, in cities, episcopacies, and countries. The higher clergy of the cathedral and collegiate chapters was also subject to similar conditions; it became harnessed to the dynastic policies of the neighbouring noble families, and the collegiate foundations degenerated into welfare institutions for the nobility. The life of the chapters was governed almost entirely by the spirit of the nobility and was only accidentally religiously oriented.

The lower clergy was held in bondage to poverty and misery. The ill-paid vicars, beneficed clergymen, and altar prebendaries became "proletarians" who most often lived from hand to mouth. If the situation is taken as a whole, the personal failure of individuals seems to have been more a result of the weakened structure of society at this time than a matter of individual responsibility.

2. Positive aspects, however, also existed. It would be wrong to overlook the deeply religious trend of the time which expressed itself in the countless gifts which were made to the church, the active church construction, the impressive religious art, and the founding of countless new brotherhoods and charitable institutions such as hospitals, alms-houses, and old-age homes. All these developments occurred in closest contact with the church, and they do not indicate that there existed a widespread or general hostility to the church. Nowhere in the fifteenth century is mass defection from the church evident. Even the Hussites had become less active when concessions were made to the Bohemians in the compacts of Prague in 1433, and the peace of Kuttenberg (1485) removed much of their residual bitterness. In fact, an increased religiosity can be noted in the later Middle Ages, a piety which shows itself most clearly in the active participation in the ecclesiastical feast days, which became great public holidays (feasts of patron saints and village feasts). Religious services and sermons were well attended, especially when great preachers such as Geiler von Kaysersberg (d. 1510) or Paul Wann (d. 1489) appeared.

Also the church itself was by no means inactive, and its "concern for the religious education of the people was considerable"

(Lortz). Luther's global accusation that the religious value of ecclesiastical life and the Catholic piety of the people were merely "justification through works" is certainly unjust. It should not be forgotten that according to background and education Luther himself was a product of this faithful class of the people. One will not be able to understand his penetrating search for a gracious God if one does not see him as a child of his time. A concern with eternal salvation deeply excited the people; consciousness of sin and striving for absolution were so general and genuine that it can be easily asserted that there probably was no age more religious than this one. St. Clement Maria Hofbauer (d. 1820) was correct when he said: "The Reformation happened because the Germans had a need to be pious."

If one were really in need of proof for the religious basis of the age, one need only look at the artistic work, for "art does not lie"; it is a genuine expression of the spirit of an age. The Gothic architecture, the church windows and sculpture, and the fervent piety in the pictures of a Matthias Grünewald (d. 1528), a Hans Holbein the Elder (d. 1524), or the masters of the Cologne school (1450–1550) speak for themselves.

3. Yet this religiosity was often intermixed with other interests; at a time when religion and life still were unified, it is not surprising that existing social, political, and economical concerns affected religious thought. The Reformation was more than a purely religious and ecclesiastical affair. Martin Luther did not become a Reformer by means of his theological theses on indulgences, but by utilizing in his three great reform polemics of the year 1520 all of the current demands for reform. These pamphlets appealed to everyone who was dissatisfied with the ecclesiastical, political, or social order. His religious formulations were soon used by everyone to express their demands. The "prophets" Karlstadt, Münzer, and Storch in 1522, Sickingen and the Imperial Knights in 1523, the peasants in 1524/1525, and finally the princes and authorities who combined rather worldly interests of an economical, political, or dynastic kind with their conversion to the Reformation, all made use of Luther's polemics. It had

257

become almost fashionable to give a religious coloration to all events. "The name of God and the words of the Scriptures . . . were considered as indispensable legitimation for all human actions and strivings" (F. v. Bezold). In the Free Imperial Cities the connection between the Reformation and social and political change was almost tangible.

4. The universal nature of the demand for reform in the church was certainly due in large measure to the long delay, but it also well illustrates to what a degree the church was still the leading spiritual force and permeated the whole structure of society. Because the church was everywhere present, any ecclesiastical failure was most obvious to the public. The *Gravamina nationis Germanicae* which since the Libel of Mainz (1451) had been presented again and again were compiled into 100 complaints at the Diet of Worms (1521) which criticized most vehemently the administrative and tax practices of the curia as well as the ecclesiastical juridical system. Since the High Middle Ages the church had increasingly come to be governed through rules and laws, and discontent with this institutional church had grown. Many turned away from the "visible" church towards a purely spiritual "invisible" one. The idea of an *Ecclesia spiritualis,* of a "Church of the Holy Spirit", which would take the place of the existing papal church, had been developed by abbot Joachim de Floris (d. 1202) and widely disseminated by the Spiritual Franciscans of the thirteenth and fourteenth centuries. This concept became linked with the apocalyptic expectations of the later Middle Ages and created a new subjective piety which frequently sought its religious satisfaction outside of the church.

This "new piety" did not need to be hostile to the church and often could run parallel to it. The *devotio moderna* which the Dutchman Gerhard Groote (1340–1384) founded in Deventer in 1380, for instance, remained totally loyal to the church. It emphasized inward and personal piety and received its strength not so much from participation in the ecclesiastical liturgy and the sacraments as from silent meditation on the passion of Christ and the spirit of the Sermon on the Mount. In his famous book

258

Imitation of Christ, Thomas à Kempis (d. 1471), who belonged to the circle of disciples of Groote, the "Brethren of the Common Life", gave slight emphasis to church and sacraments. Individual reading of the Bible became central to this devotion, and the sacraments, particularly the Holy Mass, were no longer experienced as a realization of the sacrifice on the cross, but were viewed as occasions for the private performance of devotions. This emphasis of the church and the sacraments, the *devotio moderna,* which had as its purpose internal church reform, nonetheless "laid the groundwork for Luther's spiritualism" (Iserloh).

5. The nominalism of the English Franciscan theologian William Ockham (1290–1349) contributed in large measure to the internal undermining of the concept of the church. Ockham's *via moderna* not only rejected the *via antiqua* of Thomas Aquinas, but even fought strongly against it. The inner connection, which Thomism sees everywhere in nature and which enables it by analogy *(analogia entis)* to infer God from nature (natural proof of God), Ockham rejected as impossible. He maintained that no bridge existed between the natural and the supernatural; God and man are separated for human reason by an unbridgable chasm, and only when God reveals himself, can man know him. The depth of Ockham's skepticism toward human reason and nature corresponded to his great trust in revelation; only the revealed Holy Scriptures constitute a foundation and source for faith. Luther's *sola scriptura* principle is intimated by this view. Additionally, Ockham regarded reason as powerless; only faith alone can lead man to a knowledge of God and to salvation. Luther's *sola fides* principle is here clearly recognizable. Finally, Ockham asserted that human nature is capable of nothing on its own; everything is based on pure grace. Thomas's doctrine that grace presupposes nature and builds on it, found no approbation in Ockham's view of nature. Luther later seized upon this *sola gratia* doctrine and developed it further. Luther's heresy lies in giving absolute value to the three *sola.*

To the same degree that nominalism put its faith *exclusively* in faith and revelation, it reduced the importance of the role of sacraments and the church in the process of salvation. If necessary, man can get along without these institutions. Luther expressly accepted Ockham's doctrine, and the significance of his acceptance for the development of the Reformation is evident.

6. Finally, humanism and the biblical movement or evangelism must be mentioned as prerequisites of the Reformation. Modern investigation has shown clearly that there was a world-wide biblical movement even before the Reformation. Luther did not bring Holy Scripture out of hiding; rather, he himself grew out of the evangelism of his time. *Devotio moderna,* Ockhamism, and Christian humanism were the wellsprings of the concern with the Bible. Most certainly the biblical movement would have remained stronger in its native Catholic Church, if the Reformers had not gone too far in emphasizing it *(sola)* and claiming it for themselves. Erasmus of Rotterdam, the prince of the humanists, earned great merit through his concern with the Bible. His significance for the Reformation requires examination.

39
Erasmus of Rotterdam and Humanism

Erasmus was born in Rotterdam in 1469. His father was a cleric and his mother the daughter of a physician. He received an excellent education in the famous humanist school at Deventer (1474–1484) and there became acquainted with the *devotio moderna* of the Brethren of the Common Life. In 1486 Erasmus entered the monastery of the Augustinian Canons and was ordained a priest in 1492. As secretary to the bishop of Cambrai (1493–1495) and as a student in Paris (1495–1499) he ardently pursued humanistic studies. Erasmus spoke Latin better than his native tongue, and his numerous Latin grammars and exercise books established his reputation as a humanist and contributed to making Latin the language of scholars.

In England (1499–1500) he encountered a deep and pious Christian humanism through his acquaintance with Thomas

More and John Fisher (two saints of the church) and John Colet, whom he knew particularly well. It was these men who directed his attention toward the Bible. His knowledge of Greek and Hebrew enabled him in 1516 to issue the first critical edition of the Greek New Testament, an event which overnight placed him among the most important exponents of humanism and biblical scholarship. The New Testament was prefaced with an extensive introduction in which Erasmus outlined his ideas concerning the reform of the church and theology, ideas which had been influenced by the Holy Scriptures.

Previously Erasmus had criticized the abuses in church and life with a sharp pen in his *Enchiridion Militis Christiani* (1503) and *Laus Stultitiae* (1509). Now in the introduction to the New Testament he developed his *Philosophia Christi,* a Christian way of life based on the Sermon on the Mount. The simple unpretentious spirit of the gospels was to govern, and the ballast of ecclesiastical traditions was to be done away with. *"Tollantur abusus, non substantia."* His guiding principle was that the abuses were to be remedied, but the substance of the Christian faith was not to be touched.

Erasmus had taken up the most burning questions of the day when he combined the need for reform with the gospels. All eyes were directed toward him. Would he be the man to start the longed-for reform? The humanists applauded him, and the world was ready to listen to him. His principle of a genuine reform of all Christian life on the basis of Holy Scripture and a pure and simple biblical theology struck a deep chord in the minds of the people; his practical reform suggestions found enthusiastic acclaim.

At this point Martin Luther made his appearance. Erasmus noticed him only after the Leipzig disputation, and he saw in Luther a humanistic ally whom he encouraged. Soon, Luther's fate was put into his hands; in November, 1520, Erasmus conferred in Cologne with Luther's sovereign, Frederick the Wise, who asked his opinion of Luther. Erasmus confirmed the Elector in his support of Luther, but soon after he dissociated himself from the impetuous Wittenberg monk. The sensitive scholar, whose humanistic optimism detected the good in nature and in *libertas spiritus* the necessary precondition of all human training and all true piety, saw through Luther's nominalistic skepticism toward nature and reason. In his essay *On Free Will* (1524) Erasmus criticized Luther on these points. Luther immediately and violently responded with his counter argument *On Unfree Will* (1525). Later Luther remarked that Erasmus alone of all his opponents understood the essential point of his doctrine. Erasmus polemicized against Luther once more in 1526–1527; from this time on he sharply opposed Luther, and his example was followed by most of the older humanists.

In 1521 Erasmus lived in Basle and here published texts on the Church Fathers. When, in 1529, the Reformation was violently introduced in Basle he fled to Freiburg im Breisgau. While living in Freiburg, Erasmus influenced the discussions of the Diet of Augsburg (1530), where he unceasingly pleaded for peace. He rejected any use of force against the new faith; it would be better, he thought, to tolerate the Lutheran movement than to have a religious war break out. Time would heal; in the meantime the best course to follow would be to isolate the monk (Luther) and other fanatics for a time; then knowledge and man's gentle nature would point the way back to unity. "Through freedom of the spirit to true piety", was his motto. Not knowledge threatened the true Christian religion and genuine piety, but ignorance and lack of education which always enslaves men and makes them intolerant, fanatical, and quarrelsome. The tumultuous, fanatical, and ruthless behavior of the innovators was an abomination to him, but he also untiringly warned of narrow-minded, obstinate clinging to old traditions on the part of Catholic orthodoxy. Erasmus always tried to find a way between the two extremes.

In 1536, Erasmus died in Basle, where he had returned shortly before his death. His last great writings were devoted to reunification (*De sarcienda ecclesiae concordia,* 1533). Through these writings he founded the so-called theology of mediation, which particularly among Catholics had many adherents for a long time (Witzel, Pflug, Cassander), but which was also accepted by

262

such Protestants as Melanchthon and Butzer. In some areas, especially the lower Rhine, Erasmianism remained strong and effected a peaceful coexistence between Lutherans and Catholics until it was finally ground to bits in the 1560's by the hardening lines of denominationalism.

Contemporary scholarship gives varying assessments to the value of the Erasmian humanistic attempt at conciliation. Some see in it the "Third Force" in the struggle of the confessions and regret that it never acquired sufficient strength (Fr. Heer); others accuse it of having blurred the theological distinctions and by its vagueness having damaged the Catholic Church, particularly in matters of dogma (J. Lortz); finally, others believe "that it was precisely Erasmus who was on the right track" (K. A. Meissinger). Recently it was asserted that the aged Erasmus, the Christian humanist, was neither an undogmatic skeptic nor a freethinker, but a profoundly convinced and loyal Catholic and theologian who became concerned with revelation (Oelrich). Final judgment has not yet been made.

40
MARTIN LUTHER: HIS DEVELOPMENT AS A REFORMER

"It is seldom that a single individual has as much importance for a tremendous and radically transforming historical process — for a really great revolution — as Martin Luther has for the Reformation" (J. Lortz). Although the Reformer rarely expressed a thought which had not been thought and expressed before him, he nevertheless put his mark on everything in such a way as to make it new, and his ideas were received as new by his contemporaries. The Reformation was very much Luther's own personal achievement. This does not imply, however, that he started the whole movement intentionally; he merely threw a spark into a barrel which was filled to the brim with all of the religious, intellectual, political, and social unrest of his time. But it was the overwhelming power of Luther's personality which endowed the fire with its force.

263

1. The Catholic picture of Luther has changed drastically since the descriptions by H. Denifle (1904–1909) and H. Grisar (1921–1930). The unpleasant polemic has given way to an attempt to understand and to interpret the Reformer in the light of his time and his intentions. The purity of his desire for reform is as little doubted as the justification of his wish to reform thoroughly the grievous conditions of the late medieval church. Indeed, upon closer inspection one notes that in reality Luther was only representative of a powerfully growing demand for reform within the church; it is utter tragedy that with his forceful personality he did not remain within the church but instead became a Reformer against it.

When in 1517 Luther turned against Tetzel's trade in indulgences, he thought of himself as the advocate of pure church doctrine opposing an abuse of sacred matters which was truly disgraceful. From the beginning, his altercation with the Dominican was overshadowed by the opposing views of the scholastics. Luther's nominalistic and Ockhamistic view saw questions quite differently from that of the Thomistic Tetzel. At this time, many problems of pre-Reformation theology had not yet been decided officially, and the uncertainties were not removed until the council of Trent. Until then, these theological problems could be discussed freely in the schools. Because Tetzel claimed his opinion to be church doctrine and made himself a judge, he provoked Luther's response, a response which because of Luther's temperament was one-sided and coarse. Thus a scholastic dispute turned into a fundamental controversy. We may say today, however, that the Thomistic position was by far the better one.

Many of the Lutheran attacks on church doctrine would have been superfluous if pre-Reformation Catholic theology had been clearer. This is evident with regard to such questions as indulgences, the doctrine of justification, the meaning of the sacrifice of the Mass and the sacraments, and the doctrine of the church and papal primacy, to mention only a few essential points. Nominalistic theology must bear the chief responsibility for this obscurity. Luther had been educated by nominalists and had accepted this view; he had scarcely been acquainted with real Thomistic scholasticism. By seeing everything from the standpoint of nominalism, he regarded many things as Catholic doctrine which in actuality were merely nominalistic opinions. As a result, his inner struggles were against a concept which actually was not Catholicism (Lortz), and moreover, because his representations of Catholic doctrine were distorted, he contributed substantially to subsequent confusion. This factual criticism maintains its justification, and in it one finds the real tragedy of the Reformation. Out of his misunderstanding and his personal peculiarities, Luther's theological position developed.

2. Luther was born on November 10, 1483, into a smallholder's family in Eisleben, and he grew up at Mansfeld, where his father Hans Luder (= Lothar) had become a miner. Everywhere Martin breathed the atmosphere of the late medieval piety which we previously mentioned, and obsession with witches and devils beside other strong superstitions played a not insignificant role. However, life in these times was tied to the church; one lived in and with the church, just as the church lived in and with the people. Martin's training and education also were embedded in the ecclesiastical life: elementary school at Mansfeld (1489–1495), Latin school at Magdeburg (1496–1497) where he lived with the Brethren of the Common Life and by them was inspired with the *devotio moderna,* and then further schooling at Eisenach (1498–1501), where in the person of vicar Braun he encountered a loyal priestly friend. In 1501 Luther began studying at the University of Erfurt where he graduated in 1505 with a master's degree in basic philosophy.

The University of Erfurt became of the greatest import for Luther's theological orientation. Philosophy and theology were taught there in the form of the *via moderna,* i.e. of nominalism and Ockhamism, and the young impressionable man was placed into a religious field of tension between God and man. He experienced the magnitude and majesty of God's will before whom the insignificant human being becomes nothing, and learned to understand everything as the will and judgment of God. Sin and grace, good and evil, depend not on man but on God; if God looks upon man graciously, he is good; if he looks upon him with anger, he is bad. If he so wishes, God can look graciously upon a sinner also; then the sinner is justified, i.e. righteous; he remains the same sinner as before, but God views him as just *(simul iustus — simul peccator)*. God is absolutely free in the distribution of grace, indeed even arbitrary. Man can do nothing; he can only hope and trust that God will be gracious and he must turn to God in unconditional surrender. Neither the sacraments nor the church as an institution of salvation can help him; everything depends on his own subjective attitude.

According to the wish of his father, Martin was to study law. In the summer of 1505 he was on a return journey to Erfurt when a violent storm occurred. Lightning struck next to him and believing his life in danger he made a vow on July 2, 1505, to enter a monastery. Hastily, yet not entirely unprepared, Luther reported only fifteen days later, on July 17, to the strict Augustinian Eremites at Erfurt. After his novitiate he was ordained to the priesthood on April 3, 1507, and now began his actual theological studies in Erfurt. These studies were based on the strictly nominalistic theology of Gabriel Biehl. Later Luther spoke frequently of the terrible inner torments which befell him during his monastic stay. Occupation with Augustine's doctrines of grace and predestination, his own personal sense of sinfulness, and the voluntary nature of the Ockhamistic and nominalistic theology combined to bring him to the brink of a religious and theological catastrophe. Fear of predestination overcame him; he sensed his failure and believed himself to be deserted and damned by God. He became deeply depressed, and neither frequently repeated confessions nor the other sacramental aids of the church were able to help him. Owing to his nominalistic background, Luther never had a good relationship with the sacraments; he found consolation only in the calming words of the vicar of the order, Johann von Staupitz, who instructed him not to brood about whether he was predestined or not, but simply to meditate on the wounds of Christ who sacrificed himself to God for us.

Meanwhile Luther continued his theological studies at the University of Wittenberg (1508–1509) and, after an intervening journey to Rome (1510–1511), received the degree of doctor of theology. In 1512 he succeeded to the professorship in Bible, which Staupitz had held previously, and lectured on the Psalms (1513–1515), the Epistle to the Romans (1515–1516), Epistle to the Galatians (1516–1517), Epistle to the Hebrews (1517–1518), and once again on the Psalms (1518–1519). These initial lectures, which are extant partially in his own manuscripts and partially in notes by his students, provide some information on his inner development as a Reformer. For this development, the "experience in the tower" of the monastery of Wittenberg played a decisive role. Here in a quiet hour he gained a new understanding of the "justice of God" according to Romans 1, 17. During his deeply religious quest Luther was constantly occupied with the question: "How do I find a merciful God?" This problem was less an autopsychological than a theological one; Luther had begun to doubt God and was struggling to find a new image of him. Now he discovered that the "justice of God" mentioned in Romans 1, 17 did not mean the harsh justice by which God judges a culprit vindictively and remuneratively, but rather a justice of mercy by which God for the sake of the sufferings of his son looks with pure compassion upon the faithful sinner and thereby makes him "just".

When did this tower experience occur, one asks, and what is so new about it? Protestant theologians were generally inclined previously to date it very early (K. Holl: 1511–1512; O. Scheel: 1512–1513); they were motivated by the desire to place the awakening of the Reformation as far back as possible. Catholic theologians, on the other hand, asked what was so typically reforming about the discovery of a compassionate, merciful God. Luther, they remarked, had simply surmounted within himself the image of a capricious God from which he had previously suffered; but the newly won image of God was the Catholic one to which he had merely found the way back. The experience in the tower, therefore, must be given a Catholic interpretation, and this is in keeping with the early date, because at that time Luther's thoughts and emotions were certainly still Catholic.

Only the Catholic historian H. Grisar dated the experience in the tower later, in 1518–1519. He relied on Luther's own testimony in his autobiographical fragment of 1545 in which he stated that the realization had come to him before he had lectured on the Psalms a second time. Luther conducted these second Psalms lectures in 1518–1519. Recently the Protestant theologian E. Bitzer agreed with Grisar's date and showed that Luther around this time had experienced an inner change. Luther's preceeding lectures on the Epistle to the Hebrews in the summer of 1517 indicate that he had begun to doubt the traditional Catholic concept of the church and the sacraments and had begun to construct a new concept of justification through faith alone.

According to Thomist scholastic doctrine the sacraments are signs instituted by Christ which *ex opere operato* contain and secure grace as long as one receives them in good faith and does not put an obstacle in the way of grace; faith is prerequisite for reception; but the sacramental symbol confers grace. Luther emptied the sign of its content and saw the bestowal of grace through *faith alone (sola fide)*. This gives faith a new face. Thomas Aquinas had strongly connected faith with the intellect; for him, faith meant above all that one must regard the truths of revelation as true and accept them. That this acceptance was also a matter of the heart had receded far into the background during late scholasticism. Luther discovered it anew during the tower experience and drew consequences from it. *"Corde enim creditur ad justitiam"* (Romans 10, 10). Faith becomes a matter of trust once more and Luther discovers something which has only been obscured and put into the background. Luther, however, monopolizes this truth and, by absolutizing it, recognizes only this new fiduciary faith in the process of salvation (fides = fiducia, trust). From Romans 1, 17 Luther concludes that God gives his grace to him who approaches him with faith in the atonement of Jesus

Christ and that God "imputes" to the sinner the merits of his son.

The result of the experience in the tower is not only Luther's new concept of God, but also Luther's new inner attitude toward God: Faith, which is based on the assurance of salvation in the word of God, i.e. in Holy Scripture, alone decides; *sola fides* and *sola scriptura* belong together. The church as an institution of salvation and the sacraments as conveyors of grace fade into the background. Only faith, which is built on the special assurance of salvation in the word of God, determines eternal salvation. From Holy Scripture alone man receives faith and grace: *sola scriptura* is designated as the formal principle of Protestantism; *sola fides* and *sola gratia* become its material principles.

With this realization Luther became the Reformer; the origin was a subjective experience. He became a Reformer not because he criticized ecclesiastical abuses, but because he found a new religious and theological position which was outside of the sacramental church and irreconcilable with the ecclesiastical life of the traditional church. In contrast to the case of Erasmus and other reformers, Luther called the church itself into question; it was no longer a matter of reform in the sense of an internal ecclesiastical cleansing, it was a Reformation!

3. As father confessor, Luther learned of the grievous results brought about by the superficiality of Tetzel's sermon on indulgences. Subsequently he wrote the 95 theses on the nature and use of indulgences and on October 31, 1517, sent them to the appropriate bishops, the archbishop of Magdeburg–Mainz, Albrecht of Brandenburg, and the bishop of Brandenburg, Jerome Schulz. The theses did not attack the indulgence per se; they were only designed to call attention to Luther's concept, developed in the summer of 1517, that faith was the sole decisive factor in the process of salvation, and to compare this with the abuses of indulgences and their false and coarsely materialistic representation (As soon as the money in the coffer rings, the soul from purgatory's fire springs). Luther was aware that he had raised an open question; his private letter to the bishops which

accompanied the theses asked for clarification and also requested that the indulgence sellers be restrained. Luther sought a disputation, not a controversy. According to most recent findings by E. Iserloh, there can be no talk of Luther having nailed the theses to the door of the castle church of Wittenberg in solemn protest, as a constantly repeated old legend, first told by Philipp Melanchthon in 1546, maintained. Luther simply sent the theses to the above mentioned bishops and a few educated friends, John Lang in Erfurt and Christoph Scheurl in Nürnberg. Scheurl had them printed, without the knowledge or consent of Luther, and soon they were circulated throughout Germany. Their unsuspected effect in the beginning genuinely alarmed Luther.

The excitement caused by the theses illustrated how widespread were resentment and anger at the unholy trade with indulgences, which the curia, the archbishop of Mainz, and the Fuggers were conducting, and to which the Dominicans were lending a helping hand. Most people saw in Luther's theses only protest, not a deeper theological concern. Without considering Luther worthy of a direct answer, archbishop Albrecht sued the author in Rome. The bishop was financially harmed since the preaching of indulgences had to be discontinued and Albrecht did not receive the sum of money which he had been advanced by the Fugger bank (altogether the indulgence trade should have yielded the amount of 52286 ducats). In June 1518 a heresy trial was instituted against Luther in Rome; its concern was the erroneous parts of Luther's theses.

Luther was instructed to answer the charges against him in Rome, but Luther's prince, Elector Frederick the Wise of Saxony, arranged for Luther to be examined by the papal legate, cardinal Cajetan, who had been sent to the Diet of Augsburg in October 1518. Luther refused to recant, secretly fled from Augsburg, appealed to the pope, and thereafter to a general council (October 28, 1518). Events were gaining momentum.

Among the few who correctly assessed the significance of the theses was the Ingolstadt theologian John Eck (1486–1543). He saw immediately that they went far beyond a criticism of the usual indulgence practice and, unknown even to Luther, called into question the nature of indulgences, the authority of the popes to declare indulgences, and finally the sacramental nature of the church itself. During the Leipzig disputation (June 27 – July 16, 1519) he argued heatedly with Luther. It was no longer just a matter of indulgences, but of the authority of the pope, the freedom from error of councils, and the whole sacramental order of the ecclesiastical community of salvation. Luther denied that papal primacy was founded on Holy Scripture (Mt 16, 18), and claimed that even general councils could be wrong, for, he maintained, the council of Constance had erred in the question of Hus. He had taken a dangerous step toward separation from the church. With this result Eck journeyed to Rome. The trial of Luther, which had been suspended because of the views of Frederick the Wise and the political situation in Germany prior to the election of Emperor Charles V, was resumed again in Rome early in 1520. The result of the trial was the determination of Luther's heresy. The bull *Exsurge Domine* (June 15, 1520), in which Luther was threatened with excommunication if he did not recant within sixty days the forty-one erroneous sentences which had been culled from his writings was carried to Germany by Eck.

4. The points of controversy in the meantime had shifted. The concern was no longer over the indulgence controversy but over Luther's attack on the church. Was Eck to blame for this? It might appear as though he alone had forced the issue of the church with Luther. Indeed, Eck was the first to recognize the problem and with his theological acumen to put his finger on it, but we have already noted that the problem could long be inferred from Luther's inner development. Luther's new interpretation of faith would certainly have led him to the point of deviation from the church; Eck only served to clarify his position.

In fact, after the Leipzig disputation Luther rethought his concept of the church for the first time. Now he became aware that his concept of faith, which rested on a direct and completely subjective surrender to Christ, left no room for an intermediate

271

agent. Suddenly the sacraments and the whole religious and ecclesiastical life appeared as an obstacle on the way to God. He called these aids "justification through works", in which man no longer desired to leave room for grace alone but wanted to achieve salvation on his own. This, then, meant that trust no longer reposed in God, and such a thing could only be the work of the devil. The whole visible, institutional church, which Luther had already begun to doubt, began to appear to him as the work of the devil; the pope himself became the anti-Christ, the evil foe of Christ, who led man into error; the pope had taken the place of Christ and thereby provoked the anger of God. These concepts grew into a complex which Luther could not overcome: the pope remained for him the personification of the anti-Christ.

His attitude makes Luther's vehement and angry reaction to the threat of excommunication in the form of his three great major writings of 1520 more comprehensible. In these pamphlets he relentlessly attacked the papacy and the whole existing church with all of its faults and weaknesses and summoned the people to battle against them. This was no longer reform and inner recuperation:

1) *To the Christian Nobility of the German Nation on the Improvement of the Christian Estate* (August 1520),
2) *The Babylonian Captivity of the Church* (October 1520), and
3) *The Freedom of a Christian* (November 1520).

Instead of theological treatises Luther now composed appeals to the people to mobilize them against Rome and the church. With an overpowering strength of language he crystallized all the points which for so long had been in need of reform and by making himself the speaker for the general discontent became the leader of a widespread national and humanistic opposition to Rome. In these months Luther became a national hero. Of course, most of Luther's contemporaries were not aware that Luther's reform program grew out of the soil of a new theology. Genuine and generally desirable reform attempts combined with Luther's theological opinions and before long led to a radical movement directed against the church. Although Luther became a reformer, he still remained a theologian, and it was this particular combination which caused the Reformation. Reforms were necessary; but they could and should have been performed within the church. Luther's new theological doctrine, however, was no longer reconcilable with church doctrine. Thus the reform changed into the Reformation.

From now on the idea of reform was ambivalent; today we usually distinguish between "reform" (within the church) and "Reformation" (outside and against the church). To the contemporaries such a distinction was largely without meaning. The ambivalence of the reform concept was fatal for many, particularly for the humanists who were enthusiastic about reform, but who, together with Erasmus of Rotterdam, later turned away from the Reformation when they recognized its true nature.

On December 10, 1520, Luther visibly broke with the church by publicly burning at the Elster Gate of Wittenberg the bull *Exsurge Domine,* which threatened him with excommunication, together with the books of canon law. He was formally excommunicated in Rome on June 3, 1521, and the separation was complete.

41

THE CONTINUATION OF THE REFORMATION IN GERMANY

1. After travelling from Spain with a great train, Emperor Charles V (1519–1556) arrived in Aachen, where on October 23, 1520, the coronation took place. The young Habsburg, the grandson of Emperor Maximilian I (1493–1519), had been unanimously elected on June 28, 1519, after an exciting election campaign against Francis I of France. Until he was actually elected, Pope Leo X (1513–1521) had agitated against Charles. Owing to the anti-curial sentiment in Germany, this had not been to Charles's disadvantage. Now many expected Charles to pursue an anti-curial policy, and he was greeted enthusiastically. Luther dedicated to Charles the strongest of his polemics which was

entirely designed to incite resentment and hate against Rome (*To the Christian Nobility . . .*) and exulted: "God has given us a young noble sovereign and has awakened much great hope in our hearts". He welcomed him longingly and wrote: "Where are you, admirable Emperor Charles? Where are you, Christian Princes? You became Christians by baptism, how can you now suffer the hellish voice of the Antichrist?"

But Charles, the heir of a great empire in which "the sun did not set", quite in the spirit of the great medieval tradition conceived of his imperial duty of protector of church and western Christianity as a sacred office. He was as serious about the traditional Catholic faith and the unity of the church, as Luther was about his new theology. While Luther was constantly guided by his subjective experience, Charles, who was completely rooted in the Christian community, was accustomed to subordinating his personal interests to those of the community and to differentiating between person and office. Charles was never moved by feelings of antipathy against the person of a pope to impugn his holy office; in this trait he differed fundamentally from Luther who always regarded everything subjectively. Both men were typical representatives of their kind; in Worms they faced one another.

From the beginning Charles left no doubt that in Luther's case he would take the side of the traditional church. In Louvain and Cologne (November 12, 1520) Charles had witnessed the burning of Luther's writings and he was willing, as soon as Luther had been officially excommunicated by the church, to place Luther under the imperial ban. However, he was persuaded by Elector Frederick the Wise of Saxony to consent to giving Luther a hearing at the Diet of Worms, and on March 6, 1521, he signed Luther's letter of safe conduct.

It was an extraordinary spectacle of medieval life as the excommunicated Luther, solemnly accompanied and led by the imperial herald Kaspar Sturm, arrived at Worms on April 16, 1521, amid a throng of people. The excommunication notwithstanding, the entire journey had been a triumphal procession. Now high and low thronged about his inn, trying to catch a glimpse of the famous man. He had become the center of importance at the Diet. On April 17, Luther was summoned to a hearing; he frankly acknowledged his writings before the emperor and the assembled imperial estates. When he was asked whether he wanted to defend them, Luther asked for time to consider the matter. On the following day he made a well-prepared resolute speech in which he refused any retraction. "Unless I am convinced by the testimony of the Scriptures or by clear reason (for I do not trust either in the pope or in councils alone, since it is well known that they have often erred and contradicted themselves), I am bound by the Scriptures I have quoted, and my conscience is captive to the Word of God. I cannot and I will not retract anything, since it is neither safe nor right to go against conscience. May God help me, Amen."

The address made a deep impression on the imperial estates. But the emperor on the following day also made a speech which was no less impressive; it represented the first independent statement which Charles made in public. Charles V, the young sovereign of the empire, also made the most of his hour at this historic occasion. Two men and two worlds confronted one another. "You know", he addressed the German imperial estates, "that I am descended from the most Christian emperors of the noble German nation, from the Catholic kings of Spain, the archdukes of Austria, and the dukes of Burgundy; they all have remained up to death faithful sons of the church and have always been defenders of the Catholic faith, the sacred rituals, decrees, ordinances, and holy customs. After death they have left to me by natural right and heritage these holy Catholic observances in which I have up to now lived. For this reason I am determined to support everything that has been laid down at the council of Constance as well as others. For it is certain that a single friar errs in his opinion which is against all of Christendom and according to which all of Christianity will be and will always have been in error both in the past thousand years and even more in the present. For that reason I am absolutely determined to stake on

275

this cause my kingdoms and my seigniories, my friends, my body and blood, my life and soul. For it would be a great shame to me and to you, who are the renowned German nation, if in our time not only heresy but suspicion of heresy or decrease of the Christian religion should through our negligence dwell after us in the hearts of men. After having heard the obstinate answer which Luther gave yesterday, I declare to you that I regret having so long delayed to proceed against this Luther and I am no longer willing to hear him speak more. May he have his safe conduct! And as I have said before, I am determined to proceed against him as a notorious heretic, requesting of you that you conduct yourselves in this matter as good Christians."

Positions were thus taken in the empire. On April 26, Luther left Worms; he had a safe conduct for twenty-one days. He was "kidnapped" by knights of his Prince Elector Frederick and spirited to the Wartburg to keep him from harm. There he spent the next months and worked on his translation of the New Testament. Although it was certainly not the first German translation, Luther's effort represented nonetheless "an ingenious achievement of creative language" (Lortz). Because of the power of its language and the fame of its translator, the translation soon obtained wide circulation. Luther also wrote smaller pamphlets, such as *Concerning Monastic Vows*; these were the beginning of a long series of polemics in which, often through grotesque distortions, he degraded Catholic doctrines and customs and did not hesitate to drag through the mud that which so recently had been sacred to him: monasticism, the Mass, priesthood, celibacy, papacy, and many other aspects. The coarse language and form of this literature contributed much to the poisoning of the general atmosphere. The new art of printing enabled the polemics to be widely disseminated.

The emperor meanwhile had signed the Edict of Worms on May 8, 1521, which placed Luther and his adherents under the ban of the empire. After many members had already departed, Charles on May 25 concluded the Diet. For a long time the implementation of the edict posed a problem with which the

276

Imperial Diets and politics had to be concerned, because Charles, who so emphatically had made it his own program, was required by foreign wars to be absent from Germany for nine years; during this time Luther's doctrine could take root and spread unhindered.

2. The development in Germany from 1521 to 1530, i.e. from Worms to Augsburg, shall appear only in outline. This period of Catholic history presented the painful spectacle of a superficial and irresponsible Christianity which thought only of its egotistic advantage. The church was sorely buffeted by Luther's stormy sermons of reform, which had an unanticipated effect: all of Germany was set in motion.

As early as the spring of 1521 a few priests dared to get married; the first was Prior Bernardi of Kemberg near Wittenberg. Luther applauded this action, even though it violated imperial law. Increasing numbers of monks deserted their monasteries; by November only thirteen Augustinian Eremites remained at Wittenberg. In January, 1522, the chapter of the order of the Augustinians at Weimar permitted all of its members to leave; and soon the German congregation of Augustinian monks became extinct. Mass apostasy now followed. Those monks and nuns freed themselves who without a calling had lived in orders, and whole monasteries closed their doors. There were, however, inspiring examples of loyalty, for example the Clarisses at Nürnberg, under the direction of their abbess Caritas Pirckheimer, who bravely withstood all pressure and persecution from the city council.

In December, 1521, violence broke out in Wittenberg against the officiating priests of the parish church. Karlstadt and Zwilling began to introduce a new church system with radical innovations, and iconoclastic riots took place in the parish church. The so-called Prophets of Zwickau, who claimed to be guided by a special inspiration of the Holy Spirit and who denied the validity of infant baptism, appeared on the scene and created havoc. This disorder caused Melanchthon in March 1522 to ask Luther to leave his exile on the Wartburg and to return to Wittenberg to restore order. Luther had much trouble with the "fanatics", who were joined by the revolutionary Thomas Münzer when he was driven out of Zwickau in 1521 on account of his seditious sermons. These radicals claimed that God revealed himself not through "Scripture alone", but also through an "inner light", through the "spiritual word". Münzer fled to Mühlhausen (Thuringia) in 1524, and there, together with the apostate monk Heinrich Pfeiffer, preached the new communistic state of God and demanded that the existing "godless" government be extirpated. When he was driven out by the local city council upon Luther's request, Münzer revenged himself through malicious pamphlets. During the Peasants' War Münzer was to acquire a sad fame for himself until his capture and execution in 1525.

Meanwhile the Imperial Knights had become active under the leadership of Franz von Sickingen and had started a campaign against the archbishop of Trier with the ostensible purpose of "opening the door for God's word". In actuality, they wished to enrich themselves by confiscating church property in the name of the new doctrine. After the knights had pillaged villages and towns they were finally defeated by the troops of the archbishop and his allies, their castles were razed, and Sickingen was killed in battle.

Still social unrest continued to spread; excited and confused by Luther's reform literature, the peasants revolted in 1524. The "largest politico-social mass movement in German history" (W. J. Fuchs) spread from the southern Black Forest via Swabia, Franconia, Alsace, and Thuringia to the Tyrol and Salzburg. At first it seemed as though the movement would follow a peaceful course, and the association of Memmingen in 1525 claimed to be "a Christian association according to the gospel". Using some of Luther's own words the leaders of the peasants compiled their demands into the "Twelve Articles of the Peasantry" (March 6, 1525) and submitted them to Luther. In April 1525 Luther answered with his *Exhortation to Peace* in which he appealed to the conscience of the princes and lords and asked them to cooperate with the peasants, and also considered peace and patience on the part of the peasants. When, however, Luther learned of the arson and murder which had been committed by some peasant bands, Luther wrote one of his most intemperate pieces, *Against the plundering and murdering mobs of the peasants.* In this pamphlet Luther took the side of princes and authorities without reservation and exhorted them to intervene without mercy: "It is not now the time for patience and mercy. It is the time for the sword and anger." He admonishes the mercenaries of the princes: "Stab, strike, and strangle where you can; if you die in the process, it is to your benefit, for you can never obtain a more blessed death than to die in obedience to God's word and order, according to Romans 13, in the service of love, and in the attempt to save your neighbor from hell and the fetters of the devil."

The catastrophe of the Peasants' War which ended in the defeat and suppression of the peasants, also marked a turning point in the history of the Reformation. The Reformation as a popular movement was now burdened from below with a heavy mortgage and became more and more a matter for the authorities. Many of the peasants, disillusioned by Luther's reaction, returned to the old church or joined sects and the Anabaptists, and Luther lost much of his popularity.

Luther's connection with the territorial princes led to the so-called "Reformation of the Princes" and to the formation of evangelical territorial churches. In place of the free religious community and individual personal religious decision, the authorities supplied ordinances which "ordered" the Reformation. Ecclesiastical authority was given to the territorial princes *(summus episcopatus),* which meant the abandonment of the *ecclesia spiritualis* for which Luther had fought, and the growth in its place of a rather massive corporate and institutional territorial church. Only now did the further spreading of the Reformation begin, but even though the development was quite varied in the different territories and cities, the time of spontaneous development was over. The question of the church became a political issue to be decided by the Imperial Diets.

Even though Pope Adrian VI had his delegate read to the Diet of Nürnberg in 1522–1523 a moving admission of guilt by the curia and the promise to undertake the reform of the church with all possible vigor, his counterdemand for the implementation of the Edict of Worms threw the estates into political furor. The first Diet of Speyer (1526) put the decision concerning the church question into the hands of the territorial princes. In 1525 the Grand Master of the Teutonic Knights, Albrecht of Branden- burg, secularized the order's domain and seized it as a secular principality for himself. In 1526, the Electorate of Saxony systematically began to introduce the Reformation throughout the entire state by means of church visitations and instructions. Luther put aside the religious habit in 1524 and married Katha- rina von Bora, a former Cistercian nun. In 1525, during the Peasants' War, Luther and Melanchthon wrote the visitation instructions. Hesse followed the example of Electoral Saxony (synod of Homberg, 1526) in introducing the Reformation.

When in 1529 the second Diet of Speyer decided upon the implementation of the Edict of Worms, the imperial estates who had adopted the new faith openly protested the decision. These estates now were known as the "Protestants" (Electorate of Saxony, Brandenburg, Lüneburg, Hesse, Anhalt, and fourteen imperial cities, among them Strassburg, Nürnberg, Ulm, and Constance), and on April 22, 1529, they concluded a secret treaty. Landgrave Philipp of Hesse wanted to form an extensive alliance against the emperor and tried to include Switzerland in the league. The theological differences of Zwingli and Luther were to be removed during a discussion at Marburg in 1529, but the two Reformers could not agree with respect to the doctrine of the Eucharist: Luther believed in the real presence of Christ *("hoc est corpus meum")*, while Zwingli interpreted *"est"* to be understood significatively (= it "means"). Thus the league could not be attained.

3. Emperor Charles V returned to Germany at this time after a nine-year absence and was determined to solve the church question. Through peaceful negotiations the religious contro- versies were to be discussed and reforms were to be debated.

Luther's friend and colleague Philipp Melanchthon (1497–1560) prepared a document for the new believers, the *Confessio Augustana,* which has attained universal significance for Protestantism. It was read to the Diet of Augsburg on June 25, 1530. Melanchthon, the humanist among the Reformers, who always tended toward conciliation and who received support in this from Erasmus in Freiburg, presented the new doctrine as though it were scarcely different from the traditional church doctrine. At this time people still thought in terms of a common religious foundation, and no one fundamentally questioned the unity of church and faith. So strong was this view that Melanchthon could conclude the document with: "That is in sum the Catholic doctrine; as one can see there is nothing in it which deviates from Scripture or from the Catholic i.e. the Roman Church insofar as can be determined from the literature." He insisted that the controversy was not over the faith but only over reform demands such as the reintroduction of lay communion in both kinds, the abandonment of the countless masses of all sorts, of confession, of fasting, of monastic vows, and of episcopal jurisdiction. On June 26, he wrote to the papal legate Campeggio, who was then in Augsburg, "To this day we honor the papacy. We have no doctrine of faith which differs from the Roman Church. We shall be loyal to Christ and to the Roman Church until our last breath, even if the church should condemn us, although only quite irrelevant differences in the rites prevent unity."

Such a conciliatory position appeared to present a good foundation for reunification. The emperor himself was no intransigent papist but was full of hope and in his soul an open-minded humanist in the sense of Erasmus. Charles appointed two committees comprised of theologians of the traditional and the new faith; their spokesmen were Philipp Melanchthon and John Eck. The Catholics decided to use as the basis for negotiation the *Confutatio Confessionis Augustanae* which had been worked out by Eck, Faber, and Cochlaeus and which had been read to the Diet on August 3. Both sides made concessions during the discussions and the spirit of Erasmus was alive in all participants.

281

Agreement at any price, the most extreme willingness to compromise, and the lowering to a minimum of the individual demands were the guiding attitudes, particularly on the part of the emperor. Finally, only five points remained undecided: granting of the chalice to the laity, priestly celibacy, monastic vows, restitution of the church property which had been confiscated by the Protestant princes, and the sacrifice of the Mass as it was expressed in the *Canon missae*.

The first four points concerned ecclesiastical discipline, and only the last one touched on faith. How far the willingness to compromise extended on the Catholic side can be seen by the delegation which the emperor sent to Campeggio on September 14, 1530, with the request that the papal legate also agree to concede the last five points to the Protestants. The legate refused; but the issues were considered in Rome where he sent his report. Pope Clement asked the advice of cardinal Cajetan, one of the greatest theologians of his time. Cajetan's answer was essentially positive with regard to lay communion and priestly marriage, as these were only questions of discipline and not of faith; the decision, however, should be made by a council. From then on both questions played a large role in public discussion. Because Melanchthon had declared that if these two points, at least, were conceded, no further obstacle to reunification would remain, the imperial policy was to obtain both concessions from Rome. They were only dealt with, however, by the Council of Trent in 1563, and by the time that the laity, at least, was granted the chalice, it was thirty years too late.

No union was achieved in Augsburg in 1530, and the spirit which reigned there was that of Melanchthon and Erasmus, not of Luther. As an excommunicate Luther had not been permitted to participate in the Diet; however, from the castle Koburg he paid close attention to the proceedings and influenced his adherents through constant letters. Luther had nothing but harsh rebuke for Melanchthon's conciliatory attitude; he was basically opposed to any talks. "I have no liking at all for negotiating about the unity of doctrine", he wrote to the Saxon Prince

Elector in Augsburg on August 26, "for it is impossible as long as the pope is unwilling to give up the papacy. It was enough that we gave an account of our beliefs and asked for peace; do we really hope to convert them?" The influence from Koburg proved to be stronger than that from Freiburg. Philipp of Hesse had already left Augsburg in protest in August. Melanchthon became uncertain, the negotiations foundered, and the *Ratio Fidei* by Zwingli and the *Confessio Tetrapolitana* of the four cities of Strassburg, Constance, Memmingen, and Lindau, offered no basis for agreement. The closing resolution of the Diet on September 23, 1530 declared the religious negotiations at an end and demanded from the Protestants that they submit to Catholic doctrine with regard to the undecided questions by April 15, 1531. Reference was made again to the council which was planned for the following year; and again the Protestants protested the resolutions of the Diet.

One must ask whether a reunion was possible at all on the basis of the *Confessio Augustana*. After all, Melanchthon in his discussions — consciously or unconsciously — simply left out such important doctrinal disagreements as the question of freedom of the will, of the change in essence in the Mass (transubstantiation), of justification ("by faith alone"), of the divine origin of primacy (Mt 16, 18), of the veneration of saints, of purgatory, indulgences, and many other points. Additionally, the whole course of the negotiations had shown that the *Confessio Augustana* corresponded neither to the opinion of Luther nor to that of the Protestant Estates, even though it had been signed by them. The *Confessio* was fundamentally a creation of Melanchthon. How did it become nevertheless the official statement and the lasting document of Lutheran doctrine (as revised by Melanchthon in 1540 and now known as the *Variata*) to which to this day Lutheran ministers must pledge themselves? The answer is not an easy one. In any case, it served to create the foolish illusion that it formed a basis for reunion and that the differences involved were not great. Upon this assumption the Catholic party of mediation rested its attempts to achieve reunification. This party, which functioned in the spirit of Erasmus, tried unceasingly until the 1560's to achieve reunification and believed to have found a reliable basis for negotiations in the *Confessio Augustana*. The confusing effect of this document was particularly damaging to the Catholic Church in the future.

4. Again the emperor lacked the time and the strength to execute the resolutions of the Diet. The most pressing duty of the universal emperor at this time was to stop the advance of the Turks in the Balkans; in September 1529 they stood outside of the gates of Vienna. In order to gain the assistance of the Protestant princes, who had formed the League of Schmalkalden in 1531, Charles agreed to a truce in religious matters (Truce of Nürnberg 1532) "until a council" could decide further. When the council was repeatedly postponed, a renewed truce was agreed upon (Truce of Frankfurt, April 10, 1539), and it was decided to end the discord in Germany by means of religious discussions between theologians and laymen. The emperor desired nothing more than agreement, and he personally appointed the participants: John Gropper, Julius Pflug, and John Eck for the Catholic side; Melanchthon, Butzer, and John Pistorius for the Protestant side. All of these men were great advocates of conciliation; even Eck, the unyielding opponent of Luther, had meanwhile softened his position. After preparatory talks at Hagenau (June 12, 1540) and Worms (October 28, 1540), negotiations were conducted at the Diet of Regensburg which opened on April 5, 1541. The high-minded cardinal Contarini, the leader of the reform party in Rome, took an active part in the discussions as papal legate, and he would have been prepared to concede lay communion and marriage of priests to the Protestants. The attempts at union broke down, however, over the doctrines of the sacraments and the church. Once again Luther, and now for the first time Calvin, who stayed in Strassburg, disrupted the negotiations. The *Book of Regensburg* which summarized the results was finally repudiated by both sides. Charles V had learned another bitter lesson; after 1543 he had no longer any doubt that only the sword could bring about a decision and he intended to gain the union by force.

Since defeating Duke William of Cleve, who had claimed
Geldern (Treaty of Venlo, September 1543), and following the
fifth victory over Francis I of France (Peace of Crépy, September
1544), Charles's position had improved, when an internal German
quarrel provided him with the opportunity to declare war on the
Schmalkaldic League. In 1542 the Elector of Saxony and Philipp
of Hesse had driven duke Henry of Brunswick, a convinced
adherent of the emperor and the old church, from his domain
and forcibly introduced the Reformation. When Henry fell into
the hands of the Protestant princes in 1545 during a vain attempt
to regain his dukedom, the emperor intervened as protector of
law and order. Charles was not yet fully prepared when the
Schmalkaldic League attacked, but through a diplomatic and
military masterstroke he succeeded in defeating them decisively
in the battle of Mühlberg on April 24, 1547. Landgrave Philipp
of Hesse as well as Elector John Frederick, the leaders of the
Protestant party, were taken captive and the emperor finally
became master of the situation. To his military successes now
were added the deaths of his major opponents: Martin Luther
at Eisleben on February 18, 1546; Henry VIII of England on
January 28, 1547; and Francis I of France on March 31, 1547.

The emperor was now only in disagreement with the pope;
Paul III had deserted Charles during the Schmalkaldic War when
the emperor had most needed him. Now, when Charles endeavored
to have the religious question settled at a council, Paul transferred
the council against the wishes of the emperor from the German
imperial city of Trent to the papal city of Bologna. This step
foiled Charles's plans, for he was aware that he would never be
able to persuade the Protestants to attend the council at Bologna.

Consequently Charles determined to take matters into his own
hands. At the Diet of Augsburg (opened on September 1, 1547),
Charles decreed a solution according to his own concept: The
"Interim of Augsburg" (May 30, 1548), conceived by theologians
of both denominations in a spirit of Erasmian mediation, was to
be in force "temporarily" (= interim) until a final settlement
could be made by the council. The Protestants were granted

285

the right to clerical marriage and the chalice was given to the laity, but the doctrine remained fundamentally Catholic even though it was expressed in moderate form. A separate document was drawn up for the Catholics which did not contain these two concessions. Against all expectations it proved to be difficult to implement the two decrees; the Protestants as well as the Catholics were dissatisfied. Opposition against the emperor grew and cut across denominational lines. With the addition of political grievances, the result was the "revolution of the princes" led by the young Maurice of Saxony, a friend on whom the emperor had been certain he could rely. Through a treasonous treaty (1552) with king Henry II of France, Maurice obtained backing and money in exchange for the imperial cities of Metz, Toul, Verdun, and Cambrai. Thus strengthened, Maurice attacked the astounded emperor at Innsbruck. Only at the last moment was Charles able to flee to Villach in Carinthia. The council which had gathered for the second session at Trent was dissolved.

The betrayal and the collapse of all of his plans left the emperor grievously disappointed and no longer capable of taking decisive action in Germany. He left the settlement of the German religious problem to his brother Ferdinand, who in 1552 concluded the Treaty of Passau with the rebels. In the treaty both religious parties promised mutual toleration and also consented to negotiations at the Diet of Augsburg, which Charles V called. The Diet ended with the Religious Peace of Augsburg, concluded on September 25, 1555. The agreement provided that Catholics and Lutherans in Germany should have equal rights (Zwinglians, Calvinists, and Anabaptists remained excluded; they received the status of recognized religions only through the Peace of Westphalia in 1648). The territorial princes and authorities were granted the right of choosing the denomination for their domains *(cuius regio, eius religio)*. Subjects were not permitted the right of religious self-determination and could at best migrate. An agreement was reached between the Catholic Estates and Ferdinand by means of the so-called "ecclesiastical reservation" (although the Protestants refused to assent) that if in an ecclesiastical territory (prince bishopric, prince abbacy) the ruling bishop or abbot wished to adopt Protestantism he might do so personally, but must resign his office as well as his political control and permit the chapter to elect a Catholic successor. On the other hand, Ferdinand assured the already Protestant ecclesiastical princes of permission to keep their territories *(Declaratio Ferdinandea)* and the Catholics protested strongly against this. In the denominationally mixed imperial cities there should be parity.

The Peace of Augsburg consummated the religious schism in Germany. Constant controversies arose regarding the interpretation of the peace; the age of the religious wars had begun. Its culmination was the devastating Thirty Years' War (1618–1648) which made Germany a playground for foreign armies and in the end almost reduced it to a desert.

The spread of Lutheranism continued rapidly; between 1560 and 1570 about two thirds of Germany became Protestant. Protestantism also took root in Poland, Hungary, Bohemia, and Austria, but without being able to make large inroads. The Scandinavian countries, on the other hand, became totally Lutheran.

5. In summary, let us return to the initial position at Worms in 1521: The monk from Wittenberg was victorious. The emperor had failed, and the unity of the church and of the Christian West was gone!

Luther gave himself to his work with burning devotion until his last breath and always remained the religious leader and prophet of his movement. He was not, however, a saint. Dark shadows are thrown on Luther's character by his personal irascibility which increased with the years, his obstinacy, and his unexampled coarseness and boorishness with which he frequently assaulted friend and foe. He claimed for himself with insulting harshness, "like a new pope of Protestantism", the infallible magisterial authority which he denied to the Roman pope. With grotesque prophetic self-assurance he sometimes identified himself and his work with the will of God and Jesus Christ; all opposition was the work of the devil. The passionate hatred which is evident in his later writings, such as *Against Hanswurst* (1541), *Against the Papacy at Rome, founded by the Devil* (1545), and *Portrait of the Papacy* (1545) as well as *Of the Jews and their Lies* (1542) and the other anti-semitic literature cannot be excused totally by reference to the common vulgarity of the times. And these previous examples do not even mention the filthy language which Luther employed with regard to the Mass, monasticism, and other matters which once had been sacred to him and had remained sacred to many other people. One no longer finds any trace of the sensitive and pure religiosity of his youth. Yet Luther remained committed to his beliefs, and his devotional death on February 18, 1546 testifies to his profound relationship with God.

Luther's role offers an immense contrast to that of the emperor. Charles V was convinced of his total failure; it had been his duty to preserve and to protect, for he was the guardian of the sacred order in church and world; he had been entrusted with western Christianity. He had tried to safeguard this unity and thereby peace among Christian peoples, the *Pax Christianitatis,* but his power had not been sufficient. The Reformer Luther, the "Most Christian King" Francis I of France, and, most tragically, the popes denied him their cooperation. Charles stood alone. *"Christianitas afflicta"* (H. Lutz); poor, afflicted Christianity! The last years of Charles's life were overshadowed by this tragedy. To the last moment Charles was still in conflict with the fanatical Pope Paul IV (1555–1559), whose despicable nepotism and narrow-minded anti-Habsburg Italian policy presented constant obstacles. When Paul had the gall to call his war (1556–1557) against Charles and his son Philipp II a crusade for the saving of Christianity, Charles's spirit was broken. Duke Alba quickly put an end to the war plans of the pope, but Charles's inner will to resist had been destroyed by all these failures and disappointments. Tired of everything, he put his house in order. On October 25, 1555, Charles granted the Netherlands to his son Philipp II and added to them the Spanish holdings on January 16, 1556; to his brother Ferdinand he relinquished the German Empire on September 12,

1556. Then Charles retired as a private person to Spain where he prepared for his death at the monastery San Yuste in Estramadura. Charles died on September 21, 1558, at peace with God. He had never doubted the church, a church whose excessive worldliness he had reason to know as few other people. But above all the failures of individuals, particularly of the popes, Charles always regarded as sacred the office which they held; it was God's office and Christ's deputy which he saw, and his entire life was consumed in the service of unity.

"Charles V belongs to those great figures of history who at the close of their lives had the depressing conviction of having fought for nought, of not having attained their greatest aim and who were, despite all, as Jacob Burckhardt says, 'irreplaceable' in world history; for the historic event of the Council of Trent is unthinkable without him" (Hubert Jedin).

Luther and Charles V! Will they not, after all, have to be measured by what they meant for the church? Luther's achievement stands or falls with the "right or wrong of a revolt against the church" (Lortz). Charles's struggle for the preservation of Christian unity and the inner reform of the church, which it needed so much, resulted in the Council of Trent. This council largely owes its realization to him, and thus there stood at the end of Charles's life, after all, the greatest event in church history, the revival of the church at the Council of Trent. Before we examine the events of the council, let us survey the other reform movements.

42

ULRICH ZWINGLI AND THE ANABAPTISTS

It is not possible to measure Zwingli and the Anabaptists with the same yardstick, yet they have some elements in common: both began in Zürich and both had a spiritualistic tendency in their doctrines which caused Luther to refer to them as "fanatics".

Luther together with Zwingli, Calvin, and the Anabaptists held certain basic principles of the Reformation in common: sole

289

reliance on Holy Writ *(sola scriptura)*, the concept of faith and justification *(sola fide, sola gratia)*, a new image of what the church should be, and the struggle against the traditional church. Each of these men or groups, however, had his own peculiarities. Zwingli cannot simply be regarded, as is frequently done, as a follower of Luther, because Zwingli not only followed his own outward course, but also developed his own form of religious thought. Even Zwingli's educational development, which was strongly influenced by the scholastic *via antiqua* and humanism, distinguished him from Luther.

1. Zwingli was born in 1484 at Wildhaus in the Toggenburg valley. He grew up at Weesen in the home of his uncle, who was a pastor. From 1494 to 1498 he attended schools at Basle and Bern, and then he studied in Vienna (1498–1502) where he was taught the *via antiqua*. He concluded his studies in the humanistic Basle (1502–1506), and always maintained friendly relations with the Basle humanists. Zwingli, in the humanist manner, saw in Erasmus his idol. He was ordained a priest at Constance in 1506, and worked as a parish priest in Glarus (1506–1516) and in Einsiedeln (1516–1518). Twice during this time Zwingli acted as chaplain for Swiss mercenaries who fought in the papal service in upper Italy (Reislaufen), and for this work he was awarded a papal pension. Zwingli admitted to having led a lax life with regard to women even as late as his sojourn at Einsiedeln, but deliverance from a severe illness (plague) and the assignment as people's priest at the Great Minster at Zurich in 1519 made him more receptive to religious and ecclesiastical problems.

Concern with the Bible was "modern". The city magistrate which wanted to be modern required Zwingli to incorporate scriptural interpretations into his sermons. As a humanist, Zwingli had no objections and he began at once to interpret Holy Scripture. Until 1522 his sermons were totally influenced by Erasmian thought, and it was by Erasmus that he was also inspired with thoughts of reform. Zwingli became interested in Luther only after the Leipzig Disputation (1519), and Luther's theological influence on him, as modern investigation has shown, remained weak. He was and remained a humanist. The reforms which Zwingli began to advocate in 1522 did not spring from a deep personal religious struggle and search as they had with Luther, but from practical considerations. Zwingli defied the ecclesiastical law of fasting and clerical celibacy. He had long lived with a wealthy widow, and in 1524 he publicly married her.

When the bishop of Constance remonstrated with him about the marriage, Zwingli was able to profit from the dissension between the bishop and the magistrate of the city and to win the magistrate to his side. The city council arranged two public disputations (in January and October 1523) at which Zwingli was to debate with the "monks", i.e. with the Old Believers, on the subjects of the dependence on Scripture alone, the Mass, and the veneration of images. Only that was to be held valid which could be proven from Holy Scripture; after the debate the council was to make its decision known. When the October disputation was over, mayor Marx Röist candidly admitted: "I cannot very well judge the subject matter; I speak of it as a blind man speaks of colors; yet that is the way in which God's word must be decided on by the council. We ask God to let us make the right decision." The final decision stated: "Gentlemen of the orders, listen to the decision of the council members: From now on you shall confine yourself to preaching only Holy Scriptures in the form of the gospels, St. Paul, and the Prophets; ignore Scotus and Thomas and the others of that group."

Although the city council in its term "scriptural" sermons had referred only to the traditional interpretation of God's word in *sermons,* Zwingli now applied this scriptural principle to *reform;* all of life was to be refashioned according to Scripture. In his *Conclusions* and *Short Christian Introduction* (1523) Zwingli developed his radical reform program: the abandonment of all ceremonies and benedictions, the removal of all images from the churches, the transfer of all ecclesiastical benefices to the jurisdiction of the magistrate, and the establishment of a municipal marriage court which was to assume the function of the episcopal

291

marriage court as well as the entire spiritual jurisdiction of that court later.

When in December 1523 Zwingli wanted to introduce the Lutheran Eucharist instead of Mass, the council delayed and finally denied the change. Since the time of the second disputation there had been much criticism of the changes within the city and much resistance from outside. On January 26, 1524, the other twelve cantons agreed to prevent any further infringement on the Catholic faith. This decision was directed against Zurich, where excessive reforming zeal had caused worry to the others. The Zurich council therefore hesitated to take any new steps. When Zwingli obeyed the order of the magistrate he encountered the fierce opposition of a radical element among his followers and was accused of treachery. The radicals demanded that Zwingli proceed without compromise and stated that the secular power had no authority in these matters.

The final break between Zwingli and his adherents was pre-cipitated by the question of infant baptism. The radicals, among them Zwingli's best friends Conrad Grebel, Felix Manz, and George Blaurock, by logically pursuing the idea of justification by faith alone came to the conviction that the baptism of infants was wrong and without purpose, since the infant could not yet have any faith. The radical's idea was the complete restitution of the early Christian "congregation of saints" into whose company one could be admitted only by a voluntary acceptance of the faith. This group began by not having its own newborn children baptized until they were old enough to think for themselves. They ended by denying grace to all those who had been baptized as infants, and required them to be baptized again. In December 1524, Blaurock had himself re-baptized by Grebel and then devoted himself to the propagation of Anabaptism. The sect developed a following and started a movement against infant baptism. In Zollikon the baptismal font in a church was overturned; Zwingli opposed this and retained infant baptism.

At this point, Zwingli succeeded in persuading the council to intervene. On January 18, 1525, the council ordered the immediate baptism of all hitherto unbaptized children and forbade the Anabaptists to meet. This persecution caused fanatical excitement among the Anabaptists and they began to consider themselves inspired by the Holy Spirit, the only group qualified to interpret Holy Scripture, and as the "true" church of Jesus Christ. Manz justified his opposition to authority by relying solely on the Bible. Persecutions and arrests continued, but the persecutions only caused Anabaptism to spread rapidly from Switzerland to southern Germany, the Tyrol, upper Austria, and Moravia. When Manz returned to Zurich and became active once again, he became the first Anabaptist to be sentenced to death by the city council, and on January 5, 1527, he was drowned in the Limmat river. Zwingli is believed to have been involved in this affair.

In the meantime, Zwingli had extended his influence over the city council; a born practician, organizer, and politician, Zwingli was able to persuade the council to his point of view. In April, 1525, Mass was abolished by magisterial order and the break with dogma had been accomplished.

Also at this time, in April 1524, the original five cantons of Schwyz, Uri, Unterwalden, Zug, and Luzerne concluded an agreement in Berckenried for the defense of the Catholic faith. In questions of disciplinary reform the cantons wished to co-operate with Zurich, but they did not want to alter theological dogma. In January 1525 they reaffirmed their position in the Helvetical Concordat of Faith. The Swiss Diet in 1526 arranged a public disputation at Baden in Aargau, where the Eucharist, original sin, purgatory, veneration of images and saints, and the form of worship were discussed. John Eck, John Fabri, and many other theologians attended the disputation. The new faith was represented by Oecolampadius and others, but not by Zwingli. The Swiss Diet voted by an overwhelming majority in favor of Catholicism. However, Zurich, which was completely under Zwingli's influence, rejected the decision.

Zwingli now started an ecclesiastical and political offensive which extended beyond the borders of the canton of Zurich. In January 1528 he succeeded in winning over Bern. Zwingli's aim was the reformation of the whole Helvetic Confederation. He formed an alliance which called itself the "Christian League" and which consisted of Zurich, Bern, Constance, St. Gallen, Basle, and Strasbourg. When the five Catholic cantons mentioned previously formed a defensive alliance, together with Fribourg and Wallis, against Protestantism, the first war of Kappel occurred in June, 1529 and was only averted by a compromise peace. In October 1531 hostilities were renewed, and the first religious war between Protestants and Catholics began. Zwingli took to the field with sword and battle axe, but the Catholic cantons were victorious and Zwingli was killed in battle on October 11, 1531.

The Zwinglian reform movement initially was also strong in southern Germany; at the Diet of Augsburg in 1530 the cities of Constance, Strasbourg, Memmingen, and Lindau adopted the Zwinglian denomination *(Confessio Tetrapolitana),* but later shifted to Calvinism (*Concensus Tigurinus,* 1549). A union between Luther and Zwingli which was desired by both Philipp of Hesse and Zwingli miscarried at the Marburg Disputation in October 1529. The two Reformers were unable to harmonize their doctrines regarding the Eucharist. For Zwingli, the Eucharist was merely a memorial of Christ's passion, while Luther vehemently insisted upon the real presence of Christ. Although Luther denied the (Catholic) change in the essence (transubstantiation), he explained the real presence (which was physically impossible) by appealing to God's ubiquity. The deciding factor in the case of Zwingli and Luther was their differing interpretation of Scripture. Luther understood *"hoc est corpus meum"* literally ("The Word is too immense") and refused to accept any other meaning of *"est"*; Zwingli held that *"est"* was only significative ("it means"). Since neither would alter his position, their paths divided, and Luther always rejected and disliked Zwingli.

2. The subsequent history of the Anabaptists was totally separate from that of Zwingli. Yet they retained a common reliance on Scripture and spiritualism, particularly in their understanding of the Eucharist and the sacraments.

"It is among the most dismaying experiences of the Reformation that the circle of those who had been won for the new faith separated into splinter groups because of differing scriptural interpretation and endangered their own credibility with the result that they became enemies in the no-man's-land between the fronts" (Fuchs). Luther, Zwingli, Calvin, and all the other Reformers bitterly opposed those sectarians whose interpretation of the Scriptures differed from their own and who appealed to an "inner voice" and "spirit".

In Saxony, the original area of the Reformation, the idea of Anabaptism and the new kingdom of God appeared among the Prophets of Zwickau and Thomas Münzer at almost the same time as in Zurich. The hostility of these men to the authorities and their radical repudiation of the prevailing public and ecclesiastical order made the Anabaptists appear as revolutionaries and enemies of the state. The spread of the movement was especially rapid in the countryside where the peasants' disappointment after the Peasants' war caused them to join the movement in droves. This attraction made the movement particularly suspect and as early as 1529 and 1530 laws were passed at the Diets of Speyer and Augsburg which threatened the Anabaptists with the death penalty. Luther as well as Melanchthon were in favor of these laws.

The idea, first expressed by Thomas Münzer, of the imminent beginning of the millenium, in which all the godless would be destroyed and only the baptized would rule, found great response among the socially depressed peasants and artisans. In western Europe this idea was propagated by the lay preacher and apostle of Anabaptism, Melchior Hofmann who worked and preached in northern Germany, the Netherlands, and finally Strasbourg. Hofmann prophesied that the city of Strasbourg, after bloody occurrences, would become the center of the new Heavenly Jerusalem, and he calculated that this transition would happen in the year 1533. He found followers, especially in Amsterdam and the Netherlands, but in 1533 he was imprisoned in Strasbourg and died in confinement ten years later.

Now the scene for the millenium shifted from Strasbourg to

Münster in Westphalia. Chaplain Bernhard Rothmann had preached there since 1531. In the beginning, concern with the Bible and humanism were still intertwined, and Rothmann remained undecided. He turned first to Wittenberg and then to Strassburg, where Capito acquainted him with the doctrines of Zwingli. By way of Zwinglianism Rothmann arrived at Anabaptism, and when the religious turmoil in Münster became extreme, he was able to gain influence. While Catholic and Protestants fought one another, Rothmann's views made unexpected headway. After May 1533 he was fully committed to Anabaptism and preached the necessity of adult baptism.

In Amsterdam at the beginning of November 1533 Jan Matthys had become the leader of the Anabaptist movement in the Netherlands. Unceasingly he preached the beginning of the new kingdom of God as well as the sword for the destruction of the godless. Matthys sent out apostles to preach and to baptize, and two of them arrived in Münster at the beginning of January 1534. Bernhard Rothmann together with others had himself baptized by these men. The news that Münster had been chosen as the new kingdom spread like wildfire; from everywhere the Anabaptists converged on the city, and 1400 people were baptized in one week of January 1534. Jan Bockelson and Jan Matthys hurried to Münster to help establish the new kingdom of Zion.

What now followed was like a nightmare. In February 1534, the Anabaptists seized power in Münster and one of their leaders, Knipperdolling, became mayor. Jan Matthys ruled the city as a Prophet, and all people who refused to be re-baptized were driven out as the godless. The bishop besieged the city, and when Matthys was killed during a sortie early in April 1534, Jan Bockelson, known as Jan von Leiden, succeeded him. Now the reign of terror began. In the midst of the deprivation of the siege Bockelson had himself proclaimed as the "new King of Israel" and appointed Rothmann, Knipperdolling, and Krechting as dignitaries. He also established a body-guard for himself, and the resulting situation was characterized by communal property holding, polygamy, starvation amidst glittering parties, and the execution of those regarded as godless. On June 25, 1535, the bishop finally succeeded in capturing the city; after bloody streetbattles the kingdom of Christ at Münster was ended. Rothmann was killed in the fighting, Jan von Leiden, Knipperdolling, and Krechting were imprisoned for seven months and publicly tortured to death in front of the cathedral in January 1536. Their corpses were displayed in cages hung from the Lamberti tower.

After these excesses in Münster, there followed a particularly harsh persecution; yet there also took place a significant internal change in Anabaptism. The radicals were excluded, and Menno Simons, a former East Frisian priest, became the leader of the moderates. By completely renouncing the use of force, Simons strove for a purely spiritual kingdom of God stringently divorced from any secular power. His adherents, the Mennonites, lived as "the quiet in the land". Their doctrine and custom were influenced by Zwingli and they were close to the Reformation without, however, accepting as binding its statements of confession. For a time the Mennonites had a large following, chiefly among the lower classes.

43
John Calvin and the Reformation in Geneva

The third and youngest, but certainly most effective, Reformer was John Calvin, who made Geneva the center of a worldwide movement.

1. John Calvin was born on July 10, 1509, at Noyon and also came from a social class which was close to the church. His father was procurator general, i.e. business manager, of the cathedral chapter of Noyon. He secured a benefice in Noyon for his son when John was only twelve years old and decided that John was to follow an ecclesiastical career. John grew up in the company of the nephews of the bishop. His devout mother, who early introduced him to ecclesiastical piety, died very young. It

is possible that the lack of motherly love was important in Calvin's development. "The feminine and love play no role in Calvin's life, theology, and actions" (Fr. Heer). In comparison, Calvin's head-strong father exerted a powerful influence on his six children. "The father demanded . . . unconditional submission. There was no backtalk, no criticism, no disobedience. The young John Calvin was deeply impressed by the will and authority of his father: He was to shape God's majesty and his own person according to this model" (Heer).

In 1523 Calvin began the study of philosophy and theology at Paris. He lived in the Collège Montaigu in which Erasmus had resided before him and in which Ignatius of Loyola would live a few years after him. At Paris the *via antiqua* was taught. In 1529 Calvin suddenly broke off the study of theology and turned to law. The change has been attributed to the difficulties which Calvin's father experienced with the cathedral chapter and the bishop and which resulted in his father's excommunication. Calvin's older brother, a chaplain, also broke with the church. He was apparently infected by the new religious thought, refused to read Mass, and even declined extreme unction at his sudden early death.

Calvin became acquainted with humanists while he was pursuing the study of law in Orléans and Bourges (1529–1532). After 1532 Calvin again devoted himself to humanistic studies. In his commentary on Seneca's *De Clementia* (1532) there was no trace as yet of the spirit of the Reformation; Calvin was still totally engrossed in the reform ideas of the humanists. Then, as Calvin states in his autobiography of 1557, a *subita conversio* occurred, a sudden turning to Protestantism. This event may have taken place during the winter of 1533–1534. In any case, Calvin resigned his two benefices in Noyon, and when he became subject in 1534 to the persecution of Protestants which had been decreed by the *Parlement* of Paris, he fled to Basle. There Calvin wrote his famous *Institutio religionis Christianae,* his masterly principal work. It was first printed anonymously in 1536 and then under his name in Basle in 1537, and overnight Calvin became

298

famous. Actually his masterwork had been intended as an apologia of Protestantism for Francis I of France, but instead it became the fundamental work of Calvinism down to this day. It was revised and expanded by Calvin several times prior to 1559.

Calvin's path accidentally took him to Geneva in 1536 where the Reformer William Farel (1489–1565) asked him to remain. Geneva had come into conflict with the hierarchical church because of political opposition to its sovereign, the duke of Savoy, and to the bishop of the city, who was related to him. Zwinglianism became influential in the city because the military support of Bern was needed by Geneva. Since 1532 Farel had been almost alone in his opposition to the will of the majority of the population. The amalgamation of religious concern with politics led the city toward the Reformation; "the victory of the evangelical movement in Geneva did not originate in a religious movement by the population, but in a struggle for the political independence from the duchy of Savoy" (Heussi). Calvin immediately intervened and in a short time succeeded in gaining influence in the city council. He enforced his iron will upon everyone and even wrote a new creed and a catechism for the young which were printed at the expense of the city and distributed to all citizens. In April 1537 the whole population was obliged to gather information and, in groups of ten, swear an oath to the new creed. Whoever refused lost his rights as a citizen and could not remain in the city. Calvin, who since the beginning of 1537 had held the office of public preacher, demanded with rigoristic severity the unconditional acceptance of Christian principles in both public and private life. The ethical and religious life of the city was to be reformed according to God's word. On July 29, 1537, the city council gave its approval to an ecclesiastical discipline which Calvin had designed.

The rigorous implementation of the discipline met mounting resistance, and the council, which was a slave to Calvin, was not reelected in February 1538. The new council removed Calvin from office on April 23, 1538 and banished him from the city together with Farel. Calvin then went to Strassburg where he established contact with the German Reformers; as a delegate of the city he participated in the talks concerning union at Hagenau, Worms, and Regensburg. In 1539 Calvin married Idelette von Büren, when friends urged him to do so; but Calvin, who was so completely engrossed in his task, had little time or liking for domesticity and love. After Idelette's death in 1549 Calvin stated only that she had never been a burden or a hindrance to him.

When the adherents of Calvin regained power in Geneva, he was recalled in September 1541. With indefatigable energy he immediately began to introduce his religious ideas. Their culmination was the establishment of a theocracy for the city. On September 20, 1541, the council passed into law Calvin's church constitution, the *Ecclesiastical Ordinances*. It provided for four classes of church offices: pastors, teachers, elders, and deacons. The pastors and teachers together formed the *vénérable compagnie*, entrusted with the actual pastoral care of preaching and teaching. The elders and deacons represented the consistory which, independently from the first group, managed the external affairs of the church and sternly supervised the religious and moral life of the community. The elders had free access to every house at any time and unannounced scrutinized the behaviour and attitude of all members of the community, and proceeded with unrelenting harshness against all transgressions of the religious and civil order. If spiritual punishments such as censure, penance, public apology, and excommunication were of no avail or considered too lenient, the elders requested secular punishments from the city council.

As early as 1541 the council commissioned Calvin with the drafting of a civil code which would fuse ecclesiastical and civil laws; the "secular arm" now had to grant the requests of the elders and mete out the cruel penalties. Impugning the truths of the faith, blasphemy, and high treason were punished by death at the stake; adultery, fornication, and irreverence to parents also exacted the death penalty. Failure to appear at divine service, card-playing, dancing, visiting an inn, and worldly pleasures were also punished severely, because, as Calvin explained, "the corruption of man is so great that he cannot enjoy himself without forgetting about God".

These measures were ruthlessly applied; in the first five years (1541–1546) no fewer than fifty-six death sentences were carried out and seventy-eight sentences of banishment imposed. The opposition of the people was great, but Calvin did not hesitate to employ the necessary means to break it. As late as 1553 he had the Spanish physician and philosopher Michael Servetus burned at the stake for denying the dogma of the Trinity, and such humanists as Castellio, Bolsec, and many others escaped the same fate only by flight.

Partially through the assistance of French refugees who were granted civic rights while old-established citizens were banished, all opposition was silenced by 1555. The new Geneva was a thoroughly organized theocracy and the center of a new "Reformed" Church which far surpassed Lutheranism in firmness, determination, and organization. The newly founded Geneva Theological Academy (1559) soon surpassed Wittenberg and became the outstanding training institute for "Reformed" teachers and preachers who soon spread Calvin's ecclesiastical system to all parts of Europe. From Geneva, Calvin methodically guided the triumphal progress of his Reformation which was especially successful in the western countries. In a worldspanning correspondence with theologians and laymen and in numerous messages to princes and kings, Calvin asked all of them in prophetic tones to do away with Catholicism and to introduce his Reformation. Because of his strong sense of mission Calvin could in the same breath remonstrate with Catholic princes and accuse them of intolerance against the Reformed Church in their countries and also make the eradication of Catholicism the highest duty of Protestant sovereigns and regard tolerance of Catholics in these countries as a sin against God. In contrast to Luther, who always postulated obedience to the authorities, Calvin granted his followers the right of resistance against a "godless" government and declared it their religious duty. Wherever Calvinists lived in a Catholic state, such as in France and initially in Scotland, "they refashioned the idea of submission of the state to the sovereignty of God into a *duty* of the faithful in a relentless struggle to replace a *differently believing government* by a believing government" (Heussi). In this context, the killing of tyrants was accepted as the right of the nobility and the estates. One must see the ramifications of this in full clarity, in order to understand the severity of the Huguenot wars in France and the fear of Calvinism on the part of the princes. Measuring with two kinds of yardsticks is an invention of Calvin, and it became one of the basic roots of the intolerance which led to the religious wars. Calvin died in Geneva in 1564.

2. The three *"sola"* were common to all Reformers of the sixteenth century. Even more radically than Luther, Calvin made Scripture and faith into the foundations of his Bible theology. The Holy Spirit imparts belief to the soul with the help of sacramentally understood Scripture. This belief is the free gift of God, a sign of his election. Whoever believes the word of God is therefore elected and will and must live accordingly. In a good Christian life faith must prove its effectiveness; therefore, life on earth is also the proof and the foundation for the certainty of election to eternal life. Whoever does not live a good Christian life also does not believe correctly and cannot be assured of his salvation. The awareness of being chosen becomes, therefore, the strongest motive force in everyday Christian life for Calvin's adherents.

There is, however, also a reverse side. Whoever closes his heart to God's word does not obtain God's grace of election. Calvin did not hesitate to add that that person is also outcast by God; even more, God wills the rejection of some people, just as he predestines others freely to grace. This doctrine of double predestination, i.e. the prior determination of some to be elect and others to be damned, is characteristic of Calvin's hard theological thought. He obtained the doctrine from certain parts of the Bible which he then made one-sidedly absolute. "A gloomy, yet glowing rigorism" (Lortz) is behind it. This doctrine of predestination, with regard to the concept of the church and the con-

302

sciousness of being elect, did not have the effect of paralyzing Calvin's followers, but instead inspired them. For them there was a second sign of being elect, namely membership in the reformed church.

For Calvin, the church was "visible" and "invisible" at the same time. No one can be of the right inner faith, i.e. belong to the spiritual, invisible church unless he confesses it outwardly and adapts himself totally to the visible church community. A true faith and salvation, therefore, can not exist outside of the reformed church. The true church can only be that one in which God's word is correctly preached and the sacraments are rightly administered. Since Calvin believed that the Catholic Church failed in both of these functions, it consequently became for him a false church and a work of the devil which must be avoided. Calvin not only regarded the Catholic Church with contempt, he also attacked it with unremitting hostility and imbued his followers with this hostility as well. It was Calvin who kindled a denominational war mentality long before Lutheranism and Catholicism had fallen into this deplorable state. Calvinism, with its implacable aggressiveness, soon became the principal foe of the Catholic Church everywhere, and additionally was at odds with Lutheranism.

Regarding the doctrine of the Eucharist, Calvin taught a spiritual pneumatic presence of Christ at the moment of reception. Luther's real presence he rejected as being as idolatrous as the Catholic doctrine, and Zwingli's doctrine of the significative symbolical presence he considered inadequate.

3. France became the first battlefield. Francis I (1515–1547) and Henry II (1547–1559) supported the German Protestants, but bloodily persecuted the innovators at home. Nevertheless, reformed communities were established, maintained, and extended through great sacrifice of blood and heroic devotion. Calvin untiringly exhorted his followers to unique heroism by letters, writings, and messengers. In 1559 the Calvinists were able to hold their first synod at Paris, for which Calvin drafted a confession of faith, the *Confessio Gallicana*. These Calvinists

became known as Huguenots (= *Eidgenossen*), and the conversion of several high-standing noble families in the 1560's involved the Huguenots in the struggle between noble factions and finally turned them into a political party. Their leaders were admiral Coligny and the princes Anthony and Louis of Condé of the house Bourbon-Vendôme. The Catholic party was led by the Lotharingian noble family of Guise. In 1562, religious and civil war broke out. The Huguenot Wars of 1562–1598 were conducted with unbelievable severity and brutality. Under Charles IX (1560–1574), whose mother Catherine de Medici had held the regency during his minority, there was a prospect of reconciliation which was to be sealed by the marriage of the leader of the Protestants, Henry of Navarre, to a sister of Charles IX. Catherine and the Guises used the marriage on St. Bartholomew's eve August 24, 1572, as an opportunity for a ghastly massacre of the attending Huguenots. The "bloody wedding of Paris", one of whose victims was Coligny, was followed by massacres of Huguenots in the provinces. The number of victims is not known exactly, but it was very large. The entire event can only be described as one of the most horrible crimes in world history. The nature of the crime was, however, more political than religious. It is not historically tenable to regard Pius V as having had advance knowledge of it; and if Gregory XIII, who had just become pope, had a Te Deum sung, it was because he was informed only of a "victory" over the Huguenots.

After the massacre, the struggle continued. With the death of Henry III (1574–1589) the royal house of the Valois became extinct, the Bourbons inherited the government, and none other than Henry of Navarre, the leader of the Huguenots, became the heir to the throne. This demonstrates the close connection of the Huguenot problem with royal policy. Henry IV (1589–1610) had to convert to Catholicism in order to claim his heritage ("Paris is worth a Mass"), and France remained Catholic. In the Edict of Nantes in 1598, however, the Huguenots were granted a limited freedom of religion and more than two hundred fortified towns for their security. The influence of the Huguenots continued to be considerable until the absolute monarch Louis XIV (1643–1715) revoked the Edict of Nantes in 1685 and required the Huguenots to return to Catholicism. More than 200,000 Huguenots fled from France at that time for the sake of their faith. Only during the Enlightenment in the middle of the eighteenth century did Protestants in France receive freedom of religion.

In the Netherlands, the political conflict with Spain kindled the war of liberation (1566–1609), which at the same time resulted also in the religious and ecclesiastical rejection of the Catholic Church. Under the shadow of warfare, Calvinism entered the Netherlands, and in 1571 the first Netherland national synod took place at Emden. Calvinism became the established religion in the northern Netherlands while the Spanish southern provinces remained Catholic. Calvinism reached the lower Rhineland in the late 1550's by way of the Netherlands and the Electoral Palatinate.

Coming by way of Scotland, Calvinism also made great advances in England. Holland and England, as the two strongest sea-powers of the time, carried it overseas and raised it to worldwide importance.

44
THE REFORMATION IN ENGLAND

The Reformation in England was largely an act of state — in a sense, a political revolution. Henry VIII's conflict with the papacy over his marriage to Catherine of Aragon and the subsequent Act of Supremacy in 1529, popularly viewed as the advent of the English Reformation, represented the culmination of a trend toward an independent national church that had been at work for nearly two centuries.

During the Hundred Years' War the English, suspicious of the French-controlled papacy, lessened papal authority in England by the statutes against Provisors (1351) and the statute of Praemunire (1353). Appointments to English benefices by papal provision were declared invalid. Appeals to ecclesiastical courts outside of England were unlawful and violators were subject to severe punishment. Early English reformers, such as John Wyclif (1320–1384) and the Lollards, attacked the principle of papal supremacy and ecclesiastical hierarchy. Thomas Wolsey (1475–1530), Lord Chancellor and Papal Legate, ruled the church in England after 1518 with little or no interference from the Pope. Yet anti-Romanism was not as pronounced in England as it was on the continent.

During the Western Schism the English crown had supported the pope in Rome; during the conflict between pope Eugene IV and the Council of Basle, it had upheld the pope. In 1521 Henry VIII wrote a reply to *On the Babylonian Captivity of the Church*, in which Luther had attacked the sacramental system and the sacrifice of the Mass. In return, Leo X bestowed upon the English crown the title of Defender of the Faith.

It was Wolsey's failure to gain an annulment for Henry in his marriage with Catherine of Aragon that brought the Chancellor's downfall and a jurisdictional break with Rome.

Catherine had failed to produce Henry with a male heir, her only living child having been Mary, later queen. Henry saw the need for a male heir to provide security for the Tudor dynasty and wished to marry Anne Boleyn, his mistress.

Appealing to Leviticus 18, 16 and 20, 21, he claimed his marriage with Catherine was invalid because she had previously been the wife of his older brother, Arthur, who had died at age fourteen. He further asserted that the dispensation for the marriage, granted by Julius II in 1503, violated divine law. Clement VII was too weak politically to refuse Henry's demand outright, yet he could not declare the act of a predecessor invalid without bringing into question his own authority. More compelling for a negative reply, however, was the fact that the Emperor Charles V, Catherine's nephew, had captured the pope in 1527 and sacked Rome, which he still held. On Charles' insistence, the canonical trial, which was to decide the issue of the consummation of Catherine and Arthur's marriage and decide the validity of her marriage with Henry, was transferred to Rome.

Henry began arranging for another sort of solution — one without the pope. Wolsey was charged with high treason and died en route to his trial in November, 1530. Parliament had been summoned in 1529 and a number of bills were drafted for reforming the ecclesiastical administration. The statute of Praemunire was gradually widened by the courts and in 1531 was turned against the English clergy for administering Roman canon law in their courts. The Convocation of the Clergy was allowed to buy royal forgiveness with 108,000 pounds and were forced to recognize the king as "Supreme Head of the English Church" with the vague appendage "as far as the law of Christ allows".

Thomas Cranmer (1489–1556), newly appointed Archbishop of Canterbury, declared Henry's marriage to Catherine null in May, 1533, belatedly "justifying" Henry's secret marriage to Anne Boleyn the previous January. Clement VII now intervened, threatening Henry's excommunication unless he dismissed Anne and took Catherine back as his lawful wife.

Henry, however, heartened by the easy submission of the Convocation and having conditioned public opinion through anti-papal pamphlets, had no intention of submitting and was preparing for the break with Rome. Parliament, in the spring of 1534, passed five acts which laid the basis for schism. The king was given sole right to nominate bishops; obtaining dispensations from, or paying fees to Rome was forbidden; sworn acceptance of the royal succession of children born of Henry and Anne's marriage was required; the clergy were made subject to civil law; and it was declared that no statement against the primacy of the Bishop of Rome was heresy.

The climax was reached with the passage of the Act of Supremacy of November 3, 1534, which conferred on the king the title of "the only supreme head on earth of the Church of England", and extended his power to maintaining the purity of doctrine. A second Act of Succession required all officials and ecclesiastics to take an oath upholding the succession of Anne's children, while the Treason Act branded as high treason refusing to recognize the new royal title. The definite break with Rome was an accomplished fact.

There was some grumbling among the lower clergy, though most remained silent out of fear. Three Carthusian priors were the first to fall victim to the Act of Supremacy and were executed with the learned Richard Reynolds in May, 1535. The higher clergy more readily accepted the church's new status, though again there were exceptions — Bishop John Fisher of Rochester and former Lord Chancellor Thomas More were beheaded for refusing to take the required oath.

Henry and Thomas Cromwell, who had risen to the office of Lord Chancellor, turned their attention to the suppression of monasteries, which had begun on a limited scale with Wolsey's administration. The smaller monasteries were suppressed by Parliamentary decree in 1536, while the larger monasteries "voluntarily" surrendered. Though historical accounts of a catastrophic social upheaval following the dissolution of the monasteries have been greatly exaggerated, it cannot be denied that England suffered the loss of educational, medical and charitable institutions, as well as countless manuscripts and artifacts.

From 1535–1539 modest patronage was given to moderate reformers, but in 1539 Henry found it necessary to assert his Catholic faith through the Act of Six Articles. These established penalties for denial of transubstantiation, private masses, private confession and the need for clerical celibacy.

Henry VIII died on January 28, 1547, leaving Edward VI, a son by his third marriage (with Jane Seymour), heir to the throne. Edward was nine years of age upon his accession and under the regency of the Earl of Hertford, power soon fell to the supporters of reform. Between 1547 and 1553, under the Duke of Northumberland, the reforming party produced a new and simplified liturgy in the vernacular with a Swiss doctrine of the Eucharist, published a new statement of doctrine based on Zwinglian theology, stripped the churches of images and side altars, and replaced the high altar with the holy table. Further, they forbade the use of ceremonies other than those provided in the Prayer

Book of 1552 and appropriated to secular use a large portion of church property. They weakened the authority of the bishops, substituting for it royal supremacy and where bishops refused to approve reforms, they were removed from their sees and replaced.

Upon the death of Edward in 1553, and after a few days "reign" of Lady Jane Grey, Mary Tudor, a zealous Roman Catholic, was placed on the throne. The brief restoration of Roman Catholicism during her reign (1553–1558) indicated how difficult it would be to reestablish the ancient faith in England. The persecution of evangelists as well as papal politics, reactionary Catholicism and Mary's marriage to Philip II of Spain did much to encourage a popular trend toward Protestantism.

Mary's death in 1558 left the task of eradicating strife to Elizabeth. Her settlement was political, rather than theological. Though she was attached to the Protestant faith and introduced a Protestant equivalent to Mary's persecutions, she sought to enforce religious conformity upon her realm primarily in order to weld it into a strong state firmly under her control. She did not seek so much to impose doctrine upon her subjects as to create unity and harmony within her realm. Heresy was a crime in Elizabethan England more in the political sense than a theological one, in that heresy encouraged schism and schism was treason. The so-called Elizabethan settlement was an attempt to satisfy as many of her subjects as possible in terms of religious belief. Toward the end of the sixteenth century, Catholic intrigue, Elizabeth's belated excommunication in 1570, political rivalry with France and Spain, and especially the Armada in 1588, did a great deal to encourage the acceptance of a more radical reform and heightened the persecution of Roman Catholics in England. A new generation of Calvinist and Bucerian enthusiasts from the continent began to appeal to the intellectuals of the kingdom. By the reign of James I, the anti-Catholicism of Calvin and the early Puritans was well established.

45
ECCLESIASTICAL REFORM ATTEMPTS
BEFORE THE COUNCIL OF TRENT

Ecclesia semper reformanda! The church is always in need of reform
and never must be content. It would be tragic indeed if the church
were no longer able to sense the distance between itself and its
model, Jesus Christ. As depressing as the grievances against the
church at the end of the Middle Ages may have been, it is reas-
suring to know that the church itself suffered from them. The
entire fifteenth and sixteenth centuries were filled with bitter
complaints not only against the church but also originating from
its own midst. The force of reform continued to grow and it
developed into a storm which broke as a huge reform movement
inside and outside of the church. After all, the Reformation itself
was only an expression of this desire for reform. The push for
reform within the church took a little while longer, but was no
less insistent.

Seen in detail, the process of reform within the church was at
least as many-sided and complex as the events of the Reformation.
It started at the beginning of the fifteenth century and lasted until
the end of the seventeenth century. Hubert Jedin divides it into
four stages:

1. From the reform councils until the *Sacco di Roma,* 1527.
2. The actual antecedents of the Council of Trent.
3. The Council of Trent.
4. The implementation of the Tridentine decrees.

First stage: Church reform had been one of the major problems
at the Councils of Constance and Basle (1414–1418 and 1431 ff).
During these councils there was no lack of people who recommended removing the whole question of church reform from
the papacy and transferring it to the councils. Martin V and
Eugene IV, however, were able to ward off this threat to their
prerogatives, and subsequently attempts were made by the
papacy in the fifteenth century to realize the *reformatio in capite et
membris.* But owing to the reasons which were discussed pre-

viously, the Renaissance papacy was spiritually too weak to carry out such reform measures.

Reform proposals were submitted under the following popes: Martin V (1417–1431) by cardinal Capranica; and Pius II (1458–1464) by the cardinals Domenichini and Nicholas of Cusa. Nicholas presented an extensive program for a general reform of the whole church and Pius had already drafted the bull of implementation when he died. Even under such popes as Sixtus IV (1471–1484) and the notorious Alexander VI (1492–1503) reform attempts were made. After his son Juan had been murdered in the summer of 1497, Alexander in an hour of severe shock reflected and for a short period considered an inner change. In 1512 Julius II (1503–1513) appointed a commission of eight cardinals which was to draft reform suggestions for the Fifth Lateran Council (1512–1517). The Camaldolese monks Giustiniani and Quirini submitted to Leo X (1513–1521) the most radical program which had been drafted so far.

Were these projects only pretense and delusion? With all due skepticism about the Renaissance popes, this charge cannot be made without modification. If these reforms failed or were not even attempted, there were many reasons; the most important one was that the popes themselves and the curia lacked the inner religious strength for their implementation.

When the papacy failed, the reformers provided their own help. The observer who looks behind the traditional dark shadows of the fifteenth century can partly perceive a very astonishing picture. Particularly in Germany this epoch was rich in ardent and efficient reform bishops (Dietrich von Bülow at Lebus, d. 1523; Matthias Rammung von Speyer, d. 1478). Among the orders there was also great activity, and reform branches and movements of observants sprang up (reform congregation of the Benedictines at Bursfeld, 1446; reform movement of the Augustinian canons at Windesheim; and others among the Franciscans and Dominicans). Luther belonged to such a strict reform group, the Augustinian Eremites, on whose business he visited Rome in 1511. The number of the great preachers of penance (Savonarola, Capistrano) was considerable, and they often effected marvellous conversions among the people, as the example of Savonarola in Florence demonstrated.

The second stage of reform is characterized by the struggle between Emperor Charles V and the popes over the calling of a council. Charles early began to call for a council, and in order to assess correctly the negotiations between the monarch and the popes one must look at the ecclesiastical and political situation as a whole.

Luther had appealed to a general council on November 28, 1518. In 1521 the idea of bringing the matter of Luther before a council came up again at the Diet of Worms. When the moving confession of guilt of the noble-minded Adrian VI, which promised immediate reforms, was read at the Diet of Nürnberg in 1523, the German princes responded with a call for "a free Christian council in Germany". The demand was repeated in the following year, and since a general council could not be held without a pope, the German princes simply convoked a German national council on November 11, 1524, at Speyer. The emperor had forbidden this council with the remark: "How can a single nation dare to change the ecclesiastical order?" He did, however, insist even more vigorously than before on the convocation of a general council by the pope.

Pope Clement VII (1523–1534) feared a general council because he remembered the conciliarism of Constance and Basle. All too clearly the imperial estates had indicated what they understood by a "free Christian council in Germany": it was to be free of the pope, i.e. the pope was to have no influence and the council fathers were to be released from their oath to him. The pope's concern, then, was not completely unjustified.

Clement also had another reason for not desiring a council which was connected with his policy toward the Papal States. Just as his predecessors, Clement regarded concern for the Papal States as a supreme law. He had inherited from Julius II (1503–1513), the statesman general, patron of the arts, and most outstanding of the Renaissance popes, a state which appeared healthy, but which actually was internally weak and susceptible. The cultured hedonist Leo X (1513–1521) had done little to strengthen the Papal States, and the devout and sincere Adrian VI (1522–1523), the former teacher of Charles V and the last German on the papal throne, had had even less time and interest in politics. He had been concerned solely with the reform of the church, and he had died too early. Now Clement pursued a policy similar to that of Julius II. Although personally without a blemish, Clement, as a natural descendant of the Medici, like Leo X, was oriented entirely toward the secular and political. He wanted to complete the work of his predecessors, and this work seemed to be most endangered by the universal monarchy of the Habsburgs, which encompassed the kingdom of Naples-Sicily as well as the imperial part of northern Italy. Therefore, Clement sought an alliance with France.

Charles V had just won his first war with Francis I (battle of Pavia, 1525; peace of Madrid, 1526) and now intended to return to Germany to clear up the problem of the German church. Charles's intervention was urgently needed (Diet of Speyer, 1526), but Francis I again declared war and the pope followed suit (League of Cognac, 1526). So much treachery and disloyalty made Charles indignant and he threatened the pope with a trial by a general council unless he left the league immediately. Charles then let his troops march on Rome to give the pope a show of strength; he did not foresee the consequences. Because their commanders George of Frundsberg and the Connétable of Bourbon had been killed, the rough and undisciplined Spanish and German mercenaries were leaderless when they stormed Rome on May 6, 1527; the pillaging, plundering, and murdering in the Eternal City lasted for weeks. Clement took refuge in the castle of San Angelo, but on June 5 had to surrender and endure half a year of harsh imprisonment.

This *Sacco di Roma* was regarded as a natural catastrophe by contemporaries; it was thought to be a terrible visitation by God to bring about penance and change in the secularized curia and to put an end to the Renaissance in Rome. Afterwards, reform

313

began. Admittedly, the change of heart was a slow one; Paul III (1534–1549) was still a child of the Renaissance, but he did take the first serious steps toward reform.

The emperor and the pope were reconciled through the peace of Barcelona in June 1529. In Bologna, where they were together for several months (November 1529 to February 1530; coronation of the emperor on February 24, 1530), they discussed the German religious question which was of such great importance to Charles. In the event that no agreement could be reached at the Diet of Augsburg (1530) it was agreed to call a general council. However, when the emperor, after the fruitless Diet, asked for the redemption of the pledge, Clement withdrew his promise; his apprehension was too great. "Oh", he sighed, "the Germans will bring confusion to the council and to the whole world", and he could not be induced to hold a general council together with the German Protestants.

New opportunities for council and reform only opened up under Paul III of the house of Farnese. Paul had not yet been affected by a desire for reform and was wholly unsuited for his high spiritual office. He had three illegitimate sons and a daughter, and as pope indulged in unrestrained nepotism. As cardinal, however, his views had become somewhat more serious. The *Sacco di Roma* had brought him to the realization that reform and change of heart were necessary, and so he began where he felt reform was most urgently needed, in the college of cardinals. He appointed a number of champions of reform to the college, among them Contarini, Fisher, Simonetta, Caraffa, Sadoleto, Pole, Servini, Fregoso, Morone, and others. He used these cardinals to form a reform congregation (1536), and in 1537 it submitted its report, the *Consilium de emendanda ecclesia,* which later served as model for the Tridentinum. Paul also furthered the new reform orders of the Theatines, Barnabites, Somaschi, and Capuchins. In 1540 he also approved the order of the Jesuits and worked honestly and hard to bring about a general council. Paul and Charles V agreed to call a council at Mantua for May 23, 1537.

Francis I did everything in his power to thwart the council; because of his struggle for hegemony of Europe, he feared a strengthening of the emperor's position during a general council. Francis did not hesitate to incite the Turks against the emperor and to conclude an alliance with the German Protestants, but Charles was again the victor in this third war with Francis I (1536–1538). After fruitless attempts at peaceful religious union at Hagenau, Worms, and Regensburg (1540), a council now seemed more urgently needed than ever. At Charles's urgent request the pope called the council for June 29, 1542 at Trent. Francis now declared war on Charles for the fourth time (1542–1544), and only after its conclusion was the victorious emperor able in the peace of Crépy (September 19, 1544) to force Francis I to agree to a general council. Again Paul III convoked the council at Trent, this time for March 15, 1545, but the council was able to assemble only in December.

46
THE COUNCIL OF TRENT, 1545–1563

The third stage of reform, the work of the council itself, is as rich in controversy and complexity as the antecedents of the council which already have shown how immensely difficult and involved it had been to make it a reality. On December 13, 1545, only thirty-one council fathers led by the papal legates Del Monte, Cervini, and Pole were present for the opening ceremonies, and no one suspected that this was the beginning of the greatest event in all modern Catholicism.

1. The debates began immediately with a fierce discussion between emperor and pope over the fundamental question of what the council should regard as its first and major order of business. The emperor was concerned with reform and the reunion with the Protestants; we have seen his reasons. The pope wanted attention to be centered on the clarification of dogmatic questions; it was necessary to clarify matters of faith as it was

315

becoming apparent only now how devastating the Protestant attack on Catholic theology had been. Luther's action, after all, had not originated in problems of reform, but in problems of dogma. A new doctrine of grace formed the foundation of the Reformation; a new principle of Scripture, a new understanding of justification, the sacraments, and the church, all determined the life of the new communities. A valid answer to this problem could, then, only be attempted with regard to dogma. On the other hand, disciplinary reforms also could not be neglected, and by January 22, 1546, it was agreed to treat dogma and reform simultaneously.

In its total effect, the council was entirely an internal Catholic affair. The council could afford to do without any Protestant participation, because it wanted to be neither a religious disputation along the lines of the German Diets nor a theological controversy between individual theologians, but simply a manifestation of the magisterial office of the church. At no place in the decrees of the council was the name of any of the Protestant Reformers mentioned. The debates in every case were based on a heretical article which had been excerpted from the writings of a Protestant Reformer or dissident theologian and which was then treated by redefining and establishing the Catholic doctrine which opposed it. When the pope was asked whether an indication of source should be made with regard to the particular writings of the Protestant Reformers, Paul decided in the negative and remarked that the council fulfilled its task adequately by unequivocally and clearly expounding Catholic doctrine; its task was to say *what* was heretical, not *who* was a heretic.

Thus the council performed its task objectively; in view of the subjective emotional eruptions of Luther and the personal polemicizing of Calvin, the factual argumentation of the Tridentine theologians provided a comforting and calming picture. Among the theologians present were men of impressive theological training, such as Seripando, de Soto, the Jesuits Laynez and Salmerón, and the German John Gropper of Cologne.

There has been criticism that the Germans were too weakly

316

represented at the council and that the Roman representatives had no real understanding of the underlying problems of the Reformation. To be sure, no German bishops and theologians at all attended the first session in Trent, but during the second session in the fall of 1551 the archbishops of Mainz, Trier, and Cologne, the bishops of Strasbourg, Constance, Chur, Chiemsee, Vienna, and Naumburg, and the suffragan bishops of Mainz, Speyer, Würzburg, and Münster appeared and were accompanied by their theologians: Gropper and Billick of Cologne, Pelargus of Trier, and others. Bishop Frederick Nausea of Vienna, Bishop Julius Pflug of Naumburg, a mediator and Erasmian, and particularly the theologian Gropper were highly respected in Trent. There is no doubt, however, that the principal influence was wielded by Rome: Italians were always in the absolute majority, although the Spaniards were also well represented, especially by their excellent theologians. The church is universal and non-German countries were also affected by the Reformation, if less strongly. Perhaps for this very reason they were in a better position to approach matters objectively than the far more subjective German theologians.

2. The rich results of the council can only be sketched here. The First Period, 1545–1548: In the fourth session (April 8, 1546) the council opposed the Protestant *sola scriptura* principle with the doctrine of the two sources of faith: Scripture and apostolic tradition. According to established Catholic custom, *pari pietatis affectu,* tradition was to be considered a source of faith, and the one-sided emphasis on Scripture alone was declared to be heretical. The fifth and sixth sessions treated the subjects of original sin and justification. In answer to the Protestant doctrine of *sola gratia* and imputation, the belief in the absolute depravity of the fallen human nature was rejected and the significance of sanctifying grace, inherent in the soul, for salvation was emphasized; the believer who stands in grace and who acts out of faith and out of love can perform rewarding good works. In the seventh session, doctrine concerning the sacraments in general, and baptism and confirmation in particular, was defined. Again

317

the council had dealt with a central problem of the Reformation. In the spring of 1547 the work of the council, which in the meantime had grown to sixty-four bishops and seven generals of religious orders, was suddenly interrupted. The outbreak of an epidemic in Trent and the threat from Schmalkaldic troops occasioned the transfer of the council to Bologna (March 11, 1547). The emperor protested in vain; he was then in the process of defeating the Schmalkaldic League and wanted the princes represented at Trent. Charles knew that the Protestant princes would refuse to attend a council assembled in a city of the Papal States and that the transfer would foil his plans. Yet the change was not unwelcome to the pope. The relationship between emperor and pope had become critical once again. Charles had protested the wretched nepotism of Paul when the pope had made his wicked son Pier Luigi Farnese duke of Parma and Piacenza, a part of the Papal States, and Paul III was unable to forgive Charles his interference. Driven by Pier Luigi, Paul withdrew the papal troops and money from the support of the emperor, just as Charles was about to strike the decisive blow against the Protestants. Paul also resumed treacherous relations with Henry II of France who was continuing the anti-imperial policy of his father. When Pier Luigi was murdered in September 1547, the anger of the pope against the emperor was without bounds. The controversy came into the open and on September 14, 1549, Paul suspended the council which had ceased to hold sessions a year before. Charles threatened a new *Sacco di Roma,* and only the demise of the pope prevented the outbreak of hostilities.

Second Period: 1551–1552: The council legate del Monte was elected as papal successor and as Julius III (1550–1555) reopened the council of Trent on May 1, 1551. In the beginning, attendance was even smaller than during the first period, but in the autumn the Germans arrived. The Eucharist was debated intensely and the real presence and transubstantiation were clearly defined (13th session). Then the sacraments of penance and extreme unction were discussed (14th session), and particularly the sacramental character of absolution, auricular confession, and atonement were emphasized.

In January 1552 the Protestants finally appeared. The victorious emperor had persuaded them to attend the council and he had hopes of great success. Charles was of the opinion that there still existed a uniform basis for mutual negotiations, and that one only needed to get discussion started. The deputies of Saxony, Brandenburg, Württemberg, and the city of Strassburg, however, had their instructions which they presented to the general assembly on January 21, 1552: The council must not promulgate any further decrees on matters of faith until the Protestant theologians had arrived; then all hitherto promulgated decrees would have to be revoked and re-discussed on the exclusive basis of the *sola scriptura* principle. Finally they wanted the council to function independently from the pope, with all bishops released from their oath of obedience, and the council was to be superior to the pope. The Council of Trent, as one of the Protestant theologians had maintained, so far had been neither general, because not all nations were represented, nor free, because it was not free of the pope, nor even Christian, because in its earlier sessions it had damned the correct Christian doctrine (J. Brenz, as cited by Hubert Jedin). That the council not be under the chairmanship of the pope was one of their basic demands, and for this reason the Württemberg delegates had been expressly forbidden to present themselves and report to the papal legates at Trent.

That there no longer existed a common basis for discussion was only too evident. The pope prohibited any further negotiation with regard to the Protestant demands and soon after, a revolt of the princes in Germany brought the council to an end (April 28, 1552).

The third council period, 1561–1563, was the most fruitful. It was called because of the threatening situation in France where the Huguenots were making much progress and where there was real danger of a French national council. The German bishops did not participate, as they dared not leave their bishoprics in view of the dangerous denominational tensions.

319

The most important points of debate were once again the Eucharist and the sacrifice of the Mass (twenty-first and twenty-second sessions) and the sacraments of orders and marriage (twenty-third and twenty-fourth sessions). During the debates on marriage the delegates were concerned with the question of clandestine marriages, and in the decree *Tametsi* it was decided that in the future no marriage would be valid unless it were entered into before a parish priest and two witnesses. During the twenty-fifth and final session on December 3 and 4, 1563, decrees were published concerning purgatory, indulgences, veneration and invocation of saints, and relics and images. 199 bishops, 7 abbots, and 7 generals of orders signed the numerous decrees on faith and reform, and they were then passed on to the pope. On January 28, 1564, Pope Pius IV confirmed all decrees without exception. The implementation of the decrees was now in the hands of the popes, bishops, and the church as a whole. This task was to occupy the following decades.

"The Council of Trent was the answer of the supreme magisterial office to the Protestant Reformation" (H. Jedin). It was not a solution to theological controversy, but a magisterially clear delineation of the Catholic doctrine of faith and represented internal reflection and genuine reform.

47

The Reconstruction after the Great Council

The beginning implementation of the council decrees constitutes the fourth stage of reform. This stage is marked by an extraordinarily stubborn struggle against entrenched grievances in all countries and bishoprics which now began an extremely complex process of growth. In spite of this, the restoration of Catholic life belongs among the most wonderful phenomena of church history. The attitude of resignation which had fallen upon the Catholic people, much like that of a retreating army, slowly gave way to a new battle spirit and a rediscovered self-assurance. The shocking effect of the time of the great apostasy was slowly overcome and the people who had remained loyal to their beliefs once again rejoiced in their faith.

A genuine ecclesiastical reformer requires the charisma of a saint. Only a saint has the strength to bear the full measure of human wretchedness and to offer it to God as a sacrifice. This is the precise distinction between a true reformer and a false one, that the true reformer is prepared to bear patiently the cross of the weaknesses and faults of his fellow human beings and to destroy neither himself nor others in the process. The Protestant Reformers often ignored old traditions "with a terribly ruthless irreverence" (Lortz). Like all fanatics they lacked genuine historical understanding and believed themselves able to reform the church with just a few manipulations. They certainly removed a few grievances, but they could bring neither sanctification nor inner recuperation.

Life in the service of reform is a difficult renunciatory burden. Only deep religiosity, heroic virtue, and unshakable belief in the sanctity of the church endowed the men of the ecclesiastical reconstruction with the strength, endurance, self-discipline, discretion, and, most of all, the skilful adaptation necessary to heal and not to destroy and to gather and not to disperse. They also were not spared bitter disappointments, failures, and malicious slanders, but the time had called them and they became the great helpers in this time of need.

On all levels of life in this century following the Tridentinum we again encounter so many great saints that we like to speak of the "era of saints". Each was busy with a particular task and was in truth "God's answer to the need of the time".

1. In Pius V (1566–1572) we see for the first time in three hundred years a saint as pope. This was especially important because the determination for ecclesiastical revival was thus convincingly and believably portrayed through the *reformatio in capite*. Pius owed his election to St. Charles Borromeo, and as a Dominican he continued, while on the papal throne, that ascetic life and those virtuous practices which combined a mystical

union with God in prayer with a fervent zeal for reform. He considered his most important papal duty to be the internal revival of the whole church in conformity with the resolutions of Trent. Pius logically began with a reform of the college of cardinals to which men of immaculate ethics and religiosity were appointed and which then was put to work with full responsibility for the task of reform. The pope also expanded the congregation which had been established by his predecessor, Pius IV, for the interpretation and evaluation of the Tridentinum. Then Pius founded a new congregation of cardinals to propagate and maintain the faith (1568). Yet another congregation was given the task of advising the bishops and prelates of the church and providing them with the supervision which had proven to be necessary in the time of the great apostasy. Finally, the pope ordered visitations and synods throughout the whole church to introduce the reforms into the dioceses. For the use of pastors he issued the *Catechismus Romanus* in keeping with the resolutions of Trent (1566), the revised *Roman Breviary* (1568), and a new *Missale Romanum* (1570). Of great importance for the internal functioning of ecclesiastical life was the rigorously accomplished rejuvenation of the papal curia and the correction of simony and other abuses in the curial offices. Because of these actions Pius V is regarded with justification as the great reform pope after the Council of Trent.

Because of Pius's great acts of reform, we can gladly overlook his failings in the arena of international politics, and willingly forgive him his inept handling of Elizabeth of England. In 1570 he excommunicated and deposed her, an action which was totally senseless inasmuch as Elizabeth had been outside the church for a long time. Pius only succeeded in increasing the persecution and oppression of English Catholics. The pope's conduct toward Spain and France was just as unfortunate, but in Germany he did obtain the official recognition of the Tridentine decrees by the emperor and the Catholic estates at the Diet of Augsburg in 1566, and he did see to it that numerous visitations of dioceses, such as the one in Cologne in 1569, and provincial councils actually were held. His greatest triumph was the naval victory over the

Turks at Lepanto (October 7, 1571) which he initiated with the help of Papal, Spanish, and Venetian troops (Holy League).

The successors of Pius V, Gregory XIII (1572–1585), Sixtus V (1585–1590), and the subsequent popes continued his work successfully.

2. The revived episcopate soon was personified by such magnificent episcopal figures as Matteo Giberti of Verona (d. 1543), Gabriele Paleotti of Bologna (1566–1597), and above all by St. Charles Borromeo, archbishop of Milan (1560–1584). Charles, the nephew of Pope Pius IV (1559–1565), had become a cardinal at the age of 21, and as his uncle's secretary had strengthened the pope's determination with regard to reform. Although Charles was not the driving force during the last period of the Council of Trent, as is sometimes erroneously asserted, his episcopate so expressly carried on reform that he may be regarded as the very model of the new Tridentine pastoral bishop. His influence extended far beyond Milan, and his reform measures, which were collected in the *Acta ecclesiae Mediolanensis* (1582) and were printed frequently, were the standards for the whole episcopal reform work in Italy, Switzerland, and Germany. Among the important bishops of the subsequent period we must also mention the illuminating example of St. Francis de Sales (1567–1622). Although bishop of Geneva (1602–1622), Francis resided in Annecy after Geneva had adopted Calvinism.

3. The most beautiful fruit of the reform was produced by the orders which had been affected both internally and externally by the Reformation. Almost all of the old orders resumed the reform attempts of the fifteenth century and experienced a profound reform. Among these orders were the Benedictines, Franciscans, Dominicans, and Augustinians. Only the Carthusians were not in need of reform and had preserved their original way of life throughout the late Middle Ages and the Reformation. New orders with simple vows were now formed in the more mobile societies and congregations. These combined with the reformed branches of monasticism to affect a rejuvenation of inner spiritual life and to help with the active work of ecclesiastical

reform, either by ministering to the people, educating the clergy and the population in general, or by caring for the poor and nursing the sick. Italy and Spain, and later France, were the chief centers of monastic regeneration.

Genuine saints must also be genuine human beings; their human kindness distinguishes them from spiritually crippled fanatics who are always of the devil, even if they appear to place their fanaticism in the service of religion. The humorous and happy St. Philipp Neri (1515–1595), the founder of the Oratory (1552), became the apostle to the city of Rome and succeeded through novel pastoral methods in miraculously transforming this Renaissance city and instigating a religious and ethical revival. He was a friend of St. Ignatius of Loyola and worked with him in Rome. For a short time, Philipp had to suffer the wrath of the sinister and fanatical Paul IV (1555–1559) who wished to extinguish his natural joy, but soon he was able to continue his work with papal blessing and support. He healed many thousands in spirit, body, and soul. His love of life is typical of the renascence of Catholicism and found its artistic expression in the Baroque.

The great St. Theresia of Ávila (d. 1582) lived in Spain, and with her deep mysticism and inexhaustible charity not only rejuvenated the Carmelite order but also affected extensively the spirituality of both Spain and France in the seventeenth century. She was assisted by the Carmelite St. John of the Cross (d. 1591). In 1535 St. Angela Merici (d. 1540) founded the Ursulines in Brescia. The order was approved in 1544 and was transformed in 1582 into a congregation of women for the fostering of charity and the education of girls. The Hospitaller Order of St. John of God (Fate Bene Brothers) developed in 1572 out of an association of devout laymen which had been started by St. John of God (d. 1550). In 1578 St. Charles Borromeo started a congregation of secular priests, the Oblates. St. Camillus de Lellis (d. 1614) founded the Camillians in 1584 for the nursing of the sick and dying. St. Jane Francis de Chantal (d. 1641) in 1610 created the order of the Visitation of Holy Mary with the help of St. Francis de Sales. These sisters later called themselves Salesians after him, and their duties were the nursing of the sick and the education of girls.

In France, Peter of Bérulle (d. 1629, cardinal since 1627) founded the French Oratory in 1611 which was devoted particularly to the education of the clergy. As modern research increasingly shows, Bérulle's influence on the clergy of France in the seventeenth century was immense. He is responsible for the founding of the École Française which conducts a very special training of priests with its impetus in the spiritual theology concerning the mystery of Christ's becoming man. Through the École, Bérulle was able to effect an internally directed revival of the French clergy which lent its own accent to the entire Catholic reform in France. The École Française provided the French clergy with a deep inner life and an excellent theological education. Soon the training of theologians in France was almost exclusively in the hands of the Oratorians, and Charles de Condren (d. 1641), General Superior of the Oratorians, and Jean-Jacques Olier (d. 1657), pastor at St. Sulpice in Paris and founder of the congregation of secular priests, the Sulpicians, continued to emphasize the spirit of Bérulle. Until the beginning of the twentieth century the seminary of St. Sulpice in Paris was one of the most important schools of theology in France, and an example and model for all French seminaries. It was also effective in England and America. St. John Eudes (d. 1680) must be mentioned here also. In 1643 he resigned from the Oratory, founded his own congregation of secular priests, and established seminaries. He also became one of the great revivers of the religious life of France in the seventeenth century.

This attention given to the priesthood was to prove beneficial to France in a high degree. The ascendance of France to the leading intellectual position in the seventeenth and eighteenth centuries rested to a large degree on this rejuvenated ecclesiastical and religious spirit. The new clerics were also ardent pastors and ministered to the people in all their spiritual and human needs. In the same way that John Eudes and the Eudists, in addition to training priests, had ardently devoted themselves to the mission of the people, so St. Vincent de Paul (d. 1660) became the great saint of Christian charity. Together with Louise le Gras he founded the society of the Daughters of Charity, later called Vincentians, which received papal approval in 1668. The Vincentians devoted themselves to the care of the poor and the sick. Vincent also founded a clerical congregation for popular missions, the Lazarists (who were so named after their motherhouse St. Lazare in Paris, although they are also known as Vincentians), who were to concern themselves with the spiritual care of the common people.

After 1644 the Cistercian abbot Armand Jean Le Bouthillier de Rancé (d. 1700) created the strict order of the Trappists. The Borromaeists were founded by E. and J. Chauvenel in Nancy in 1652 as a "secular community" for the care of the abandoned sick; also in 1681 the Institute of Brothers of the Christian Schools was founded by St. John Baptist de la Salle (d. 1719).

Such an abundance of great saints, new orders, and works of charity and education gives proof of the genuine Christian spirit of the epoch. The re-awakened Catholic life, which many had regarded as destroyed during the sixteenth century, attained an impressive fulfillment in the lives of these men and women.

The most important order, its founder Ignatius of Loyola, and his Society of Jesus have not yet been mentioned, and we must deal with them separately.

4. Ignatius of Loyola (1491–1556) will often be completely misunderstood if he is regarded merely as a great strategist, organizer of the Counter-Reformation, and keen observer of human nature and psychology. Above all, Ignatius was a profound mystic, supplicant, and saint. He was born at the castle of Loyola in the Basque country in 1491, received a courtly education (1506–1517), and served as an officer in the army of the Spanish vice king of Navarra, i.e. in the service of Emperor Charles V. During the defense of Pamplona against the French in 1521, Ignatius was severely wounded in the leg. During the course of his extended recuperation he underwent a change of conscience which was completed by a subsequent pilgrimage to

the shrine of the Mother of God of Montserrat; and while in the seclusion of Manresa (March 1522–February 1523), Ignatius experienced his mystic transformation. Here he also wrote the first draft of his famous little book of exercises, the *Exercitia Spiritualia,* and made the decision to seek in the future only the greater glory of God. "Omnia ad maiorem Dei gloriam" became his guiding principle. While on a pilgrimage to the Holy Land (June 1523– January 1524), he decided to become a priest as well, and in spite of all difficulties he survived the Latin school of Barcelona (1524–1526), the philosophical studies in Alcalá and Salamanca (1526–1527), repeated persecutions by the Spanish inquisition, and theological studies in Paris (1528–1535). While in Paris, Ignatius lived in the Collège Montaigu where earlier Erasmus and Calvin had received their education.

In Paris, Ignatius gathered his friends around him: Peter Faber, Francis Xavier, Jacob Laynez, Alfons Salmerón, Simon Rodriguez, and Nicholas Bobadilla, and in Montmartre on August 15, 1534, together they took vows of chastity and obedience and added to them another: to work as missionaries in the Holy Land or, if this should not be possible within a year to put themselves unconditionally at the disposal of the pope for any ecclesiastical task. Ignatius concluded his studies in Paris with the Master's degree in philosophy and theology. Unable to undertake the journey to Palestine, Ignatius and his friends went to Rome in 1538. He was ordained a priest on June 24, 1537, just before his departure. At this time Ignatius decided to found an order, and on September 27, 1540, Paul III approved the statutes. As the first general of his society, Ignatius now remained in Rome and devoted himself completely to his duties; the order grew rapidly.

It is commonly recognized and accepted today that Ignatius's purpose in founding the order was not to fight Protestantism as such, but rather to serve Christ in the church and to work for the internal revival and deepening of Christian life. His thought and his direction did oppose Protestantism, however, because of the diametric opposition of his views to those of Luther and

327

the Reformation. Only now, when the publication of sources is nearly complete, is it possible accurately to assess Ignatius. He was one of the greatest mystics, but his mysticism was without subjectivistic fanaticism. It has been called a "mysticism of service", a sober unselfish dedication to Christ the Lord. Ignatius saw the living Christ in the church, and in the Roman Church exclusively. He took the mystery of the incarnation seriously; human nature, human poverty, and human frailty were part of the incarnate Jesus Christ, who had united them in his person in order to redeem them. The *Ecclesia Spiritualis* was, therefore, unreal and also un-Christian. Ignatius affirmed the human element and wished only to fight sin. The institutionalized church was for Ignatius the living Christ; therefore, he did not hesitate to put himself at the disposal of this church, soberly, realistically, courageously, and without reservations. His gaze was open to the "world" which belongs to Christ, and he believed that in it the mystery of redemption is realized. Ignatius lived in a very "mysticism of secular affirmation" (K. Rahner).

Ignatius also experienced conflicts with the institutional church. As a student he was arrested by the inquisition. He also had stormy encounters with the fanatical cardinal Carafa who brought about a difficult period for Ignatius after he had been chosen pope (Paul IV, 1555–1559). Nevertheless, Ignatius never doubted the church, because he was able to distinguish the human elements from the divine, and to acknowledge and bear them. In this he not only differed from the Reformers, he was diametrically opposed to them; because of his "Catholicity" his thought and volition had to conflict with the Reformation. In contrast to the Reformation's subjectivism and spiritualism and its appeal to individual conscience, Ignatius posited obligation to the church as a higher authority. For him, obedience to the church, which was the very core of his life and that of his order, was obedience to Christ; his unquestioning devotion to the Holy See, to the office of the deputy of Christ, was, therefore, service to Christ.

The maxims for his ecclesiastical conduct he laid down in his *Spiritual Exercises* and thus made them available to many millions of people. These instructions or "rules for the correct churchly attitude" determined the spirit of the post-Tridentine time. Everything which the Reformation with its lack of comprehension and blind zeal had rejected because it was not in keeping with its particular spiritualism, i.e. confession, the sacraments, the Mass, vows, adoration of saints, pilgrimages, indulgences, and liturgical ceremonies, Ignatius made understandable from a profound incarnatory point of view and put into a greater context. He emphasized that one should not speak of faith alone *(sola fides)* but also exhort people to good works, for otherwise they would become lazy and indifferent. One should not only mention that grace alone *(sola gratia)* was responsible for everything, because this "causes the poison which destroys freedom". One also should not point only to predestination, because although there is selection by God without which no one is saved, grace and human participation also should be emphasized. In this and in all other questions of redemption that which was taught by the hierarchical church should be regarded as valid. No one has the right to interpret Holy Scripture according to his own subjective opinion *(sola scriptura);* it is the prerogative of the supreme magisterial office of the church to interpret it authentically.

Again and again Ignatius emphasized the traditional Catholic doctrine of collaboration between God and man, grace and nature. To the one-sidedness of the Reformation Ignatius opposed the Catholic synthesis. "Pray as though everything depended on God alone; but act as though it depended on you alone whether you will be saved." Ignatius did not desire a revival of pre-Reformation conditions but an internal rejuvenation by means of a healthy religious and ecclesiastical spirit. He did not expect anything from a fight against errors and vice. Nowhere in his writings did he refer to the Reformers or heresies. He only wanted to guide people on the right path and save their souls with love and instruction.

In a remarkably short time his followers spread this new spirit and once again Catholics took pleasure in their faith. Nothing mirrors this joy more impressively than the new Baroque style of art. It has been called the Jesuit style, and actually it is not only a form of art but the expression of a new religious and ecclesiastical attitude toward life. As such it has nothing at all to do with Counter-Reform ("Art of the Counter-Reform") but is an expression of the Catholic renascence which followed the Reformation. In color and form the Baroque expresses in inexhaustible profusion the new outpouring vitality of faith. Soon the Baroque adorned the Catholic churches, particularly those of the Jesuits, and its joyful internal and external excitement was communicated to the people gathered for divine service. Soon gay processions of Baroque splendor once again wended their way through the countryside, and the traditional Catholic feasts and customs were again revived and celebrated.

The Jesuits had a large hand in all of this. At the death of St. Ignatius (1556) the order already had about 1,000 members; twenty years later there were 4,000; around 1,600 as many as 8,520; and at the end of the seventeenth century as many as 20,000. The rigid centralized administration of the order permitted its members to develop into a well prepared, extremely effective instrument in the service of ecclesiastical revival. The great number of saints which the order has produced testifies to its inner religious strength. Among them are St. Peter Canisius (1521–1597), the first German Jesuit (since 1543) and "Second Apostle of Germany"; St. Francis Xavier (1506–1552), the great missionary of India and Japan; Francis Borgia, the third general of the order (1565–1572); Aloysius Gonzaga (1568–1591); and Robert Bellarmine (1542–1621).

48

COUNTER-REFORMATION: INQUISITION, PERSECUTION OF HERETICS, AND WITCHCRAFT

1. Calvin and his disciples were determined fighters who without compromise declared a war of destruction on the traditional church. Beza, Calvin's successor, remarked: "It is a Mohammedan doctrine that everyone can be saved in his religion", and freedom

of conscience was detested in Geneva. Compared to Calvin, Luther was a moderate, a man of the middle, despite his bluster against the papacy and the Roman Church, and he was accused by Calvin and Zwingli of having stopped halfway. Lutheranism always remained more willing to compromise with Catholicism than Calvinism, and into the seventeenth century Lutherans and Catholics often worked together against the Calvinists. Real freedom of conscience, however, in the sense of freedom of religion, was an impossibility for the age, because it was essentially at variance with the absolute conception of truth, the religious and political unity of culture, and the unanimous ideological foundation demanded by public life. Only the Enlightenment created the necessary prerequisites for such a change of attitude.

There have been heretics in the church at all times, but on the whole their number always has been small. They were treated as errant members of the church and therefore it was possible to proceed successfully against them by means of ecclesiastical penalties. The Reformation, however, changed the situation; now there were entire religious and ecclesiastical corporations whose members no longer could be viewed as disobedient and misguided members of the *one* great church, but had to be acknowledged as independent confessors of a separate religious faith. In Augsburg in 1555, the Lutherans had been recognized officially as a denominational community and an organized church. Although Calvin, the Anabaptists, and others were still excluded, they also could no longer be overlooked. The big question was: What should be the basic attitude toward the followers of another denomination?

2. "The evolution of denominationally different church types belongs to the major developments of European history in the sixteenth and seventeenth centuries" (E. W. Zeeden). In addition to the religious and ecclesiastical factors, political, juridical, and even economic interests played important roles. Territorial churches had developed even before the Reformation, and those which adopted Lutheranism soon became completely independent. Ecclesiastical, religious, dynastic, and political questions

331

became fused; by 1555 the Reformation was no longer an individual religious decision. The sovereign alone decided the faith of his territory.

The inhabitants of the Electoral Palatinate, for example, were forced to change their faith six times: Prince Elector Louis V (1508–1544) had taken an Erasmian position of mediation in the religious question; Frederick II (1544–1556) opened the doors for the Reformation; Ottheinrich (1556–1559) expelled all Catholic pastors and replaced them with Lutherans; Frederick III (1559–1576) introduced Calvinism and expelled all Lutheran pastors and in 1563 introduced the Calvinistic *Heidelberg Catechism;* Louis VI (1576–1583) restored Lutheranism and with great harshness harried the Calvinistic pastors out of the country; and Frederick IV (1583–1610) forcibly returned the Electoral Palatinate to Calvinism. Following the havoc of the Thirty Years' War, Catholicism was again permitted under the Pfalz-Neuburgers Philipp William (1685–1690) and John William (1690–1716), without, however, replacing the other denominations.

It is obvious that under such conditions the so-called Counter-Reformation also had to use ecclesiastical and political methods. Inasmuch as the religious peace of Augsburg (1555) had transferred the right to determine the religion of the population to the German princes, the future of Catholicism in Germany now depended on how well the church would succeed in instilling the spirit of the inner Catholic revival in the few remaining German Catholic dynasties (Habsburg, Wittelsbach, and, since 1613, also Pfalz-Neuburg) and whether it would be able to put them into the service of maintaining and expanding the Catholic Church in Germany. In this pursuit, Jesuits and Capuchins performed yeoman work among the royalty and nobility as educators, father confessors, and advisors, not only at the German courts, but also in Paris, Madrid, and the Italian principalities. Now ecclesiastical and political alliances played an even more decisive role not only in the marriage arrangements of the princely houses, but also in determining the bestowal of bishoprics and abbacies. Often this necessitated the accumulation of bishoprics in one hand, even though this practice had been severely condemned by the Council of Trent. If the Catholic principalities and bishoprics were to be protected against further inroads of their Protestant neighbors, their political and military position had to be strengthened, and this was only possible by decisive merger with one of the more powerful Catholic principalities. When, for instance, through the apostasy of its archbishop John Gebhard, Truchsess of Waldburg, Cologne was in danger of being lost to the church in 1582–1583, Rome did not hesitate to confer the archbishopric, torn from John Gebhard with Bavarian help, on the Bavarian prince Ernst and to add to it four other West German bishoprics (Liége, Münster, Paderborn, and Hildesheim). From this time, for almost two hundred years, Bavarian princes, as archbishops of Cologne and in personal union with the other bishoprics, governed and protected the entire northwest German area. Occasionally the exigency of the time demanded that great moral weaknesses in these princes be ignored. It was a question of the existence or the destruction of the church in Germany; this crucial issue was part of the spirit of the Counter-Reformation.

3. It is painful to mention the effectiveness of the inquisition in this context. The papal office for the purity of faith and morals, also called *Sanctum Officium,* became active again after its reorganization by Paul III (1542) and under the fanatical Paul IV (1555–1559) displayed a new and sinister effectiveness. Even cardinals were not immune, and Sadoleto, Pole, and Morone were indicted and persecuted because of suspicion of heresy. Morone languished for two years (1557–1559) in the prison of the inquisition, and Ignatius of Loyola also trembled before Paul IV. The inquisition raged most terribly wherever the Spaniards ruled. In June 1561, the Waldensians were bloodily persecuted in Calabria. The Spanish inquisition should be distinguished from the papal one; it was an establishment which had been created by the state in 1481 to protect Christian Spain in its struggle against the Mohammedan Moors. After Christian baptism had been made compulsory, many Jews and Moors converted to Christianity only for the sake of form, the so-called Marranos and Moriscos.

These groups were regarded as politically unreliable and they often served as spies against the state. They were treated like traitors. In order to further deter these groups, executions included a solemn ceremony and were designated as Autos da Fé (= *actus fidei*). At a time such as this when all life was regarded as a unit, it is difficult to evaluate to what extent religious or political, economic or human interests played a role in these terrible executions. It is equally difficult to state how many people lost their lives. The phantastic figures which are occasionally mentioned must be viewed very critically.

In Germany, the persecutions were mainly directed against the Anabaptists; here the social background is visible, because since the excesses of Münster (1534–1535) the Anabaptists were feared as social revolutionary agitators. Again, however, reputations may be misleading: For centuries the Catholic imperial city of Cologne, for example, was known as particularly hostile to heretics, and yet a recent very critical investigation of legal procedures by H. Stiasny (Münster, 1962), in which he examined the trials and transcripts of all Anabaptist trials in the city in the century of the Reformation (1529–1618), reveals that although ca. 170 Anabaptists were arrested in Cologne during this period, almost all of them escaped with expulsion from the city or with "rather short incarcerations on water and bread". Only nine of those arrested were actually executed; four of them in the year 1534–1535, the others in the years 1558–1565, and in all cases the martial and political background of the time was evident and decisive. In Protestant countries the persecution of the Anabaptists was harsher and the number of executions was greater. This must be said not as an excuse but as an admonition to caution, as every victim is to be pitied. However, "criticism is too facile if it places itself unhistorically on the ground of liberal political thought" (Erler, in *Religion in Geschichte und Gegenwart*, 3rd ed., vol. III, 771).

4. The witch mania and the trials of witches, however, constitute an even greater blot on the record of the inquisition than the persecution of heretics. Today we lack all means of com-

parison for these mass neuroses and their sinister connection with religion and the procedures of the inquisition. There was not the slightest degree of difference between Catholic and Protestants with regard to the persecution and burning of witches. On the contrary, each stimulated the other, because neither side wanted to be surpassed by the other in the pursuit of what they imagined to be a manifestation of the devil. When the *Hammer of Witches* (1487), which had been written by the Dominicans Institoris and Sprenger, was prefaced by Pope Innocent VIII with a bull against witches, belief in witchcraft spread very rapidly. Luther, Calvin, and the other Reformers also believed in the existence of witches and also fought them with burnings. The superstition reached its peak between 1590 and 1630, and only began to decrease and finally stopped during the eighteenth century (the last burnings of witches: Kempten, 1775; Glarus, 1782; Posen, 1793). "No age and rank was immune. There were even centers, mainly in the mountainous areas, and with varying intensity the superstition seized Savoy, Switzerland, Tyrol, Lorraine, and the Scottish Highland, to mention only a few. Focal points of the witch mania were the French court (1400), Arras (1461), England (after 1576), Franconia (1623–1630), Luxeuil (1628–1660), Vaduz (1634–1680), Scotland, Scandinavia, and North America (1645–1693) . . ." (F. Merzbacher, in *Lexikon für Theologie und Kirche,* 2nd ed., vol. V, 318).

The first opponents of this belief in witchcraft were the physician John Weyer, an Erasmian at the court of duke William of Jülich-Cleve and the Jesuits Adam Tanner (1627) and Friedrich von Spee. In Paderborn in 1630–1631 Spee wrote his famous pamphlet *Cautio criminalis* (i.e. Caution in the trials of criminals!), and almost was burned himself because of his courageous intercession on behalf of the innocence of witches and protest against the absurd criminal conduct of the trials.

The entire witchcraft mania with its manifold roots can only be characterized as a sad aberration of humanity.

49
THE NEW AGE OF WORLD MISSION

The church received from Christ the express command to evangelize (Jo 17, 18; 20, 21; Mt 28, 18; Lk 24, 47; Acts 1, 8). The Christian character of an epoch can be recognized by the manner and intensity with which it acknowledges and realizes this essential commitment. For it is through the mission that the church as institution of redemption and continued incarnation of Christ finds its most complete realization. The church becomes internally "Catholic" by means of the unabridged and unadulterated preaching of the full message of the gospels and through opposition to all heretical and sectarian narrowing, but it remains externally "Catholic" through its mission among all peoples and races of the earth.

1. The church was often in danger of identifying itself and becoming satisfied with the culture in which it had just found a home. We have seen the first tremendous excitement which seized the entire early church during the transition of Christianity from the confines of Judaism to the wider scope of the pagan Roman world. For a long time the Jewish Christians had continued to believe that they had the right to act as guardians to gentile Christianity and had to keep it within their own narrow channels of life and thought. Only when finally the young Christianity cut its ties with Judaism and took root in the Hellenistic-Roman world was it able to expand effectively. The same tensions and difficulties arose again during the transition of Christianity from the Greek-Roman culture to the Germanic-medieval one. It was several centuries before Christianity achieved its full expression within the new culture. The early and high Middle Ages were times of intense missionary activity during which all of Europe was Christianized. At this time, however, something depressing also occurred. While during antiquity the Mediterranean Sea had welded the bordering peoples of Africa, Asia, and Europe in a great cultural unit, in the seventh century Islam acted as a wedge which split the people of Europe from most of those of Asia and

Africa. Only a few outposts of Christianity were able to maintain themselves in the Islamic countries of Asia Minor and North Africa, and even Byzantium only maintained its position with difficulty. Christianity now became limited essentially to Europe, and when this Europe was finally split into an eastern and a western Christianity during the tragic Greek schism of 1054, the Roman Catholic Church became limited to only the West. The attempt to remove the barrier of Islam by military force during the crusades ultimately ended in failure, and the attempt to unify Byzantium and eastern Christendom with the western community by force (1204) was equally unsuccessful. The Latin Kingdom of the East (1204–1261) was a regrettable mistake, and with the conquest of Constantinople by the Turks in 1453, the ring around the Christian West was tightened further.

The final step on the path toward the impoverishment and narrowing of the universal western church was the Reformation of the sixteenth century. After the loss of the largest part of the northern countries, the Catholic Church saw itself principally confined to southern Europe, where Italy and Spain were for a long time its last great bulwarks. The universal church now had become severely truncated.

2. It may be regarded as providential that at just this time the age of great geographical discoveries provided the church with a new worldwide mission. Since the middle of the fifteenth century, the Spaniards and the Portuguese had turned their ships south; following the western coast of Africa, the Portuguese reached the Cape of Good Hope in 1486. In 1498 Vasco da Gama continued this course around Africa in the direction of India. The Portuguese Cabral discovered Brazil in 1500, and Portuguese colonies sprang up everywhere on the coasts of India, Africa, and Brazil (1505–1515). Magellan sailed around the world for the first time in 1519–1522. Portuguese merchants had reached China by 1516 where they settled in Canton, not as conquerors but as peaceful traders. With the official permission of the Chinese government a colony was founded in Macao in 1567, and by 1542–1543 Portuguese seamen also had reached Japan.

The Spaniards, meanwhile, had been no less successful. The Genoese Christopher Columbus while in their service made the first discovery in 1492, when he reached the islands of the Central American archipelago. These were named the West Indies, as he believed that he had reached India by sailing around the world in a western direction. In 1519–1521 Fernando Cortez conquered Mexico; the discovery and conquest of Chile followed in 1520, of Argentinia in 1525, and of Peru in 1532. The sun truly did not set on the empire of Emperor Charles V.

The religious question played a not unimportant role in all of these discoveries. In addition to love of adventure, and economical, political, and military interests, missionary zeal was one of the main motive forces for these enterprises. Even the most unruly "Conquistadores" felt a commitment to disseminate the Christian religion among conquered peoples. Their methods, however, were often not only simply questionable, but shameful and cruel. The destruction of paganism and the establishment of the Christian faith was regarded by them as an achievement to be reached simultaneously with that of military conquest, and the Conquistadores were always accompanied by missionaries.

3. The history of the church in Latin America can be understood only in the light of the close relationship that existed between the church and the crown in Spain during the years of discovery and exploration. The Spanish popes, Alexander VI and Julius II, gave the Spanish kings what amounted to complete control over the church in America. Under Philip II, who governed the colonies through the Council of the Indies, almost every activity of the church in the New World was controlled by the government. No missionary could leave for America without approval of the government. The creation of new dioceses and the appointment of bishops came from Madrid rather than Rome; all ordinations and decrees of local councils and synods were reviewed by the Spanish crown.

The greater part of the early missions work in Latin America was carried out by the mendicant orders, Franciscans and Dominicans, and later by the Jesuits. The first bishopric was that of

Santo Domingo, created in 1511. Eleven years later, the ecclesiastical organization of the Antilles, comprising eight bishoprics, was completed. Ten years after the conquest of Mexico by Cortes in 1515, a diocese of Tlaxcala was established, followed by that of Mexico City, in 1526. By 1548, the latter had become a metropolitan see with seven suffragan dioceses. Although Caracas was the first diocese established in South America, Lima, Peru, soon became the most flourishing ecclesiastical center in that continent. Created in 1541, it was, by 1575, the metropolitan see of a province that included what are now Ecuador, Bolivia, Peru and Chile. Brazil's first diocese was that of San Salvador de Bahia, established in 1552. In the La Plata area, four bishoprics were created, the most important of which was that of Buenos Aires, established in 1582.

One of the chief obstacles to the introduction of Christianity among the native Indians was the extreme cruelty with which they were treated by the Spanish colonists. A system known as *encomienda,* whereby a number of natives were handed over to the colonists with the right to exact work and tribute from them, provided also for their instruction in the Catholic faith. Serious attempts were made to learn the native dialects and to offer at least a rudimentary Christian literature. A notable example of this effort was the case of the first bishop of Mexico City, Juan de Zumárraga (1468–1548). The college of Tlaltelolco was established with the purpose of producing an indigenous clergy and educating the Indian élite for service in both church and the state. It was the bishop's aim, in the Erasmian tradition, to translate and disseminate the Scriptures in the native tongues.

The great champion of the Indians was the more famous Bartholomew de Las Casas (1474–1566). Largely at his urging, the Emperor Charles V promulgated a series of new laws which mitigated some of the severity of the *encomienda* system. In a famous debate held at Valladolid in 1550, Las Casas argued for the equality and freedom of the native Indians, opposing the views of the theologian Juan Gines de Sepulveda. The latter used the arguments of Aristotle to justify his view, and that held

339

by much of the hierarchy that certain peoples are by nature born to slavery. Because of the new type of plantation agriculture developed in the New World, both the Portuguese and Spanish became strong defenders of slavery. It was not until 1888 that slavery in the New World was abolished. On the occasion of the abolition of slavery in Brazil, Pope Leo XIII, in the encyclical *In plurimis,* proclaimed that slavery was "entirely in opposition to that which was originally ordained by God and nature".

One of the great problems facing the church in Latin America was that of integrating the native population into full membership. The first synod, held in Lima in 1552, limited the participation of the Indians in the reception of the sacraments. In 1555, the first Council of Mexico forbade ordination into the priesthood of mestizos, those of mixed Spanish and Indian blood, and of mulatlos, those of mixed Spanish and Negro origin. Most of the religious orders excluded those not of European stock. It was not until 1772, at the third Council of Lima, that the ban against ordaining Indians as priests was lifted.

The first Spanish missionaries to the Philippine Islands were Augustinians, who arrived in 1565. When the diocese of Manila was established in 1579, it was a suffragan see of Mexico. It was raised to an archbishopric in 1595. The Jesuits opened a number of schools in the Islands in 1601 and the famous Dominican University of Santo Tomaso was established in 1611. The Philippines remain to this day the only Christian nation in the Far East.

As the fortunes of Spain and Portugal declined in Europe, so did conditions in their vast overseas empires. The revolutionary wars of independence which swept Latin America during the early 19th century had a drastic effect on the church in these areas. The removal of Charles IV from the throne of Spain in 1808 brought the repudiation of the new government by the cirollos of the colonies. After Napoleon's defeat and the restoration of Ferdinand VII, the colonies continued to revolt, defeating the royal armies in the Peruvian battles of Junin and Ayachuch in 1824. Most of the royally-appointed hierarchy fled to Spain.

By 1825 there were eleven vacant sees in Greater Colombia. In Mexico, the hierarchy was all but extinct.

The Spanish king, refusing to admit the loss of the American colonies, continued to appoint bishops, who were automatically rejected by the new republics. The papacy, on the other hand, aggravated the situation by urging the bishops to disavow the revolutionary governments. Meanwhile, the new governments assumed the prerogatives of royal patronage. *Patronato real* now gave way to *patronato nacional*. In 1824, Greater Colombia passed a Church State law called the *Ley de Patronato,* according to which the state governed the church. The Congress was empowered to reorganize dioceses and summon ecclesiastical councils. In the United Provinces of La Plata (Argentina), similar laws were put into effect by the Memorial Ajustado. The liberator Bernardo O'Higgins, President of Chile (1818–1823), exiled the bishop of Santiago.

Free Masonry played an important role in the anti-clericalism of the 19th century in Latin America. In Venezuela, the *caudillo* Blanco, a high ranking Mason, dealt the church a blow from which she has only slowly recovered. In Ecuador, the leader Garcia Moreno (1860–1875) established a virtual theocracy, infuriating the liberals, thus bringing about his assassination. The tendency of the church to support dictators in much of Latin America has not enhanced the cause of Catholicism. Two important Concordats with the Holy See in Ecuador (1862) and Colombia (1887) set the pace for subsequent agreements with the governments of Haiti, Guatemala, Nicaragua and Costa Rica. Although Mexico has a long history of anti-clericalism, intensified during the 1920's, the present policy is one of a more liberal attitude toward the church.

An interesting chapter in the history of the church in Latin America is the story of the Jesuit missions, or "Reductions", in Paraguay, the so-called "Republic of the Guaranis". Here the practice of bringing natives into Christian villages for protection and instruction in the Catholic religion achieved its greatest success. The first settlement was founded at Loretto in 1610, and

341

by 1623 there were more than 23 Christian villages with a population of 100,000. To protect these settlements from marauders and a hostile colonial population, the king of Portugal, in 1641, forbade his subjects to enter the region under Jesuit control and allowed the missionaries to arm the natives.

Within the Reductions, the Indians were lodged in well-constructed houses, given sections of arable land to cultivate and were provided with elementary education. Certain industries were also introduced. The entire process was not unlike the present day attempts to create Catholic villages in Viet Nam. The weakness of the system, like much else in past Catholic missionary endeavors, was that it failed to give responsibility to the natives. Authority rested firmly in the hands of the Jesuits, who did little to develop a sense of initiative among their subjects. Paternalism and a refusal to view the natives as adults were policies that remained unaltered for more than a century. No Indian was ever ordained, nor were religious orders for women introduced. By the end of the 18th century, and with the suppression of the Jesuits, the entire effort collapsed.

4. The great Jesuit missionary Francis Xavier (1506–1552) worked under Portuguese domination in India and Japan. As papal legate in the service of the Portuguese king John III, Xavier arrived in Goa in 1542, conducted a very successful mission in Malacca (1545–1547), and visited the newly discovered Japan in 1549. On a voyage to China, Xavier died on the island of Sancian in 1552. From that time onward the Jesuits systematically expanded their missions, and above all made an attempt to break with the Portuguese narrow-mindedness regarding missionary methods. The Jesuit Robert de Nobili (1577–1656) introduced the idea of adaptation by seriously trying for the first time to bring his mission in line with the way of life and thought of the Indian population. After 1605, de Nobili lived as a Brahmin in Madura (southern India), led the resigned life of an Indian penitent, and isolated himself from all Europeans, including his brother Jesuits. He wished to be a Hindu among Hindus, because he had recognized how much the aversion to the Portu-

guese and the spiritual connection of Christian theology with the western spirit was an obstacle to the Christian mission. De Nobili learned Sanskrit, the religious language of the Indians, mentioned the Holy Books of the Indians in his sermons, and completely incorporated the gospel of Christ as the fifth Veda into the world of Indian thought. Formerly Paul and the Christian apologists had pursued a similar course with respect to Hellenism, and success was also not long in coming to de Nobili. As early as 1609 he was able to establish a Christian church for the Brahmins and to begin baptizing them.

Robert de Nobili permitted the Indian converts to retain all of their Hindu customs as long as they were not clearly pagan; even in liturgy and communal life he adopted Hindu customs, and permitted the wearing of the Brahmin thread and the *kudumi*, as well as the use of sandalwood and the ritual washings. Extreme tolerance was exercised toward all native religious questions, and in similar fashion other Jesuit missionaries soon worked among the other lower castes of the population. By 1650 Madura already could count 40,000 Christians. Pope Gregory XV approved the method in 1623 and admitted the Brahmin rites with certain reservations. At the end of the seventeenth century, however, a controversy arose over the permissibility of the adaptation method. After long and acrimonious debates Benedict XIV condemned the "Malabaric rites" in 1742. That decision sealed the fate of the Indian mission, and Christianity no longer found a fertile soil in India.

The Jesuit mission suffered a similar fate in China, where the great Matteo Ricci (1552–1610) had introduced the method of adaptation with extraordinary results. After 1600 he lived at the imperial court in Peking as an astronomer and mathematician, and as a friend and advisor of the emperor was able to proclaim Christianity openly. At his death there were more than 2,000 Christians within the leading ranks of China. His associate Adam Schall von Bell (1592–1666) even advanced to the rank of a mandarin and in 1645 became the Director of the Imperial Astronomical Service. In 1650 von Bell built a public church in Peking and obtained religious freedom for Christianity in the whole of the empire (1657). At von Bell's death there were almost 270,000 Christians in China. The imperial edict of toleration in 1692 rewarded the service of the Jesuits on behalf of China and the imperial house, and thus an independent Chinese Church was in process and had the best prospects of success.

The Chinese mission, however, also met with misfortune. This time not external pressures but an internal ecclesiastical controversy over adaptation led to the collapse of the China mission. How did this come about?

Ricci had deliberately utilized the existing conceptions of God in his sermons. He had to avoid presenting the Christian faith to these advanced and religious people as something entirely new; it must not seem that he regarded the Chinese as atheists who had never revered God before. Therefore, Ricci acknowledged that the Chinese had always been devout and showed them that the knowledge of God reached supreme perfection in the Christian faith. The "Lord of the Heavens", whom they so long had revered, was Christ; Christian revelation would teach them to understand him better. As long as it did not reach the proportions of pagan idolatry, Ricci permitted the worship of ancestors and Confucius as expressions of civic culture. All the natural values of Chinese culture were to retain a place in Christianity, so that Christianity might be brought closer to the Chinese.

Had adaptation gone too far? Dominican and Franciscan missionaries who had been working in China since the 1630's felt that it had and brought action in Rome against Ricci and the Jesuits. In 1645 Innocent X forbade adaptation, but Alexander VII moderated the proscription in 1656. Petty rivalries among the orders aggravated the conflict, and because of the influence of Jansenism, which had so strongly slandered the morality of the Jesuits (Blaise Pascal), Rome grew more timid. One year after Emperor Kangh Hsi's edict of toleration, adaptation was once again sharply condemned by Rome. Although the Jesuit missionaries submitted recommendations and the emperor himself personally intervened in their behalf, Rome remained adamant and Clement XI renewed the proscription in 1704. In 1707 the papal legate Tournon was dispatched to China and his unfortunate conduct at the Kang imperial court finally led to the alienation of Emperor Kang Hsi. Tournon was confined and finally died in China in 1710. Now the emperor prohibited Christian service unless it complied with the Jesuit version. He reproached the next papal delegate Mezzabarba vehemently: "You have destroyed your religion, exposed the resident Europeans to misery, and profaned the good name of the dead." Although Innocent VIII had again conceded a modification in 1723, Benedict XIV in 1743 decreed a basic prohibition of any adaptation. This shortsighted victory of Europeanism brought the death of the East Asia mission, and the long persecution of Chinese Christians soon began. The appropriate moment for the mission in China had been missed. Not until the twentieth century were Christian missionaries slowly able to establish themselves again in China. Pius XI (1939) and Pius XII (1940) finally retracted the interdiction of Chinese rites for mission in China, but too late! In 1949 three years after the first Chinese bishop Tien had been appointed cardinal (1946), the communist troops of Mao Tsetung were victorious. In the new communistic China the old traditions and rites were without importance. New persecutions once again destroyed the young Christianity and the recently established ecclesiastical hierarchy of twenty archbishoprics, seventy-nine dioceses, and thirty-eight apostolic prefectures. Tragedy has always governed the mission in China.

50

FROM THE BAROQUE TO THE ENLIGHTENMENT

The period of dissolution which succeeded the religious schism was followed by the Council of Trent and a strong ecclesiastical concentration. For the papacy, the Reformation was both a crisis and a turning point. The Council of Trent permitted the papacy to emerge strengthened and rejuvenated from these hard times.

By placing the continuation of the work of reform expressly into the hands of the pope, the council fathers not only acknowledged his position of primacy but also supplied him with the means of exerting an effective influence on the life of the whole church. The curia intervened more than ever in the internal conditions of the countries and dioceses by means of reform controls and visitations. Papal jurisdiction also grew internally as well as externally; the reorganization of the (15) congregations of cardinals by Sixtus V (1585–1590) gave each of the congregations a definite administrative task, and permanent nunciatures were established at the focal points of ecclesiastical life. The officers of the nunciatures, the nuncios, who were provided with extensive powers, contributed considerably to the strengthening of ecclesiastical centralism.

This concentration of powers was quite necessary, salutary, and successful as long as the need existed for reconstruction and ecclesiastical rejuvenation. However, it was certain to encounter increasing resistance once the restoration of ecclesiastical life had been accomplished, for then the bishops and princes regarded the papal support no longer as aid, but as tutelage and unwelcome interference.

1. During the seventeenth century the opposition forces grew and it was no accident that they received their most decisive impulses from France. That country was just then experiencing a tremendous intellectual revival which affected all levels of the population, but was particularly effective in giving fresh impetus to the ecclesiastical and religious life. At the same time, nationalism and absolutism awakened, and in Louis XIV (1643/61–1715), the "Sun King", France saw its glorious apotheosis. France was too strongly oriented to internal conditions to have much sympathy for Rome's centralism.

All of the movements which made life so difficult for the church between 1600 and 1800 originated in France: Gallicanism, absolutism, Jansenism, and episcopalism.

a) Gallicanism claimed for the *Ecclesia Gallicana* rights which would sorely curtail papal primacy. It was the right of the French king, wrote P. Pithou *(Les libertés de l'Église gallicane,* 1638*)*, to convoke national councils, to limit the jurisdiction of the papal nuncios in France, to appeal to a general council even against the pope, and to make the validity of papal decrees dependent upon his agreement (Placet). The leading French ministers, the cardinals Richelieu (1624–1642) and Mazarin (1643–1661) seized upon these ideas and France soon stood on the brink of a schism. In addition, the situation was aggravated further by Jansenist and anti-Roman sentiments. The anti-Roman tendencies of the national church reached their peak under the absolutist monarchy of Louis XIV. As early as 1663, the *Parlement* of Paris forced the theological faculty to acknowledge the Gallican doctrines that a council stood above the pope (conciliarism) and that authoritative papal decisions on doctrine *(ex cathedra)* were not infallible. In 1682 the *Four Gallican Articles* were solemnly proclaimed in the name of the French clergy. Admittedly, Louis XIV retracted them on the protest of the pope in 1693, but in practice they remained in existence and retained their validity in France into the nineteenth century. Only the First Vatican Council destroyed their effectiveness with the dogma of papal infallibility.

b) The absolutism of the state intervened ruthlessly in the affairs of the church. The state welcomed the curtailment of papal rights in France, since Gallicanism tended to reinforce national absolutism.

c) Jansenism was a dangerous error which under the guise of special piety and rigorism introduced into Catholic theology a distortion of the Augustinian doctrine of original sin and grace strongly influenced by Calvinism. The Calvinist doctrine of predestination was given here a Catholic cloak. The originator of Jansenism was the Belgian bishop Cornelius Jansen (d. 1638). In 1642 and again in 1653 and 1705–1715 the Jesuits demanded and obtained from Rome the condemnation of some of the statements in his book *Augustinus* (1640). Out of this a conflict arose over the meaning of the sentences and the papal prohibition. The center of Jansenism was the Cistercian convent of Port Royal near Versailles, whose devout nuns, under the direction of Angelica Arnauld, led such a godly life that it exerted a great attraction. A group of scholars, theologians, and laymen began to gather around the convent, among them Anton Arnauld (d. 1694) and Blaise Pascal (d. 1662). This group reproached the Jesuits for an allegedly too lax moral theology. The Jansenists themselves introduced such a rigoristic practice of the sacraments that they in fact succeeded in keeping the average believer from receiving communion. Their extended disputes with Rome placed them in bitter opposition to the papacy, made them into allies of Gallicanism and episcopalism, and involved them in many political struggles. The high point of the battle was reached around 1710 when P. Quesnel (d. 1719) was expelled from France by Louis XIV and Port Royal was torn down. The Jansenists survived in Holland where they even established their own schismatic church with a validly ordained hierarchy.

d) Many bishops were also concerned with narrowing papal influence in the dioceses. The defenders of episcopalism opposed Roman centralism with the independence of the episcopal office. In Germany also a grave crisis, which threatened the German Church ·with schism, occurred in the seventeenth century. In the eighteenth century, the Trier suffragan bishop J. Nicholas von Hontheim in his book *De statu ecclesiae et legitima potestate Romani Pontificis* (1763), written under the pseudonym Justinus Febronius, compiled episcopal thought and supported it with conciliaristic and territorial ecclesiastical principles. The pope was granted only a very limited guiding authority, and papal monarchy in the church was to be supplanted by a multitude of autonomous national churches, represented through the supreme ecclesiastical organ, the general council.

These ideas, called Febronianism, found a willing ear. In the Punctation of Ems of 1786 the German archbishops of Cologne, Trier, Mainz, and Salzburg concluded an alliance for common action against the recently established nunciature in Munich (1785). Their aim was the fundamental limitation of absolute papal power as represented by the nuncios.

After the middle of the seventeenth century, the respect of the European peoples for the papacy continued to decrease. There was no room within the absolutist states for the claims of the universal church to universal jurisdiction. Soon the church had to look on helplessly as the deserving and once powerful Jesuits were subjected to a campaign of destruction by the Catholic countries of Portugal, France, Spain, and the Two Sicilies. When the Bourbon courts ruthlessly called for the prohibition of the order on pain of a schism or even an attack against the Papal States, Pope Clement XIV (1769–1774) was powerless to do anything except concede to the demands. On July 21, 1773, Clement decreed the suppression of the Society of Jesus.

e) The concept of a national church enjoyed its greatest triumph in Catholic Austria, where Emperor Joseph II (1780–1790), the "enlightened" son of Maria Theresia, used his system of absolute state sovereignty over the churches (= Josephinism) to perform arbitrary reforms, claim ecclesiastical jurisdictions, and suppress monasteries and church establishments to a large degree. When Pius VI (1775–1799) journeyed to Vienna personally in order to intervene, he was forced to suffer bitter disappointment and grievous insults. The position of the papacy had reached a new low.

2. Meanwhile a new spirit had conquered Europe, the Enlightenment. This new philosophy broke with the old traditions and, spreading from England via France to Germany, fought under the banner of reason for a new freedom of the spirit. The world view of more than a thousand years was discarded. In 1784, Immanuel Kant (1724–1804) declared that the goal of the new movement was the liberation of the autonomous human being who is able "to make use of his mind without the tutelage of others".

Indeed, modern society owes much to the Enlightenment. It was an indispensable step in the evolution of a progressive human outlook. As the last of the great movements in Western thought, it overcame the medieval forms of life and thought which still gripped humanity and made possible the development of modern society. Not only did the Enlightenment pre-

349

cipitate the end of trials for witchcraft and heresy, of torture as part of the judicial process, and of religious discrimination in public life, but the movement also brought about the recognition of those basic human rights which were incorporated as law for the first time in the American Declaration of Independence (1776) and later in the declaration of the French National Assembly (August 27, 1789). It is scarcely an exaggeration to say that the unhindered development of science and of our whole modern culture had its roots in the Enlightenment.

For Christianity as a revealed religion, and for the Catholic Church in particular, the rationalism of the Enlightenment created one of the greatest and most dangerous crises of its entire history. In the 16th century, the Frenchman Jean Bodin (1530 to 1596) and the Englishman Lord Herbert of Cherbury (1581–1648) had developed a theory according to which all human beings were born with a "natural religion" which made any special revelation superfluous and even deleterious. John Locke and subsequent philosophers expanded these ideas into the philosophy of Deism and placed it in opposition to traditional Christianity. The awareness of a "Supreme Being", the expectation of an eternal life, and the belief in a day of judgment were to constitute the entire core of true religion. Matthew Tindal (*Christianity as old as the Creation,* 1730) demanded that Christianity also be reduced to this nucleus, and Lord Shaftesbury (1671–1713) saw the essence of religion only in the harmonious development of a noble humanity. While Deism itself may have been no more than a typically English phenomenon, it was a short step from this view to that of the doctrine of Jean Jacques Rousseau (1712–1778) that true religion consisted only of love for everything good and beautiful. Within the framework of this philosophy the result is a Christianity without Christ, without revelation, and without redemption, and religion becomes merely a humanitarian element of education or, by further extension, a substitute for religion! By equating religion and morality, the Deists reduced the church and Christianity to mere factors of human education and the servants of the church to popular agents of the Enlightenment. An optimistic belief in education and progress — which today we can comprehend only with difficulty — caused the men of the Enlightenment to view the future in the rosiest of colors.

Rational Deism penetrated deeply into all levels of educated society. One of the foremost instruments for its propagation was Freemasonry. Organized in London in 1717, Freemasonry quickly spread from England to all of its colonies and to other Western countries. The first Masonic lodge was established in Calcutta in 1730, another followed in Boston the same year, and soon lodges throughout North America became centers of intellectual and political life. By 1750 there were numerous influential lodges in all European countries. Their cosmopolitan attitude and their battle for the right of free expression, social justice, and freedom of thought lent prestige and attraction to the movement. With respect to religion the Masons limited themselves to the belief in a "natural religion" and a supreme being whom they acknowledged to be the "great architect of the Universe". Thus Freemasonry was not atheistic and in the Anglo-Saxon countries was neither anti-Christian nor anti-clerical. In the Netherlands numerous clerics of all faiths and even some Catholic priests joined the Freemasons. Only in France did Freemasonry assume an increasingly anti-clerical and anti-religious character. Denis Diderot, the editor of the Encyclopedia, in particular regarded religion as the source of all evil. Although d'Alembert and many others retained a belief in revelation, and the volumes of the Encyclopedia which appeared before 1759 received the imprimatur of the Sorbonne, the spirit of the enterprise grew increasingly hostile to church and Christianity. In the end the Encyclopedists were to regard everything that was holy to the faithful Christian as an object of scorn and derision, and Voltaire, who had declared war to the death on the church *("écrasez l'infâme")*, let no opportunity pass to undermine ecclesiastical authority. The French Revolution soon was to form the bloody sequel to these deliberate provocations.

The Enlightenment adopted a different and friendlier attitude

351

toward religion in Germany where its leading advocates were the philosophers G. W. von Leibniz (1646–1716), Christian Thomasius (1655–1728), and Christian Wolff (1679–1754). Leibniz throughout his life was concerned with the desire to reunify all Christians and to promote toleration in questions of faith and sectarianism. But even the philosophy of Leibniz provided little room within natural religion for the revealed faith of Christianity and assigned it only a secondary role in human existence. For Immanuel Kant (*Religion within the Limits of Reason Alone*), religion lost any aspect of supernatural character, and religious activity directed toward a transcendental god could only appear as illusion unworthy of an enlightened humanity. The attitudes of these men exercised a powerful influence throughout the 19th and 20th centuries among poets, artists, and intellectuals, an influence not totally overcome to this day.

In spite of its obvious disadvantages, the less aggressive German Enlightenment did leave room for the inclusion of more moderate, milder enlightened thought and endeavors, and even if radical elements were unable to gain a foothold in the church, the need to cleanse ecclesiastical life of outmoded traditions and expressions of piety could no longer be ignored. If the church was concerned with appearing believable to the world around it, it had to face the criticism of its ossified scholastic-theological doctrinal system openly, and turn its attention to the still widespread manifestations of superstition and witch-hunting and abuses growing out of backward practices and customs. With this realization as a starting-point, faithful clerics and laymen attempted in the spirit of the Enlightenment to bring about long overdue church reforms. Whatever deficiencies the reforms of Empress Maria Theresia and her son Joseph II of Austria may have contained, the intention behind them was good and they were not without their salutary effect. The achievement brought about in the areas of education, ecclesiastical organization and administration, the revival of preaching, liturgical reforms, and the reform of ecclesiastical customs is of particular importance today in light of the Second Vatican Council.

In the second half of the 18th century almost all German bishoprics were occupied by "enlightened" prelates who were eager for reform and who were in the main irreproachable clerics, as faithful as they were educated. The abbeys and monasteries also often were permeated by the spirit of reform. Johann Michael Sailer (1751–1832) and Prince-Abbot Martin Gerbert of St. Blasien (1720–1791) as well as Vicar-General Ignaz Heinrich von Wessenberg (1774–1860) in Constance earned great merit for their services in the rejuvenation of ecclesiastical life. Unfortunately, the entire movement was discredited and the church ultimately harmed by the ruthless and excessive criticism of some of the Catholic advocates of Enlightenment. In Germany, however, this radical clerical group remained in the minority and may be regarded as merely a fringe element.

Second Epoch: 1789–1918
From the French Revolution to the First World War

51

THE FRENCH REVOLUTION AND SECULARIZATION

The storm of revolution suddenly broke over France and quickly spread to all of Europe; with it came a new era for the church as well.

1. In its beginnings the French Revolution was not hostile to the church. When the Estates-General met in Versailles on May 5, 1789, there was great agreement between the Third Estate and the clergy which was represented in the First Estate. 149 pastors and four bishops joined the revolutionary Third Estate on June 23, 1789, when it constituted itself as the National Constituent Assembly. During the storming of the Bastille (July 14, 1789) religious interests did not yet play a role; however, soon after, throughout the country, castles, churches, and monasteries were burned. During the famous "Night of Sacrifices" (August 4/5, 1789) in the national assembly the clergy in France competed with the nobility in giving up old feudal rights and in renouncing its privileges in favor of the peasants and the bourgeoisie. In one convulsive action the entire medieval feudal order of the French Church collapsed. A Te Deum was sung in the national assembly on the morning of August 5, and all distinctions of rank were discarded. Every citizen was now equal before the law. On August 27, 1789, the Rights of Man and the

Citizen were solemnly declared law: "Liberty, Equality, and Fraternity". Article 10 granted freedom of religion and conscience to all Frenchmen.

But a more radical course was soon followed in the question of church property. In order to solve the pressing financial needs of the state, the national assembly adopted the suggestion of Bishop Talleyrand (1754–1838) and confiscated all church property for use in paying public debts. During the ensuing debate public opinion was divided, and the clergy left the assembly in protest. The radical left greeted the exodus with sneers, and the climate of the assembly now changed drastically. On February 13, 1790, all non-charitable orders and monasteries were closed, and on April 14, 1790, a law concerning the confiscation and secularization of all church property was passed. On July 12, 1790, the new constitution introduced the Civil Constitution of the Clergy, which incorporated the French church into the French state on a purely national basis and separated it from Rome. Faith and morals had not yet been touched, but in November 1790 the clergy was required to swear an oath to the new constitution. When approximately two-thirds of the clergy refused the oath, bloody persecutions ensued, in the course of which about 40000 priests were imprisoned, deported, or executed.

The Terror, which lasted until October 1795, was initiated with the frightful September Massacres (September 1792). Danton and Marat now governed the country; on January 21, 1793, king Louis XVI was executed and queen Marie Antoinette followed him to the guillotine in October. When Marat was assassinated on July 13, 1793, Robespierre succeeded to the dictatorship of terror. In November 1793 Christianity was abolished in France and the "Cult of Reason" was introduced. The raving against royalists and clerics continued unabatedly. The bloodthirsty Jacobins, who were so named after their meeting place, the convent of St. Jacob, were eliminated from power by Robespierre early in 1794. Robespierre then had the national convention decree the recognition of a "Supreme Being" and the immortality of the soul. On June 28, 1794, his life also ended on the guillotine. Now the government was assumed by a five-member Directory (1795–1799). The Catholic clergy was again slowly accorded toleration, yet the fundamental separation of church and state had become law (February 21, 1795). Further persecutions and deportations of priests occasionally took place, and only when the young victorious general Napoleon Bonaparte staged a successful coup d'état on November 9, 1799, were the hostile actions against Christianity ended.

Napoleon was completely indifferent to religion which he regarded as nothing but a political factor. To restore order in France he concluded a concordat with the pope on July 15, 1801. The preamble stated that the Catholic apostolic Roman religion was the denomination of the majority of French citizens and as such was to be restored. The church relinquished its claims to the nationalized church property, and the state assumed responsibility for the salaries of clergymen. Bishoprics were to be redesignated and appointments made for them. Napoleon secretly added 77 "Organic Articles" to the concordat which partly cancelled the effectiveness of the treaty, and the pope protested in vain against them. Pius VII (1800–1823) suffered greatly from Napoleon. In 1804 Napoleon had himself elected emperor of the French, and although the pope anointed the emperor, Napoleon placed the crown on his head himself. In 1808 Napoleon occupied Rome and the Papal States, and the pope was imprisoned when he excommunicated Napoleon. At Fontainebleau near Paris, where the pope was interned since 1812, Napoleon tried to blackmail Pius into relinquishing claim to the Papal States. Napoleon's rule collapsed after the unsuccessful Russian campaign (1812), and the victory of the allies at the battle of Leipzig (October 1813) enabled them to occupy Paris (March 31, 1814). The Congress of Vienna (1814–1815) could begin the reordering of Europe.

2. Everywhere French troops had penetrated, the institutions of the revolution were introduced. The secularization of ecclesiastical states was of utmost importance for Germany; the Imperial Delegates Enactment of Regensburg (February 25, 1803) decreed the confiscation and secularization of twenty-two

archbishoprics and bishoprics, eighty free imperial abbeys, and more than two hundred monasteries. Thereby the German Church lost its material foundation as well as its administrative strength in the empire. The loss of the clerical states resulted in the closing of eighteen Catholic universities, and in the future the impoverished church was unable to do very much for the education of its members. Wherever the previously Catholic territories were incorporated into Protestant states, Catholics found themselves hopelessly in the minority. The new tensions which the incorporation produced in the Protestant states and among their Protestant majorities resulted in furious struggles with the national churches and produced the typically German denominationalism of public life. One benefit to the church, however, was its freedom from several antiquated practices: The monopoly of the nobility over the appointments to bishoprics and high benefices was done away with, and the entire medieval feudal order with its complex system of benefices and its distinctions between higher and lower clergy was removed with the stroke of a pen. The emasculated and impoverished church established a new relationship to the people. Bishops, priests, and laymen were drawn closer together, and the popular church of the nineteenth century was able to develop. The "mercy of the nadir" offered the chance for a healthy reconstruction.

52
THE RESTORATION OF THE CATHOLIC CHURCH IN THE NINETEENTH CENTURY

A. Germany

Reconstruction contained two parallel processes: a) the material reordering of the German Church with reference to public and canon law and b) the internal reshaping of ecclesiastical and religious life.

1. At the Congress of Vienna the curia silently forewent the

restitution of the secularized church property, although it fundamentally condemned the secularization as sacrilege. Instead, the church attempted to obtain a reorganization of the bishoprics through negotiation and concordats with the individual states. A concordat is an international treaty between a state and the church which presupposes a mutual recognition of sovereign persons; it is understandable that such a recognition was difficult for some of the states because of their religious denomination or because of an established state church. These states, therefore, preferred to avoid concordats. In such cases the curia was satisfied with an administrative arrangement by means of bulls of circumscription. Concordats were successfully concluded with Spain, Naples, Sardinia, France, Russia, and Bavaria, while Austria and the other German states were influenced through bulls of circumscription. Thus the bull *De salute animarum* (1821) provided for the new episcopal organization in Prussia, the bull *Provida sollersque* (1821) in Württemberg, Baden, and the three Hessian provinces, and the bull *Impensa* (1824) in Hannover.

2. The inner reconstruction of ecclesiastical life and the development of a great Catholic movement which seized not only Germany but also all other European countries, had many roots. In the history of ideas, German Romanticism was of great significance for the reawakening of religiosity in general and for the new esteem of Catholicism in particular. The Romanticist's enthusiasm for medieval art and literature also awakened an interest in the church, and many of them converted to Catholicism. Soon Catholic "revival" groups formed the nuclei of a new religious life: in southern Germany the group led by J. Michael Sailer (1751–1832); in Münster the *"familia sacra"* of the princess Gallitzin (1748–1806); and in Vienna the circle around St. Clement Maria Hofbauer (1751–1820). Similar work was performed by the Würzburg suffragan bishop Georg Zirkel (d. 1817), and many others. The most lasting effect probably came from the endeavors of Sailer, a pastoral theologian and subsequently bishop of Regensburg, although other theologians such as Johann Adam Möhler (d. 1838) in Tübingen and Munich and other members

of the Tübingen school were also helpful. Even the theologian Georg Hermes (d. 1831) in Bonn and his students, the Hermesians contributed in their way. Although still rooted in the Enlightenment, the Hermesians aided the development, but their method, with examined faith with Kant's and Fichte's categories of thought and attempted to make it appealing to their fellow human beings, was later (1835) condemned as semi-rationalistic.

During the so-called "Cologne Affair", the masses of the people were touched for the first time. In 1837 the archbishop of Cologne, Clement August von Droste-Vischering was arrested by the Prussian government because he had taken the side of the church with regard to the question of mixed marriages. Pope Gregory XVI immediately protested against this use of force, and Joseph Görres's fiery indictment *Athanasius* (1837/1838) caused reverberations throughout the world. The collective Catholic conscience was awakened and everywhere the necessity for closer cooperation was recognized. Therefore numerous new organizations suddenly sprang up in the 1840's all of which had a purely ecclesiastical and religious character. Among these new groups were the Borromaeus Association (1844), the Association of Journeymen (1846), the Society of Boniface (1849), the Elizabeth Society (1840), the Francis Xavier Missionary Society (1842), and the Pius Association with its annual gatherings of Catholics (1848). Even Catholic orders took on a fresh buoyancy. Pius VII had restored the Jesuit order in 1814 and in 1847 they returned to Cologne. The Jesuits were followed by the Redemptorists, Pallottins, and numerous women's congregations and their branches. Old Benedictine monasteries revived and were newly settled. In many instances the new constitutions after the revolutions of 1848 granted greater freedom of movement and independence to the Catholic Church. Soon extensive popular missions were conducted, a rich system of pilgrimages and devotions developed, and everywhere new ecclesiastical life emerged. A Catholic press slowly developed. In 1852 Catholic delegates in the Prussian Diet formed for the first time a Catholic fraction which after 1858 designated itself as the Center Party.

Thus fresh ecclesiastical life emerged everywhere. In the common age of industrialization and mass man it was to be important for the church to have an open mind toward social problems. Through new pastoral methods the church was able to accommodate itself to the people and to try to take care of them by means of charity and education. Adolf Kolping (d. 1865), the "Father of Journeymen", became the prototype of the new pastor. The countless priests and "chaplains of the people" also must be mentioned who worked untiringly in the industrial centers of the Rhine and the Ruhr. At a time when there was no social legislation and the solution of social problems was left entirely to Christian charity, the effectiveness of the new charitable congregations of sisters and orders for the nursing of the sick was particularly important. Throughout Germany organizations for charity and welfare sprang up. The great popular writers also exhorted love for one's fellow man. The Borromaeus Association viewed its activity as a "work of spiritual charity".

B. France

Even after Napoleon's fall there was no internal peace for the country in which the great upheaval had originated. On the one hand, the sufferings of the church in the period of terror had awakened a willingness on the part of the faithful to make religious sacrifices and had increased their loyalty; but on the other hand, the anti-religious propaganda produced long-term repercussions among the generation which had grown up under the domination of the Jacobins and the influence of an irreligious Enlightenment. Among the French bourgeoisie a large anticlerical group in accord with the works of Voltaire and Rousseau continued to exist and passed this spirit on to the rising "Fourth Estate" comprised of socially discontented industrial workers.

1. Louis XVIII (1814–1824), through whom the Bourbon dynasty had been restored, outwardly attempted to restore the old ecclesiastical order in the country and negotiated with the Holy See for a new concordat which would supersede the agree-

ments of 1801. But when he presented a draft to the legislature in 1817, he was unable to obtain its consent with the result that the Napoleonic concordat remained in force essentially unchanged. His brother and successor, Charles X (1825–1830), felt even closer ties to the *ancien régime* and enlisted the church in the service of restoring the former conditions. Charles was a committed Catholic and regarded the bond between throne and altar as the foundation for his rule, even though he did not hesitate to apply Gallican concepts when making appointments to the bishoprics. Like his pre-revolutionary predecessors, Charles gave precedence to the nobility in making appointments, and soon the church appeared more closely tied to the monarchy than ever before. It was thus unavoidable that the so-called "July Revolution" of July 30, 1830, which swept Charles from the throne and replaced him with Duke Louis Phillipe of Orleans (1830–1848), had serious effects upon the church. The new liberal democratic government broke immediately with the principle of an established Catholic Church and introduced full freedom and equality of religion. The church lost its special position and, at least at the beginning, faced a decidedly anti-clerical government. Not until the revolution of 1848, which deposed the "Citizen King" Phillipe I and proclaimed a republic, was a course friendlier to the church adopted by the republic's first president, Louis Napoleon, the nephew of Napoleon I.

In order to win over the French Catholics, Louis Napoleon went to the assistance of Pope Pius IX, who in 1848 had been driven out of Rome by revolution. In July 1849, French troops regained Rome and remained for the protection of the city against the attacks of Giuseppe Garibaldi until 1870. Louis Napoleon continued to favor the church after he became Emperor Napoleon III (1852–1870), even though ill feeling arose between the crown and the French Catholics with respect to the Vatican when, in July 1858, Napoleon concluded the alliance of Plombières with the Piedmontese Prime Minister Camillo di Cavour (1852–1861). This alliance was directed against Austria and thereby also affected the interests of the Papal States, but was somewhat mitigated in September 1864, when Napoleon signed a convention with the newly created Kingdom of Italy guaranteeing the existence of the Papal State. Only in July 1870, when Napoleon was forced by the outbreak of the Franco-Prussian War to withdraw his forces from Rome, did the papal rule collapse (September 20, 1870).

With Napoleon's defeat, another shift occurred in the fortunes of the church in France. Under the presidency of Marie Edmé de MacMahon (1873–1879), an ardent Catholic, the religious life of the church was at first free to unfold. But beginning in 1876, and even more so after 1879, an anti-clerical counter-movement developed. The permission of full freedom of education (1875) which the Catholics used to found numerous institutions of higher learning, such as the *Instituts Catholiques* in Paris, Angers, Lille, Lyon, and Toulouse, sparked this development. The legislature, which in the majority was anti-clerical, intervened and in 1880 closed 74 Jesuit schools, thereby causing increased tension. Shortly afterward 261 religious houses were closed, in 1881 all clerics and members of religious orders were forbidden to teach religion in public schools, and after 1886 the teaching of religion was eliminated from French public elementary schools. A battle was in the offing which tended toward a complete separation of church and state. In 1901 the radicals won the upper hand and found a leader in the strongly anti-clerical Justin Combes. Monasteries were closed and religious instruction continued to be banned in all public schools. The coping stone of these anti-clerical measures was the law of separation of church and state (1905) through which the state terminated all subsidies to the church and confiscated all church property.

2. The internal ecclesiastical life of France in the 19th century also displayed strong agitation. On the one side there was a pronounced conservative trend, centered around Count François de Chateaubriand, who had changed from an unbelieving revolutionary into a faithful Catholic and had influenced his contemporaries toward the traditional religious values in art and literature through his book *Le génie du christianisme* (1802); Count

Joseph de Maistre (1754–1821), who with his book *Du Pape* (1819) had re-awakened love and admiration of the papacy; and finally the journalist Louis Veuillot (1813–1883), whose exaggerated cult of the papacy will concern us later. Opposing this group were the representatives of a liberal Catholicism, led by Hugues Félicité Robert de Lamennais (1782–1854), who after having been seized by the rationalism of the revolutionary period in his youth had been led back to the faith by his older brother Jean Marie de Lamennais, a saintly priest and future founder of the Brothers of Christian Instruction. Under the influence of the anti-rational doctrine of Vicomte Louis Gabriel de Bonald (1754–1807), de Lamennais had become a convert to traditionalist theology and had become a prominent literary defender of adherence to ecclesiastical tradition and authority in opposition to Cartesianism and Gallicanism. Gradually de Lamennais began to doubt these precepts and in reaction to the narrow-minded rule of Charles X became a passionate champion of the separation of church and state. After 1830, "God and Liberty" was the motto under which he fought for the church, and after the July Revolution of 1830 he became increasingly the leader of the liberal Catholics who favored an alliance between the church and an extended democracy.

Together with his friends Phillipe Gerbet (1798–1864), Henri Lacordaire (1802–1861), and Count Charles de Montalembert (1810–1870), de Lamennais put out the first modern Catholic daily newspaper *L'Avenir,* and fashioned it into the voice of Catholic liberalism. He demanded separation of church and state, freedom of the press and of instruction, and the adoption of a democratic philosophy in government. The growing influence and European-wide significance of *L'Avenir* was most unpopular in Rome, and the European courts, which also opposed de Lamennais, were successful in having Gregory XVI condemn his program in 1832. When de Lamennais defiantly published his book *Paroles d'un croyant* and passionately defended his position, the encyclical *Singulari Nos* (July 7, 1834) once again condemned his doctrines, particularly that of the separation of church and state. A definite break with Rome now followed. The man who had once been leader of the ultramontane party, who had admired the pope as the defender of the rights of the church and humanity against the despotism of Napoleon, and who had contributed greatly to the strengthening of papal centralism and the recognition of the infallible authority of the pope, now became the spokesman for the opposition. Increasingly de Lamennais was seized by the revolutionary socialist current and, at the end of a life governed by a kind of tragedy, died unreconciled with the church.

Events in the lives of Montalembert and Lacordaire developed along more effective lines. In 1839 Lacordaire joined the Dominican Order and gained an unusually wide audience as the most impressive preacher of the time in France. Closely bound in friendship to this group of men was Frédéric Ozanam (1813–1853). In 1833 Ozanam set up the Vincent Conference of Charity, a forerunner of the Society of Saint Vincent de Paul. Equally influential as a Christian and a scholar, he taught foreign literature at the University of Paris after 1841. Through the work of men such as these, charity and education received a strong impetus in France. In the field of ministerial work, the saintly pastor of Ars, Jean Baptiste Marie Vianney (1786–1859), set an example which was influential far beyond the limits of his small village near Lyon. Also of lasting impact on the religious life of France were the visions of Mary given in 1858 to Bernadette Soubirous of Lourdes, which soon changed the small town in the Pyrenees into a pilgrimage center for all of France.

Theologically significant, albeit less well founded scientifically, were the theological collections published around the middle of the century in Paris by the enterprising Jacques Paul Migne (1800–1875); and in particular his issue of the Fathers contributed much to a revival of patristic studies. Migne's *Patrologiae Cursus Completus* consisted of 221 volumes in a *Series Latina* which comprised the Latin Church Fathers from Tertullian to Innocent III, and in the 161 volumes of the *Series Graeca* encompassed the Greek patristic literature from the Pseudo-Barnabas to the Council of Florence (1483). Even today both series are indispensable tools

364

for the theologian, although many writings of the Church Fathers have meanwhile become available in better editions. Also active in France at this time was Prosper Guéranger (1805–1875), the great abbot of Solesmes, from whom originated the first impulse toward the liturgical movement. In the persons of the bishops Dupanloup, Pie, and others, the French episcopate was able to appoint eminent theologians to the First Vatican Council.

C. Spain

The modern history of Spain is characterized by strange cross-currents of political and religious ideas encompassing the reactionary, conservative, and progressive. Since the country was pervasively Catholic and the great Catholic tradition accepted by all parties as the basis of all political thought, internal political disputes almost always assumed the character of impassioned religious controversies as well. The bloody civil wars which repeatedly racked the country in the 19th and 20th centuries were always also religious wars concerned with ecclesiastical issues, but never questioned the Catholic religion itself.

In the 18th century the Bourbon rulers, following the Gallicanism of the country of their origin, developed a unique type of established church which was characterized by divine absolutism and the full sovereignty of the king over the church. The concordat which they had wrested from Rome in 1753 confirmed their unlimited right of patronage over all churches of the country, a right which they had exercised since 1508 in their colonies, and conceded to them the right of nomination to all ecclesiastical offices. The Jesuits who defended the right to resist this divine right monarchy (Juan de Mariana) were expelled from Spain and the American possessions in 1767 and mercilessly persecuted until the complete dissolution of their order in 1773. The property of the church was ruthlessly exploited by the monarchy in its own interests (Amortization Laws of 1763 and 1798), and when the Bourbons, who had been deposed by Napoleon, were restored in 1814, Ferdinand VII (1814–1833) not only returned to the *ancien régime* but also reestablished the absolute monarchy. The liberal constitution of the Cortes of Cadiz (1812), which had continued to acknowledge the Catholic faith as the sole religion of the Spanish nation, was abrogated; the nobility and the clergy regained their old privileges; and the Inquisition together with the entire medieval ecclesiastical system was re-instituted. To the dissappointed fighters for independence of 1812/1813, this short-sighted political restoration, seemingly supported by religious principles, indicated that the church had willingly and without criticism entered into the alliance with a reactionary monarchy. It is not surprising, therefore, that the liberal revolution of 1820 evidenced anti-clerical overtones. The causes for this anti-clericalism again may be found in the dominating attitudes of clericalism itself. The law which had established Catholicism as the state religion was revoked; church property was secularized; and all orders, with the exception of the mendicant orders, were banned. However, after Ferdinand returned to the throne in 1823 with the aid of French bayonets, these measures were annulled; the country returned to an absolutist form of government; and established clericalism became stronger than ever before. Both church and clergy suffered greatly in the civil war (Carlist War, 1834–1840) which broke out soon after Ferdinand's death. Although it was basically a dynastic war, it temporarily assumed the trappings of a religious war against the Catholic Church. A further disastrous result was the extension of the war to the Spanish colonies. The peak of this religious war was reached under the despotic government of Minister President Baldomero Espartero who acted as regent for the minor Queen Isabella (1833, and 1843–1868). Only his fall produced a calmer atmosphere and in 1851 a concordat was finally concluded with Rome. In 1868 another revolution broke out which led to Isabella's expulsion and to new legislation directed against the church. Relations with Rome were again broken off and after a brief monarchy under King Amadeus of Aosta (1871–1873) a republic was proclaimed in 1873 which once again adopted anti-clerical attitudes. When the monarchy was restored two years later (1875), the new King Alfons XII (1875–1885) once again gave the country a conservative constitution (1876) which declared Catholicism to be the state religion and prohibited the public performance of other religious rites, but which did not permit the persecution of individuals because of religious faith. A constitutional monarchy was introduced under which liberals and conservatives might participate in the functions of government. In 1909, new unrest originated in Barcelona, and soon 68 monasteries and churches had been burned and 138 clerics killed. From 1910 to 1912 diplomatic relations were discontinued between Madrid and the Vatican. The almost anarchic conditions in the country produced successful officer juntas. Under the dictatorship of Primo de Rivera (1923–1930), the Catholic Church again was maintained as the established church but otherwise forced to submit to the harsh conditions of life. The fall of the monarchy (1931) and the new republic finally brought about the complete separation of church and state and freedom of religion for all citizens. However, all religious orders were forbidden and church and monastic property was confiscated. Anti-clerical demonstrations were staged which led to the burning of numerous churches. Even this new situation brought no rest to Spain. To an ever greater degree than before, the country became a battle-ground of radical socialistic, communistic, and anti-clerical groups. The country moved inexorably toward the war of 1936–1939, and from this bloodiest of all the civil wars the regime of General Francisco Franco emerged victorious.

Only those who are well acquainted with this turbulent history are able to understand what otherwise must remain incomprehensible to any observer of Spanish church conditions. The Spanish philosopher Donoso Cortés (1809–1853), who together with Jaime Balmes (1810–1848) was one of the most influential political thinkers and theological rejuvenators of 19th century Spain, under the influence of civil war had developed from an emphatic liberal and anti-clerical in his youth into an enthusiastic advocate of strict monarchical government. Cortés had come to the conclusion that only a dictatorial form of government would be able to save Christian society from the anarchy which liberalism and radical socialism seemed to engender. In his *Ensayo sobre el catolicismo, el liberalismo y el socialismo* (Barcelona, 1851) Cortés endeavored to justify philosophically and theologically his experiences, particularly those of the revolution in 1848. A dictatorship with a religious base appeared to him as the best form of government. Such a concept, coming after those of de Maistre, Bonald, and the younger de Lamennais, were to prove disastrous in the future since many Catholic politicians and political theorists undeviatingly clung to monarchy and Christian dictatorship as the ideal form of government. As late as the first four decades of this century Cortés exercised a considerable influence in Germany. Some of the forerunners of the Third Reich, such as the political theorist and National Socialist theoretician Carl Schmitt, referred to the ideas of Cortés in justifying the dictatorship of Adolf Hitler.

Thus Catholicism in Spain typified a serious weakness in the Catholicism of the nineteenth and twentieth centuries. In creating the close tie between church and state in order to maintain itself as the established church, Catholicism also erected a great barrier to the development of a free and fruitful ecclesiastical life; and the emphasis upon absolute monarchy or dictatorship, justified by natural law, consistently had evil results. This position on the part of the church prevented it from accepting democratic ideas and caused it to become hopelessly retrogressive. Dominated by the utopian theory that with the aid of the state it could exercise ecclesiastical control over all aspects of the lives of the faithful, the church failed to become part of today's pluralistic society and permitted a dangerous unexpressed anti-clericalism to develop. Today, even in Spain this problem is acknowledged and the church is gradually inching away from Franco's regime, although at the expense of some of its privileges. The decree on freedom of religion which was proclaimed by the Second Vatican Council on September 14, 1965, although still needing implementation, has irrevocably broken with the old attitude.

How these attitudes and influences developed in Italy (Papal State), England, and America will be treated in separate chapters.

53
THE CHURCH IN ANGLO-SAXON LANDS

1. Although Catholicism survived in England after the Elizabethan period, it was constantly beset with persecution and isolation. The Gunpowder Plot and the marriage of Charles I to a Catholic princess helped to confirm the conviction that Roman Catholicism was a foreign religion. The old Catholics were largely from among the landed gentry, who maintained the faith by supporting chaplains and home missions and sending their children to the continent for education. They were barred from the professions, the universities and, until 1829, from the political life of their country. As late as 1780, there was a law which made the teaching of Catholic doctrine or the performance of the rites of the church a felony in the case of a foreign priest, and high treason for an English priest. No Catholic could purchase land. Any Catholic educated abroad in the Roman Catholic religion lost the right to inherit land.

In spite of the efforts of the Irish statesman Henry Grattan, who strongly supported the Act of Union of Great Britain and Ireland (adopted in 1800), it was not until the formation of the Roman Catholic Association in 1823 by Daniel O'Connell that sufficient political force could be mustered to alter the situation. Finally, in 1829, the Roman Catholic Relief Bill was passed. One of its important provisions was that Catholics could be admitted to Parliament. Two important developments helped to obtain political equality for Catholics. One was the favorable change in England's attitude toward Catholicism during her long struggle with the French Revolution and Napoleon. During this period, some 190 bishops and 5,000 French priests took refuge in England. The other development was the large influx of the Irish, intensified by the famine of 1846. These immigrants poured into London, Bristol, Liverpool and the industrial midlands. By 1851, the number of Irish-born residents in England and Wales was 600000, out of a total population of eighteen million.

The Oxford movement, initiated by the Anglican scholar John Keble in 1833, and called Tractarianism because of the large number of pamphlets called *Tracts for the Times* (some 90 in number), held that the Church of England, as part of the Catholic Church created by divine authority, was more than a merely human institution. The Tractarians, soon joined by John Henry Newman (1801–1890), claimed that the bishops of the Church of England were successors to the Apostles and that the Church of England represented a *via media* between Roman Catholicism and Protestantism. Tract 90, published by Newman in 1841, attempted to prove that the Thirty-Nine Articles of Religion of the Church of England were not inconsistent with the dogmas of the Church of Rome. The Tract was formally condemned by the hierarchy of the Anglican Church the same year. As a result, several hundred clergymen of the Church of England entered the Roman Catholic Church. Newman himself was converted in 1845. Nicholas Wiseman (1802–1865), later leader of the restored hierarchy, welcomed the Oxford converts with great enthusiasm. However, Wiseman was not an old English Catholic. Born in Spain of Irish parents, he represented the religious romanticism of men like Görres and Chateaubriand. More representative of the old Catholic group was historian John Lingard (1771–1851). His *History of England,* the first serious effort on the part of a Catholic to write the history of that country, was aimed at removing Protestant prejudices, and displayed remarkable scholarship. Lingard was suspicious of Wiseman's aggressiveness and predilection for continental Italian devotional practices.

The reestablishment of the English hierarchy took place in 1850. The Papal Brief, *Universalis Ecclesiae,* which established the hierarchy, created the metropolitan see of Westminster and twelve other dioceses. Later, other dioceses were created. In 1911, Liverpool and Birmingham were made Archepiscopal sees and in 1916, Cardiff was made the see of a Welsh province. Political opposition to the reestablishment of the Catholic Church in England was led by the Whig Peer, Lord Russell. The result of this agitation was the Ecclesiastical Titles Bill of 1851, which threatened the new hierarchy with fines and loss of property. It was repealed under Gladstone in 1871.

It was not until 1895 that the hierarchy permitted Catholics to attend the universities of Oxford and Cambridge, although restrictions in this regard had long been lifted. This defensive mentality of the church helps to explain why most of its famous apologists have been converts — e.g., Newman, Manning, G. K. Chesterton and Christopher Dawson. Yet this group of converts has been notably active in the field of journalism and letters. The *Downside Review*, founded by Gasquet in 1882, is a Benedictine publication dealing with philosophy, theology and monastic history. *The Blackfriars*, a Dominican monthly founded in 1920, is considered an excellent intellectual publication.

The social and political division of Catholics has been an obstacle to the formation of any acceptable social and political program. The British government's approval of the seizure of the Papal States was not supported by the Catholics. During the 1930's Catholics were in the forefront of those who supported Chamberlain's efforts to reach an understanding with Mussolini. They worked in close contact with the Foreign Office in attempts to counter German propaganda and keep Fascist Italy out of the war.

Although Cardinal Manning attempted to stimulate interest in the labor movement and trade unionism, there has been very little serious effort on the part of the English Catholics to participate in the problems of industrialized society. One of the reasons for this failure is that the chief spokesmen of English Catholicism, Chesterton, Hilaire Belloc and Vincent McNabb, followed one another into the dazzlingly blind alley of distributism. This protean social viewpoint, ranging from an advocacy of extending property-holding to a return to a green and peasant England, together with condemnations of capitalism and socialism, has been completely negative in results. It conjured away social problems and political action by anticipating a universality of conviction and moral reform. The policy of the determinists continues to provide for many Catholic sociologists in England a means for witty and amateurish denunciations of the money-power and capitalism, and of most social legislation as forging further chains of slavery. Their journalistic influence has been thrown to the Conservative Party.

2. Although the first Catholic parish in what is now the United States was established in 1565 at what was then the Spanish colony of St. Augustine, Florida, the history of American Catholicism must be traced to the efforts of George Calvert, first Baron of Baltimore, who established a colony for English Catholics in 1627. His first efforts in Newfoundland were frustrated by the extreme climate and the French. It was not until 1632, two months after his death, that a charter was granted by Charles I to form the colony of Maryland. The first colonists, led by Calvert's son Cecil, landed on an island in the Chesapeake Bay — a place they called St. Clements — in March of 1634. The outbreak of the English Civil War in 1642 and the political interference of the neighboring Virginians, under William Claiborne, forced the Maryland colonists to draft an Act of Toleration in April, 1649 — a declaration that granted freedom of worship to all Christians. The act, however, was repealed in 1654 and Catholics were outlawed. In June of 1691, Maryland became a Royal Colony and a year later the Church of England was established in the colony. For almost a century, and until the War of Independence, the Catholics of Maryland were excluded from public life and forbidden to conduct schools of religious instruction. Faced with these difficulties, many of the Maryland Catholics migrated to the Colony of Pennsylvania. Here, William Penn, a Quaker and likewise the victim of intolerance, offered a modicum of freedom to the Catholics. In 1743, the Jesuit Joseph Greaton established a parish

in Philadelphia. A number of German Jesuits also arrived to minister to the needs of the German immigrants from the Palatinate, who were arriving in large numbers. Farther to the North, in New York, a former Dutch Colony, the Catholic Thomas Dongan was appointed Governor in 1682. The small community enjoyed religious freedom until 1689, when Jacob Leisler overthrew the government and outlawed Dongan and the Catholic clergy. The Church of England was established by law in the four leading counties of New York in 1693, and penal laws against Catholics continued to exist there until 1806.

Since the English Catholic hierarchy had become extinct in 1585, the affairs of the church in the colonies were in the hands of the Jesuits, some 186 of whom worked there between 1634 and the suppression of the order in 1773. These priests were under the direction of the General of the Jesuits in Rome, who dealt with the Congregation of the Propagation of the Faith and the missionary bishops. After 1688, these bishops functioned under the title of the Vicar Apostolic of the London District. It was not until 1790 that the Holy See appointed the first Catholic bishop of the United States — John Carroll. He was consecrated in England. Of a total population of four million, there were approximately 25,000 Catholics in the United States at this time.

The Revolutionary War found a number of Catholics active in the struggle for independence. Charles Carroll was a delegate at the Continental Congress from Maryland and Thomas Fitz Simons represented Pennsylvania. John Barry was active in the founding of the American Navy. The alliance of the new nation with the French government after 1778 did a great deal to lessen prejudices against the Catholic minority. It must be borne in mind that the political ideals of the revolution were not of a religious origin. Contrary to popular opinion, the majority of the colonists came to America in order to improve their social and economic status. The influence of John Locke, especially his *Treatises on Government,* was notable. Puritanism, especially in New England, had long advocated the idea of popular sovereignty, but the majority of the revolutionary figures, like Thomas

Jefferson and Benjamin Franklin, were Deists. The Quakers in Pennsylvania, as well as other religious refugees — Huguenots, Moravians and various German confessions — gave to the early colonies that element of religious pluralism which fostered freedom and toleration. The decades following the War of Independence witnessed what was called the Great Awakening of American Protestantism. Characteristic of the movement was the revival, or camp meeting. Begun by Presbyterians, it was taken up by the Methodists and Baptists. The revivals gave a distinctive quality to American Protestantism along the growing frontier and added that element of Evangelicalism which was to predominate among non-Catholic Christians in America. Pietistic in origin, the Evangelicalism emphasized personal repentance, conscious conversion and a life showing the fruit of the Spirit.

By the end of the Revolutionary era, there were over 3,000 religious organizations and congregations in the states. The Congregationalists were the largest, followed by the Presbyterians, Baptists and Episcopalians. The first amendment of the Constitution of the United States, which took effect in 1791, declared that: "Congress shall make no law respecting an establishment of religion, or prohibiting the free exercise thereof . . ." It was not, however, binding on the various states. The established Church of Georgia was not dissolved until 1798. A state church was supported out of tax monies and legal privileges in Massachusetts until 1834. The new Constitution of the state of South Carolina spoke of "Christian Protestantism" as the official faith of its citizens. Although the Catholic minority benefitted from the eventual disestablishment, it contributed very little to its implementation. It was largely the Baptists, Quakers and Methodists who contended that free churches supporting and governing themselves could do more for the revival of religion than an establishment. The religious freedom that resulted was not, however, an act of hostility toward the various churches. The Congress and the armed forces of the Federal Government supported chaplains. The President of the United States takes his oath of office on the Bible. The freshness and enthusiasm for construction of a new society which would conform with Christian ideals are symbolized in the Great Seal of the United States. Below the basis of a partially constructed pyramid is the eye of God. The inscription reads, *annuit coeptis, novus ordo seculorum,* or "He approves of beginnings, the new order of the ages."

What was new in the American religious experiment was that for the first time in history, religion was to be the product of a voluntary commitment. It was based upon the belief that men could be good fellow citizens even though they went to different churches. This had the end result of achieving security of person and integrity of conscience for the citizen who had no religious convictions. It gave both the state and the church a new freedom to fulfill their true destinies. The 19th century church historian, Philip Schaff, summed up the uniqueness of the American experiment: "The glory of America is a free Christianity, independent of the secular government, and supported by the voluntary contributions of a free people. This is one of the greatest facts in modern history."

The first federal census of 1790 indicated that the population of the thirteen states was 3,929,214. Of this total, there were approximately 35,000 Catholics, who were settled largely in the Middle Atlantic states and in the French villages of the western country. The purchase of the Louisiana Territory in 1803 added some 15,000 Catholics of French and Spanish descent. As the new nation moved westward with its sense of manifest destiny, the church was often in the vanguard of the new settlements. The first Catholic bishop was appointed for California in 1840, eight years before the famous discovery of gold that expedited the movement to the coast. The Vicariate Apostolic of Oregon was erected in 1843. Four years before Texas was annexed by the United States, a bishop was appointed for that area. It is estimated that by 1850, a total of 1,071,000 Catholic immigrants had landed in the United States. Most of them were of Irish and German extraction. Those of German birth constituted one quarter of the foreign-born population of the country in mid-nineteenth century. The first German Catholic newspaper, *Wahrheitsfreund,* was published in Cincinnati in 1837. The territorial expansion and the flood of immigrants is reflected in the First Plenary Council of Baltimore in 1852. Of the thirty-two assembled prelates, nine were native-born, sixteen had been born in France or Ireland, four in Belgium or Canada, and one each in Austria, Spain and Switzerland. Catholicism was truly the church of the immigrant.

Early efforts at education also reflect the immigrant status of the church in America. Georgetown Academy, later Georgetown University, was opened in 1791. A year later, St. Mary's Seminary, the first institution in the new country for the training of American priests, was founded in Baltimore. Most of its faculty were French Sulpicians, expelled from their own country by the Revolution. The subsequent training of the American clergy was largely in the hands of the Sulpicians and other European-based religious congregations. By 1829, the seminary had ordained 52 priests, of whom thirteen were natives of Ireland, and eighteen were either German or French. The Jesuits took control of Georgetown in 1806 and in 1808, a second Catholic college was founded at Emmitsburg, Maryland. Elizabeth Seton, a convert to Catholicism, founded a religious order for women and opened a school for girls at Emmitsburg in 1809. Her foundation, the Sisters of Charity, soon spread rapidly throughout the country and formed the first source of teachers for parochial schools, which by 1840 totaled over 200. Most of these parochial schools were located in the Middle West. As the Catholic population increased, so did the resentment of the predominantly Protestant citizenry.

During the third and fourth decades of the 19th century, a depression and the growing scarcity of employment, augmented by the cheap labor of the immigrants, gave birth to a strong anti-Catholic movement. Already in 1830 an openly anti-Catholic publication, *The Protestant,* threatened and maligned the newcomers, declaring that the principles of popery were "subversive of civil and religious liberty". In August of 1834, a convent of Ursuline Nuns in Charlestown, Massachusetts, was burned. The following years, riots in Philadelphia resulted in the burning of two Catholic churches and the loss of thirteen lives. In 1852, the Know-Nothing Party was formed with a platform that fomented hatred of the foreign-born and of Catholics. Its policies were a definite harassment for the church until the outbreak of the Civil War. Under the sponsorship of the Know-Nothings, the Putnam Bill was passed in New York, which forbade Catholic bishops to hold property in their own name.

The Civil War and the great issue of Negro slavery found the Catholic population of the United States in no way united. The official doctrine of the church taught that slavery, *per se,* was not necessarily evil, nor was it opposed to divine and natural law. One of the leading Catholic theologians of the period, Francis P. Kenrick, was strongly opposed to the idea of abolition. The early Jesuits in Maryland were slave owners, as was the first American bishop, Carroll. The large mass of the Irish Catholic immigrants supported the institution of Negro slavery, because it was a system that allowed them to be placed for the first time one rung up from the bottom of the social ladder. Once the war had broken out, the bishops in the South generally supported the cause of secession. In Baltimore, the clergy of the Cathedral refused to read a prayer for civil authorities, composed by Bishop Carroll in 1791, since it contained a petition for the preservation of the American Union. The Bishop of Nashville was forced to resign and retire to a Dominican monastery in Ohio because of his views on the subject.

Orestes Brownson (1802–1876) was perhaps the most distinguished convert to Catholicism in America during the 19th century, and certainly its greatest intellectual. He was outspokenly critical of his fellow Catholics in their attitude toward slavery. His *Quarterly Review* did not hesitate to scold the clergy and bishops for what he felt was a lack of support for the Union. One of the dark pages in the history of American Catholicism was its failure to aid the newly freed slaves. Now, in the twentieth century, it is reaping the harvest of this indifferent, if not hostile, attitude. One of the excuses for this failure is that, following the emancipation, the church had to direct all of its energies toward the preservation of the faith of the new wave of immigrants from eastern Europe. Thousands of Italians, Hungarians, Poles and Lithuanians, not to mention increased immigration from Ireland and Germany, poured into the United States following the Civil War.

Occupied with the problem of protecting the newly arrived immigrants from the evils of Protestantism, the church authorities were more concerned with establishing parochial schools than they were with directing the laity to the higher realms of education.

Although a large number of institutions for higher learning were established in the nineteenth century, among them the University of Notre Dame in 1842 and the Catholic University of America in 1889, few of them were little more than extended seminaries. One European critic wrote: "In no western society is the intellectual prestige of Catholicism lower than in the country where, in such respects as wealth, numbers, and strength of organization, it is so powerful." Largely responsible for the anti-intellectual climate of American Catholicism was the fact that few of the hierarchy were educated at universities. Most of them were more deeply involved in administration, real estate and the construction of churches and schools. In addition, the Irish and their descendants who came to dominate the hierarchy, lacked a tradition that fostered an interest in intellectual matters. The simple and unquestioning faith of the peasant, often bordering on superstition, characterized the great majority of American laity.

The implications of rapid economic and technological changes that took place during the last decades of the 19th century did not go unnoticed by all Catholic leaders. In the transformation of the country from a predominantly agricultural to a predominantly industrial economy, Catholics, largely a wage earning group, sympathized with radical labor movements and often participated in their violence. Yet the majority of the hierarchy feared that even non-socialistic trade unions would wean Catholic working-men away from their faith. In 1874, the Archbishop of Baltimore, James R. Bayley, condemned labor movements as "miserable associations" and expressed the view that no Catholic with any idea of the spirit of his religion would encourage them. One Catholic lawyer, T. W. Collens, who supported the Christian Labor Union, suggested that the Catholic solution to labor questions might be communities modeled on the historic Paraguay Missions. The condemnation of the Knights of Labor by Rome and the excommunication of the labor-minded priest, Reverend Edward McGlynn, are indicative of the Catholic mentality toward organized labor at that time. The bishop of New York, Michael A. Corrigan, unsuccessfully attempted to have the work of the laborite, Henry George, *Progress and Property,* placed on the Index. Archbishop John Ireland, in condemning the famous Pullman Strike of 1894, spoke of the "unthinking ones who transgress the golden mean and rush into the war against property". It was his belief, one shared with most of the American bishops, that the half-Americanized immigrant workingman could not distinguish between liberty and license. Ceaselessly, he preached the economic virtues — thrift, temperance and education — urging his subjects to do their best to acquire property and social standing. His social philosophy, like that of his fellow bishops, was little more than a Catholic version of Puritan individualism.

Far more positive and enlightened in his approach to the moral problems of an industrialized society was the Reverend John A. Ryan (1869–1945). His first publication, *A Living Wage,* was hailed as "the first attempt in the English language to elaborate a Roman Catholic system of political economy". While others before him had been satisfied with trade unionism pure and simple, Ryan advocated industrial democracy in the form of worker participation in management and ownership as a more effective answer to socialism.

Interest in philanthropy and social service also characterized the years before the First World War. The National Conference of Catholic Charities was organized in 1910. In order to encourage and train personnel for Catholic social service, special schools were established, usually associated with universities. The University of Loyola, in Chicago, and Fordham University, in New

York, were outstanding examples of this effort to secure social justice for the masses.

The entrance of the United States into World War One occasioned the creation of the National Catholic War Council as an organ of the American hierarchy in August of 1917. This organization, at the urging of Pope Benedict XV, became the National Catholic Welfare Council in 1919. Significantly, at papal insistence, it changed its name to the National Catholic Welfare Conference in 1922 and announced that its decisions were of counsel and not binding on the individual bishops. It was not until 1966, as a result of Vatican II, that anything resembling a synod of bishops appeared in the United States. Perhaps the most significant pronouncement of this early organization was the Bishops' Program of Social Reconstruction, issued in 1919. The program called for a federal child labor law, the legal enforcement of labor's right to organize, stringent regulation of public utility rates, government competition with monopolies, worker participation in management and social insurance against unemployment, sickness and old age. Many of these proposals were realized during the New Deal of Franklin D. Roosevelt and the later Kennedy and Johnson administrations. Strangely, the bishops at that time had little to say of the festering racial problems. Yet many feel that the Bishops' Program for Social Reconstruction is the key document in the history of the social philosophy followed by the American Church in the present century. By mid-century, eleven of its twelve basic proposals had become law.

The apparent success of the policy of Americanization caused a minor crisis in the Catholic world at large. A large number of European Catholics, noting the success of the Americans, desired to extend the program in an effort to place the church on the side of democracy and modern progress. The Catholics of France, particularly, harassed by the anti-clerical laws of the Third Republic, found the American experiment worthy of emulation. The principle agent in the controversy was the *Life of Father Hecker,* by Walter Elliott (1842–1928). Father Isaac Hecker, a convert and successful proselytizer, had brought many Protestants to the Catholic fold, and in 1865 had begun publishing the *Catholic World,* a monthly journal that soon reached out to a nation-wide audience. The biography of Hecker, translated into French, brought forth a plethora of denunciations. European traditionalists were appalled at the methods of Hecker — methods which emphasized partial agreement, rather than disagreement, with Protestants. The controversy became known as the heresy of Americanism. In January of 1899, Leo XIII published a papal letter, *Testem Benevolentiae,* addressed to Cardinal Gibbons, wherein he summarized the false doctrines imputed to the Americans. The errors sounded much like the suggestions of the Second Vatican Council. The church should adapt itself to modern civilization, relax its ancient vigor, show indulgence to modern theories and methods, deemphasize religious vows and give greater scope for the action of the Holy Spirit on the individual. These tendencies, asserted the Pope, would restrict the Church's right to determine questions on matters of faith and morals. The docility of the American hierarchy of that period is reflected in the fact that not a single American bishop refused to give up the errors reproved by the Pope.

While active in national politics from the days of the Revolution, American Catholics, until the mid-twentieth century, had been limited to participation that usually terminated at the ward level. There were some few exceptions. Roger B. Taney was appointed to the cabinet of Andrew Jackson as Attorney General in 1831 and later filled the post of Secretary of the Treasury. In 1836 he was elevated to the post of Chief Justice of the Supreme Court. In 1853, President Pierce named James Campbell of Pennsylvania to be Postmaster General. A number of Catholics have held this latter, somewhat undistinguished, post. Before the Kennedy era, there had been only fourteen Catholics in cabinet posts; ten of these were appointed after the coming of the New Deal. The failure of Alfred E. Smith to be elected President in 1928, due largely to prejudice, was for many years a barrier to the aspirations of politically-minded Catholics. The decades before and after the Second World War saw a number of Catholics in the limelight of political controversy. During the 1930's, Reverend Charles E. Coughlin, the "radio priest", enthralled national audiences with his interpretation of the *Quadragesimo Anno* and the *Rerum Novarum,* yet he was more interested in monetary inflation and banking control than a modernized guild system. His open anti-Semitism and his support of ideas and techniques of Fascist lineage lessened his prestige and influence. During the 1950's, Senator Joseph McCarthy championed a Communist witch hunt that gave rise to the expression "McCarthyism". Largely supported by both lay and clerical Catholics, he held the dubious distinction of dispelling the lingering suspicion that Catholics were anti-American. The emergence of a more prosperous suburbanite Catholic elite has found many of them supporting conservative and rightist groups, including the John Birch Society and the Dean Manion Forum. Few support the military involvement of the United States in Southeast Asia with greater determination than the American hierarchy. Yet the Second Vatican Council has unleashed in America a movement of reform that has questioned ancient beliefs and practices. Clerical celebacy, birth control and the continued support of parochial schools are but a few of the issues that now disturb a once docile and papally oriented Church.

The Catholic Church in Canada, like the Church in Latin America, owes its origins to the almost inseparable aims of 17th century colonialism and missionary enterprise. Religious and nationalist elements were nowhere in the New World so closely intertwined. The great explorer, Champlain, inspired with missionary zeal, secured the service of four Recollets for French Canada in 1615. In 1625, the first Jesuits appeared. From that time until 1674, with the coming of the Sulpicians to Montreal, the Jesuits exercised a control of the new colony that amounted to a veritable theocracy. The question of Gallican liberties and early rivalry between Quebec and Montreal troubled the newly established church. However, in the person of François de Montmorency-Laval, who became bishop of Quebec in 1674, the struggling colonial church was placed on a firm basis. In 1663, he founded a seminary with an eye to providing native-born clergy and nuns. The Jesuits founded their first college in Canada in 1635. The Recollets established a seminary at Three Rivers, and the Sulpicians, in Montreal. The Ursulines opened schools for young ladies in Quebec and the Congregation of Notre Dame in Montreal. In contrast to the English Colonies to the south, there was little intellectual life in New France.

The Jesuit mission to the Hurons, in the region south of Georgian Bay, enjoyed a temporary success under the Jesuits Brebeuf and Lelemant. However, the Iroquois War in 1648 terminated the effort as the English-allied tribe destroyed the settlements of St. Ignace and Ste. Marie. Later missionary efforts were carried out in the Great Lakes area and the Mississippi valley. Following the discoveries of Jacques Marquette, who accompanied Louis Jolliet to the upper Mississippi in 1673, a network of Jesuit missions extended from Lake Michigan to the tributaries of the Ohio and Mississippi Rivers.

The conquest of the French colony by the British and its surrender, ratified by the Treaty of Paris in 1763, placed the Catholic colonists in a unique position — 70 000 French speaking Catholics, vastly outnumbered by two million British North Americans, predominantly Protestant. The situation brought forth a culture that was characterized by defensiveness and insecurity. The Quebec Act of 1774 guaranteed not only freedom of worship for Catholics, but also provided the church with a feudal, authoritarian system that was to perdure until the 20th century. Cut off from France by the conquest and the revolutions of 1789 and 1848, the French-Canadian Catholics turned to Rome with even greater docility than their Catholic brethren to the south.

Strongly evident in French-Canadian Catholicism is the idea that the ancient tradition of *Gesta Dei per Francos*. They regard themselves as a right-thinking spiritual island in the materialistic and atheistic sea of North America. This dominant conservatism was strengthened during the 19th century with the advent of religious teaching orders from France — among them, the Jesuits, Oblates and Congregation of Holy Cross.

One of the principal agents in the cultivation of the messianic, cultural nationalism of the French speaking Catholics has been the work, *Histoire du Canada,* by François-Xavier Carneau (1809–1866). Influenced by Lacordaire, Dupanloup and Guizot, Garneau's book provided the doctrine of the essential relationship between French language, laws and customs, which soon became an article of cultural faith for all French-Canadians.

The political struggle between British imperialism and the nationalism of the French-Canadians tended to strengthen ties with France between the Boer War and the First World War. Under the Abbé Lionel Groulx, the Action Française, now entitled Action Canadienne-Française, became the center of a separatist movement aimed at the creation of a separate French-Canadian state, "Laurentia". During the Spanish Civil War, the French-Canadians supported the forces of Franco, as they did later the Fascist party in Italy. In 1945, a French-Canadian Academy, modelled on the French Academy, was established in Montreal.

Since the Second World War, the Universities of Laval, Ottawa and Montreal have exerted disproportionate influence in the realm of philosophical thought. Following the direction of Gilson and Maritain, they have become strong centers of Aristotelian Thomism. Charles De Koninck and André Dagenais, among others, have stimulated interest in reconciling the doctrine of Aquinas with the world of science and politics of the 20th century. Interest in the Middle Ages has brought about the establishment of a number of medieval institutes in Ottawa and Montreal.

54

THE POPES AND THE PAPAL STATES

At the beginning of the nineteenth century it was debated whether the papacy and the Catholic Church had any future. Pius VI died in Valence on the Rhône in 1799 as a prisoner of the French revolutionary government, completely isolated and deserted. Yet

Pius VII (1800–1823) already noticed the winds of change, and Napoleon courted him. The power which still inhered in the papacy was demonstrated by Pius by his deposition of thirty-six bishops when the precarious condition of the church demanded it. These were bishops who resided outside of France in exile and whom Napoleon did not permit to return when the French Church was organized in 1801. The subsequent abuses of the pope by Napoleon increased the pope's moral prestige. The restoration of the Papal States which had been taken by Napoleon was, therefore, not very difficult to attain at the Congress of Vienna.

The Papal States proved to be a very great burden for the papacy and one that it could not maintain for very long. Italy was moving toward national unity and the revolutionary ferment expressed by the secret societies of the Carbonary and the Free Masons could not allow the existence of a clerical state which was governed according to strict absolutist-monarchistic principles. An additional factor was that the following popes, Leo XII (1823–1829), Pius VIII (1829–1830), and Gregory XVI (1831–1846) pursued Metternich's reactionary policies and thereby not only lost touch with the national movement of the *Risorgimento* (reawakening) but made themselves its enemies. After 1849 the Papal States were so hated that they could be maintained only with French bayonets.

Pius IX (1846–1878) was welcomed initially because he was regarded as national and liberal, and when on March 14, 1848, he gave the Papal States a constitution which permitted the people a moderate degree of participation in their government, the event was greeted with enthusiasm and jubilation. But Pius changed his mind about the Papal States when the first papal prime minister count Pellegrino Rossi was assassinated by radical revolutionaries on the occasion of the opening of the chamber of deputies in November 1848. The pope was forced to flee to Gaeta, and revolution broke out in Rome. With French military help Pius won back Rome and the Papal States and restored the old absolutist rule. The irritation of his opponents grew even greater, and the national unity movement, which was now headed by king Victor Emmanuel II (1849–1878), grew into an avalanche which could no longer be stopped. The resistance was directed by the Piedmontese prime minister Cavour (1852–1861). In 1859 the Romagna was lost to the Papal States, and after the defeat at Castelfidardo (September 18, 1860) the papal troops were forced to evacuate Umbria and the Marches. In Florence in March 1861 Victor Emmanuel had himself proclaimed king of Italy.

Rome itself was still protected by a French garrison, and the incursions of the Free Corps leader Garibaldi in 1862 and 1867 were repulsed with French assistance. But when the French troops were needed in their own country as a result of the Franco-Prussian War (1870–1871) and were withdrawn from their station in Civitavecchia, the Piedmontese immediately invaded Rome and captured it after a short bombardment on September 20, 1870. The Papal States had come to an end after more than 1000 years.

Pius IX withdrew into the Vatican. In June 1871 Victor Emmanuel transferred his residence to Rome and moved into the Quirinal. The protests and excommunications of the pope were ignored. On May 13, 1871, the new government in the Law of Papal Guarantees offered the pope an annual subsidy together with the free and unhindered exercise of all his spiritual functions as well as personal inviolability and sovereign rights. But Pius angrily rejected the offer and continued his protestations as the "prisoner of the Vatican". He forbade Italy's Catholics to participate in political elections in the decree *Non Expedit* (1874), but the effect only was that those who were loyal heeded his admonition and left a free field to the radicals. The result was an increasingly anti-ecclesiastical course in the Italian government. Pius XI finally put an end to this unpleasant condition, the "Roman Question", by concluding the Lateran Treaty with Mussolini in February 1929. In the treaty, the pope renounced all claims to the former Papal States; he received full sovereignty in the small Vatican State and the extraterritorial areas of the chief basilicas (Lateran, S. Maria Maggiore, and S. Paul), the administrative buildings of the curia, and the Villa Castel Gandolfo. A concordat also was concluded with the Italian government, whereby the Italian Church once more obtained a lawful relationship with the state.

55

THE FIRST VATICAN COUNCIL

The pontificate of Pius IX (1846–1878) was rich in both gains and losses. Just as the external political power of the papacy disappeared, his internal and moral prestige grew immensely. The definition of papal infallibility and the declaration of primacy occurred simultaneously with the capture of Rome and the fall of the Papal States. The First Vatican Council represented a culmination; but it was also for many a bone of contention, and was filled with tension from the beginning.

1. On December 8, 1854, Pius had declared as dogma the traditional belief that Mary had been conceived without original sin. "It is a divinely revealed truth of faith that Mary in the first moment of her conception was freed by special grace from the stain of original sin in view of the merits of Christ." Thus Pius decided in favor of the Franciscans a theological dispute which had been carried on for centuries by them and the Dominicans. It was not the subject of the decision which was new, but the way in which it was proclaimed. This was not a decision by a council, but an *ex cathedra* definition by the pope. New discussion was now unavoidable concerning the extent to which the pope alone, without council, could decide and proclaim dogma, and the one great topic of the First Vatican Council was provided. It should be noted that prior to proclaiming this dogma, the pope had written to all bishops of the world asking their opinion: 536 had agreed with his view, 4 had opposed it, and 36 had accepted it *iuxta modum,* i.e. they had agreed with his decision but regarded the current moment as inopportune. The solemn proclamation was attended by fifty-four cardinals and one hundred and forty bishops, but the decision was made by the pope alone. No disagreement had been heard in the church.

Ten years later, on December 8, 1864, the pope in his encyclical *Quanta Cura* sent to all bishops a "syllabus", i.e. a compilation of eighty contemporary errors, which from the Catholic point of view had to be condemned. These errors were concerned with doctrines of pantheism, naturalism, rationalism, socialism, and communism, as well as erroneous opinions concerning the relationship between church and state, the nature of Christian marriage, and the lack of necessity for the Papal States. Liberalism and the unqualified belief in progress were especially harshly rejected.

This time reaction was certainly not lacking. Catholics, and to an even greater extent, Protestants accused the pope and the Catholic Church of flagrant backwardness and hostility to civilization. To be sure, the syllabus did not claim for itself dogmatical validity; it only wished to be a guide. But what would happen if the pope by an *ex cathedra* decision declared isolated statements or even the whole syllabus as dogma? This apprehension was voiced everywhere and was soon reinforced by the papal announcement that a council was to meet.

On December 6, 1864, two days before the syllabus was issued, Pius had mentioned for the first time the idea of holding a general council. Under the seal of silence the pope inquired of the twenty-one cardinals of the curia in Rome what their opinion of the plan would be. The majority answered in the affirmative, with only two opposing it, while six had a few doubts but were not basically in opposition. The pope now appointed a preparatory congregation of cardinals (March 9, 1865), took additional bishops into his confidence and, on the occasion of the 1800th anniversary of Peter and Paul (67), announced to more than five hundred bishops his plan to convoke a council. On June 29, 1868, the bull of convocation was sent out, and the council was to be opened in Rome on December 8, 1869.

The question of the definition of papal infallibility was in the air. The German cardinal Reisch mentioned it in December 1864, and eight of the episcopal opinions of the year 1865 demanded it. The concept as such posed no great difficulties; Catholics had very little doubt that the pope as successor of Peter (according to Lk 22, 32) possessed special magisterial authority. The question was only how far this authority extended, whether it could be exercised independently from councils and the college of bishops, and what special preconditions would have to be met.

On February 6, 1869, the Roman Jesuit periodical *Civiltà Cattolica* printed a contribution from France which demanded a definition of infallibility in a way which was wrong both in content and form. After the Revolution a peculiar loyalty to the papacy had developed in this Gallican country which was designated as "ultramontanism". Its champions were H. F. R. De Lamenais (1782–1854) and J. de Maistre, a layman in the diplomatic service. After the disturbances of the revolutionary and Napoleonic eras, these men extolled the papacy as the sole repository of order and morality. De Lamenais declared that only the popes were capable of restoring the disordered human society and only a clergy independent from the state and firmly led by an infallible pope, the uncontested master of the church, had the required prestige and strength to protect spiritual freedom from the tyranny of political power. Infallibility, therefore, appeared to De Lamenais as the unavoidable, necessary, and obvious prerequisite of an effective papacy. The church must be a monarchy according to the will of God. What sovereignty was to secular monarchs, infallibility was to the popes; infallibility was nothing more than sovereignty in the realm of the spirit and of the church.

In this way De Lamenais, a convinced monarchist, transferred his concept of political sovereignty to church and papacy, and the common people echoed his desires. But De Lamenais was not a theologian and the weakness of his conceptions was soon revealed by the great Tübingen theologian Johann Adam Möhler in his work *Unity in the Church* (1825). To Möhler, the church was a mystical living community with Christ as its head. No more than the head can be separated from the living body, no more can the pope, the vicar of Christ, be isolated from the *Corpus Christi mysticum*. The pope is engaged in a permanent exchange of ideas with the entire organization of the church as represented

389

by the bishops. Even though he is the center and the apex of the entire episcopate, he still remains a bishop as well. Primacy and collegiality have a certain relationship to one another.

To determine this relationship in detail was the difficult task of the subsequent decades, and two extremes opposed one another. In France it was chiefly Louis Veuillot (1813–1883), chief editor of *Univers,* a newspaper which he had developed to universal importance, who continued to elaborate ultramontane ideas and assisted in their dissemination. In a dangerously exaggerating form, which amounted to actual worship of the papacy, Veuillot extended the concept of primacy and infallibility to all regions of the official and private statements and actions of the pope and advocated the idea of a positive inspiration by the Holy Spirit which accompanied and guided all papal actions. Supported by a numerous following, Veuillot now desired to have his views accepted by the council and made dogma. This, then, was the essence of the article in *Civiltà Cattolica.*

A group of theologians and scholars in Germany led by Ignaz von Döllinger (1799–1890), a church historian of international reputation, watched with concern the development of the ultramontane concept in France. Until about 1860 Döllinger had been one of the most outspoken public defenders of German Catholicism, but then he had increasingly raised his voice in warning. His criticism of the backward conditions in the Papal States and his agreement with the global condemnations of the Syllabus had earned him the reputation of a "liberal" Catholic. For these reasons he had not been invited to Rome to participate in the theological preparation for the council. Now Döllinger raised his voice in passionate diapproval of the ultramontane French tendencies regarding the question of infallibility. In unusually harsh words he attacked papal infallibility in a series of articles in the *Augsburger Allgemeine Zeitung* under the pseudonym of "Janus". Döllinger wished to prove historically that such infallibility had never existed and that, on the contrary, it could be shown that popes frequently had erred and fallen into heresies, as was demonstrated particularly in the case of Pope Honorius I

(625–638). He denied the pope any kind of infallible magisterial authority and even attacked his primatial position and authority in the church. These views regarding primacy and authority certainly went too far.

In July 1869 Döllinger's articles appeared in bookform under the title of *The Pope and the Council* by "Janus", and the book's polemical tone had a particularly unfortunate effect. Among liberals and Protestants, Döllinger's attack on the papacy, as which it was regarded everywhere, incited hatred of everything Catholic at a time when tensions between the denominations were already great. Among the Catholics, feelings were divided; some more or less agreed, influenced principally by Veuillot's heretical exaggerations, while others saw the attack as treachery. The great Cologne theologian M. J. Scheeben called the book a pamphlet against the papacy. Most portentous was its effect on the public; the council suddenly became a political event. In April 1869 the Bavarian minister president prince Hohenlohe sent a circular dispatch to all European governments in which he warned of the political consequences of a papal declaration of infallibility and suggested common action by the states against the council. But the plan foundered on Prussia's (Bismarck) and Austria's unwillingness to become involved. When at the end of August 1869 the German bishops traveled to the conference of bishops at Fulda, they were harassed and insulted by the people of Protestant Hesse, and were forced to give calming explanations in their subsequent pastoral letter. Since the majority of them also considered the definition of infallibility inopportune, they urgently requested the pope, in view of the general dissension, to abandon a discussion of this topic at the council.

2. Inasmuch as the discord concerning the problem of infallibility was equally great in England, France, and other countries, the pope removed the question from the agenda. Hardly had the council begun its work in December 1869, however, when it was raised again by the zealous proponents of infallibility. On December 25, Archbishop Dechamps of Malines introduced a motion to have the infallibility question put on the agenda

again after all, and four hundred bishops supported it. Since the "Congregation for the Examination of Suggestions" was also in favor of the motion, the unusually vehement reaction of the opposition, which mustered one hundred and thirty-six counter votes, could not prevent the assent of the pope, and the subject of infallibility was put on the agenda.

On May 9, 1870, the debates on papal infallibility began in the council. Thirty-seven sessions of the plenary congregation took place, and one hundred and forty long and harsh speeches pro and contra were made. The discussion became more and more passionate, and was spiritedly fanned by pressures from outside the council. Döllinger, in particular, this time under the pseudonym "Quirinus", wrote bitter articles which increasingly lacked objectivity. In the council, Bishop Hefele of Rottenburg, the learned author of the famous *History of the Councils,* and Bishop Strossmayer of Djakovar in Bosnia led the opposition against a definition; they were supported also by numerous other cardinals and bishops, among them the majority of the Germans. But by far the majority of the council members affirmed the fact of papal infallibility as such; they were only of the opinion that at that time it was inopportune to proclaim it as dogma. The debate was conducted freely and frankly and with the advantageous result that all arguments and counter-arguments could be expressed without hindrance and nothing was concealed or suppressed which was required for a clarification. As a matter of fact, the vehemence of the opposition, which was so brilliantly represented by Bishops Hefele and Strossmayer, caused their objections to be examined particularly carefully. Because this careful attention was given to the opposition views, the absurd content of Veuillot's exaggerations was soon excluded, and the remaining nucleus was so much more irrefutable and reliable.

At the first ballotting on July 13, 1870, 451 council fathers voted in favor of the definition of infallibility, 88 opposed it, and 62 accepted it with reservations. The final voting on July 18, 1870, demonstrated that among the opponents the greater majority had voted against the definition for reasons of inopportunity, and now had no difficulty in voting affirmatively. There were still others who were uncertain, but as they did not wish to prevent the definition, fifty-five bishops with the consent of the pope left Rome before the final vote. That same day at the solemn fourth session of the council the constitution *Pastor Aeternus,* which contained the doctrines of the primacy and the infallibility of the pope, was adopted with 533 affirmative against only 2 negative votes. The constitution stated: a) The pope as successor of Peter, vicar of Christ, and supreme head of the church, exercises the full regular direct episcopal authority over the whole church and over the individual bishoprics (primacy, universal episcopate). This authority extends to matters of faith and morals as well as to discipline and church administration. It is not designed to supplant the regular local episcopal jurisdiction which each bishop has for his diocese and which was instituted directly by the Holy Spirit but incorporates this local jurisdiction in and subordinates it to the totality of the universal church. Therefore, the individual bishop owes the pope true obedience, "not only in matters concerning faith and morals, but also in those of habits and administration of the church". b) When the pope in his official capacity *(ex cathedra)* makes a final decision concerning the entire church in a matter of faith and morals, this decision in itself is infallible and immutable, and does not require the prior consent of the church.

3. The council had to be discontinued immediately after the vote on infallibility, because the outbreak of the Franco-Prussian War (July 19, 1870) forced many council fathers to return home. Later, the occupation of Rome by the Piedmontese on December 20, 1870, also prevented a continuation. Therefore a debate did not occur on the other important points of the schema "On the Church". Most important of all, a definition of the church itself, and a more precise determination of the position of the episcopate within the church, were not established. Primacy had been defined, but its relationship to the episcopate had been only intimated and not defined exactly. As a result of the abrupt discontinuation, the primatial aspect

dominated the collegial one, and a certain discontent necessarily remained.

There were other questions, however, with which the council had dealt and which had been worked on by the committees. The important dogmatic constitution *On the Catholic Faith* was adopted on April 24 and approved by the pope, but of a total of fifty-one schemata only two were disposed of. The importance of the question of primacy and infallibility overshadowed everything else which was discussed and it was yet to have a sequel.

56

AFTER THE COUNCIL:

OLD CATHOLICISM AND KULTURKAMPF IN GERMANY

It is a traditional privilege in the church for everyone to express his opinion concerning a question of faith as long as the question has not been conclusively settled. Only the denial of a dogma is formal heresy. How would the opposition of the council react now that papal infallibility had been accepted? Many asked this question apprehensively. It is an impressive illustration of the genuine Catholic attitude toward the faith that the entire episcopate adhered to the position either immediately or after only a short period of time. Those bishops who had left the council before the ballotting submitted to the higher decision of the church; most of these bishops, such as Archbishops Melchers of Cologne and Scherr of Munich, had only opposed the definition because they considered it inopportune. On the other hand, it certainly was not easy for Hefele of Rottenburg and Ketteler of Mainz, who had opposed the position for so long, now to be compelled to submit to it. After a difficult inner struggle, Bishop Hefele published the decrees in his diocese in April 1871. In an open letter to Döllinger's followers, who had denounced him for abandoning his position, he wrote: It took several months of inner struggle "until I was able to come to terms with the council decree and frankly and freely submit to the supreme authority of the church. What

I foresaw has come about: This step has brought down upon my head much vilification, but it has also restored my inner peace." Catholic principle had won a victory over private judgment.

1. The opposition group in Germany was even more disappointed, because until the last moment it had believed that with the support of the German bishops it could oppose the council decision even after papal infallibility had been accepted. Many of the German opposition flattered themselves that they would be able to overturn the council decision by the weight of their scientific reputation, and moved toward schism. It must not be denied that these men also underwent severe inner struggles; some of them later found the way back to unity, but others persisted in their opposition. These events are marked by profound tragedy.

On August 14, 1870, a theology professor from the University of Bonn staged a protest meeting in Königswinter at which furious accusations were hurled against the Vatican "meeting", which was denied the character of a free council. On August 27, 1870, another meeting of an even larger nature took place in Nuremberg. Now both signatures and followers were sought, and in Cologne and Munich so-called "central committees" were formed for this purpose. Döllinger provided the catch-word when he had spoken of the "Old Catholic Church" which had been adulterated by the Vatican Council; the struggle was now to be in defense of the "Old Catholic Church". Numerous professors of the theological faculties of Bonn, Breslau, Munich, and Braunsberg, when requested by their bishops to submit to the dogma, refused obedience and were excommunicated. In September 1871 the first congress of the "Old Catholics" was held in Munich. Now even Döllinger warned against pitting altar against altar and thus bringing about a schism; nevertheless, an "Old Catholic Church" was founded, which Döllinger never joined.

The Breslau professor of theology Reinkens was elected as bishop of the new community in June 1873. In order to guarantee a genuine apostolic succession, he had himself consecrated by the Jansenist Bishop Heykamp of Deventer. The schism had become complete. The "Old Catholic Church" still believed that it could adhere to all Catholic doctrines with the exception of the last dogmas, but "reforms" soon began. Auricular confession, fasting, and abstinence were "reformed" (1874); indissolubility of marriage, canonical obstructions to marriage, and many feast days were put aside (1875); and celibacy of priests was abandoned (1878). Because of the desire to create similarities to the other Christian communities and thus make union with them possible, several other Catholic doctrines and customs were abandoned. Hatred and hostility to the Catholic Church also continued to grow when their hopes of attracting large numbers from the Catholic Church remained totally unfulfilled. The rejection which they received from the Catholic population was great, and the fronts between the two groups hardened, a condition which unforunately has continued to exist to this day.

2. Only the governments welcomed the Old Catholics. Bismarck saw them as welcome helpers in his forthcoming battle against the Catholic Church in Germany. With the help of the Old Catholics, Bismarck believed that he would be able to realize his dream of a German national church free from Rome. The schism, therefore, received his support and the Old Catholics were provided by the state with all possible assistance.

The *Kulturkampf* in Germany had many roots: The dissension over imperial politics between the (Protestant Prussian) Little Germans, whose leader was Bismarck, and the (largely Catholic) Great Germans; the hostility of liberalism to the church, especially since the Syllabus and the Vatican Council; and last but not least the ecclesiastical opposition of the Old Catholics in Germany, who, to their own advantage, intensified the struggle against the Catholic Church. The new empire, which Bismarck was then in the process of forging after the victory over France, was to be as uniform as possible. Having grown up with the idea of a national church, Bismarck could only envisage a Catholic Church which like the Protestant territorial churches would be completely and exclusively subordinated to the will of the state. The existence of the Center Party, which had reorganized itself in 1870 and which now constituted separate political representation for Catholics, became a painful thorn in Bismarck's flesh when the Centrists entered the Reichstag in considerable strength.

Thus there began in the new empire the bitter struggle, instigated by Prussia against the Catholic Church, which was termed the *Kulturkampf.* In 1871 the Catholic department in the Prussian ministry of public worship and education was closed. On December 10, 1871, the Pulpit Law limited the freedom of the sermon. These events were followed by the School Supervision Law (March 11, 1872); the imperial Jesuit Law (July 4, 1872), which expelled the Jesuits and "related orders" (Redemptorists) from Germany; and finally by the May Laws (1873), in which the state decreed regulations for the training and hiring of clergy, the handling of purely internal ecclesiastical matters, and for the facilitating of cancellation of church membership. Obligatory civil marriage was introduced, first in Prussia in March 1874, and then (February 6, 1875) in all of Germany. In May 1874 additional "May Laws" followed; among these was the "Old Catholic Law" which on July 4, 1875 gave Old Catholics the right of using the Roman Catholic churches along with the regular Roman Catholics and in spite of their extremely small numbers. All monasteries and establishments of orders in Prussia were dissolved in May 1875 and the members of the orders expelled; only the orders active in the nursing of the sick were permitted to remain by express ministerial sanction. The "Breadbasket Law" (April 22, 1875) cut off all obligatory financial payments to the church by the Prussian state. Future payments were made dependent on a signed declaration acknowledging and consenting to obey the *Kulturkampf* laws. As only the Old Catholic priests were willing to do this, they alone received these monies. The *Kulturkampf* laws were implemented by the use of the police and such methods as fines, prison sentences, and expulsion from the country.

The Catholic people, clergy, and episcopate opposed these forcible measures with complete unanimity. The struggle was waged in Baden, Hesse-Darmstadt, and Saxony as well as in Prussia. Even Catholic Bavaria, which under Döllinger's influence had rejected the decisions of the Vatican Council and ardently promoted Old Catholicism, joined in the battle. Yet although they inflicted immeasurable damage, the governments were unable to achieve anything. On the contrary, the Catholic population only drew closer together. In 1873–1874, the Center Party occupied as many as ninety-one seats in the Reichtstag, and had many gifted leaders such as Windthorst (d. 1891), the brothers Reichensperger, and von Mallinckrodt. In the end, Bismarck was glad to be able to make peace, which was facilitated by Pope Leo's XIII (1878–1903) conciliatory attitude, and in 1880 began the dismantling of the *Kulturkampf* laws.

57
THE POPES AFTER THE FIRST VATICAN COUNCIL

The growth of the moral prestige of the papacy both within and without the church formed a strange contrast to its external impotence in the years following the demise of the Papal States. The definition of the two dogmas concerning papal primacy and infallibility in matters of faith and morals had a positive rather than a damaging effect on the relationship of the church to the nations. Only in Germany did hostilities occur; in France there was no resistance, and the French Church lived in peace under the presidency of MacMahon (1873–1879). In England, Ireland, Belgium, and America the returning bishops were received with all honors.

During the pontificate of Leo XIII (1878–1903) the prestige of the papacy steadily increased. This was illustrated by the continually rising number of diplomatic representations to the Vatican (even non-Catholic countries maintained relations with it in Rome), and was further demonstrated by the unanimous homages which were paid to Leo by all sides on the occasion of his personal jubilees (1883, 1887, 1893, 1903: 50th anniversary as cardinal and 25th anniversary as pope). In 1890 the German Emperor Wilhelm II visited Leo at the Vatican. The product of their discussion regarding the difficult social and political problems in the industrial states was the famous social encyclical *Rerum Novarum* (1891), which developed for the first time a Catholic solution to social questions without limiting its action, as had so far been the case, to charitable measures.

It was Leo's desire to abandon the reactionary course of his predecessor with respect to acute social, political, and cultural questions. Above all the problem of church and state occupied him. In several encyclicals he developed his doctrine of the Christian state, which largely followed that of Thomas Aquinas (1881, 1885, 1888, 1890). The remarkable thing about Leo's doctrine was its emphasis upon the independence and the dignity of the state. In the encyclical *Aeterni Patris* (1879) Leo called special attention to the importance of Thomist theology and philosophy and declared it to be the basis of ecclesiastical theology. Leo also demonstrated his progressivism in questions of biblical exegesis (*Providentissimus Deus*, 1893). He also won great credit from history by opening the Vatican Archives in 1881 for scholars of all denominations. In 1879 he had appointed the Würzburg historian Josef Hergenröther (1824–1890) as prefect of the archives and at the same time made him a cardinal; the learned Heinrich Denifle O. P. (1883–1905) was appointed to work with Hergenröther as assistant archivist, and Franz Ehrle S. J. (1895–1914, since 1922 cardinal, died 1934) became prefect of the Vatican Library. Since this time, the archives and library of the Vatican have become centers for historical scholarship of international significance. In 1886 Ludwig von Pastor used their resources in writing his monumental *History of the Popes since the End of the Middle Ages* (22 volumes, last printing Herder, 1961).

Leo's conciliatory attitude, which contrasted sharply with the inflexible position that Pius had maintained toward the states, had visible successes on the diplomatic level. The pope secured the end of the *Kulturkampf* in Germany, and nothing indicated the new German situation better than Bismarck's request that

399

the pope mediate in the dispute between Germany and Spain over the possession of the Caroline Islands. In Belgium (1885) and in Switzerland (1888), Leo also adjusted difficulties between state and church.

It was important that Leo in all of his extensive magisterial activity not once invoked the decision of the council regarding the *ex cathedra* infallibility of the pope. Thereby the pope defused the accusations which had been made during the heat of battle in 1869–70, and allayed the dire prognoses for the future. Dogmatic definitions are only formulated with regard to crucial questions of faith and morals, and papal infallibility is not claimed for the doctrines contained in papal encyclicals. The next infallible statement of faith was made only in 1950 by Pius XII.

In France the church-state relations came to a head once again. The Republicans were in power after 1879 and they immediately began new efforts against the church which reached their climax in the years 1900–1906. It was the aim of the Republicans to abolish Christian education and training and to completely secularize public life. Their motto was the separation of church and state. The Law of Associations in 1901 expelled the orders from France with the exception of a few congregations active in nursing of the sick. After Leo's death, diplomatic relations between France and the Vatican were broken off in 1904. Leo had urged the French Catholics, who were still strongly monarchistic and anti-republican, to cooperation (Ralliement) with the republic, but he had made little headway. His efforts only produced a delay, but did not avert open war.

In his last years, even Leo, now a nonagenarian (1810–1903), showed certain reactionary tendencies, primarily as a result of his reactionary environment. In 1903, for example, he established a Pontifical Biblical Commission consisting of several cardinals and a number of consultants which "was designed to supervise strictly the work of Catholic exegetes" (R. Aubert). It was in the nature of things that Leo's strongly authoritarian personality contributed to Roman centralism in the church. During his increasingly necessary interventions in the church political disputes of individual countries, the pope negotiated directly with the governments through his nuncios rather than through his bishops and this contributed as much to creating centralism as did his numerous instructions to the bishops. An intensive encouragement of pilgrimages by Catholics of all countries, which modern transportation made possible, also helped to make people conscious of Rome as the center of Christendom.

Pius X (1903–1914) was completely different from Leo; he was an apolitical, innerly devout man, who "gave the impression of a saint to everyone", and was indeed canonized in 1954. *Instaurare omnia in Christo* (encyclical, 1903) was his motto, and he concentrated entirely on internal ecclesiastical and religious problems. As a pastoral pope and one of the greatest reformers in history, Pius contributed immeasurably to the church. His intensive reform activity was tied directly to the First Vatican Council; the numerous reform decrees which had not been realized because of the discontinuance of the council in 1870 were taken up and put into effect. His decrees regarding communion (since 1905), in which he promoted frequent communion and early communion for children; his liturgical reforms with respect to the breviary, the missal, and choral singing; and his pastoral letters on the ascetic and scientific rejuvenation of the clergy were of enormous benefit. Also important were his reform of the curia, whose administration he reorganized and modernized, and his preparatory work for the revision of all canon law. These actions also were based to a large degree on the preparatory work of the Vatican Council, and on the whole he performed an inestimable achievement for the internal growth of the church.

But even saints are human beings and have their limitations. His unflinching stand for the purity of the faith and the rights of the church was coupled with a certain narrowness and inflexibility which was to have fateful results in the area of church politics. The prestige which Leo had acquired for the papacy was quickly lost by Pius, with the result that the condition of the church worsened in many countries. In France the controversy regarding the right to nominate bishops led to the severing of diplomatic relations in 1904. The government, which was hostile to the church, provided in its measures for the separation of church and state in December 1904, for the establishment through out France of local religious associations which were to administer church property and to whom the appointment and payment of the clergy were to be transferred. Inasmuch as Pius X forbade the participation of Catholics in these institutions, the associations were soon controlled by non-Catholics and enemies of the church. The law regarding the complete separation of church and state came into force on January 1, 1906; church property then became ownerless and its administration passed to the state. The material damage to the Catholic Church in France was great, and total impoverishment led to its displacement from public life. Contact was lost with the republican-minded masses of the French people, and secularization in France assumed terrifying proportions.

New tensions also arose with respect to Russia, Germany, and the United States. In 1910 diplomatic relations with Spain were severed, and in 1911 an open conflict with Portugal occurred. Pius X, who was as monarchistically inclined as his predecessors, rejected democratic ideas and lost contact with the republican tendencies of the age.

Within the church the condemnation of Modernism by the decree *Lamentabili* and the encyclical *Pascendi* (1907) produced a grave crisis. Modernism was the result of the serious and to some degree erroneous efforts of progressive Catholic theologians and scholars to bring Catholic teaching into line with contemporary scientific and philosophical thought. In America, the convert Hecker energetically demanded a greater participation of Catholics in public life, and in France, the exegete Loisy accepted the "modern" biblical criticism of liberal Protestant theology. Blondel, Laberthonnière, and Le Roy incorporated thoughts of modern evolutionary philosophy into the Christian doctrines of faith and morals and thus relativized dogma. In Italy, modernism was followed by Minochi, and in England chiefly by the convert Tyrrell. There is no question that it was necessary for the magisterial office of the church to take a stand and to condemn the errors.

Unfortunately, however, the papacy did not sufficiently distinguish between those who merely desired a greater openness of the church toward modern life and those who either had gone very far in their adaptation (in Germany, for instance, J. Müller and J. Schnitzer) or who had already become heretical (Loisy). A strongly reactionary circle around Pius X suspected heresy everywhere, and the integralists soon organized a fanatical hunt for real or suspected modernists. In order to supervise Catholic teachers, in 1910 the anti-modernist oath was required of every priest who was active as either a pastor or a teacher. Later it was required also of clerics before holy orders, of theologians before they began to teach, and of pastors, prelates, and superiors before the investment of their canonical office. It is still required in this form. In the beginning, anonymous accusations and hasty proceedings often led to the unjustified accusation of men with unmixed loyalty such as Hermann Schell and Albert Ehrhard. This narrow-minded approach by the church created an awkward and depressed mood, and Benedict XV in his first encyclical (November 1, 1914) immediately condemned the heresy mania of the integralists.

The pontificate of Benedict XV (1914–1922) was overshadowed by the First World War. With utmost sincerity the pope worked untiringly to counter the hatred among peoples. When Benedict submitted a lengthy peace note to the belligerents on August 1, 1917, the political shortsightedness of all powers caused them to reject his mediation suggestion. After the war the pope did everything in his power to alleviate the distress and to heal the wounds by means of large scale aid, which particularly benefited defeated Germany. Forcefully Benedict warned of splitting Europe into victors and vanquished, and he did not approve of the Treaty of Versailles. Unfortunately, no one listened to him. After the war, the number of diplomatic representations at the Vatican grew to twenty-five; among them were Protestant Holland, England, and even Japan. Of internal importance for the church was the new ecclesiastical law code, the *Codex Iuris Canonici* (1917), which came into force in 1918.

Third Epoch: 1918 to the Present
From the First World War to the Present

Approximately 10 million dead and 20 million wounded comprised the sad ledger sheet of the great massacre of World War I. The violent emotions which the war had caused and its experiences brought about new spiritual conditions. Old ties were discarded, and a new beginning was to be made. This epoch was a period of tremendous change also for the church. An accounting was made of the mistakes of the past and new paths were sought. The result was the rediscovery of the common foundations of Christianity and a new profound awareness of the church. The "Age of the Church" had begun.

58
RETURN FROM EXILE AND NEW BEGINNINGS

1. In Germany it was realized that Catholicism would have to accept greater responsibility for world civilization and correct its backwardness. Since the turn of the century men such as Georg von Hertling, Schell, Ehrhard, and Carl Muth, the publisher of *Hochland* (since 1903), had untiringly pointed out the real "inferiority" of Catholics in cultural, scientific, and political life and had appealed to the Catholic people to face the tasks of modern times. These men, like many others, had suffered gravely from the anti-modernist psychosis of Pius X, and now they outspokenly

demanded redress. The philosopher Peter Wust has termed the discussion of these events the "return from exile".

An examination of the past revealed that despite its successes in the nineteenth century, Catholicism had become inwardly stunted. National churches, denominationalism, nationalism, and liberal arrogance had involved the church in a permanent petty war, and during such struggles as the German *Kulturkampf*, the Italian *Risorgimento* with its war against papacy and Papal States, and the French church war at the turn of the century had occasionally posed threats to Catholicism's very existence. The church had been pushed into a permanent defensive attitude, and Catholics had withdrawn from public affairs. The way into the ghetto, however, meant that Catholics excluded themselves from participation in science, politics, and culture and lost touch with the most important developments of the modern age. Two excellent examples were the attitude of the church toward democratic ideas and its failure to give adequate support to social legislation.

The republican and democratic tendencies of the nineteenth century had not affected the Catholic Church; the popes had been fundamentally opposed to all democratic ideas. Since the French Revolution the papacy had fallen prey to "a complex of fear and shock regarding democracy" (H. Meier). In the period of restoration the popes again had established a closer "bond between throne and altar". De Lamennais and de Maistre had pronounced monarchy the only god-willed form of government and a misguided conservatism fashioned this opinion into a basic dogma of ultramontane Catholicism which the popes did everything to strengthen. The rejection of the republic by French Catholics resulted in a struggle against the church in France at the end of the nineteenth century. In Germany this view even after the First World War prevented the growth among many Catholics of a real democratic understanding of the Weimar Republic.

The significance of the social question also was not recognized early enough by the church. In their naive conservatism, Catholic social theoreticians of the first half of the nineteenth century believed on the one hand in fighting the rising capitalistic

405

form of society and on the other in being able to alleviate the distress of the industrial workers through charity alone. They demanded renewal of the old ban on usury, extirpation of capitalism, and a return to the order of estates found in the Middle Ages. As late as 1848, pastor Wilhelm von Ketteler, the future "social bishop", proclaimed emphatically at the first union of Catholics at Mainz that it now would be shown "that the final solution of the social question is reserved to the Catholic Church, for the state, no matter what regulations it will decree, has not the strength for it".

Indeed, almost another four decades were to go by before the state adopted social legislation (1882–1883 ff); but the church also required a long time, too long a time, before it arrived at a clear social concept and recognized that what was involved was a structural problem in society which could not be mitigated by charity alone. In the meantime, Marx and Engels won to their side increasing masses of workers who became lost to the church; Leo's XIII social encyclical came too late (1891), and even the Catholic Workers' Movement which was organized in Munich (1892), Berlin (1895), and Mönchen-Gladbach (1904) was able to capture only a fraction of the working masses. The church remained in its bourgeois environment, and the proletariat transferred its allegiance to atheistic Marxism.

2. An internal development which decisively determined Catholic spirituality after the war and tied it to the church, proceeded parallel to this reflection on responsibility in church and state. Romano Guardini proclaimed prophetically in 1922: "A religious development of unforeseen impact has begun: The church is awakening in the souls of men"; his prophesy proved correct. The common experiences in the trenches and the common ideals of the youth movement led to a rediscovery of the church as a community. Hand in hand with this went the liturgical movement and "ecumenical" understanding between the denominations. A change in the image of the church was basic to this new church consciousness.

The new image of the church moved away from the hitherto

valid Counter-Reformatory and juridically accented definition of Bellarmine, who saw the church as a denominational and redemptory community under the direction of the pope; instead the church was rediscovered as the living Christ and a work of God. This anti-individualistic attitude was inspired by the community oriented concept of the *Corpus Christi Mysticum,* of which individuals are only the members. An appreciation of community prayer led to the rediscovery of liturgy, and the people of God began to participate more responsibly in the celebration of divine service.

The modern liturgical movement originated in Mecheln in 1909. At a Belgian meeting of Catholics the demand was first voiced that the prayers of the Mass be made accessible to the people. "Il faudrait démocratiser la liturgie", L. Beauduin OSB demanded; and thereby started a development which soon spread to Germany, Austria, and many other countries. Benedictine abbeys such as Maria Laach and Klosterneuburg (Pius Parsch) became champions of the movement, and the German Catholic Youth Movement also came to its support. Romano Guardini, the spiritual leader of the Quickborn, in his countless writings and lectures, preserved and passed on the spirit of the liturgy in a profound way. The majority of the younger clergy were seized by this enthusiasm, and at the time of the national socialistic persecution of the church, when outward activity was curtailed, the unifying strength of liturgy was experienced afresh. During the distress of the Second World War and the misery of the postwar years, liturgical participation in divine service gave strength and support to many people.

After careful consideration, the movement was also accepted by the hierarchy of the church. It is possible to trace a direct line from the encyclical *Mystici Corporis* (1943) and the encyclical *Mediator Dei* (1947) to the liturgy constitution of the Second Vatican Council on December 4, 1963. The liturgical movement is more than a revival of liturgy, it attempts to effect a revival of the faithful through the spirit of liturgy and to have them experience the "passage of the Holy Spirit through his church" (Pius XII). It is the present church's strongest source of power.

The *Una Sancta* Movement and Catholic "ecumenism" also have their roots in this new image of the church. With the defeat of the Counter-Reformatory attitude and the encounters between Christians of all denominations during the war, the need arose for better interdenominational understanding.

In the non-Catholic world, this encounter had already assumed firm organizational forms. As early in the "ecumenical movement" as 1910, a Protestant missionary conference in Edinburgh had suggested that agreement on certain basic cooperation in the missionary areas was most necessary, particularly where the competition between the many Christian groups had been painfully apparent. Out of this effort had grown the decision to organize a world conference of all Christians at which questions of the common faith and ecclesiastical constitution were to be discussed. These topics were then seized by two movements; the first one adopted the topic "Faith and Order" and treated questions of doctrine and ecclesiastical structure. The second one, "Life and Work", for the time being wished to effect nothing but a practical encounter of Christians and common action by them. The first world conferences were held at Lausanne in 1927 and at Edinburgh in 1937. At Utrecht in 1938 and Amsterdam in 1948 the two movements combined into a "World Council of Churches" with its seat at Geneva. In Lund in 1952 the movement defined itself as "a community of churches who accept Christ as God and Savior". At the world conference in New Delhi in 1961 the acknowledgement of the Trinity was added: "The Ecumenical Council is a fraternal association of churches who in accordance with Scripture confess to the Lord Jesus Christ as God and Savior and who endeavor jointly to perform their common calling to the honor of the one God the Father, the Son, and the Holy Spirit." One hundred ninety eight Christian churches are united in the council today; the Catholic Church is not a member.

At first, Rome took a very negative attitude toward the Protestant ecumenical movement; the idea of an interdenominational "superchurch" which was constituted as a "world church" was far too opposed to the Catholic doctrine of the "one true,

Catholic and apostolic church" which has as its sole head the successor of Peter. The Catholic Church, therefore, was unable to cooperate with the other churches as an equal among equals; it logically rejected the so-called branch theory, according to which all churches are only branches of one and the same trunk, because the Catholic Church regarded itself as the only God-willed church. All efforts toward a reunification of faiths could, therefore, only result in the Catholic Church inviting the "erring brothers" to return and in its asking them again to adhere unconditionally to the Roman Catholic Church. The encyclical *Humani Generis* (1950) thus still warned of a false "irenicism" (peace and reunification at any price) instead of counseling an open mind.

During this time, however, there grew from year to year in the Catholic Church an increasingly active and deep interest in the other Christian brethren and in reunion. A new understanding of Luther's reformatory concern, as well as of the underlying reasons for the split between eastern and western churches, created the foundations for a more open-minded encounter.

A dialogue with the eastern church was the first to be initiated. The Catholic Church has in common with the eastern church the same sacramental system and, with the exception of primacy and infallibility, generally the same body of dogma. Special centers were founded to foster relations with the eastern church and to provide opportunities for evaluation and exchange of mutual information (Oriental Institute 1917 and Russicum 1929 in Rome; Union monastery Amay-Chevetogne 1925 in Belgium; Istina, 1927). The popes of the modern age have repeatedly extended the hand of peace to the eastern church; but only with the pontificates of John XXIII and chiefly Paul VI have earlier injustices been admitted and has the emphasis on Rome's legitimacy been dropped. With these events, the dialogue has entered a fruitful phase. The meeting of Paul VI with the Patriarch Athenagoras of Constantinople in Jerusalem (January 4–6, 1964) was more than a superficial gesture. Their embrace and the confession of guilt on Mt. Golgotha were both realistic and symbolic, and promise a better future for the cause of reunion.

The approach to the Protestants began with "talks across the fence" conducted between individuals and small groups. In Germany communication became more intense under the common threat to the churches from national socialism. Contacts were given a firm basis by Max Josef Metzger in 1938 through the *Una Sancta* Brotherhood. The "Association of Christ the King" in Meitingen became the center of the movement. Metzger himself, who was also an untiring champion of the peace movement, was executed by the Nazis in 1944; he died as a martyr for the cause which he had defended so uncompromisingly.

A papal instruction of December 20, 1949 transferred to the bishops the responsibility for the *Una Sancta* movement and thereby for the first time provided the unofficial contacts with a permanent footing in the church. In 1952 the unofficial "Catholic Conference for Ecumenical Questions" was founded, and out of it developed the "Secretariat for Promoting Christian Unity" established under the direction of Cardinal Bea in 1960 by John XXIII with its seat in Rome. The announcement of the Second Vatican Council also gave unsuspected encouragement to the ecumenical movement.

3. The church prospered after the First World War in other areas as well. In France the orders were permitted to return to their houses, the lay laws were no longer enforced, and the state transferred the administration of church property to newly established lay diocesan associations. Now it was also possible to build numerous new churches, and the country became covered by a network of Catholic schools. Liturgical and biblical movements took a long time to become established, but then showed uncommon activity, especially with the founding of the *Centre de Pastorale liturgique* in Paris (1943). For a time the chauvinism of the *Action française* seemed to pose a threat; it was removed by the suppression by Pius XI in 1926. The Catholic Action was the more active and effective after 1927. The goals for which the numerous new professional and youth organizations (*Mission*

de France and worker priests) worked, were the recovery of France
and a reawakened Christian life in general. Their success was great;
after the Second World War France not only had a large Catholic
political party and Christian unions which soon counted 40% of
the organized workers, but also today France is leading the
Catholic missions with 3500 missionaries, is establishing standards
for the liturgical and biblical movements through its intensive
pastoral activity, and is exercising through its theologians a great
influence upon Catholic theology.

In Italy the Catholic Action was founded in 1922 and in the
post-war years achieved singular significance even under the
fascist-dominated government. The settlement of the "Roman
Question" by the Lateran treaties and the concordat of 1929
provided conditions which soon affected all Christian life
favorably.

The nineteenth century had witnessed a new flowering of
Catholic missions. After the collapse of Portuguese and Spanish
colonialism, which had paralyzed the missionary effort of the
eighteenth century through its governmentally directed missions,
the Roman Congregation of Propaganda (founded in 1622) assumed the total direction of world missions. Numerous new
orders were founded and new missionary areas were added, with
Africa, India, China, and the South Sea Islands as the preferred
areas of missionary activity. After the First World War, emphasis
was placed on the establishment and strengthening of native
churches, and in 1926 the first native bishops were ordained.

59

THE PONTIFICATES OF PIUS XI AND PIUS XII

Pius XI and Pius XII had much in common, even though their
origins, training, and characters were radically different. A continuity of the pontificates was assured by the fact that after 1930
Pius XII as secretary of state directed the policies of his predecessor.

Pius XI (1922–1939) was a quiet scholar and a renowned alpinist before he became pope, and this peculiar combination was expressed in his nature. On one side he was sober, factual, intelligent and thorough; on the other, temperamental, self-assured, strong and tenacious. Both sides of his nature were connected by a firm trust in God and a daring optimism. He appeared, therefore, as a man who would be able to give peace and inspiration to a world in disorder.

Achille Ratti was born in 1857 in Desio near Milan, and became a priest in 1879. After a short period as a teacher, he spent his life in libraries, first as a librarian at the Ambrosiana in Milan and then after 1914 as the prefect of the Vatican Library in Rome. In his spare time Ratti undertook his mountain tours; his ascent of the Dufour peak of the Monte Rosa (1889) found its literal reflection in his *Scritti Alpinistici,* a book which made him famous. After a short and not very successful diplomatic sojourn as nuncio in Poland (1918–1920), he became archbishop of Milan and then cardinal. In the following year he was elected pope.

He announced his program in his encyclical *Ubi Arcano* in 1922: *Pax Christi in regno Christi!* Untiringly Pius preached the idea of the kingdom of Christ. In 1925 he introduced the feast of Christ the King (last Sunday in October); and in 1925 and 1933 he initiated the holy year under the guiding principle: "Christ must rule" (1 Cor 15, 25). Some people saw a certain anachronism in the pope's emphasis on kingship at a time when monarchies were disappearing, but in the kingdom of God other criteria are used than on earth. With the revelation as a background, the pope used his great magisterial letters to confront the burning problems of the time; in his encyclical *Divini illius Magistri* (1929) he dealt with Christian education, in *Casti Connubii* (1930) with Christian marriage, in *Quadragesimo Anno* (1931) with the Christian social order, and in *Ad Catholici Sacerdotii* (1935) with the priesthood of the church. Pius gave special attention to the Catholic Action which he provided with a firm form in 1925. The concept of a "participation and cooperation of laymen in the hierarchical apostolate of the church", as he formulated it in October 1933

412

in Rome before the German Catholic Youth, was "one of the key-notes of his pontificate" (Pacelli). With this concept, the pope provided the impetus for a reexamination of the position and duties of laymen in the church. If today we again have a "theology of the laity" (Y. Congar) and if the Second Vatican Council was opened to laymen, we owe this development to this pope's initiative. The century-old process, which since the Middle Ages had led to increasing clericalization of the church, was stopped, and value was once again given to the mature cooperation of the layman in the church as it had been during the time of early Christianity.

Pius's farsightedness and energy gave missionary work new impetus and direction toward the establishment of independent native churches. His church policy revealed a sober awareness of the realities of life. Just as a mountain climber safeguards himself with pitons, Pius attempted to create firm foundations by means of concordats and treaties. To his great merit he was able to settle the old controversy with the Italian government. On February 11, 1929, Pius concluded the Lateran treaties which liberated the pope from his voluntary imprisonment and restored his full sovereignty over the small Vatican State. Under his pontificate a new era of concordats began: in 1922 with Latvia; in 1924 with Bavaria; in 1925 with Poland; in 1927 with Rumania and Lithuania; in 1929/30 with Italy; in 1929 with Prussia; in 1932 with Baden; in 1933/34 with Austria; and finally also in 1933 with Germany.

The controversial German concordat of July 20, 1933, if viewed alone (as is so often the case) looks quite different than it does if taken within the context of the entire policy of the church. The concordat was part of the framework of a tested and extensively practiced Vatican treaty policy. The centralization of Germany under Hitler had for all practical purposes nullified the concordats with Bavaria, Prussia, and Baden and confronted the curia with the question of whether to abandon the existing concordats or to accept Hitler's offer of a concordat for all of Germany. What was more obvious than to choose the latter? Pius XII later (July 19, 1947) described the concordat with Germany as an "effort, in view of an uncertain future, to save the provincial concordats by widening the area of application while attempting to maintain the contents". No one knew at the time how malicious, insincere, and mendacious the German policy really was. Nevertheless, the Vatican did not fall blindly into a trap; because it was able to maintain a critical distance from Hitler's violence, it believed itself able to force Hitler to moderation through the binding force of formal law. Had this same policy not just succeeded with Mussolini? The Lateran treaties and the concordat with Italy had removed to a large degree the difficulties between state and church and had created a bearable situation. International law and decency, which were the basis for the implementation of the treaties *(pacta sunt servanda)*, were still valid then; the German deceit had not yet become obvious. As intensely shameful as this last statement must be for a German, we have little justification for criticizing the Vatican for its treaty policy. The experience of German treachery in the future was to be one of Pius's most bitter realizations. His disillusion was reflected in the countless notes he sent to the German government and in the severe outburst of his encyclical *Mit brennender Sorge* (March 4, 1937).

His pontificate was beset with church afflictions throughout the whole world. There were martyrs in very large numbers in Russia, in Mexico, in Spain (Civil War 1936), and in Germany, and the pope suffered intensely from these tragedies. Pius regarded atheistic communism as the greatest enemy of Christianity (encyclical *Divini Redemptoris*, March 19, 1937). In 1933 it was not yet evident that national socialism was no less malicious; this knowledge only came after the experience in the following years of the unimaginable brutalities and bestialities of the national socialistic regime. Pius died on February 10, 1939, shortly before the outbreak of the Second World War. He must certainly be counted among the best and most able of the popes of the modern age.

Pius XII (1939–1958) was unanimously elected by the cardinals as the papal successor on the second ballot, because no one else seemed capable of steering the ship of Peter through this troubled time. His election was greeted with universal acclaim.

Eugenio Pacelli was born in 1876. He was the son of an old family of jurists which for generations had been in the service of the curia. His brother as papal justiciary had played a decisive part in the drafting of the Lateran treaties of 1926–1929. Since his ordination as a priest, Pacelli had been in the diplomatic and legal service of the curia and not only gained experience as a successful nuncio to Bavaria (1917–1920) and to the government in Berlin (1920–1930) (concordats with Bavaria and Prussia), but also had developed a special preference for Germany. As curial secretary of state under Pius XI, he had determined the political course of the curia since 1930, including its attitude toward Hitler and Germany.

"Justice creates peace" was the philosophy of his pontificate. Pius was an intelligent man with a refined, noble, and devout character, and in addition he was a sober politician with a grasp of reality, who had experience in making critical evaluations of alternatives and who would not gamble unless he had previously weighed all the consequences. Perhaps this quality most distinguished him from his predecessor and was in even greater contrast to his successor, who governed with spontaneity and considerable daring. His policy was resolute and clear, and tenacious negotiations were his weapon. It was not his fault that his policy failed in the face of a mendacious and malicious German diplomacy based on force. Was an alternative course open to the pope, who had no power backing as did the great states and world powers? He could only appeal, as he did, to law and justice, and put his moral prestige at stake. In countless speeches and encyclicals Pius untiringly asked for justice, gave instructions, and preached Christian principles. Was he permitted to remain silent about the crimes of the Nazis, particularly the murder of the Jews? That is the bitter question which is directed now against his pontificate. Was he silent? Could he have said more? These questions will be discussed in detail in the next chapter.

Pius XII tried to prevent the outbreak of the up to the last minute and, when his appeals were of no avail, at least to keep Italy neutral. His diplomatic appeal to Hitler in May 1939 brought no results. Mussolini also reacted negatively, and inasmuch as he had begun to imitate Hitler's racial mania, the relationship between fascist Italy and the Vatican again deteriorated. During the war the pope was forced to tread a path of painstaking neutrality. This position was necessary not only because of the specific clauses in the Lateran treaty of 1929, but also because of his own helpless condition. Not only did the pope reside in the midst of a belligerent country, but also he occupied a position as leader of a supranational religious community whose members belonged to both sides. It is not the duty of a pope to make political decisions. It would have been superfluous to discuss internally the moral or immoral aspect of Hitler's conduct of the war as all responsible persons, particularly the bishops and Catholics of Germany were well aware of it and condemned it unconditionally; a public papal pronouncement would only have become a political plaything, and it was only for this purpose that the people who urged the pope to break his silence wished to use such a pronouncement. Although Pius remained politically neutral, he earnestly appealed to the conscience of both sides to return in peace to humanitarianism and Christian love.

If the pope appeared to grant a modicum of meaning and justification to Hitler's foreign policy in the beginning, he did so only insofar as he regarded it as a defense of Christian Europe against atheistic bolshevism. This attitude was limited to the Russian threat and never extended to Poland or other countries for whose peoples he always felt the deepest compassion. Pius did not stand alone in his fear of bolshevism. Millions in and outside of Germany agreed with him, and post-war developments in the countries behind the Iron Curtain have proved them right. But could Belzebub be driven out by the devil? That was the question! It might have been possible to check the Soviet Union if the Allies had utilized their victory in 1945 better, but they were not this far-sighted.

After the war, Pius continued to urge peace, to bring assistance through organized charity to the suffering peoples of Europe, and to denounce the concept of German collective guilt and the campaigns of hate which were based on it. Simultaneously the pope turned his loving concern to the prisoners of war and the refugees. The absorption of whole Catholic peoples such as the Poles and Hungarians by the communist power bloc caused him great suffering, as did the persecution of Christians and the imprisonment of bishops and clergy which was soon initiated in these countries. Pius responded to these acts with excommunication for those responsible for them, and his attitude toward bolshevism which had inflicted such great losses on Christianity and the church was implacable.

"Rarely in history has the Roman Church suffered more extrinsic losses and yet risen to higher esteem in the world than during the pontificate of Pius XII", wrote a non-Catholic historian (K. G. Streck, in *Religion in Geschichte und Gegenwart,* 3rd ed., vol. V, 400). Rarely have the speeches and writings of a pope exercised such a profound and international influence as those of Pius XII. His pronouncements were heard and heeded everywhere, not only within but also outside of the church and even in the non-Christian world. When Pius XII died on October 9, 1958, the entire world was shocked; it sensed that a great human being had gone.

The greatness of Pius XII is especially evident in the internal sphere of the church. He opened the college of cardinals, which was then dominated by Italians, to all nationalities and races, and numerous new appointments soon reflected the universal nature of the church. In his encyclical *Mystici Corporis* (1943) Pius produced a new understanding of the church which was determined by the *Corpus Christi Mysticum* and broke with the traditional juridical and hierarchical interpretation; now laymen were to be given a greater opportunity to participate. The biblical encyclical *Divino afflante Spiritu* (1943) and the liturgical encyclical *Mediator Dei* (1947) took into consideration the influence of contemporary trends in the church. *Menti Nostrae* (1950)

417

discussed the sanctity of priesthood, and *Provida Mater* (1950) dealt with virginity; in the latter encyclical he also gave the sanction of canon law to the secular institutes, those novel ecclesiastical associations whose apostolate is conducted in the world and in the midst of the professions, workings, and situations of secular existence. Almost all religious and ecclesiastical principles received the benefit of Pius's attention and his deeply Christian insight. His unflagging energy concerned itself with everything, and in particular with the administrative reorganization of the curia. The theological climax of his pontificate was his *ex cathedra* definition on November 1, 1950, of the dogma concerning the *Assumptio Mariae,* i.e. of the bodily assumption of the immaculately conceived mother of God. Thirty-three canonizations were performed during his pontificate.

In spite of his many accomplishments, Pius XII was a member of the older generation. It was to be reserved to his highly gifted successor, John XXIII, to open the gates to a fresh understanding of the church and a renewed dialogue with the world. Pius demonstrated only a limited sympathy for ecumenical ideas and new theological endeavors (encyclical *Humani Generis,* 1950). In spite of his affability and open-mindedness, which was repeatedly demonstrated to the people during his audiences and liturgical celebrations, Pius always remained an autocrat who governed the church centrally. Even though he devoted his Christmas speech in 1944 to the idea of democracy, his basic views were monarchical. This may explain to some degree the weakness which he always had for great "leaders".

60

THE CHURCH IN THE THIRD REICH

Rarely have politics and ideology been so intertwined or their interaction so cleverly manipulated as in the Third Reich, which was the most disgraceful and darkest period of the German past. Rarely has deceit been so unscrupulously employed as in

418

the policies and diplomacy of Adolf Hitler. These observations must precede any discussion of church history during this period, because they are indispensable to the understanding of the situation in which the church found itself during the Third Reich.

1. Hitler was born in Braunau (Upper Austria) on April 20, 1889, and lived in Vienna from 1906 to 1912, where he worked at odd jobs and filled his mind with anti-semitic and anti-religious ideas. During the war in 1914–1918 he served voluntarily in a Bavarian regiment and, finding himself unemployed after the war, decided to enter politics. Hitler assumed the leadership of the "German Workers' Party", which was founded at this time and which after 1920 added the adjective "national socialist" (NSDAP) to its title. In addition to this, the stages of Hitler's political development included: participation in Ludendorff's putsch (November 9, 1923), nine months imprisonment at Landsberg, and the refounding of the NSDAP in 1925. In view of the general economic crisis, Hitler's broad and unscrupulous promises enabled the party after 1929 to grow into a mass organization. In 1930 the party received 6.5 million votes and 107 seats in the Reichstag; in 1932 it became the largest German party with 13.75 million votes and 230 mandates. The radical course of the party's history is marked with terror, blood, and fear. The suffering of millions of people and the dissatisfaction of more than six million unemployed help to explain this tragic development. President Hindenburg refused to offer the position of chancellor to Hitler, even though he could lay claim to it as leader of the dominant party. After von Papen and others had exerted pressure on the aging president, he finally consented to appoint Hitler chancellor on June 30, 1933. That was the unhappy day of the "seizure of power".

Long before 1933, men in ecclesiastical circles had decisively attacked national socialism. As early as 1931, the Jesuit Father Friedrich Muckermann had warned against the "widespread misunderstanding" which regarded Hitler's party as merely a political entity and not as a pseudo-religious ideology. Muckermann called the "prophecy of the Third Reich" and the intended

419

salvation of the world by means of the Aryan race "the heresy of the 20th century". Alfred Rosenberg's book *The Myth of the Twentieth Century* more than Hitler's *Mein Kampf* served to make people aware of the sinister background of the movement. This book appeared in Munich in 1930, but only became well known after 1934. The bishops forbade membership in the NSDAP (Cologne diocese, March 5, 1931; Mainz, etc.), and a war of ideologies was unavoidable.

After seizing power, Hitler then suddenly pursued an entirely different policy. In his first official statement on February 1, 1933, he solemnly declared that his "national government" regarded it as its "first and foremost duty to restore the spiritual unity of our nation as desired by the people. It will preserve and defend the foundations on which the strength of the nation rests. It will firmly protect Christianity as the basis of our whole morality, and the family as the germinal cell of the people and the body politic . . ." War was declared only against anarchism and communism; and he immediately stopped the agitation of his followers against Christianity. He led people to believe that he and his party, now that they had assumed the responsibility for governing the state, were concerned only with political realities and considered ideology as nothing but a transitional manifestation of previous political battles with which they no longer wished to be burdened. Article 24 of the Party program in 1925 stated: "We demand freedom of religion for all denominations in the nation . . . The Party as such is in favor of a positive Christianity, without committing itself to any one denomination." Reference to the Germanic race and the fight against the Jewish materialistic spirit was carefully neglected. This apparent acceptance of religious values was even more clearly formulated in the Enabling Act of March 23, 1933: "The national government sees in the two Christian denominations the most important factors for the preservation of the nation. It will respect the treaties concluded between them and the states. Their rights shall not be infringed upon . . . Similarly the government, which sees in Christianity the unshakable foundations of morality and ethics in the people, places the utmost value on friendly relations with the Holy See and seeks to expand them . . ."

Such words were certain to create confusion. Had earlier judgments of the man really been wrong, after all? If one took him by his word and bound him with treaties, could one perhaps actually tame and shackle him? Therefore, when Hitler, probably at von Papen's suggestion, made the offer of a concordat for Germany, he found a receptive audience in Rome. It is not the concordat itself which should cause consternation, because it was, as we have seen, only an extension of general Vatican policy, but it is rather the fact that any doubts about this dictatorial government were ignored because of religious benefits that is truly reprehensible. This failure to judge correctly is the penalty which the Catholic Church had to pay because of its failure in finding a positive relationship with democracy. Out of a misunderstood interpretation of the term "Führer", which was influenced by the pope's monarchical view, the church fell prey to the national socialistic phantom of the unitary state. The uncertainty and helplessness of Catholic politicians is illustrated by the concurrence of the Center Party to the Enabling Act (March 24, 1933) and its (enforced) dissolution within the framework of the general suppression of parties during June and July of 1933.

With the loss of participation in the political arena, the church now rested all hopes in the concordat (July, 22, 1933); these contractual assurances appeared to guarantee the necessary and desirable freedom of movement in the religious and cultural sectors. To many Catholics, who were dissatisfied with the Center Party, this solution of the contested questions between church and state appeared more promising than the constant parliamentary warfare which had taken place during the Weimar Republic. Although the church at no prior time had asked for anything unreasonable or unusual, no previous German government had been nearly as generous in its concessions to the Catholic Church as Hitler was during the negotiations for the concordat. The gratitude which the bishops showed Hitler was understandable.

421

No one knew at the time that the negotiations for the concordat were only a tactical maneuver by Hitler; they gained him time and enabled him to drive a wedge between the Center Party and the episcopate. Hitler needed this time to establish himself and his government and to win the Catholic voters. Unceasingly he tried to imbue Catholics with the conviction of the reprehensible nature of "political Catholicism"; he declared himself willing to give the church what it needed, but the church in turn must refrain from political activity. All this sounded loyal and plausible.

Hitler's actual intentions became known only when his table talks and the diaries of his associates were published after the war. From an examination of these sources there can be no doubt that from his youth onward Hitler hated Christianity and wished to destroy it. Rauschning (*Conversations with Hitler,* Zurich, 1940, 188 ff) mentions statements by Hitler which demonstrate that his hatred for the Jews was only equalled by that which he felt for Christianity and that he intended to exterminate Christianity in the same way as Judaism. In Hitler's empire only the Aryan master-race had the right to exist, even though this race was yet to be bred. "My educational theory is uncompromising", Hitler declared, "the weak must be removed. In my schools for political leaders, youths will be trained who will terrify the world. I want a brutal, domineering, fearless, and cruel youth . . . A free and masterful beast of prey must look again out of their eyes . . . I want no intellectual training. Knowledge only will ruin them . . . But they must learn discipline . . . they must learn to conquer the fear of death. Heroic youth is the first phase. The second phase is the man who is the measure and the goal for the world, a God-man . . . In the schools of my order the beautiful self-governing god-man will become the cultic image . . ." (Rauschning, *ibid.*).

Hitler's policy must be seen only against this ideological background. "Within ten years we will be able to dictate the law of Adolf Hitler to all of Europe", declared Heinrich Himmler, the leader of the SS. The total state was oriented toward the cultivation of a new Nordic-Germanic racial type and the creation of a pagan Germanic empire.

Hitler regarded Christianity as the sequel to Judaism, an invention of the Jew Paul. Christian morality simply went counter to his image of man. His program was unequivocal rejection and destruction of Christianity. He believed that providence had appointed him to destroy the Catholic Church as well as Judaism and Bolshevism, two groups which he viewed as one. Now we also know what he thought of the concordat. Two weeks after the Reichstag session of March 23, 1933, in which he had declared as his foremost task the protection of Christianity and the churches, he remarked to his closest collaborators in the Reich Chancellory: "Let Fascism make peace with the church, in God's name, and I shall do so also. Why not? But that will not prevent me from extirpating Christianity from Germany lock, stock, and barrel. One is either a Christian or a German; one cannot be both." (F. Zipfel, *Kirchenkampf in Deutschland 1933–1945,* Berlin 1965, 9).

The war against the church which began almost immediately after the signing of the concordat must be silhouetted against a background such as has just been described. The persecution progressed through three phases: the first phase (1933/34) consisted of disguised measures. Hitler kept himself in the background, left the ideological battle to his followers, and professed to know nothing about it (since 1934 Rosenberg had been officially in charge of the ideological training of the NSDAP). During the terrible massacre connected with the "revolt" of Röhm (June 30, 1934), Hitler also had such Catholic leaders as Klausener and Jung, two outstanding laymen, assassinated. The boycott of Jewish stores had begun in April 1933. Second phase (1934–1939): The struggle against the church now became a more open one, although at first it was disguised as an attempt to de-emphasize the role of the church in public life. Religious influence was limited in all areas: all religious associations and youth organizations were prohibited; religious instruction in schools was impeded and then suppressed; financial subsidies for religious kindergartens and other social and charitable establishments were stopped; the religious press was suppressed; preaching was forbidden; and priests and laymen were arrested. Trials against the orders for currency violations were conducted in 1936. In order to undermine the trust of the people in the clergy and the church, show trials of clergy on morals charges were conducted to prove "that is how all of them are". In 1938 and 1939 the last parochial schools and many monasteries, including Catholic seminaries and the theological departments of universities (Munich) were abolished; the latter were to be replaced by "Departments for Racial Studies". The Nürnberg Laws of September, 1935, stripped the Jews of their rights, and by the fall of 1938 about 170000 Jews (a third of the total number) had emigrated from Germany. The first large organized pogroms took place during the so-called "Chrystal Night" of November 9, 1938. Third phase (1940–1945): In spite of the war, the persecutions of the church continued; in defeated Poland (Warthegau) the church and the practice of Christianity were entirely rooted out (1940 ff). An assault against the monasteries in Germany finally was stopped by Hitler himself, because it created too many disturbances, particularly in the Münster diocese (Bishop von Galen). Limitations on the recruitment for the orders and on the number of theology students were explained as necessitated by the war, as were such crimes as the killing of the mentally ill (euthanasia) and the brutal measures directed against the church in Alsace (1943). In 1941, Martin Bormann, probably the most fanatical opponent of the church, assumed the leadership in the war of destruction which after the war was to lead to the liquidation of both church and Christianity in the whole domain of the Nazis and which was to crown the final victory.

In 1941 the "final solution" of the Jewish question had already begun. At first special SS units were ordered to exterminate the Jews in occupied areas. Ghettos (in Warsaw since October 1940) and extermination camps (since fall 1941) were established, and Jews from Holland, Belgium, France, Norway, Hungary, and other southeast European countries were transported to them. After October 1941, Jews from Germany also were sent to camps.

In Auschwitz alone three to four million people were killed in gas chambers after 1941. Other death camps were established in Chelmno, Treblinka, Belsec, Sobibor, and Maidanek, and approximately six million Jews were murdered. In addition to the death camps, there were regular concentration camps at Dachau, Sachsenhausen, Belsen, Buchenwald, Theresienstadt, and Mauthausen, where mass murders by torture, starvation, epidemics, and shootings took place. No one can read this atrocious balance sheet of an atheistic, anti-Christian system without being profoundly moved. The suffering of these millions of people, to whom the war victims must also be added, exhausts the powers of the human imagination.

2. The resistance of the churches to such criminal excesses may look inadequate to us today in view of the sheer magnitude of the outrages: at least that is the accusation leveled against them. In reality the churches were the only force which waged an uninterrupted and furious fight against the Nazi regime. It is evident from the subsequently published secret reports of the Gestapo that it recognized the churches as the regime's most dangerous enemies (Zipfel, *Kirchenkampf,* 272 ff). Catholic and Protestant Christians closed ranks in this struggle; the Protestant Church during this time was, after all, no better off than the Catholic. It was a time when believing Christians in their need found one another.

The number of episcopal protest notes and pastoral letters is immense. They began as early as the fall of 1933 and increased with the years in significance and sharpness. No action hostile to the church occurred without being answered with furious protests. Rosenberg's appointment as ideological leader (January 1934) was immediately answered with a flood of episcopal protests. Cardinal Schulte of Cologne went to Hitler in February 1934, called Rosenberg's *Myth* a pamphlet against Christianity, and demanded his recall. Hitler pretended to disavow Rosenberg, but of course took no action against him. Schulte was deeply shocked and noted after his return: "Hitler is a sphinx, a sinister man. We shall yet receive a terrible treatment by him" (*Festschrift*

425

Frings, 1960, 574). Only one year after the signing of the concordat, the bishops in a pastoral letter accused the government of violating its provisions. An appeal to the concordat from this time on formed the constant foundation of their complaints.

The concordat actually turned out to be a not inconsiderable support in the struggle. Above all, it entitled the pope to a say in ecclesiastical matters within Germany. Indeed, the bishops soon agreed for tactical reasons to have the Vatican submit by way of diplomatic channels the more important and grave grievances as violations of the concordat. The language of these Vatican notes is unbelievably severe, as can be seen in their recent publication (D. Albrecht, *Der Notenwechsel zwischen dem Heiligen Stuhl und der deutschen Reichsregierung,* I, 1965). In a note of May 14, 1934, official complaints were lodged concerning the most serious violations of the concordat, and the *Osservatore Romano* on July 26, 1934 spoke of an open battle in Germany against the church. The struggle reached its apex with the unprecedentedly sharp encyclical *Mit brennender Sorge* (March 14, 1937). We now know the history of its origin. The first draft was written by cardinal Faulhaber during a visit to Rome at the urgent request of the pope. This draft, however, appeared too weak to Pius XII, who was then secretary of state Pacelli. He personally added concrete and extremely pointed accusations to the most important passages, and in-this form it was released to the world in the name of the curia. The entire encyclical is a massive indictment of the Hitler regime.

Shortly before the release of the encyclical, the Holy See had even considered cancelling the concordat because of constant German violations, but the German bishops were opposed to this. After the encyclical was released, the Nazis, in angry reaction, also considered abandoning the concordat, but Hitler wanted to retain it. Thus, despite dissatisfaction on both sides, the concordat remained in force. During an administrative meeting on July 4, 1942, Hitler called the concordat a regrettable shackle on his church policy in Germany, but held it necessary "in consideration of the war; after the war the end of the concordat would come also". (H. Picker, *Hitler's Table Talk,* 1964, 435–7). It was necessary also for the Vatican to adhere to the concordat because it provided Rome with the right and the opportunity to intervene directly in the church struggle in Germany (something of which the German Catholic Church heartily approved). The courageous sermons of Bishop von Galen of Münster and many other bishops show that the German church itself did not remain silent. Galen's sermons of July 13, and 20 and August 3, 1941, were circulated throughout Germany and even throughout the world. Bormann wanted him hanged because of them, but while the war lasted it was not prudent to act against him in view of the attitude of the population.

Could the popes and the bishops have done even more, particularly with regard to the Jews? That is a question which should not be posed lightly nor answered without grave consideration. Because all of the sources are not yet published, particularly those in the Vatican archives, a decisive answer must be postponed. The objective scholar will shun the passing of premature verdicts.

61

The Pontificates of John XXIII and Paul VI

1. The brief pontificate of John XXIII (October 28, 1958 — June 3, 1963) marks a turning-point in the history of the church. The pope turned from old traditions with charismatic assurance. He gave the church a new image of the papacy, and opened the doors of the church to the separated brethren in the churches of East and West.

John was born on November 25, 1881, into a poor peasant family with many children in Sotto il Monte (Bergamo). He was ordained in Rome in 1904, and in 1905 became an episcopal secretary and professor at the seminary at Bergamo. During World War I, 1914–1918, he was a soldier and hospital chaplain. As director of the Society for the Propagation of the Faith in Italy (1921–1925) and apostolic delegate in the East (ten years in

Bulgaria, 1925–1934; and ten years in Turkey and Greece, 1934–1944) he gained diplomatic experience and developed a love and understanding for the Greek Orthodox Church. In 1944 John was appointed nuncio in Paris, where he was particularly active in behalf of the German prisoners of war. He founded the prisoner-of-war seminary in Chartres, and also promoted the French workers' mission. As cardinal and patriarch of Venice (1953–1958), he was always particularly concerned with pastoral care; it was foreseeable that as pope he would also wish to be more bishop and *"il parroco del mondo"* than sovereign. John was the exact opposite in all things of the austere, aristocratic and autocratic Pius XII.

John XXIII sincerely wanted to personify the bishop of Rome and as such the pastor of the universal church. He broke through the narrow confines of the Vatican, mingled with the Roman populace, visited Roman orphanages and hospitals, spent hours conversing with the prisoners at the Regina Coeli, and celebrated the liturgy in the suburban parishes of Rome. The pope began his reform work by calling a synod of the Roman diocese which was to adjust the pastoral care of the city to the completely changed modern conditions. His plan was through his episcopal office in Rome to develop the office of Peter, the universal episcopate. The first step was to be the synod of the Roman diocese; then a general council was to be called, at which the accommodation *(aggiornamento)* of the whole church to the urgent requirements of the modern age was to find expression in revised canon law. John completed the first stage successfully. The second stage he began by convoking the twenty-first ecumenical council, the Second Vatican Council, on October 11, 1962. The brevity of his pontificate prevented his completing the third stage, although in April 1963 he appointed a commission for the revision of the *Codex Iuris Canonici.*

John ordered the necessary steps everywhere for an adjustment to the modern age; they included not only methods of implementation but also changes in the very structure of the church. The office of Peter, papal primacy, was once again visibly associated with the college of bishops, and the change was striking. Under Pius XII administrative concentration in the curia had just reached its greatest intensity; now John started the process of decentralization and returned to the principle of collegiality. Bishops were entrusted with tasks affecting the church as a whole, and the college of cardinals was considerably enlarged. It was decreed that in the future the Roman Congregations should invite to their plenary sessions all archbishops and cardinal bishops then in Rome; in this way, the work of the supreme administrative offices was to be united with the entire episcopate and protected against absolutism.

His goal was the adaptation of the pastoral methods in the dioceses and the orders. High priority was given to the problem of adaptation in the missions; native hierarchies were erected and "Europeanism" in the missions was finally discarded. The church was to reach out to peoples and cultures, not uproot and absorb them. It must also approach the separated brothers of the Orthodox Church and the churches of the Reformation; it must not remain in an ivory tower and wait for others to act. John was aware that a mere invitation to non-Catholics to repent and return to the fold would not solve the problem of a divided Christendom. He spoke of a *mutual* search for unity and assigned this task to the ecumenical council. As a beginning, every community, including the Catholic one, was to examine itself to see where it encountered obstacles and where it created them for the other churches. The pope did not hesitate to say a *mea culpa* and to beat his own breast; not since Adrian's confession at the Diet of Nürnberg in 1523 had such words been spoken by a pope. They could not fail to influence non-Catholic Christendom, and their echo throughout the ecumenical movement was great. The pope opened the door to the ecumenical movement, and at the height of his pontificate declared clearly and insistently that the Catholic Church had the duty of encouraging the non-Catholic Christians to unity by returning to the purity of its beginnings. He asked Catholics to strive earnestly and lovingly for a more precise knowledge and greater appreciation of the separated Christians. A special secretariat for the promotion of unity was established under the direction of Cardinal Bea.

The words of John XXIII were so unpretentious, simple, and sincere that they could not fail to find their mark. He even attempted to speak to the governments behind the Iron Curtain. Here also he tried to find more flexible methods and to dissociate himself from his predecessors' rigid rejection of the Communists while maintaining his rejection of atheistic Communism. The visit of Krushchev's son-in-law Adjubei to the Vatican in the spring of 1963, the visit of Cardinal König to Budapest, the new relationship to the patriarchs and bishops of the autocephalic orthodox churches of the east, and Krushchev's telegram of condolence on the occasion of the pope's death, all characterize the change of climate which his initiative brought about.

In the Roman vernacular he continues to live as "John the Good" and "father of the poor". The secret of his power was his kindness. He died on Whit-Monday 1963.

2. On June 21, 1963, G. B. Montini succeeded John as Pope Paul VI. It was not an easy task to administer and continue John's heritage; so far Paul has conducted his pontificate with determination and in his own manner.

Paul VI was born in Concesio near Brescia in 1897. He was ordained a priest in 1920, and subsequently prepared himself at the Academia dei Nobili in Rome for service in the curia. In 1924 he joined the secretariat of state. In the course of time, Montini advanced to under-secretary of state (1937) and after 1944 under Pius XII, who acted as his own secretary of state, was chiefly concerned with the internal ecclesiastical business of that office. In 1954 he became archbishop of Milan and was made a cardinal in 1958. During his years as bishop of Milan, Montini became acquainted closely with the problems of pastoral work at all levels of society. Paul had an open mind to all modern questions, and loved the dialogue with all who were "distant". He was motivated by his own convictions to pursue the line of his predecessor. This intention was immediately expressed in his address at his coronation Mass. He enumerated as his particular goals the continuation of the council and the extension of the dialogue with the Orthodox Churches of the East, the separated Christian Churches of the West, and the modern world. His pilgrimage to the Holy Land (January 4–6, 1964) was an event of universal significance. The confession of guilt on Golgotha, the meeting with the "Ecumenical" Patriarch Athenagoras, the spiritual leader of the Orthodox Churches, and with the Patriarchs Benedictos and Derderian were the historical highpoints. Again and again the pope emphasized the appeal to forgive and forget the past and to concentrate all efforts on the future and the restoration of unity. The patriarchs answered the pope in this same vein.

Paul said: "The paths leading to unity will be long for both sides and will be obstructed by many difficulties. But the paths of both sides lead toward one another and are joined at the well springs of the gospel." The encounter served the "deepening of Christian love" and "mediation"; it was a promising beginning.

62
THE SECOND VATICAN COUNCIL AND ITS EFFECTS

The announcement of the Second Vatican Ecumenical Council by John XXIII on January 25, 1959, was entirely the result of the pope's personal initiative and, as he emphasized repeatedly, had come about through the inspiration of God. The more cautious of the pope's contemporaries shook their heads in doubt when they heard that John, possibly with the presentiment of an early death, wished to have his plan executed within two or three years. Added to this doubt was a misunderstanding arising from the fact that although in traditional ecclesiastical and Catholic usage the term "ecumenical" means "universal", i.e. encompassing the church in the entire world, in recent times it has been increasingly applied to the ecumenical movement toward Christian unity. Therefore, the announcement of an ecumenical council was understood by many to be the papal announcement of a council to reestablish the ecclesiastical unity of all Christians on earth, a sentiment which caused a mixture of great enthusiasm and astonishment. In view of this, the Vatican issued a clarifying statement in which it said that the council was not intended to be a meeting of all Christian communities with an eye toward union, but solely an internal Roman Catholic event. On the other hand, the pope was most aware of the universal longing for unity in faith. In order to deflect unreasonable expectations, John denied that the council would be able to effect an immediate union, since the time for such a union simply had not arrived, but that it would not be averse to removing those old prejudices and obstacles within the Roman Catholic Church which stood in the way of such a course and would attempt to kindle a new ecumenical spirit. Thus the pope assigned to the council the double task of internal reflection and external openness to non-Catholic Christians. The foundation was laid for an unprecedented stimulation of the ecumenical idea both inside and outside of the Catholic Church.

The courageous act of John XXIII was fittingly reflected in the selection of the expression *aggiornamento* as the guiding principle of the council. The term encompassed not only an "adaptation" to the outward life of contemporary society but also the presupposition of a complete inward change of thought. It expected that the council turn away from the past pattern of thought and devote itself to the requirements of the present and its totally new environment. If applied with this definition in mind, *aggiornamento* could but lead to a revolutionary change of ecclesiastical life equal in magnitude only to that of the Constantinian Turning-Point or the Reformation. The result would be an overcoming of the close connection of religion and politics, power and church which had originated in the Constantinian Age, a renunciation of the narrow spirit of denominationalism engendered by the Counter-Reformation, and a transition from an epoch of Tridentine theology and way of life to a church which would reflect modern theology and contemporary mentality. All of these things were embraced by the term *aggiornamento*. It was a powerful program! Would the council be capable of fulfilling it after so brief a time of preparation?

432

Skeptics viewed with concern the work done in the ten preparatory commissions. In spite of the consultation of Catholic theologians throughout the world, the influence of a strictly Roman theology as represented in the papal universities and the administrative offices of the curia was predominant. The 69 drafts drawn up by the commissions and presented at the beginning of the council appeared to be more of a recapitulation of conservative theological and ecclesiastical views than guideposts for the present and the future. The question arose whether the coming council would constitute a hardening of obsolete conditions or whether it would open the gate to fresh developments. Dramatic disputes between conservatives and progressives were expected as a matter of course, but it could not be foreseen how the majority would decide and what weight the attitude of the Curia and that of the pope would carry.

The confidence of the optimists rested above all on the person of the pope. Unlike his predecessors, John XXIII from the beginning indicated clearly that he wished to break with the traditional principle of authority based on a narrowly judicial concept of primacy which had been in effect since the First Vatican Council. He also intended to demonstrate at the council that he seriously intended to implement the principle of collegiality in the church. Without sacrificing a particle of the primatial position of the Roman bishop within the universal church, as this had been defined by ecclesiastical doctrine in accordance with God's will, the pope repeatedly emphasized the importance of the responsible participation of the bishops. John placed himself among the bishops as bishop of Rome, and used to say "we bishops" when he spoke to them. But, the most anxious viewers asked, would he be able to prevail at the council against the well-oiled machinery of the curial bureaucracy? How did the pope conceive of the relationship between his position of primacy at the council and the responsible collegiate participation of the entire episcopate in the supreme administration of the church? These questions were posed by Catholics and non-Catholics alike. For many non-Catholic Christians, the council might well

433

prove to be the test of the genuineness of the Catholics' desire for union and of their will to be open-minded toward the beliefs of the orthodox as well as the reformed churches.

The opening session was conducted on October 11, 1962, and was carried to the whole world by radio and TV. The 2,540 voting council fathers together with the pope entered St. Peter's Church, which had been remodeled inside into an auditorium, and on October 12, 1962, the selection of new council commissions headed the agenda for the first working session of the general congregation. The decision regarding the direction of the council was made at this first session. The Curia at once suggested the confirmation in their functions of those fathers who had been active members of the preparatory commissions. Such a course would have transmitted the conservative spirit of the old commissions to the new commissions. To the general amazement of everyone, the council rejected the proposal and on October 16 elected new members for the commissions comprised of theologians from all over the world. This act not only indicated the will of the council fathers freely to reserve decisions for themselves but also the forward direction which events were to take. The pope did not intervene, although he did order the addition of one curial official to each of the nine commissions, probably in order to pacify the dismayed Curia. Work could now begin.

If this meeting of so many bishops from all of the world constituted an exceptional ecclesiastical event in itself, the degree of exchange of views in such a brief period of time and the change and progress effected was viewed by all observers and council participants as bordering on the miraculous. Many bishops from the more distant dioceses came into contact with the new theology for the first time and they "did not consider it beneath their dignity to become students at the council and to penetrate deeper into theological and pastoral problems" (H. Jedin). Moreover, these bishops demonstrated sufficient courage to make independent decisions during the voting and to defend their new positions. "This development transformed the Second Vatican Council into the opening of a new era of church history."

The work of the council proceeded in four chronologically distinct meetings. The first session lasted from October 11 to December 8, 1962. The opposing views came into the open immediately with respect to the schema on liturgy. The progressives which included all bishops of those countries in which the liturgical movement had long been pronounced, such as Germany and the German-speaking countries, France, and Northern Italy, desired the introduction of modern languages instead of Latin into the Mass, a more active participation of the people, and the granting of communion under both kinds at least on special occasions such as weddings. Surprisingly, they were joined by the bishops from the mission countries and Latin America who were cognizant of the significance of bringing the service closer to the people. Thus the liturgical reform party was victorious, the schema was sent back to commission for final formulation, and the way was opened for the decisive developments of our day. Even more important and graver was the next debate on the schema on the sources of revelation. Here not merely opposing theological views were involved but also a question of basic doctrine. The terms "scripture" and "tradition" recently had been reassessed within the context of ecumenical theology, and they played an important role in the dialogue with the Protestants. While the conservative curial group opposed the advance of modern biblical criticism, the progressives, among them Cardinals Frings, Döpfner, König, and Alfrink, battled for recognition and acceptance of the undeniable fruits of critical exegesis. Each group presented a draft of its position. As neither of the two drafts received the required two-thirds majority in plenary session, the pope took the topic off the agenda and referred it back to commission. The first period ended without further tangible success when the schemata on modern communications media (radio, TV, the press, and film) and on the Eastern Churches also failed to be accepted.

On June 3, 1963, in the midst of the preparations for the

435

next session, Pope John XXIII died and his loss was deeply mourned by the whole world. He was succeeded on June 21, 1963, by Cardinal Montini, Archbishop of Milan, who became Pope Paul VI. The new pope immediately announced his intention to continue the council.

The second session was conducted from September 29 to December 4, 1963. Pope Paul was particularly interested in a clarification of the concept of the church and this concept was discussed in the schema on the church. In hot debates the new progressive understanding of the church clashed with the traditional, juridical, post-Tridentine notions. Structural problems were brought to light, dealing mainly with the relationship between primacy and collegiality and the participation of the college of bishops together with the pope in the supreme church government. But questions of the internal understanding of the church and the association of the schema of Mary with the schema of the church also contributed to a heated emotional climate. At the end of October a serious crisis occurred. The schemata of decrees on bishops and the government of dioceses and on ecumenism, which contained chapters concerning the Jews and freedom of religion, immediately precipitated dispute. Sharp debates ensued and conservatives and progressives fought for the decision. A great victory was won by the progressive wing when the redrawn liturgy schema was finally adopted by an overwhelming majority (2158–19) and was accepted and promulgated by the pope in the final session on December 4. The decree on the mass media also was accepted, although a special instruction was provided as an addendum. The principles which had been discussed in the debate on ecumenism seemed to be confirmed and strengthened when, at the end of the session, the pope announced his intention to travel to Jerusalem, there to meet at the Holy Sepulcher with the ecumenical Patriarch Athenagoras. The journey which was undertaken from January 4–6, 1964, must be regarded as an extension of the spirit of the council.

The third session opened on September 14, and continued until November 21, 1964. From the first session the schema on

436

revelation still remained to be concluded, and from the second session, the discussions on the church, the bishop's office, and ecumenism. New additions of the third session were decrees on the apostolate of the laity and on the church in the world of today. Pope Paul in his opening speech embraced the principle of collegiality in the church as a useful adjunct of the episcopate to the primacy, but many details had yet to be clarified on this as well as other topics. Among the many critical debates were those dealing with the problems of ordaining married men as deacons and the imposition of obligatory celibacy on them, and whether the declaration of freedom of religion did not in fact make the truth relative and aid indifferentism. Guidelines for the life and ministry of priests, the training of priests, the renovation of rules for orders, Christian education, the apostolate of the laity, and missionary activity were discussed. Proposals for a reform of marriage laws, including in particular the hotly contested subject of mixed marriages, were treated as well in the schema on the church in the world of today. In November another crisis occurred over a discussion of chapter 3 of the schema on the church which defined the position of the college of bishops. Finally, however, after the schema on the Eastern Churches was accepted on November 20, the constitution of the church and the decree on ecumenism also passed the hurdle of the final vote on November 12.

The fourth and last session from September 14 to December 8, 1965, still had a full measure of work to do. Eleven drafts, which had been treated earlier, had to be voted on. At the outset, the pope announced the formation in 1967 of a Synod of Bishops which within the spirit of the principle of collegiality would participate in the general church administration as representatives of the episcopate as a whole. The debate on freedom of religion was long drawn out; it was clearly stated that this decree was not designed to soften the contours of absolute truth and error, but simply to assure the freedom of the individual from religious coercion in his private life. The solemn declaration of the right to freedom of conscience had the emphatic purpose

437

of proclaiming that no state had the right to prevent through external pressure the preaching and acceptance of the Gospel. At the same time the church turned away from the assumption which had been held since the Constantinian turning-point that wherever it possessed the means (as in Spain and Italy) it had the right to avail itself of public power in order to enforce, through *bracchium saeculare,* its religious demands and to further its work of salvation. By accepting the decree, the church solemnly renounced in principle any use of external force in the area of conscience. Its proclamation on December 7 marked a radical break with a fifteen hundred year old practice which had long been unacceptable.

In October the council passed a number of decrees in quick succession. On October 28, the decrees on the pastoral office of bishops, the renovation of rules for orders, Christian education, and the attitude of the church to non-Christian religions were accepted by the plenum and proclaimed by the pope. On November 18, the decrees on the apostolate of the laity and missionary activity again were presented for debate as well as the declaration on the life and ministry of priests. The debate on celibacy had been excluded by express request of the pope who did not yet consider the time appropriate for discussion. The council still had difficulties with the schema on the current role of the church in the world. After lengthy negotiations, this schema as well as the decrees on the life and ministry of priests, missionary activity, and religious freedom were solemnly proclaimed during the last open session of December 7, 1965.

It was on this day that the council witnessed an historical act which caused a sensation in the Christian world. With great earnestness and the sincere desire to make amends for an ancient injustice, Pope Paul VI announced the lifting of the mutual ban with which Rome and Byzantium had excommunicated one another in the year 1054 and had thus created the Great Schism; the memory of it was to be committed to oblivion.

An impressive celebration on St. Peter's Square ended the work of the council on December 8, 1965.

Sixteen decrees, but not a single dogma! These were the products of the council which wished not to promulgate dogma but to reform with particular emphasis on pastoral concerns. Doctrines may be registered and acknowledged in textbooks of dogma, but the pastoral decrees of the council must be complied with and carried over into life. In these decrees the council defined and elucidated problems whose solutions remain our continuing concern.

Even before the end of the council, a number of papal commissions had been appointed which were to make coin of the newly gained capital: a commission for the reform of canon law; a council for liturgical reform; a secretariat for promoting Christian unity, one for non-Christian religions, and a third for non-believers; and finally a commission for the mass media. On January 3, 1966, by papal decree six new post-conciliar commissions were set up: five were subject matter commissions, and one was a central coordinating commission for post-conciliar activity and for the interpretation of council decrees. The five subject matter commissions were to define implementation with regard to the decrees on bishops and the government of dioceses, orders, missions, Christian education, and the apostolate of the laity, all of which were to go into force on June 29, 1966. The function of the central commission was to expedite the work of the commissions, to interpret the decrees authentically, and to assure a uniform direction; above all it was to publish the papers of the council and distribute them. As all church members were to be addressed, translations into the modern languages assumed special significance. It was the function of the commission for canon law to integrate the council decrees into the existing body of canon law and to alter those canons of the *Codex Iuris Canonici* which required changes in order to meet the new definitions.

So far all commissions have done well in their pursuit of the objectives of the council. Probably the activity in the field of liturgical reform has been most conspicuous. The reorganization of the Mass was an almost stormy and alarming event for some Catholics. The institution of the vernacular into the Mass was

439

guided by the motive of making the word of God more pronounced and of inviting the faithful into more active participation.
Here the work done toward substituting native languages for
Latin went far beyond anything the council had dared to suggest.
When the German bishop for the first time permitted the use of
the German language at Advent 1967, the practice already had
precedents in other countries. The agitation for the retention of
Latin by a counter-movement of conservative Catholics under the
name of *Una Voce* can no longer stop the development.

Of great significance to the further development of the
ecclesiastical structure was the organization of an episcopal
synod which Pope Paul VI had announced during the last
council session. As a collegiate complement it was designed to
support the papal primacy effectively in the supreme government
of the church. It had not been made clear whether it would
function merely in an advisory capacity or as a co-determining
representative of the entire episcopate. The first meeting was held
in Rome on September 29, 1967, and until its conclusion on
October 28, 1967, it discussed all undecided post-conciliar
questions. Only time will reveal its permanent function.

The end of the episcopal synod was marked by an impressive
visit to the Vatican by Patriarch Athenagoras from October 26
to October 28, 1967. He reciprocated the attempts to reach a
better understanding between the Eastern and Western churches
which had been begun during the meeting of the pope and the
patriarch in Jerusalem and the visit of the pope to the patriarch
in Constantinople in the summer of 1964. On September 26,
1964, Pope Paul VI solemnly returned to the Greek Church the
relic of the head of St. Andrew the Apostle which Italian crusaders
had taken from Constantinople in 1208. This subtle gesture has
greatly improved the climate between the Eastern and Western
churches and strengthened the hope for reunion.

Today the church conducts a dialogue with the world. May
God grant that these promising beginnings bear fruit and help
the church to fulfill its divine task of *aggiornamento*.

440

INDEX

441

CHRONOLOGICAL TABLE
OF THE POPES

Figures in parentheses refer to page numbers of the book

54. Felix III (IV), 526–530
55. Boniface II, 530–532
    Dioscorus, 530–530
56. John II (Mercurius), 533–535
57. Agapetus I, 535–536
58. Silverius, 536–537
59. Vigilius, 537–555 (80)
60. Pelagius I, 556–561
61. John III, 561–574
62. Benedict I, 575–579
63. Pelagius II, 579–590 (91)
64. Gregory I (the Great), 590–604
    (90, 128 ff, 137)
65. Sabinianus, 604–606
66. Boniface III, 607–607
67. Boniface IV, 608–615
68. Deusdedit (or Adeodatus I)
    615–618
69. Boniface V, 619–625
70. Honorius I, 625–638 (81, 390)
71. Severinus, 640–640
72. John IV, 640–643
73. Theodore I, 643–649
74. Martin I, 649–653 (82)
75. Eugene I, 654–657
76. Vitalian, 657–672
77. Adeodatus II, 672–676
78. Donus, 676–678
79. Agatho, 678–681
80. Leo II, 682–683 (82)
81. Benedict II, 684–685
82. John V, 685–686
83. Conon, 686–687
    Theodore, 687–687
    Paschal, 687–692
84. Sergius I, 687–701
85. John VI, 701–705
86. John VII, 705–707
87. Sisinnius, 708–708
88. Constantine I, 708–715
89. Gregory II, 715–731 (132)
90. Gregory III, 731–741 (132, 138)
91. Zacharias, 741–752 (134, 138,
    139)
    Stephen II, 752–752
92. Stephen II (III), 752–757 (134f,
    138, 140ff)
93. Paul I, 757–767

Constantine II, 767–768
Philip, 768–768
94. Stephen III (IV), 768–772
95. Adrian I (Hadrian), 772–795
96. Leo III, 795–816 (148, 154)
97. Stephen IV (V), 816–817
98. Paschal I, 817–824
99. Eugene II, 824–827
100. Valentine, 827–827
101. Gregory IV, 827–844
     John, 844–844
102. Sergius II, 844–847
103. Leo IV, 847–855 (159, 162)
104. Benedict III, 855–858
     Anastasius III, 855–855
105. Nicholas I (the Great), 858–867
     (160f)
106. Adrian II, 867–872 (143, 147)
107. John VIII, 872–882 (160)
108. Marinus I, 882–884
109. Adrian III, 884–885
110. Stephen V (VI), 885–891
111. Formosus, 891–896 (162)
112. Boniface VI, 896–896
113. Stephen VI (VII), 896–897 (162)
114. Romanus, 897–897
115. Theodore II, 897–897
116. John IX, 898–900
117. Benedict IV, 900–903
118. Leo V, 903–903
119. Christopher, 903–904
120. Sergius III, 904–911 (162)
121. Anastasius III, 911–913
122. Lando, 913–914
123. John X, 914–928
124. Leo VI, 928–928
125. Stephen VII (VIII), 929–931
126. John XI, 931–935
127. Leo VII, 936–939
128. Stephen VIII (IX), 939–942
129. Marinus II, 942–946
130. Agapetus II, 946–955
131. John XII, 955–963 (163, 167)
132. Leo VIII, 963–965 (168)
133. Benedict V, 964–964 (?)
134. John XIII, 965–972
135. Benedict VI, 973–974
     Boniface VII (Franco), 974–974

136. Benedict VII, 974–983 (169)
137. John XIV, 983–984
138. Boniface VII, 984–985 (169)
139. John XV, 985–996
140. Gregory V, 996–999 (170)
     John XVI, 997–998
141. Sylvester II, 999–1003 (170)
142. John XVII, 1003–1003
143. John XVIII, 1004–1009
144. Sergius IV, 1009–1012
145. Benedict VIII, 1012–1024 (171)
     Gregory VI, 1012–1012
146. John XIX, 1024–1032
147. Benedict IX, 1032–1045 (172)
     Sylvester III, 1045–1045
148. Gregory VI, 1045–1046 (173)
149. Clement II, 1046–1047 (173)
150. Damasus II, 1048–1048
151. Leo IX, 1049–1054 (173, 178,
     184 ff)
152. Victor II, 1055–1057 (173)
153. Stephen IX (X), 1057–1058
154. Benedict X, 1058–1059
155. Nicholas II, 1058–1061 (178)
156. Alexander II, 1061–1073
     Honorius II, 1061–1072
157. Gregory VII, 1073–1085 (112,
     142, 178, 179 ff, 220, 235)
     Clement III, 1080–1100
158. Victor III, 1086–1087
159. Urban II, 1088–1099 (189, 192,
     194 ff)
160. Paschal II, 1099–1118 (181)
     Theodoric, 1100–1102
     Albert, 1102–1102
     Sylvester IV, 1105–1111
161. Gelasius II, 1118–1119
     Gregory VIII, 1118–1121
162. Callistus II, 1119–1124
163. Honorius II, 1124–1130
     Celestine II, 1124–1124
     Innocent II, 1130–1143
164. Anacletus II, 1130–1138
     Victor IV, 1138–1138
165. Celestine II, 1143–1144
166. Lucius II, 1144–1145
167. Eugene III, 1145–1153
168. Anastasius IV, 1153–1154

169. Adrian IV, 1154–1159 (186)
170. Alexander III, 1159–1181 (112,
     183, 207)
     Victor IV, 1159–1164
     Paschal III, 1164–1168
     Callistus III, 1168–1178
     Innocent III, 1179–1180
171. Lucius III, 1181–1185 (207)
172. Urban III, 1185–1187
173. Gregory VIII, 1187–1187
174. Clement III, 1187–1191
175. Celestine III, 1191–1198 (220)
176. Innocent III, 1198–1216 (112,
     183, 184, 196, 208, 210, 213,
     215, 220–5)
177. Honorius III, 1216–1227 (215)
178. Gregory IX, 1227–1241 (211,
     219, 225)
179. Celestine IV, 1241–1241
180. Innocent IV, 1243–1254 (225)
181. Alexander IV, 1254–1261
182. Urban IV, 1261–1264
183. Clement IV, 1265–1268
184. Gregory X, 1271–1276 (179)
185. Innocent V, 1276–1276
186. Adrian V, 1276–1276
187. John XXI, 1276–1277
188. Nicholas III, 1277–1280
189. Martin IV, 1281–1285
190. Honorius IV, 1285–1287
191. Nicholas IV, 1288–1292
192. Celestine V, 1294–1294
193. Boniface VIII, 1294–1303 (112,
     226, 229, 235 ff)
194. Benedict XI, 1303–1304
195. Clement V, 1305–1314 (228 f)
196. John XXII, 1316–1334 (230)
     Nicholas V, 1328–1330
197. Benedict XII, 1334–1342
198. Clement VI, 1342–1352
199. Innocent VI, 1352–1362
200. Urban V, 1362–1370
201. Gregory XI, 1370–1378 (231)
202. Urban VI, 1378–1389 (233 ff)
     Clement VII, 1378–1394 (233 ff)
203. Boniface IX, 1389–1404
     Benedict XIII, 1394–1423 (239)
204. Innocent VII, 1404–1406

205. Gregory XII, 1406–1415 (234)
206. Alexander V, 1409–1410
207. John XIII, 1410–1415 (236)
208. Martin V, 1417–1431 (243)
   Clement VIII, 1423–1429
209. Eugene IV, 1431–1447 (244)
   Felix V, 1439–1449
210. Nicholas V, 1447–1455 (247)
211. Callistus III, 1455–1458 (247)
212. Pius II, 1458–1464 (247)
213. Paul II, 1464–1471 (247)
214. Sixtus IV, 1471–1484 (247)
215. Innocent VIII, 1484–1492 (246)
216. Alexander VI, 1492–1503 (245, 248, 311)
217. Pius III, 1503–1503
218. Julius II, 1503–1513 (248, 251, 312)
219. Leo X, 1513–1521 (248, 273)
220. Adrian VI, 1522–1523 (255, 279, 313)
221. Clement VII, 1523–1534 (282, 306, 312 ff)
222. Paul III, 1534–1549 (246, 285, 314 ff)
223. Julius III, 1550–1555
224. Marcellus II, 1555–1555
225. Paul IV, 1555–1559 (246, 288, 328, 333)
226. Pius IV, 1559–1565 (320)
227. Pius V, 1566–1572 (304, 321 f)
228. Gregory XIII, 1572–1585 (304, 323)
229. Sixtus V, 1585–1590
230. Urban VII, 1590–1590
231. Gregory XIV, 1590–1591

232. Innocent IX, 1591–1591
233. Clement VIII, 1592–1605
234. Leo XI, 1605–1605
235. Paul V, 1605–1621
236. Gregory XV, 1621–1623
237. Urban VIII, 1623–1644
238. Innocent X, 1644–1655 (344)
239. Alexander VII, 1655–1667
240. Clement IX, 1667–1669
241. Clement X, 1670–1676
242. Innocent XI, 1676–1689
243. Alexander VIII, 1689–1691
244. Innocent XII, 1691–1700 (247)
245. Clement XI, 1700–1721
246. Innocent XIII, 1721–1724 (345)
247. Benedict XIII, 1724–1730
248. Clement XII, 1730–1740
249. Benedict XIV, 1740–1758 (345)
250. Clement XIII, 1758–1769
251. Clement XIV, 1769–1774 (349)
252. Pius VI, 1775–1799 (384)
253. Pius VII, 1800–1823 (356, 385)
254. Leo XII, 1823–1829
255. Pius VIII, 1829–1830
256. Gregory XVI, 1831–1846 (359, 385)
257. Pius IX, 1846–1878 (385 ff)
258. Leo XIII, 1878–1903 (398 ff)
259. Pius X, 1903–1914 (401 f)
260. Benedict XV, 1914–1922 (403)
261. Pius XI, 1922–1939 (412 ff)
262. Pius XII, 1939–1958 (247, 345, 413 ff, 429)
263. John XXIII, 1958–1963 (427 ff)
264. Paul VI, 1963– (409, 431 ff)